THE HISTORY OF

GLAMORGAN
COUNTY
CRICKET CLUB

THE CHRISTOPHER HELM
COUNTY CRICKET HISTORIES

Series Editors:
Peter Arnold and Peter Wynne-Thomas

HAMPSHIRE
Peter Wynne-Thomas, with a personal view by John Arlott

KENT
Dudley Moore, with a personal view by Derek Underwood

MIDDLESEX
David Lemmon, with a personal view by Denis Compton

THE HISTORY OF

GLAMORGAN
COUNTY
CRICKET CLUB

Andrew Hignell

**With a personal view by
TONY LEWIS**

CHRISTOPHER HELM

London

© 1988 Andrew Hignell and Tony Lewis
Christopher Helm (Publishers) Ltd, Imperial House,
21–25 North Street, Bromley, Kent BR1 1SD

ISBN 0-7470-1408-6

A CIP catalogue record for this book is available from the British Library

Typeset by Cotswold Typesetting Ltd, Gloucester
Printed and bound in Great Britain by Biddles Ltd, Guildford, Surrey

CONTENTS

A PERSONAL VIEW
Tony Lewis

THE STORY OF GLAMORGAN CRICKET can make you laugh, make you weep; sometimes both at the same time so sudden are the moments of triumph, so deep and long the troughs of failure and frustration. The graph of progress from 1888 to the centenary year of 1988 is one of long, up-hill scramble to playing respectability and financial solvency, a line jagged with pit-falls and occasional leaping achievement: even now, 99 years later as I write, the team has managed 17 seasons of mediocrity save a losing appearance in a Gillette Cup final and at the moment a beleaguered treasurer sometimes has to pretend he has lost the key to the Club purse. The history of Glamorgan makes Pilgrim's Progress sound like a day in the life of Peter Rabbit.

Yet there is romance in all this, woven into tales which, if not exactly true, tell us what it was like at the time—tales of the 1930s spun by Dai Davies, staunch batsman between the World Wars and Test umpire afterwards, of Maurice Turnbull taking the team dancing after a full day's fielding in order to raise cash for their week's wage: 'Dance our feet off, we would, and there would be the skipper at the door by midnight handing out the pay-packets.'

Was it really true that Frank Ryan, American born, long, left-arm spinner, lover of the alcoholic beverage, was found one early morning sleeping under the covers? Was it true that Mr John Clay could usually be seen in the Cowbridge High Street squeezing a firm rubber ball in his right hand to strengthen his fingers for spin? John Clay always referred to the 'rag-time days' when, as captain, from 1924 to 1927, he was never sure he had 11 players until the bus left and even then not sure which 11. Did it happen that they had only ten on the way to the Midlands one day in 1926, stopped at the cross roads in Tredegar, picked up a stranger named Jones who played the one match, got no runs and did not bowl, and was dropped off at the same corner on the way back without anyone knowing his Christian name? The statistical section at the end of the book suggests that our mystery man may be Edward Cyril Jones. But what was he doing at the crossroads in Tredegar? This tale may not be true, but the times were ripe for it to be so.

Glamorgan cricket has long lived in the shadow of Welsh rugby. Visit almost any of the Club's grounds used for first-class cricket and you will see rugby posts at the other end of the ground. The Cardiff Arms Park ground which we used until 1967 was dwarfed by the giant north stand of the famous rugby ground next door. Rugby for many Welsh people is identity. It excites a small, patriotic following, an emotional watering of the national daffodil every summer, but for most of the year we are a rugby nation. Glamorgan need to be chasing the English County Championship before the masses turn out.

Glamorgan, in cricket terms, has come to mean the whole of Wales. It was always a strange feeling driving for five hours over the mountainous inland to play a Glamorgan home match in Colwyn Bay in Denbighshire on the North Wales coast. This was probably Wooller's Law. Wilfred Wooller, born in 1912 at Rhos-on-Sea, which is virtually part of Colwyn Bay, has been the colossus who has held North and South together, not only by his link with both but because his unwritten edict was that any young cricketer born or residing in Wales is 'ours'. He freely quoted the act of Union of 1536 to include Monmouthshire and a lot of the Welsh Marches in that! There was no pussy-footing to Lord's with application forms to register any young player from Chester or Shrewsbury or Ludlow or Monmouth. They were Welsh until proved otherwise.

It is still an astonishment that Wilfred allowed Pat Pocock out of his Bangor birthplace in his nappies to go to London to become the Surrey and England off-spinner. David Green of Oxford University, Lancashire and Gloucestershire, born in Llanengan, Caernarvon was another babe to side-step the Wooller minefield laid between Mold and Old Trafford.

I played my first county championship match for Glamorgan a few weeks after my 17th birthday in 1955. There was nothing else in the world I wanted to do more. I had played in the second team for a few seasons, capped by John Riches, son of N. V. H. Riches who led Glamorgan into first-class cricket in 1921. The second eleven cap was a daffodil bud, but now, at Cardiff Arms Park in 1955, I was consorting not only with full flowers but also with the famous red, orange and navy-edged sweaters awarded to MCC touring players abroad. Gilbert Parkhouse and Allan Watkins wore them like gods.

Unfortunately *Wisden* never lies. I was out first ball, padding up to a giant chinaman bowled by an Australian. Jack Walsh, left-arm over the wicket, spun the ball out towards second slip: I thought 'good, a sighter, I can lift the bat out of the way'. The ball fizzed and bit and turned. Fatal. I retreated into the bowels of the rugby stand, our strange home which reeked of dubbin and draught beer, and entered a dressing room of 'bad lucks'. It was an hour or two later that I was offered consoling words, by another Jones of course, this one William Edward from Carmarthen. As a lad I had watched 'Little Willie' cut bowlers to distraction in the great championship year of 1948, when he had averaged over 40.

'Anyone tell you to play forward to Jack Walsh until you know what's going on?'

'No,' I mumbled. 'Is that what to do?'

'Ay.' Willie continued to whisper as if he could get into trouble with the skipper, Wilf Wooller, if he was caught. 'Push out Tony bach; if it turns in you're covered, if it doesn't, well you never know, God might be on your side.'

The skipper said nothing. He gave me time to recover, and he was not one for whispers.

'Mark down every Leicestershire name out there, Tony. Catch up with the bastards one day and make them pay.'

I do recall having to stand all the way to Neath on the N&C bus that night – reading the *South Wales Echo* to find that I had been out 'to a guileful delivery from the veteran Walsh'.

In fact the Cardiff Arms Park was a ground full of atmosphere, closeted as it was by the back of the rugby stand and the Westgate Street flats. Residents of these apartments had a perfect view of the play, and often had cricket parties, draping daffodil flags over the balcony rails and tinkling glasses. Their chat was sometimes audible to the deep fielders below. The river Taff flowed unseen on the far side and the sun went down, sometimes blindingly, behind the bowler's arm in the west.

Sophia Gardens, Glamorgan's present headquarters, was never so cosy, and for many seasons its pitch was even less accommodating. Colin Milburn recalls in an early county match there being bowled by a ball from Tony Cordle which kept so low it hit the base of the stump and the dislodged bail fell forwards. Sophia Gardens, though smarter these days with an attractive office 'portakabin' on the ground, still lacks the theatre of an exciting cricket venue. Its wide open spaces can be unfriendly to the players and spectators: a day watching there when the prevailing wind blows is like a week at sea. Weatherbeaten faces file out at close of play.

St Helen's, however, is an exciting stage, intimate because of its shorter straight boundaries. It is like theatre-in-the-round nestling into the high curving terrace mid-wickets on the city side. My own recollections of great Glamorgan matches are all here. As a ten-year-old I queued around the St Helen's walls, pop and sandwiches in my bag, to see the 1948 Australians. I had heard of Don Bradman – everyone in Neath had been talking about him for days before. Sadly he did not play. Exactly 29 years later I spoke to Sir Donald Bradman in Australia and told him my sad story.

'Don't worry, Tony, it was all over by then,' he said. 'I was past my best. You didn't miss a lot.' Probably the understatement of all time.

My generation was reared on the County's first Championship win and then the great win against South Africa at St Helen's in 1951. For once the rugby emotions spilled out onto the cricket field and massed crowds sang the old rugby hymns outside the pavilion.

Happily I was playing on a few occasions when Glamorgan's supporters had something to sing about – the 1964 win over the Australians (I missed the second in 1968 through illness) and a victory in 1969 against Essex on the last ball which sent us surging towards the second County Championship win in 1969.

Part of the St Helen's feeling of theatre came from the long walk down the centre steps of the pavilion. It was a grand entrance. Nowadays players rather sneak on, low down to the left, more comfortable if you are about to be out first ball but hardly time for a fanfare if you are about to play a grand innings.

A final Swansea selection would be the six sixes in an over hit by Garry Sobers off Malcolm Nash. I was the defending captain but it never came down to field-placing. I have always felt sorry for Malcolm that few mention the fact that he was experimenting with cutters on that occasion. Nash the left-arm seamer was a superb strike bowler who took over 900 wickets for the Club.

To define the character of Glamorgan cricket you have to consider the pitches played on. Most fixtures are played at Cardiff and Swansea, but occasional fixtures have gone to out-grounds which are ordinary club surfaces prepared for a special occasion. These are almost always slow. The Gnoll, Neath, for example lies at the foot of a hill wood and has a high water table. Even so in 1985 Javed Miandad and Younis Ahmed were able to beat the County's fourth wicket record, raising it to 306. The ground, decorated with sponsored marquees all around, fitted the occasion. Usually, however, the Gnoll is a slow, low turning surface. I was batting at the other end to Wilf Wooller in 1955 when he completed a seven-hour century: the pitch deteriorated over by over and after he had occupied the crease he tossed the ball to Allan Watkins, who bowled cutters instead of seamers when required, and to Don Shepherd. With a wicket or two from Jim Pressdee we won the match. So bowlers in Glamorgan have had to be able to adapt to varying conditions. Slow pitches, for example, blunted the speed of Jeff Jones, an England fast bowler, but he was a superb trier, never gave in and was developing into a big wicket-taker when an elbow injury ended his career. Welsh pitches made batsmen improvise too. Gilbert Parkhouse was magnificent. Yet pitches which did respond to spin and cut made for exciting cricket, with a cluster of brilliant fielders diving for catches around the bat. Glamorgan had a reputation for close-catching: matches were so often decided close to the bat. Allan Watkins and Peter Walker were superb backward short-legs, Majid Khan, Gilbert Parkhouse, Bryan Davis and Matthew Maynard have been outstanding slips; Wilf Wooller made the forward short-leg position his own and at 'Boot Hill', short square leg, none has been braver or more skilled than Roger Davis.

John Arlott gave his own impression of the Welsh at play in his poem 'Cricket at Swansea' (Glamorgan in the Field):

> The Ball is a withering weapon,
> Fraught with a strong-fingered spin
> And the fieldsmen, with fingers prehensile,
> Are the arms of attack moving in.
> In the field of a new Cymric mission,
> With outcricket cruel as a cat
> They pounce on the perilous snick
> As it breaks from the spin-harried bat.

However, it is possible to prepare good, firm pitches in Wales. I am in favour of a sensible balance, otherwise the skills of seam bowling and of batting on fast, bouncy pitches are blighted. Ossie Wheatley, skipper from 1960 to 1966 loved the sea breezes at Swansea. He got his late away-swinger going and, especially when the tide was in and moisture had seeped up the sandbank under the ground, he got the ball to nip off the seam.

Thus county cricket in Wales in my time usually produced results and it seems to me now that when Alan Jones was not batting through three decades for an unrivalled 36,049 runs, Don Shepherd was bowling, initially fast and then off-cutters, from 1950 to 1972 for a record 2,218 first-class wickets.

As long as I have known Glamorgan Cricket Club there has always been argument about identity, about Welshness. How much should Welsh talent be eased out of the team for signings from outside? On only the rare occasion has there been a team on the field composed entirely of Welshmen. There were the great Yorkshire saviours between the wars: Bates and Bell, then Arnold Dyson. In the 1948 Championship came the strong Middlesex influence of Len Muncer, Norman Hever and Jim Eaglestone. Ossie Wheatley in his day was the first non-Welsh captain, and in the 1969 Championship side there were two overseas cricketers, Majid Khan from Pakistan and Bryan Davis from Trinidad. The modern Glamorgan side frequently contains as few as three Welshmen.

Personally I do not believe the Welshness is the vital factor but I do believe that the side

4

should contain a high percentage of locally reared talent. Otherwise what is the incentive for the young player? It is difficult enough to persuade teenagers to choose cricket at all now that much of school cricket has disintegrated. It is equally hard for our coaches to turn club players with poor techniques born of limited-over matches into cricketers capable of performing well in three, four or even five-day games. Yet this is the job facing us, and only evangelism at the grass roots level will send Glamorgan healthily into the next one hundred years. One day surely we must turn the patchwork history into something richer and more reliable.

Even so, Glamorgan has been loyally served by some superb overseas players, none better than Majid Khan, who became devoted to the Club until the captaincy and criticism hurt him enough to leave. He played the best single innings I ever saw, against Worcestershire at Sophia Gardens in 1969. He made 156, jewelled with perfect strokes, and all the more brilliant because it was the decisive innings in the game that won the County Championship. The pitch was dry and breaking up. Only three others made it to double figures. I still see him gliding down the pitch to meet Norman Gifford's spinners. Time and again I expected to see him stranded but the Worcestershire captain, Tom Graveney, in the end had to reinforce his cover field with two fast runners on the boundary.

Bryan Davis, the Trinidadian, was another fine professional, unselfishly playing for the side and catching brilliantly. Roy Fredericks, the West Indian left-hander, sometimes found concentration difficult but he did play several devastating innings. Less illustrious when he came – not a Test player because he was South African – was Rodney Ontong, but he ranks with Majid as a great trier on the field, just the sort of cricketer who knew how to adjust his style from fast bowling to slow off-spin. With his tenacious batting, he has sustained a long and productive career as an all-rounder. There is a lot of Ontong sweat out there on Welsh pitches. Somehow the talent of Javed Miandad and Winston Davis never truly came through to turn the County into a winning side in the 1980s, but they were exceptional players and the standards of play rose. There have been too, one has to say, some motley signings which wasted the precious trump cards.

For many years Glamorgan were allocated two matches against the touring teams every season. This was because others in the County Championship were involved in local derbies. The games were huge attractions then, played with pride and the strongest instinct of competition by the players. Not so these days, when tourists use the matches against the counties as practice and the home professionals might be looking for a rest before an important one-day competition.

How the Rev Samuel would have failed to understand this. He used to lead our Gnoll Road Congregational Church on its annual Whitsun march, but as our phalanx of singers marched past the Victoria Gardens in Neath chanting 'Onwards, Forwards, Shouting out Hosannah', he would nip off to the Cardiff bus-stand and be off to the Glamorgan match against the tourists before we had completed our spin down London Road and around Stockhams Corner.

Another corner of Glamorgan history lurks in London. There has always been keen support among the exiles and they turn up at Lord's and the Oval hoping that we are about to have one of our good days.

There have been special haunts. Along from Lord's is the Star of India pub where I found it possible to stand and talk all night in spite of fielding all day. Around the corner, the Portland Arms withstood many a Glamorgan invasion. In our smarter, more adventurous moments we took to Raymond's Revue Bar, not for the strip show, which we saw many times, but because George Richardson, who managed it, was a Surrey cricket fan.

After clinching the County Championship in Cardiff in 1969 we had to drive to London to meet Surrey the next day. Our cars, as if on automatic pilot, went straight for Raymond's. The party was going well when suddenly George announced that Brian Huggett, the Welsh Ryder Cup player, had been on the telephone asking them to serve us some champagne at his expense. Our friends, if not everyone else, knew where to find us.

Three weeks before the end of the 99th season, I became Chairman of the Glamorgan Cricket Committee. It has helped me to form an impression of the recent past and compile thoughts for a future. From 1973 to 1988 there have been ten captains. This cannot be right and means one of two things – either leadership has changed into a high-risk, near-impossible job, or we have been chosing the wrong man. I am not the adjudicator of the second possibility because I was an absentee sometimes, living in London. But I would like to write about the first.

During the 1970s there were strong stirrings among the professional playing fraternity. The Cricketers' Association was the Union, though never a militant one, and there was talk of feudal relationships in the game between the counties and their employees. In 1977 Kerry Packer came along, recruited the best players in the world, and proved that old bonds could be broken. The role of the captain, traditionally, was to represent the players strongly to the committee and the committee to the players. It required a man of independent spirit, and whereas some could be brought from outside, like for example Eddie Barlow in Derbyshire, often players were elevated from the pack who found the job painful and impossible. In Glamorgan there was an absence of former players ready to stand for the committee and advise, though the business was carried on stoically in those complex times by Ossie Wheatley as Chairman, Jim Pleass, also a former player, and a committee which perhaps failed to keep in time with the swirling changes in professional attitudes.

Nothing grinds down a captain or a committee more than playing failures on the field, and Glamorgan have spent an agonising 18 years without a cup or title. To be honest, I am unable to write that the Club's reputation for cricket is high as the centenary arrives. It is a disappointment to the amateur workers involved who have given up so much time to attend meetings and matches, and to the players who, no doubt, have tried like hell.

The optimism I offer is this. The balance between a winning outfit and a losing one is delicate. A team is like a clock and attention has to be paid to every single cog and spring before the balance can be right. Once the tick of the team becomes steady, the wins will come, and winning, like losing, is habit.

There have been moments of promise and in many ways the Club is taking on a new personality. The Secretary, Philip Carling, has opened new avenues of sponsorship by marketing the Club well and by creating new possibilities for business entertainment.

John Steele, one of the successful professional players who came from outside, has been persuaded to stay in Glamorgan and work with Alan Jones at the cricket, both present and future. Yet there can be no picture of the future without knowledge of the past and this is the moment when I break off, hoping that I have whetted the appetite for the full story which Andrew Hignell is about to unfold. I have tried not to anticipate his portraits of the outstanding players and personalities who have given great pleasure or infuriating disappointment along the one hundred years, or pre-empted the themes which have driven the County forwards to a long life. The past is essential to our future. When I first played alongside my hero, Gilbert Parkhouse, I felt a frisson of disbelief – yet it was only continuity making its presence felt.

And so we are all attached to what has gone before: it is our inspiration and our mirror as well as our future. If I was asked what I enjoyed most about Glamorgan I would not talk of Championships or Tests, I would say just being part of it. You only have to play one game to feel that, because, you see, there is no Glamorgan without those Joneses, Lewises, Evanses and so on who turned out for their occasional game: nor is there a Glamorgan unless young boys playing cricket with a tennis ball on the same road in Neath where I once played, are dreaming as I did. I think of the opening lines of T. S. Eliot's 'Burnt Norton':

> Time present and time past,
> Are both perhaps present in time future
> And time future contained in time past.
> If all time is eternally present
> All time is unredeemable.

So enjoy the one hundred years, because from its strengths as well as its weakness comes the will to give Glamorgan its future.

GLAMORGAN AND THE SOUTH WALES CRICKET CLUB

SEASON 1988 FELL in Glamorgan's Centenary Year – and the team failed to win any titles or trophies, despite the presence of several keen young cricketers and a few wise old heads. This has been the normal course of events during much of the Club's existence for unlike many other counties, the history of the Welsh county has not been filled with glittering success. Rather than a series of Championship wins or one-day titles, they have won the County Championship on just two occasions, and have played in only one limited-over final at Lord's. Despite their lack of success, however, the first hundred years of the club have been packed with incident and have involved many colourful characters both on and off the field.

The Club could hardly have had a more humble· origin, being formed in July 1888 at a meeting in a smoke-filled room at a Cardiff hotel, attended by officials and patrons from the leading cricket clubs in South Wales. The small gathering was attended by ambitious men, with pockets deep enough to match their enthusiasm, and several did not mind dipping into them to launch the Club. But despite their eagerness to see the new Club succeed, I doubt if many of those at the meeting would have dared to believe that the team would contribute players and captains to the England team, besides playing and beating all of the other first-class sides and the leading Test playing nations in the world. Indeed, some of the Club's finest hours have been against Test teams, especially Australia. Glamorgan achieved outstanding wins over the Australian tourists in 1964 and 1968, and, listening to some of the stories told about these games, it seems that nearly every cricketing enthusiast in Wales was at St Helen's when Ossie Wheatley and Don Shepherd led the County to their famous victories.

An important aspect in the Club's development has been that they have achieved a national identity. Rather than keeping to the geographical boundaries of the County, the Club have staged matches throughout South and West Wales, and have even travelled north to Colwyn Bay and Llandudno for several matches. As J. H. Morgan wrote in the 1967 *Wisden*: 'the club started to serve a county and grew to represent a nation'. This national identity has been very important with the Celtic qualities of 'hwyl' and 'hiraeth' greatly assisting the club.

That almost unique Welsh 'hwyl', so typical of rugby internationals at the Arms Park, has helped both during troubled times on the field and whilst celebrating success – the singing of the Welsh national anthem on the pavilion balcony at Bournemouth in 1948, and at Swansea in 1968 after the victory over Australia is still clearly remembered by Glamorgan's loyal band of faithful supporters. The feeling of 'hiraeth', a sense of loyalty and native attachment to Wales, has also meant that wherever the team play around England and sometimes further afield, there will always be some support for the Welsh county. These feelings also explain why so many expatriate Welshmen around the world eagerly look in the papers for Glamorgan's scores, and despite being many miles away, celebrate when they succeed.

The course of events during the Club's first hundred years is the result of the deeds of a small body of men. Initially, the team was brought together by J. T. D. Llewelyn, the cricket-loving squire of Penllegaer, and Joseph Brain, who had played for Oxford University and Gloucestershire. Their rôle was taken over by 'Tal' Whittington and Norman Riches each side of the First World War, with the former being instrumental in Glamorgan's elevation to first-class status in 1921. The graceful Maurice Turnbull and the debonair Johnnie Clay took centre stage during the 1930s, establishing the Welsh team as a force to be reckoned with in county cricket.

Sadly, Turnbull was not alive when his efforts came to fruition in 1948 when Glamorgan, led by Wilf Wooller, took the county title. The former Welsh rugby international has been the major figure in post-war Glamorgan cricket, and in making Glamorgan a force to be reckoned with on the field of play. Later, as an administrator and Test selector, Wooller oversaw the creation of a sound financial base as cricket became more of a business concern.

But it has not been a totally romantic story; indeed some would argue that the events of the 1970s and 1980s were more akin to a nightmare than a fairytale, with the club making headlines more for events off the field than on. In particular, overseas players have come and gone as the Welsh team has loitered at the base of the county table. Test stars like Majid Khan, Javed Miandad, Roy Fredericks and Collis King have all joined the Club, but for a variety of reasons they have gone their own way. Captains too have been tried from within or imported, without any marked degree of success. There have been claims of poor management and the tag 'more chiefs than Indians' has been applied in recent years though both have been rather harsh as a series of injuries and early retirements has prevented the Club from fielding a full-strength side.

Nevertheless, with all the glittering array of Test-class talent that has been available, plus a number of seasoned county professionals,

9

one could have expected better things, and the team have often been frustratingly inconsistent in their quest of an elusive title or trophy. Present-day observers firmly believe that the Club are moving out of the trough. Success and failure in sport often runs in cycles, and the recent emergence of Matthew Maynard into the England team, and the acquisition of a keen squad under Hugh Morris' captaincy, augurs well for the immediate future of the Club.

Glamorgan of the 1980s can now boast a behind-the-scenes framework worthy of any other county club. A modern office complex at Sophia Gardens, and an enthusiastic supporters organisation based in Swansea, plus an energetic chief executive in Philip Carling and an enthusiastic committee, astutely led by chairman Tony Lewis, all provide the Club with a base from which success can be obtained. This effective modern-day operation, and a score of advertising boards and sponsors backing the team, is in marked contrast with the earliest days of the Club, when it was left to several wealthy patrons to put the Club on its feet.

The events leading up to the formation of the Club began in the mid-19th century – a time when South Wales was undergoing commercial and industrial growth. The local economy was booming and there was a considerable amount of migration to the area from the neighbouring counties of South-West England. Cricket clubs had been formed at Abergavenny (1834), Llanelli (1837), Neath (1844), Cardiff (1845), Maesteg (1846) and Swansea (1848), and the standard of play rose with the massive influx of wealthy merchants, tradesmen and gentlemen who could afford both the time and money to play.

A club had been formed in Newport during the 1820s, and by the 1850s its leading personality was Captain Samuel George Homfray, the son of the managing partner of the Tredegar Iron Works. He was the club's captain and secretary, as well as being their best bowler. Homfray was keen to see the standard of club cricket in the area improving and he decided to put his organisational skills and money towards achieving these goals. In 1855 a South Wales XXII was assembled to challenge the All-England XI, who travelled the country playing exhibition matches, at the Arms Park. Despite including Hinkly of Kent and Gloucestershire's Henry Grace, the South Wales team lost by five wickets. This game gave Homfray a clear indication of how to achieve his aim, and during the 1850s and 1860s he organised a number of special friendlies in Glamorgan and Monmouthshire.

In September 1859 the All-England XI travelled to Newport to play a Monmouthshire XXII. *Lillywhite's Guide* recorded how 'great interest was consequently excited. Captain Homfray was the originator and manager, and well did he perform the duties, as well as most hospitably entertaining the eleven.' Games were also played against the United England Eleven and *Lillywhite's* commented how 'Homfray could not possibly pass a season unless he had some talented cricketers to entertain.' Amongst the famous names to visit South Wales were H. H. Stephenson, the captain of the first England team to Australia (in 1861/2), George Parr, the renowned batsman from Nottinghamshire and Edgar Willsher of Kent, who was called 'the father of overarm bowling'. With so many talented cricketers involved, there were sizeable attendances at these exhibition matches, suitably rewarding Homfray's missionary-like zeal.

Following the success of these games, Homfray began to consider the formation of a team to represent South Wales. He gained the support of a number of leading cricketers in the region and members of the local gentry. Consequently, he formed the South Wales Cricket Club in July 1859 and arranged an inaugural fixture against the Clifton club from the Bristol area. It was not a successful start, as the SWCC lost by 114 runs and played with just ten men, including a substitute from the opposition. However, Homfray did not lose heart and arranged a re-match a month later at Newport, with a £50 wager on the SWCC winning! With their honour and a healthy sum at stake, the game was keenly fought, but unfortunately a furious row broke out over an umpiring decision, causing the match to be abandoned at the end of the Clifton innings.

Despite this acrimonious start, Homfray arranged five games the following year. The game with The Knickerbockers at Aldershot brought the SWCC their first-ever victory, with Samuel France, the Yorkshire-born pro from Llandovery, taking 11 for 84. Season 1860 established a pattern which became the norm for the club in the next few years. Half a dozen games were played in the West Country and an annual tour was made to the Home Counties where matches were played against some of the strongest amateur teams, including the MCC, Surrey Club and Ground, Prince's and I Zingari. Despite the standard of the opposition, social and political aspirations were as important as mere cricketing ones when the SWCC chose their party for this annual event. Indeed, most of the SWCC's games had an air of country house cricket about them, with their teams being composed of gentlemen who had learnt their cricket at English public schools and were now successful businessmen in South Wales, together with some of the talented, and not so talented, members of the local gentry who could take time off to play in these two-day games.

Some amateurs with rather tenuous residential links with South Wales also turned out for the SWCC. The most famous was W. G. Grace, who had played as an 11-year-old for Clifton in the Welsh club's initial fixture. His brother, E. M. Grace, was a regular member of the team in the early 1860s and took 15 wickets in the match against the MCC in 1861 which gave the SWCC their first-ever victory at Lord's. Indeed, it was E. M. Grace who was responsible for W.G. appearing for the South Wales team. In 1864 the officials were selecting their team at The Oval against Surrey and at Brighton against The Gentlemen of Sussex. They contacted the Grace family, hoping that E.M. would be available; but he was still travelling back from Australia, and it was suggested that the 15-year-old W.G. take his place. The SWCC agreed, but the engagement nearly fell through, with Homfray and the captain, John Lloyd, having doubts about the suitability of playing the youngster. W.G. travelled up to London with his Uncle Henry, who had also agreed to play. The famous doctor recollected how they were practising on the ground when 'the captain of the South Wales team approached Henry and asked him if he objected to my standing out against the Gentlemen of Sussex at Brighton, as he had the offer of a very good player . . . Henry objected very much. "To begin with", he said, "the boy was asked to play in both matches, and he shall play in both matches or none, and I only hope every member of the team will do as well as I expect him to do."' W.G. scored 5 and 38 against the Surrey Club and then repaid his uncle's kindness by scoring 170 and 56 not out at Brighton!

One of the leading Welsh members of the SWCC was John Talbot Dillwyn Llewelyn, the squire of Penllergaer, near Swansea, who was known to one and all by his initials 'J.T.D.' He was a most generous benefactor to many causes, including cricket, and was a typical Victorian philanthropist. J.T.D. believed there was scope for the formation of a team representing South Wales which would not be used as a social stepping stone, and would be composed of players who had stronger connections with the area than turned out for the SWCC. Clubs in West Glamorgan had been in regular contact with teams in Carmarthenshire, where a county team had been formed in 1852. J.T.D. served as a JP for Carmarthenshire, and had many acquaintances in the West Wales county. He used these to arrange a two-day game between a Glamorganshire XI and Carmarthenshire on 5 and 6 August 1861. Although it was the first team to carry the County's name, Llewelyn's team was not representative of the entire area. He invited only players from the Swansea and Cardiff clubs, together with a few drawn from his own Cadoxton team.

Unfortunately, the Llanelli wicket was in a sodden state after heavy rain in the days leading up to the game. Indeed, *The Cambrian* noted how 'the ground was from the commencement in a truly pitiable condition; wherever the ball alighted, there it remained almost motionless, as if checked or detained by some magnetic force!' Consequently, the match was a low scoring affair, with all of the batsmen struggling to make any impact. Glamorgan secured a 36–run lead on first innings, and then O'Donoghue took six wickets in Carmarthenshire's second innings to leave Llewelyn's team a seemingly modest target of 49. But the wicket had cut up even further, and they fell four runs short after some accurate bowling by the Arthur brothers from Llanelli.

Despite the result, the game showed that a useful Glamorgan team could be raised, and during the 1860s regular fixtures were held with Carmarthenshire. These matches led to talk of forming a club to represent Glamorgan, along the lines of the teams which had been formed in other parts of Wales, including Radnorshire, Pembrokeshire, Denbighshire and Anglesey. However, the hopes of J.T.D. and his friends were dashed when both Homfray and John Lloyd severed their links with the SWCC in 1865. The Grace family also broke off their connections with the SWCC and without their most important influences both on and off the field, the SWCC went into decline. This was a severe blow to the lobby calling for a County team, because it had given an opportunity for the better players from the Welsh club to play at a higher standard. John Nicholl, a cousin of J.T.D.'s from the Bridgend area, initially stepped into the void created by the loss of the SWCC games, and arranged a series of inter-county matches on his estate at Merthyr Mawr. In June 1866 a Glamorganshire XI raised by Nicholl and Llewelyn played Carmarthenshire, but only seven of the visitors arrived at Nicholl's estate and Glamorgan had a comfortable innings victory.

It was therefore left to J.T.D. to assume the catalytic rôle of promoting the game in the late 1860s and early 1870s. In 1868 he persuaded John Lloyd to bring his Breconshire team to play at Merthyr Mawr, and arranged two exhibition games. The first, at the end of May, was between a XXII from his Cadoxton club and a United South of England XI at Neath. The England team included W. G. Grace, and J.T.D. must have been relieved when the Doctor was dismissed for a duck in each innings by Howitt, who was guesting for the Cadoxton team. The second in July involved a team representing the Gentlemen of Swansea led by Llewelyn himself against the touring Australian Aborigines at St Helen's. It was something more than just a game of cricket, because after the tourists had won, there was a variety of athletic events on the Swansea ground, including the throwing of spears and boomerangs by the Aborigines.

During the winter of 1868/9, Llewelyn made a concerted attempt to form a County team, and on 13 March, a meeting was held at The Castle Hotel in Neath to discuss the feasibility of forming a County Club. There was a reasonable attendance and enough money was raised to allow J.T.D. to arrange fixtures with Monmouthshire, Breconshire and Radnorshire during 1869. In addition, a trial match

J. T. D. LLEWELYN

J. T. D. Llewelyn was the son of a wealthy Swansea industrialist, who was one of the first photographers in Wales. After attending Eton and Oxford, J.T.D. was the pioneer force behind cricket in South Wales during the 1860s and 1870s. He set up many clubs, including the Cadoxton club, which was regarded as the MCC of Wales, and led the South Wales CC on its many visits to London.

Llewelyn was a useful right-arm bowler, considered by many as the first 'length bowler' in the area, taking all the Llanelli wickets in a game in 1881, and dismissing W. G. Grace in a match in 1870. He held a dream that a County side should represent Glamorgan and was instrumental in the creation of the present club in 1888. Amazingly, he even made one appearance for the County against Monmouthshire at the ripe old age of 60!

J. T. D. was a kindly patron to many sporting bodies, acting at the President of both the Welsh Rugby Union and the Swansea Cricket and Football Club for many years. Llewelyn also held many interests outside sport, especially horticulture, and the grounds of his home at Penllergaer were amongst the best gardens in South Wales. He acted as Mayor of Swansea in 1890/1 and was the town's Conservative MP between 1895 and 1900.

He was knighted in 1890 in tribute to his services to sport and life in general in South Wales. A host of tributes were paid to him on his death in 1927, with the *South Wales Daily News* fittingly describing him as 'one of the most popular and busiest men in the county'.

J. T. D. Llewelyn, 'the father of Glamorgan cricket', in his mayoral robes. (Swansea City Council)

was held in May at The Gnoll, Neath, between a Glamorganshire XI and a Colts XXII, captained by Swansea's William Bancroft, to test the strength of the Glamorgan team and to assess the emerging talent within the County.

The squire also assembled a South Wales XII to play the MCC at Lord's. It was a successful trip for Llewelyn's team as they won by 24 runs. It gave a huge fillip to the development of cricket in the County, and Llewelyn was able to arrange a series of friendlies in the early 1870s against fairly strong sides. For example, in 1870 his Glamorgan team played a West Gloucestershire side at Cardiff Arms Park. The visitors included both W. G. and G. F. Grace, and the Doctor enjoyed far better fortunes than in his previous visits to South Wales, taking six for 5 and hitting a mighty six off the first ball he received. These matches also saw the emergence of several promising young Welsh cricketers, including T. B. Jones and C. P. Lewis, the first cricketing blues at Oxford from Welsh schools (Christ College, Brecon and Llandovery College).

Llewelyn's team was interestingly described in the 1874 edition of *Lillywhite's Annual* as 'Glamorganshire County Cricket Club'. It seemed a rather grandiose description as only two or three annual matches were played, and it had a membership of just over 50! However, it existed as a gentleman's club, run along similar lines to the SWCC and included many of their players. Nevertheless, Llewelyn had high hopes that the team could get off the ground. A club motif was designed, incorporating the County's coat of arms, and Walter Bennett, one of the founder members of Cardiff CC was engaged as match secretary, utilising his many contacts with other teams in South Wales and the West of England. But with only a select number of members to play in the handful of fixtures, and the limited financial resources, it was never likely to sprout into a substantial and representative County Club.

But J.T.D. was not without hope that one day a county team would be formed and in 1874 he resurrected the SWCC in an attempt to assist the development of cricket in the area. As before, the SWCC went on an annual tour to the London area and played many of the leading amateur clubs. However, Llewelyn made a concerted effort to widen the club's appeal and membership, hoping that it would not become another 'social cricket' club. It was agreed that a professional could be chosen, providing he was Welsh by birth, had resided for two consecutive years in the Principality, or had been engaged for two seasons by a Welsh club. Annual trials were also organised in Cardiff, Swansea and Newport in an attempt to attract more local players, which might lead to the formation of a truly representative Glamorgan side in the future.

The reformed SWCC were fairly successful; three of the four games were won in 1876, and in 1878 J.T.D. secured a fixture with the Australian tourists. The squire led the South Wales XVIII and his bowlers performed well enough to prevent any of the visitors from passing 50. However, the Welshmen had great difficulty batting against the pace of Spofforth and the steady seam of Boyle. They took 17 and 15 respectively as the tourists gained an easy win by an innings and 37 runs. It showed that the standard of cricket in Glamorgan was still below county standard, and in 1879 Llewelyn and C. P. Lewis made a valiant attempt to rectify this by inaugurating a knock-out competition called the 'South Wales Cricket Challenge Cup'. Quite fittingly, the first winners were J.T.D.'s Cadoxton club, who beat Cardiff in the final by 42 runs.

The Challenge Cup raised the competitive spirit in inter-club matches, which had previously been on a friendly basis. However, it also led to some acrimonious arguments between the participants, especially over residential eligibility, and there were a number of cases of bad sportsmanship and rows.

Things came to a head in 1886 in the match between local rivals Swansea and Morriston. The game was riddled with disputes over the starting time and when lunch should be taken. When one Swansea batsman failed to take his place at the wicket in the afternoon session, the Morriston players 'timed him out', and with the crease vacant, their wicket-keeper removed the bails. A furious row broke out and the wickets were pulled up with Swansea's score at 48 for five. *The Cambrian* reported how 'the match ceased amidst much excitement. The spectators soon covered the ground in animated groups, discussing the merits of the dispute. Several demanded their money back, but there was a sufficient number of police on the ground to prevent any breach of the peace.'

Doubts began to be expressed over the future of the competition and of the SWCC itself. They had struggled during the 1880s, winning just five of their 31 games. Yet the poor results were not a reflection of a deterioration in cricket in the region. The clubs in the expanding industrial and commercial centres on the coast and in the coalfield areas had their strongest sides to date. The declining form of the SWCC in fact was the result of the Club's failure to attract new blood, and it had to rely on the ageing stalwarts from the 1860s and 1870s.

Many of the successful players from the town clubs felt that the SWCC was still socially elitist, despite J.T.D.'s effort to broaden its appeal. Many felt that the club still preferred someone with a public school education rather than one with a working-class background, and that the club existed as a form of social entertainment rather than serious sport. Consequently, at their meeting in the autumn of 1886, the SWCC was disbanded and the Challenge Cup competition was discontinued. It seemed as if J.T.D.'s dream of a Glamorgan team was not going to be realised.

GLAMORGAN CCC IS FORMED

THE DATE OF THE BREAK-UP of the SWCC was therefore the time when club cricket in South Wales was ironically in its healthiest state. A number of people were sad at the decision to disband the SWCC but there were many more who believed the time had finally come to form a truly representative Glamorgan team, selecting the best players within the county, regardless of their social background. During 1887 J. P. Jones, an influential architect and surveyor who was both captain and secretary of Cardiff CC began a campaign with these aims. He gained the support of William Bryant, the secretary of Swansea Cricket and Football Club, who contacted J. T. D. Llewelyn and obtained the promise of financial support from the squire, who must have been delighted that there was grass roots support for his dream of a Glamorgan team.

In the spring and early summer of 1888, Jones and Bryant contacted all the officials of the clubs within the county boundaries regarding the feasibility of convening a meeting to form a county team. The replies were favourable and at the end of June, J.T.D. sent the following letter to all the club officials:

> Penllergaer
> Swansea
> June 30th, 1888
>
> Dear Sir,
> I have much pleasure in convening a meeting at the Angel Hotel, Cardiff on Friday, July 6th at six o'clock in the evening to consider the advisability of forming a county cricket club. I need scarcely say that the meeting should be thoroughly representative of cricket in the county, and shall be glad therefore if you will do your utmost to attend.
> Yours faithfully,
> J. T. D. Llewelyn

Over 30 people gathered in the small hotel room, many of them stalwarts of the days of the SWCC. The meeting was chaired by J. P. Jones because J.T.D. was delayed as a result of his duties in the quarter sessions court. The first topic on the agenda was the democratic formation of a county cricket club. It was a formality, with unanimous agreement to the proposal by Edward Jones, the former Cardiff CC and SWCC batsman 'that a county club for Glamorganshire be formed'. Everyone was delighted by this and they all keenly listened to the next item, an address by M. S. Foulger, a journalist with the *South Wales Daily News* who had been involved with the formation of Warwickshire CCC in 1882 when he had been working in Leamington Spa. Foulger told the meeting about his experiences on the Warwickshire committee and how the Midlands club had successfully got off the ground. He believed that 'there was no reason why Glamorganshire as a county should not do as well as Warwickshire. The population was large, the material to work upon better than existed in Warwickshire when that county club started, and there was money!' Foulger had taken an active involvement in Warwickshire's discussions regarding a county ground, and he told the Welsh officials that Glamorgan should earnestly consider obtaining a base of their own. This did not meet with unanimous approval, with Lewis Kempthorne of Neath CC pointing out that 'it would cost a great deal of money, and then would come the difficulty of deciding whether it should be at Cardiff or Swansea' – a comment which was to become awfully familiar as the years passed by.

J.T.D. arrived at the end of Foulger's speech, just in time for the election of officers and a committee. He was unanimously appointed Treasurer, whilst J. P. Jones was elected Chairman, with William Yorath, also of Cardiff CC, as his Secretary. A committee of 14 was then formed, including many personalities such as John Nicholl and Edward Jones, who had been involved with the SWCC. Llewelyn finished affairs by pledging his support to the new Club and its committee, stating that it was his dearest wish that 'county cricket in Glamorganshire would be successful. By good trial matches they would be enabled to unearth talent of very considerable merit, and that without going beyond the limits of the county. They have a good executive committee and out of that would come a shrewd match committee who could take pains that next year Glamorgan would be represented by a strong team. Afterwards, they could play three or four or even five of the various English counties not very far away, and later on perhaps fly at a higher game.'

There were hearty cheers at J.T.D.'s optimistic view of the Club's future but the committee recognised at their first meeting that these hopes would be realised only if they could turn offers of support into hard cash. With this in mind, J. P. Jones proposed that the Marquis of Bute, who owned Cardiff Castle, should be appointed President. Jones was an employee of the Bute Estate and had played for the Marquis's team which regularly played at Cardiff Arms Park in the 1870s and 1880s. The Estate owned, and managed, the thriving docks at Cardiff which had been the seed-bed of the region's industrial growth. They also owned the railway lines which fed the docks and several of the coal mines in the valleys, plus vast areas of land in the county, including the Arms Park. The Marquis was a kind benefactor to the residents of the region, and duly agreed to Jones's request. In addition he offered financial support and the use of the Arms Park ground, thereby solving the potentially divisive issue of purchasing a suitable ground.

The committee also invited other members of the local gentry and business world to become Vice-Presidents, including Lord Jersey, Lord Windsor and Lord Aberdare, plus all the MPs and mayors of the boroughs in the county. Ordinary members began to enrol as well and by the end of July enough financial support had been raised for the committee to get down to creating a viable team. Yorath wrote to all the clubs in South Wales asking for the names of players who the officials believed could represent the County. Replies flooded back and a series of trials and net sessions were held during August 1888, and at the end of the month, a County XI played William Morgan's Llwynypia club to test the strength of the new county side.

The Secretary also contacted the MCC and Ground, Surrey Club and Ground, Herefordshire, Somerset, Worcestershire and Staffordshire with the aim of arranging fixtures in 1889. But nothing came of his requests and the committee spent some agonising weeks during the autumn of 1888, wondering who would agree to play them. Their anxiety was relieved in the New Year when Foulger used his connections with Warwickshire to arrange a game between the two clubs at Cardiff in June 1889. However, the Midlands county would only honour the fixture if £40 was guaranteed towards the match expenses. J.T.D. (representing the West Area) and J.P. Jones (representing the East Area) acted as guarantors, thereby allowing the fixture to go ahead. There was further good news when Yorath received belated replies from the MCC and Surrey agreeing to fixtures in August as part of a short London tour, along the lines of that previously undertaken by the SWCC.

During the spring of 1889, the Arms Park wicket was carefully prepared in readiness for the big day in June. A number of practice sessions were held during May, so that the Glamorgan players would be in top form for the initial fixture. But after all the meticulous planning and publicity, Glamorgan were unable to raise a full strength team. J.T.D.'s son, Willie, later an Oxford Blue, William Morgan and Lewis Kempthorne were either unavailable or injured; and just to compound matters, Warwickshire sent down a strong side led by L. C. Docker, who had toured Australia with Arthur Shrewsbury's team in 1887/8. It also included Arthur Lilley, one of the best wicketkeepers in England, John Shilton, a revered fast bowler and William Collishaw, an all-rounder who had played for an England XI in 1886.

Edmund David of St Fagan's led the Glamorgan team and he struck

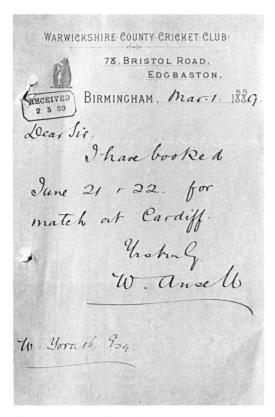

WARWICKSHIRE·COUNTY·CRICKET·CLUB·

78, BRISTOL ROAD,
EDGBASTON,

BIRMINGHAM, *Mar 1* 1889.

Dear Sir.

I have booked June 21 & 22. for match at Cardiff.

Yours truly

W. Ansell

W. Yorath Esq.

Confirmation from Warwickshire of Glamorgan's first official match.

the first blow by winning the toss and electing to bat. However, with only the second ball of the game, Lewis Jenkins fell to a catch off Shilton, and a steady procession of Glamorgan batsmen returned at regular intervals to the Cardiff pavilion. At 70 for nine it looked that an embarrassing start would be made, but there was a stubborn last wicket partnership between Astley Samuel, the Pontardawe all-rounder, and Dan Thissen, the Morriston wicket-keeper. They steadily picked off the tiring bowlers, confused the Warwickshire fielders by calling to each other in Welsh, and took the score to 136 before Thissen was dismissed. This gallant partnership gave the Welshmen a feeling of confidence and their bowlers tenaciously fought back. Despite the presence of the illustrious names in the Warwickshire line-up, they were dismissed for 138 with James Lindley, the Cardiff professional, taking five for 51.

However, the Glamorgan batsmen failed to get to grips with Shilton in their second innings. They collapsed once again and were

21

GLAMORGAN *v.* WARWICKSHIRE

Played at Cardiff Arms Park, 21 and 22 June 1889

WARWICKSHIRE WON BY 8 WICKETS

GLAMORGAN

	FIRST INNINGS		SECOND INNINGS	
L. Jenkins	c Richards b Shilton	0	c Lilley b Whitehead	7
D. E. Jones	c Lilley b Bird	12	st Lilley b Whitehead	12
A. W. Morris	c Bird b Leake	9	b Shilton	8
W. J. Bancroft	b Shilton	13	c Leake b Whitehead	1
T. Robinson	c Leake b Shilton	19	lbw b Shilton	15
*E. U. David	c Lilley b Bird	0	b Shilton	2
J. G. Clarke	c D. Docker b Bird	2	b Shilton	20
J. V. Lindley	lbw b Shilton	7	b Shilton	3
W. E. Lewis	st Lilly b Shilton	10	not out	9
A. W. Samuel	not out	28	c Richards b Shilton	1
†D. E. Thissen	c Leake b Whitehead	33	lbw b Shilton	0
Extras		3		2
Total		136		80

1st inns: 1-0, 2-11, 3-37, 4-52, 6-54, 7-60, 8-66, 9-81
2nd inns: 1-1, 2-2, 3-11, 4-37, 5-39, 6-42, 7-42, 8-53, 9-74

BOWLING	O	M	R	W	O	M	R	W
Shilton	36	16	49	5	28.4	13	42	7
Leake	17	2	38	3				
Bird	29	11	44	1	7	5	4	0
Whitehead	1.1	0	2	1	21	9	32	3

WARWICKSHIRE

	FIRST INNINGS		SECOND INNINGS	
D. Docker	c David b Lindley	8	b Samuel	0
A. Law	b Lindley	24	not out	26
W. Richards	st Thissen b Samuel	0	lbw b Robinson	21
*L. C. Docker	c Thissen b Lindley	41	not out	25
C. F. Hunt	b Samuel	11		
W. F. Collishaw	retired hurt	0		
J. E. Shilton	c Bancroft b Lindley	18		
A. Bird	c Thissen b Lindley	1		
†A. F. A. Lilley	run out	8		
J. Leake	not out	8		
S. J. Whitehead	b Samuel	3		
Extras		16		7
Total		138	(for 2 wkts)	79

1st inns: 1-11, 2-16, 3-52, 4-88, 5-108, 6-110, 7-121, 8-133, 9-138
2nd inns: 1-0, 2-35

BOWLING	O	M	R	W	O	M	R	W
Lindley	26	7	51	5	13	6	17	0
Samuel	21	7	56	3	10.3	1	37	1
Robinson	6	1	15	0	7	0	18	1

This was Glamorgan's first official match, but their opponents proved far too strong and cruised to an easy victory.

Edmund David, Glamorgan's first captain. (David Smith)

bowled out for 80, with only Gowan Clarke offering any resistance. This left the visitors needing just 79 to win which they comfortably reached for the loss of just two wickets. A fairly large crowd had turned up, so Warwickshire agreed to continue batting for exhibition purposes, adding a further 65 runs. However, the Glamorgan officials were more concerned about the poor public response than the heavy defeat – gate receipts on the first day had amounted to under £10 and those the following day around £17.

Because the Club recorded a heavy loss in both playing and monetary terms in their opening fixture, some doubt existed as to whether they could honour the London area fixtures. Their fears were eased at the end of July when J.T.D. once again came to the Club's rescue by agreeing to cover the entire running costs for the rest of the season. A further boost came when Glamorgan acquired the services of 30-year-old William Wilkinson, a fast bowler from the Nottingham area, who was attached to the Cardiff club, and was chosen for the London tour in place of the unavailable Bancroft. Willie Llewelyn, William Morgan and Hastings Watson, the talented Cardiff opener, were also available, and the County officials were able to select a strong party for the matches in London.

Even with a reinforced team, they suffered a 103-run defeat against MCC and Ground in the first game of the tour, but morale was boosted in the next against Surrey Club and Ground when Glamorgan registered their first-ever victory. Surrey batted first, but were tied down by some accurate bowling by Lindley, Llewelyn and the fiery Wilkinson, and were restricted to 161. Hastings Watson and Daniel Jones gave the Welsh county a good start with a half-century partnership for the first wicket. A mid-innings collapse stiffled their progress, but some bold tail-end blows by Thissen and Lindley saw Glamorgan to a useful lead of 62. Lindley and Wilkinson were spurred on by the tail-end resistance and once again posed problems for the Surrey batsmen. They both picked up four wickets, and the Welsh county were left needing just 21. However, they lost Watson, Jones and Llewelyn with only a handful of runs on the board and there were a few flutters in Welsh hearts. Thissen was unsuccessfully promoted to hit the winning runs, and it was left to the Cardiff pair of Gowan Clark and W. H. 'Buller' Williams to steer Glamorgan to their first success.

The victorious team returned to Cardiff that night, but there was little time for celebration as they were playing a return fixture with the MCC the following day. After their initial victory a much larger crowd attended the match and although it ended in a draw, the Glamorgan officials were delighted at the better response. At their Annual Meeting, J. T. D. Llewelyn reported that £141 had been taken in gate money, mainly at the MCC match, and that the Club had a profit of £11. It wasn't much, but at least it was a start and the committee could plan ahead for 1890.

The same fixtures were arranged for 1890, plus matches against Monmouthshire and Somerset. The newly acquired game with Monmouthshire at the Arms Park saw Herbie Morgan of Penarth CC hit the first century for Glamorgan. Morgan was still only 19 and his feat only came about because Cardiff's Daniel Jones was unavailable. The Glamorgan committee hurriedly called up the young batsman, after being impressed by his fine 52 against Cardiff at the Arms Park the previous weekend. Morgan had played for the County the previous year, but had batted in the lower order. He went in at No 7 against Monmouthshire and scored 147 with four sixes and fifteen fours, though he was fortunate enough to survive many near misses, and the hapless Monmouthshire fielders spilled several catches.

SURREY CLUB AND GROUND
v GLAMORGAN

Played at The Oval, 19 and 20 August 1889

GLAMORGAN WON BY 6 WICKETS

SURREY	FIRST INNINGS		SECOND INNINGS	
†H. C. Cooper	b Wilkinson	7	st Jones b W. Morgan	7
W. Harris	b Llewelyn	27	b Wilkinson	13
W. Brockwell	c Llewelyn b Wilkinson	0	absent	0
G. H. Watts	b Williams	48	c Llewelyn b Lindley	10
P. A. Robinson	b Wilkinson	1	b Wilkinson	0
C. Wigram	c Wilkinson b W. Morgan	26	b Lindley	0
J. W. Sharpe	st Jones b Llewelyn	1	c Clarke b Lindley	12
Lyddon	b Lindley	4	c Lindley b Wilkinson	5
C. H. Mills	c Watson b Lindley	23	c Jones b Lindley	30
*F. E. Huish	run out	5	b Wilkinson	0
Dexter	not out	5	not out	0
Extras		14		5
Total		161		82

BOWLING	O	M	R	W	O	M	R	W
Lindley	20.4	5	46	2	18	10	20	4
Wilkinson	28	10	39	3	21.3	8	39	4
Llewelyn	14	5	29	2	5	1	10	0
Williams	6	1	16	1				
W. Morgan	4	0	17	1	4	2	8	1

GLAMORGAN	FIRST INNINGS		SECOND INNINGS	
W. H. Watson	lbw b Harris	58	b Lyddon	4
†D. E. Jones	run out	25	c Dexter b Lyddon	1
W. D. Llewelyn	b Huish	19	b Sharpe	1
J. G. Clarke	b Sharpe	24	not out	6
*W. Morgan	c Cooper b Harris	1		
W. L. Yorath	run out	4		
W. Wilkinson	b Huish	4		
W. H. Williams	c Harris b Huish	8	not out	3
D. E. Thissen	b Sharpe	26	c Huish b Lyddon	9
H. E. Morgan	lbw b Huish	5		
J. V. Lindley	not out	31		
Extras		18		
Total		223	(for 4 wkts)	24

BOWLING	O	M	R	W	O	M	R	W
Sharpe	28.4	17	49	2	13	6	13	1
Watts	9	1	41	0				
Lyddon	19	9	33	0	14	8	11	3
Mills	6	2	29	0				
Huish	22	12	35	4				
Harris	6	2	18	2				

A rare victory in a season full of worries on and off the field. Glamorgan owed their success to a fine innings by Watson, and a spell of hostile bowling from both Lindley and Wilkinson.

*Herbie Morgan, the first Glamorgan centurion, in his Penarth rugby kit.
(Penarth RFC)*

Glamorgan went on to score 420, and ended up with a comfortable victory thanks to Morgan's batting. However, it was their only success of the summer, as the other six games all ended in defeats.

One of the reasons behind the moderate form was the relaxed air about the way the team played, with the amateurs viewing the games as an escape from the demands of the commercial world. One of the people who tried to mix business with pleasure was Astley Samuel, an estate agent from Swansea, who was a useful seam bowler. On the first morning of the game with the MCC in June 1890, Samuel had to make a business call, and after reporting for duty and having a net at St Helen's, he hurriedly left the ground hoping to complete his work and return in time to bat. However, Glamorgan collapsed against a strong MCC bowling attack and were dismissed for 57 before lunch, with Samuel being simply recorded as 'absent' in the scorebook. Sadly, there are no records of what Alec Morris, the Glamorgan captain, said to Samuel when he returned during the afternoon!

Samuel blotted his copy book later in the season during the tour of the London area. Fixtures had been arranged against Surrey Club and Ground and the MCC, followed by a match with Somerset at Bath on the way back home. Samuel obviously enjoyed the socialising off the field whilst up in London, because he was reported as being 'taken ill at Bath and unable to bowl with his customary effect!'

Despite losing six of the eight games, fairly large crowds were once again attracted to the Swansea and Cardiff grounds for the County's home matches. As a result the profits rose to £97 at the end of the season, allowing the committee to plan a tour of North-East England in May 1891, with matches against Durham and Northumberland.

How teams were selected in the early days; letters like the one above were sent by the Secretary to players asking whether or not they were available. In this case, J. P. Jones must have been too busy! (Chris Brain)

The officials also discussed suitable colours and a motif for the club. In their initial games, the team had sported white caps with a red dragon badge. The design however was unpopular and the committee decided instead to use green caps with a dragon motif.

Season 1891 was much better, with two victories over Monmouthshire and a very gratifying win for the first time at Lord's over the MCC. Glamorgan batted first and scored 218, with Billy Bancroft, the 20-year-old Swansea cricketer and rugby international top scoring with 56. The MCC were dismissed for 180, with Theo Robinson of Cardiff and Burton, the Bridgend professional, both taking five wickets. Robinson then shared a half-century opening partnership with William Morgan and it looked as if the Welshmen were going to build up a commanding lead. But a collapse set in with Glamorgan being bowled out for 156, leaving the MCC with a target of 195. They got off to a shaky start with Morgan taking four wickets in a fiery opening spell. Burton and Harry Letcher tied down the MCC batsmen with their accurate spin, and they ended 18 runs short when the final wicket fell, to the unashamed delight of the Welsh contingent.

The Glamorgan supporters were brought back down to earth with a jolt as the MCC easily won the return match at Swansea, whilst Gloucestershire inflicted two heavy defeats. Indeed, the West Country team fielded an extremely strong side in both of their matches with Glamorgan. The first game at Cardiff in May saw a Glamorgan XV take on a Gloucestershire XII which included W. G. Grace. After the Welsh team had been dismissed for 61, Gloucestershire declared at 140 for seven, with the 'Doctor', batting at No 8, making 34 not out. His presence ensured a large attendance, and the *South Wales Daily News* recorded how there was 'a huge round of applause at the advent at the wicket of the champion, Dr. W. G. Grace'. The Glamorgan side were bowled out for 50 in their second innings, leaving the visitors the winners by a handsome margin. The Doctor played against the Welsh county once again in a conventional eleven-a-side game at Bristol in August. He was dismissed for nought this time, but the good name of the Grace family was upheld by E.M., who scored 135! Gloucestershire amassed 351 on the first day and then proceeded to bowl out the Welshmen for 93 and 41 on the second. It was a dismal batting performance with the *Western Mail* gloomily saying that 'even the most sanguine supporters of Glamorgan did not anticipate that they would be able to avert defeat, but few imagined they would make such a very poor batting display'.

The match with Gloucestershire at the Arms Park had been arranged for publicity purposes by Joseph Brain, the new captain-secretary of the Welsh Club. J. H. Brain had played for the West

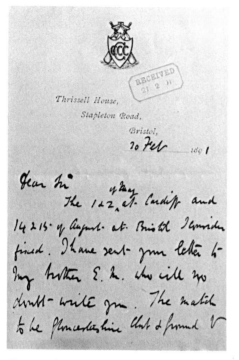

Correspondence with 'The Doctor' regarding Glamorgan's games with Gloucestershire in 1891. Obviously W.G. did not want to field too strong a team against his former colleague's side. (Chris Brain)

Country team between 1883 and 1889, but had returned to South Wales to become involved in the family's brewery at Cardiff, and was to become a dynamic force behind Glamorgan around the turn of the century, cleverly using his contacts in the business and sporting world. He was instrumental in getting several talented West Country amateurs to cross the Severn Estuary and turn out for the Welsh county. One of the recruits was the Reverend Lyonel D'Arcy Hildyard who had been in the Oxford team with Brain which beat Australia in 1884, and had first-class experience with Somerset and Lancashire.

But Brain did not rely on importing friends and acquaintances, and made concerted efforts to introduce talented Welsh youngsters, and in May the Club sent out a circular advertising a Colts match at the Arms Park over the Whitsun Holiday. Secretaries of clubs in South Wales were invited to send the Glamorgan officials names of any young players, and so great was the response that a Colts XXII took on a Glamorgan XI.

29

Brain also realised that the Club badly needed a full-time professional, and during the winter of 1891/2, the committee began searching for a suitable candidate, with J. P. Jones offering to pay some of the costs the professional would incur, as long as the County's choice was based with Cardiff CC. George Porter, the Derbyshire fast-medium bowler, was interviewed, but he demanded winter employment, preferably in a public house! Despite their close links with the Brain family, the County could not guarantee Porter's wishes, and negotiations ended.

Ironically, the Welsh team had their most successful season to date in 1892, and the search for a professional was shelved. Five of the eight games were won, including the double over the MCC and Monmouthshire. Five matches were won again in 1893, but there were also five defeats, including the game with the touring South Africans at the Arms Park. Brain had been instrumental in arranging this fixture in an attempt to raise the image of the Club. However, it failed to bring a Welsh victory as George Rowe took twelve for 106 to secure a comfortable ten-wicket victory for the Springboks.

This heavy defeat was a major setback to Brain who had hoped his team would put up a good show against the tourists. However, the Club were dealt a far more severe blow in August when Willie Llewelyn, one of their finest prospects, was killed in a tragic accident within weeks of his marriage to the daughter of Lord Dynevor. He died in a shooting incident in the grounds of Penllergaer House whilst walking down to the nearby lake to do some fishing. He had taken his double-barrelled shot gun, as he often saw hawks flying over the lake. As he walked down to the lake he saw an animal scurry into a nearby wood, so he decided to pursue it, using the butt of the gun to make an opening in the thicket. Tragically, a branch caught in the trigger, and the gun went off into Llewelyn's chest, killing him instantly. His funeral attracted hundreds of people from the local gentry and sporting world, with several members of the committee attending to pay their respects to the 25-year-old who was seen by many as a future captain and administrator of the Club.

The officials were still in a sombre mood a few weeks later when they met to discuss the Club's financial situation at the end of the season. Gate money had fallen to just £73 with fewer people watching their games and this caused the committee to agonise over the public's apparent ambivalence towards their matches. There was a growing feeling that the public of the area were far more interested in the faster moving game of rugby, in mining coal, producing iron and steel and attending chapel. Many found it difficult to understand the 'English gentleman's game', and others found hardly any spare time in the summer months during which they could try to learn how to play the

The ill-fated Willie Llewelyn, as depicted in 'Cricket – a Weekly Record of the Game', 21 May 1891. (David Smith)

game. Moreover, the geographical nature of the narrow valleys in the South Wales coalfield meant that most areas of flat land were used for housing and there was little spare land available on which a square could be laid.

Consequently, support at the grass roots level had not grown in the way in which J. T. D. Llewelyn (now Sir John) had expected. It meant that the County were increasingly reliant on his good patronage, plus the enthusiastic support of the wealthy tradesmen and businessmen such as J. P. Jones and J. H. Brain. Nevertheless, the falling financial reserves and dwindling public support led some of the

31

officials to believe that the Club should be disbanded once again. But most of the committee were successful businessmen who had made their fortunes through hard work, and although Brain was sceptical about the future, the committee were optimistic and felt a winding up of the Club would be unwise and hasty; and a resolution was passed that 'Glamorgan CCC should continue to exist'. Even so, the officials still had a lot of work to do in raising the overall image of Glamorgan cricket – for example, E. V. Lucas commented in *Willow and Leather* that 'on a fine day, when the match is not important enough to crowd the ring, when for instance the MCC are playing Glamorganshire, the Pavilion cat has the pleasant habit of sunning itself on the turf!'

Despite their determination to carry on, the County still lacked a settled XI, with a wide variety of amateurs and professionals turning out. The team often included a number of Welsh rugby internationals, whose appearance on the cricket field must have helped swell the gate receipts. Amongst those to turn out were Percy Bush, William Gwynn, George Young and the Biggs brothers, Selwyn and Norman. The latter had become Wales's youngest international, playing against New Zealand in December 1888 at the tender age of 18 years and 1 month. He appeared for Glamorgan in a friendly against a Cardiff and District XI in 1893 which the committee had arranged as a trial for three professionals – Lewin, Casbourne (Buckinghamshire) and Roffey (Surrey). None of them impressed the watching officials, with Roffey, batting at No 4 failing to score in either innings, whilst the other two bowlers picked up just four and three wickets respectively. Biggs's cricket career ended around the turn of the century, when he went off to join the Nigerian Police. Sadly, he was to meet a decidedly sticky fate in February 1908 when he was killed by a poisoned arrow during a native ambush.

Another character to appear during the 1890s was the Rev Owen Jones, the curate of Cadoxton-juxta-Neath and a tearaway fast bowler, described by one club captain as 'undoubtedly the best opening bowler in South Wales'. Jones had attended Llandovery College, and whilst at Jesus College, Oxford, was involved in an incident rather unbecoming of a potential clergyman. In November 1881, he was found guilty of gross disorderly conduct in travelling with a second-class ticket in a first-class carriage on the Great Western Railway, as well as breaking the windows and damaging the compartment. Maybe he saw the light and repented his sins after this incident, for which he was given a three-month suspension by the college, and opted to reserve his wrath for the cricket field, plus the occasional 'fire and brimstone' sermon!

There were also throwbacks to the days of the SWCC as social factors became as important as cricketing ability in selection for some of the friendlies, as the committee chose members of the local gentry, such as Lord Cope and Sir J. W. Courtis, hoping that they would financially support the Club. However, they still failed to find the right combination of players, and won only two of the seven matches in 1894. At the end of the season, Brain told the committee that he was greatly disappointed at the apathy of the players and the difficulties of putting good teams in the field. It was obvious that there was still an air of country house cricket about the way the side played, and it was agreed that the time had come to raise standards by engaging a professional. Several names were discussed, and eventually the committee hired Billy Bancroft at the princely sum of £2 a week for 20 weeks, believing that his appontment would give the team a greater Welsh identity, and thereby increase support from local people. However, Bancroft's appointment put even greater pressure on the Club's already flimsy finances, so in an attempt to boost funds and membership, Brain organised several special friendlies. The first must have rekindled old memories and friendships, because it was against a team raised by C. P. Lewis, representing the SWCC. Lewis's veterans, however, were no match for the younger Glamorgan side, and despite a fighting half-century by the 42-year-old Lewis, the County XI won by nine wickets.

In August, another two-day friendly was staged against an eleven raised by Vernon Hill, the Welsh-born batsman who was playing for Somerset and had been at Oxford with Brain. The game received much publicity from the local press, with the *South Wales Daily News* saying that 'cricketers in Glamorgan have to thank J. H. Brain more than anyone else for the continuation of the county club . . . It was a happy idea of the popular captain to invite the co-operation of Vernon Hill in bringing to Cardiff a representative eleven with a view to popularise the game locally.' Hill's team included several of his Somerset colleagues, plus the legendary C. B. Fry, yet another Oxford Blue, who was playing for Sussex. Fry top-scored with an elegant 71, showing why the England selectors included him for their winter touring party. Unfortunately, rain interfered with the fund-raising friendly and it ended in a rather soggy draw.

Although it meant a greater financial commitment, Bancroft's hiring led to major improvements in the playing standard. For the first season to date, the team went through 1895 without a defeat. Whilst rain played a hand in some of the draws, the Glamorgan team of 1895 was stronger in talent and more competitive in spirit. There were several new faces in the team – Joseph Brain's younger brother William took over behind the stumps and proved himself to be a most capable wicket-keeper, as befitting someone with first-class experience for Oxford University and Gloucestershire. Indeed, in 1893 he

BILLY BANCROFT

Billy Bancroft was one of the Club's leading professionals during the minor county era, scoring over 8,000 runs in his career between 1889 and 1914. He was also a useful change bowler, taking a hat-trick and scoring a century against Surrey II in 1899. Billy also kept wicket in a few games when the Club were struggling to raise an eleven, and without his all-round services it is doubtful whether the Club would have survived very far into the 20th century.

Bancroft was also a talented full back at rugby, and won 33 caps for Wales between 1889 and 1900. He was a fine kicker too, and scored over 1,000 points in his career with Swansea RFC. He was a member of a well known sporting family and was brought up in a cottage alongside the St Helen's ground. His grandfather was the Swansea professional, and led the Colts XXII against Llewelyn's Glamorganshire team in 1869. Billy's father was also a useful player for Swansea and the South Wales CC, and they both appeared for Glamorgan in the trial match against the Colts XXI in 1892.

Billy kept his association with St Helen's after he retired, and in the inter-war period acted as a steward in the members enclosure, often sitting at the bottom of the pavilion steps, engrossed in play and always willing to pass on advice. He also coached many youngsters, including Gilbert Parkhouse, and by Bancroft's own admission, one of his proudest sporting moments came in the 1950s when Parkhouse played for England.

The cricketing family Bancroft (circa 1890) in front of their cottage at St Helen's. Left to right: William Bancroft (senior), William Bancroft (junior), Billy Bancroft. Jack Bancroft is the small boy seated in the foreground with a rugby ball. (Swansea Cricket and Football Club)

had accomplished the unique feat of stumping three Somerset batsmen off consecutive deliveries from Gloucestershire's Charles Townsend.

Brain also persuaded William Pullen, a 29-year-old batsman who had played for Gloucestershire since 1882, to appear for the Welsh county. The bowling attack was more potent following the acquisition of two fast bowlers – Frank Binch, a Lancastrian who was the professional at Penarth CC and Sam Lowe, formerly of Nottinghamshire, who was attached to Cardiff CC.

The improvement in playing form continued in 1896 when four of the nine games were won. The match with Monmouthshire at Newport epitomised the new spirit within the County Club. Glamorgan were set 211 by Monmouthshire, but lost five quick wickets and looked in a hopeless position. However, Bancroft got his head down and struck a superb 119 to lead the side to a two-wicket victory. J. H. Brain himself hit 144 against the MCC at Lord's, whilst Selwyn Biggs, the 21-year-old rugby international, emerged as a most promising spinner, by taking eight wickets in the victory over Herefordshire and ten in the innings win over the MCC at the Arms Park.

Although defeats occurred at the hands of Worcestershire Club and Ground, and Surrey II, Brain was able to take great satisfaction from the way his team played in 1896, and there were indications that it had finally come of age, with the captain and Bancroft instilling a feeling of greater confidence and a more professional attitude. Nevertheless, there was still the odd hiccough – the Club still undertook an annual tour to London and there must have been more than one red face when young William Brain fell 'ill' after a night socialising before the game against Surrey Club and Ground at The Oval. A telegram was hurriedly sent to T. M. Barlow of Cardiff CC asking him to catch the early morning train up to London, but he was unable to arrive in time for the match and the Welsh county had to borrow Carrington of the Surrey groundstaff as a replacement. I wonder if J. H. Brain had a quiet word in his younger brother's ear when they got back home?

MINOR COUNTY DAYS

J. H. BRAIN had a firm belief that the Welsh county would further its improvement if they played in a higher standard of play, preferably on a league basis. Back in the late 1880s and early 1890s, Brain's team had been viewed as being only a third-class side, but the improving results during the 1890s had shown they were capable of holding their own with the teams who had been competing in the recently formed Minor County Championship. Support at the grass roots level seemed stronger following the creation of the Glamorgan Cricket League and Brain believed that the time was right to enter the new competition. At their autumn committee meeting, the Glamorgan officials agreed with his proposals, and the secretary wrote off to Lord's to gain the MCC's approval. They endorsed the Club's application, and everyone connected with the Welsh county eagerly looked forward to the new challenge ahead.

There were a host of articles and letters in the local press during the winter of 1896/7, all designed to promote the County's new venture. One of the letters in the *South Wales Daily News,* signed J.O.E., stated 'those who are doubtful of the ultimate success of the efforts made by J. H. Brain and his committee to bring Glamorganshire cricket to the front, should consider the rise and progress of Somerset . . . We are getting on fairly well, but the lesson of Somerset should inspire the public of the district . . . so that what has contributed to the success of Somerset since 1888 – the nimble sixpence of the working man – shall help to bring about a brilliant future for Glamorgan. Let the public show in a practical way that love of the grand summer game is by no means dead, and we may yet become one of the first-class counties. Now South Walians, lovers of sport and all manly games, bring the enthusiasm you hold for football in the winter into cricket in the summer. You need not give up football for cricket, but keep both going.'

Despite their elevation into the minor county ranks and the go-ahead policy of the committee, there were a few behind-the-scenes arguments over the selection of the Glamorgan team for their first game in the competition against Surrey II at The Oval on 7 and 8 June 1897. The side was chosen the weekend before the match, and amongst those selected was William Russell, the professional at Cowbridge, who was a talented all-rounder from Norfolk. However, his employers were somewhat reluctant to release him. The Cowbridge chairman, E. H. Ebsworth of Llandough Castle, had just laid a cricket pitch on his 1,500-acre estate with the help of Russell and

Alec Hearne, the Test cricketer from Kent. Ebsworth preferred that Russell devoted his time and energy to his job of groundsman of the new square and informed Glamorgan that the all-rounder was not available for the Surrey match.

The Glamorgan officials made an attempt to persuade Ebsworth to change his mind in the couple of days prior to the team's departure for London. But Ebsworth stood firm and refused to release Russell – in fact Ebsworth was not the sort of man to be trifled with. He was a fine shot and his lavish home contained tokens of his skill with the rifle, including an enormous stuffed brown bear which he had shot at close quarters whilst on a business trip to Russia! Russell's unavailability was a major blow to the Welsh team, with the *Western Mail* correspondent summing up public opinion by saying that Russell's inclusion 'would help the side to win a match in which the victory would do the Welsh county no end of good, for the winning or losing of this game may have much to do with the future of Glamorgan cricket.'

Despite all these background arguments, the Welsh team performed well against a strong Surrey II, nine of whom had first-class experience, and the match ended in a highly creditable draw. Ten days later, in the friendly with Monmouthshire, the club was given a further boost as William Brain scored one of the fastest centuries on record for Glamorgan. Going in at No 7, he hit the Monmouthshire bowlers to all parts of the Newport ground, reaching 113 in just 53 minutes. But the team were brought back down to earth in their next Championship match as Worcestershire, the eventual Champions, scored 356 and secured a comfrotable victory by an innings and 114 runs.

Glamorgan registered their first success as a fully fledged minor county at the end of July against Cornwall at St Helen's. The game was also notable for the fact that Sam Lowe, the Cardiff professional, took the first-ever hat-trick for the Welsh county. His feat occurred in the visitors' first innings, described as follows by the *South Wales Daily News*: 'Hosking, who had been in twenty minutes for one, was caught in the slips off Sam Lowe, who had had downright bad luck to date. But with his next ball, the Cardiff fast bowler knocked over the Cornwall captain's middle stump (Colville-Smith) and with his next, he bowled Trevarthen, so performing the hat-trick and gaining unstinted applause from the small band of spectators.'

The Welsh county had only mustered 126 in their first innings, but they fared much better in their second, with Bancroft and Letcher making half-centuries. When last man Lambert was bowled, Cornwall were left to score 259 in the three hours and 20 minutes remaining. It seemed a reasonable target, but they collapsed to 25 all out, with Sam Lowe and Lambert both taking five wickets. The Cornish innings lasted only three quarters of an hour and the victorious Welshmen were cheered off the ground by the small crowd, who could not quite believe the ease and speed with which victory had been achieved.

The good form was maintained the following weekend as Wiltshire were beaten by ten wickets at the Arms Park. Lowe and Lambert played leading roles once again, taking ten for 105 and ten for 149 respectively. A large crowd turned up for the mid-week match with Surrey II at Cardiff, confirming Brain's belief that the local population would support a successful team. They nearly saw another victory as Surrey were set 221 on the final day, and lost their ninth wicket with the score on 142 with five minutes to go. The last pair, Keene and Hussey, bravely hung on in the final over from Harry Letcher, and the crowd went away happy that Glamorgan had had the better of a tense game. It seemed that everything was finally going right for Brain's team, and further good news came when the dispute with Ebsworth was settled towards the end of the season, and the County were able to secure the services of Russell on a regular basis.

Glamorgan ended their first season in the competition in a highly promising second place, with just the Worcestershire defeat against them. The improvement continued in 1898 when six of the eight games were won, with one draw and one defeat. The Welsh county had the highest number of victories to their credit and had sound claims to the Championship title. However, the ruling was that the title would be decided by the number of defeats. Consequently, the title was shared by Northamptonshire and Buckinghamshire; neither lost a game and drew seven matches each, but won only three and one respectively. The Glamorgan committee ruefully pondered on the vagaries of the system, but their frustration was tempered by the safe knowledge that Brain's team was making fine progress, as testified by the victory over a strong MCC team by four wickets. The development continued in 1899, as the Glamorgan team ended in joint third place, winning nine matches, drawing one and losing one. A very useful team was moulded together, with the leading run-scorers being Herbie Morgan, the Brain brothers, Ralph and Sidney Sweet-Escott and Richard Lowe, the former Notts and Sussex batsman and brother of Sam. Harry Creber of Swansea took 13 wickets in the victory over Monmouthshire and 14 in both of the games against Berkshire, whilst Russell claimed 12 in the match with Wiltshire. In addition, Bancroft emerged as a fine all-rounder, achieving the rare feat of a hat-trick and a century in the game with Surrey II. Brain thus had few worries about the on-field events in 1899, but unfortunately this was not the case with the financial position. Despite the good form

GLAMORGAN *v.* CORNWALL

Played at St Helen's, Swansea, 22 and 23 July 1897

GLAMORGAN WON BY 233 RUNS

GLAMORGAN	FIRST INNINGS		SECOND INNINGS	
E. W. Jones	c Blight b Hide	6	b Hide	17
W. J. Bancroft	b Hide	9	c Trevarthen b Hide	71
H. B. Letcher	b Hide	10	c Hosking b Hide	57
*J. H. Brain	c Colville-Smith b Hide	48	c Coade b Hide	16
H. E. Morgan	c Coade b Hosking	0	c Trevarthen b Hide	0
E. U. David	b Hide	6	b Hosking	4
†W. H. Brain	lbw b Hide	5	c Hosking b Hide	12
R. Lowe	not out	30	c Colville-Smith b Hide	44
W. S. R. Sweet-Escott	b Trevarthen	7	c Trevarthen b Hide	4
S. Lowe	c Tyack b Trevarthen	0	not out	4
W. Lambert	c Treweeke b Trevarthen	0	b Hosking	1
Extras		5		17
Total		126		247

1st inns: 1-13, 2-22, 3-39, 4-40, 5-61, 6-79, 7-85, 8-126, 9-126
2nd inns: 1-0, 2-0, 3-3, 4-3, 5-8, 6-9, 7-16, 8-18, 9-18

BOWLING	O	M	R	W	O	M	R	W
Hosking	16	4	50	1	24.1	5	80	2
Hide	24	8	51	6	33	12	98	8
Blight	5	2	9	0	6	0	29	0
Trevarthen	3.2	0	11	3	7	1	15	0
Oates					4	2	8	0

CORNWALL	FIRST INNINGS		SECOND INNINGS	
Tyack	b Lambert	21	b Lambert	0
†W. Coade	c and b Lambert	39	st W. H. Brain b Lambert	0
W. H. Treweeke	st W. H. Brain b Lambert	19	b S. Lowe	3
Hosking	c Morgan b S. Lowe	1	b S. Lowe	0
J. B. Hide	c R. Lowe b Lambert	4	c David b Lambert	4
Rev. W. Pickford	b Lambert	7	c Morgan b S. Lowe	2
*E. Colville-Smith	b S. Lowe	0	not out	0
Trevarthen	b S. Lowe	0	b S. Lowe	3
W. E. Oates	b Lambert	1	c W. H. Brain b Lambert	6
Blight	not out	5	b S. Lowe	1
R. T. Mitchell	b S. Lowe	1	b Lambert	6
Extras		17		
Total		115		25

1st inns: 1-51, 2-84, 3-85, 4-89, 5-97, 6-97, 7-97, 8-97, 9-102
2nd inns: 1-0, 2-0, 3-3, 4-3, 5-8, 6-9, 7-16, 8-18, 9-18

BOWLING	O	M	R	W	O	M	R	W
S. Lowe	18.3	10	27	4	6	2	9	5
R. Lowe	9	1	21	0				
J. H. Brain	7	2	21	0				
Lambert	16	6	29	6	6.1	2	16	5

This game resulted in Glamorgan recording their first victory in the Minor County Championship and boosted the morale of Joseph Brain's predominantly amateur side. However, it was the professionals William Lambert and Sam Lowe who set up this win, remarkably within the space of 13 overs. Cornwall's 25 remains the lowest total by any county against Glamorgan.

shown by the players, the attendances had been moderate, and over £200 was owed to the Bank. In their Annual Report, the Club's officials expressed their deep regret at the 'unsatisfactory balance sheet and call upon members to do all they can to improve the finances by introducing new members or procuring further donations.'

Brain had hoped to secure a fixture with the South Africans in 1900, but the overdraft prevented Glamorgan giving the tourists satisfactory guarantees and the idea had to be dropped. The captain realised that the Club's funds had to be boosted so he used his varsity contacts again and arranged a one-day game at Arms Park against an XI chosen by W. D. Brownlee, an Old Cliftonian who had links with Oxford University. His team was composed of well-known amateurs from Gloucestershire and Somerset, including Gilbert Jessop, the Gloucestershire captain, Sammy Woods, the Somerset captain, and Charles Townsend, another Old Cliftonian, who was a leading bowler with Gloucestershire. A large crowd turned up to see this star-studded team and they saw a superb all-round performance by Sam Lowe. First of all, he recorded another hat-trick, clean bowling Peppin, Magniac and Bush to finish with the fine analysis of seven for 35. The Welsh county lost early wickets, but then Sam Lowe and his brother shared in a partnership which took Glamorgan to within 14 runs of the target.

The match against Brownlee's team was successful in terms of raising funds, and it marked the start of the Welsh county's most successful season to date. They ended on top of the table along with Durham and Northamptonshire as the title was shared. Their success was a fine reward for all the hard work Bancroft and Joseph Brain had put in, plus the committee's patience and determination, not forgetting Sir John Llewelyn's generous financial help in the earlier years when the future had seemed bleak. Without doubt the most praiseworthy of the six victories in 1900 were the two over Surrey II. Both of these victories were by an innings, as the batsmen built up large totals. At The Oval, Glamorgan totalled 388, with Joseph Brain making 88, Richard Lowe 80 and Bancroft 65, whilst in the return game at the Arms Park they amassed 369, with the captain leading the way with a fine 102. Creber was the most successful bowler once again, taking eight for 75 in the highly creditable draw with Northamptonshire at the Arms Park. Russell also emerged as a top-class all-rounder, scoring 93 against Monmouthshire and taking ten for 57 in the match with Wiltshire.

The committee were delighted at the sharing of the title, and a number of special functions were held during the autumn to celebrate the team's success. However, there were still a few dark financial clouds hanging over their heads. More people had come to watch the team, but the Club still ended the season £150 in debt. Nevertheless,

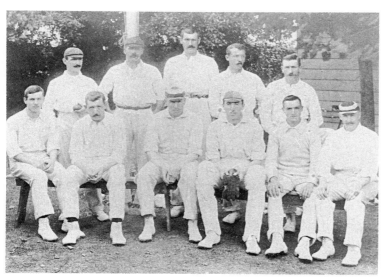

The Glamorgan team of 1901. Standing: Harry Creber, Richard Lowe, Sam Lowe, William Russell, Billy Bancroft. Seated: Norman Riches, Herbie Morgan, Joseph Brain (capt.), William Brain (wkt. keeper), Arthur Osborne and Dr Arthur Cameron.

the officials were optimistic of it being reduced in 1901, especially as the Club had secured a fixture with the South African tourists. A fair-sized crowd did turn up, but it was not a successful game for the Welsh club. The tourists proved far too strong, and despite a fighting half-century from Bancroft, the South Africans won by 132 runs.

Indeed, the team failed to maintain their progress and slipped back to fifth place in the table. For once, luck was not on their side and they suffered two narrow defeats against Wiltshire and Surrey II. In addition, batting was not as strong as in previous years, partly because Herbie Morgan's business commitments prevented him from playing regularly. However, he made a major contribution when he was available, none more so than in the game with Monmouthshire, when he scored 254 out of the Glamorgan total of 538. It was the highest score to date by a Glamorgan batsman, and he lived up to his name of 'The Penarth Slogger' by hitting one six and forty fours. Morgan's absence gave some other players an opportunity to stake a claim for a regular place, including his club-mate Arthur Osborne, who was an attacking opener, a useful change bowler and a fine cover point. Season 1901 also marked the debuts in Glamorgan colours of 18-year-old Norman Riches, a stylish batsman from Cardiff CC and 20-year-old Thomas ('Tal') Whittington, a batsman from Neath. Both went on to play leading roles in the affairs of the Club.

Unfortunately, the attendances in 1901 did not improve, and the committee were left to bemoan the lack of support. Joseph Brain realised that this was partly because of the limited facilities and amenities at both the Cardiff and Swansea grounds. Therefore, several improvements were made during the course of 1901, including an experiment with up-to-date scorecards (now taken for granted) during the game with Surrey II at the Arms Park. The seating accommodation at the grounds was rather rudimentary, and the club knew that it would be very expensive to improve. Fortunately, Sir John Llewelyn came to the aid of the County once again and donated over £1,200 to Swansea Cricket and Football Club to allow a bank and terraces to be built at the St Helen's ground.

The worries over the financial position were further eased when Brain secured a fixture for 1902 against the Australian tourists at Cardiff. The committee were delighted that the captain-secretary had been able to acquire such a 'plum' game, though because of their previous record against touring teams, it was agreed that the 'Glamorgan' team would include Arthur Silverlock of Monmouthshire, plus John Stevens, Walter Medlicott, Audley Miller and William Overton from Wiltshire. The Australians' only previous visit to the Principality had been in 1881, and after a gap of 21 years it was not surprising that a record-breaking crowd in excess of 10,000 attended the first day's play. The *South Wales Daily News* correspondent was delighted to report how the crowd was 'nearly ten times bigger than has ever assembled in Wales. Spectators seemed to so thoroughly appreciate it that the game may gain such encouragement as in a few seasons may make it a generally popular a pastime in Wales as it is truly national in England.' Although the match ended in a five-wicket win for the tourists, it gave a much needed boost to the Welsh county's finances. Gate receipts exceeded £1,300 and at the end of the season the Treasurer, T. M. Barlow, was able to report a profit of £273.

Whilst 1902 was easily the best financial year the Club had witnessed so far, it could hardly be called the best season on the field of play. Glamorgan rose just one place to finish fourth, and overall failed to find any consistency. The batting was hindered once again by Morgan's unavailability and also by an injury to the promising Riches. Although the bowling was accurate, it lacked its customary penetration, and relied heavily on Creber and Sam Lowe. Indeed, the club were very fortunate to keep Lowe's services. He was offered a position with a leading South African club, and there were rumours that the terms were an attractive £100 for a ten-week season. The temptation was great, but everyone connected with the Welsh county heaved a huge sigh of relief when Lowe turned the offer down, after having a long chat with Joseph Brain.

The docks at Cardiff had continued their growth, and by the early 1900s, they had become one of the major ports in Europe. The population of Cardiff grew and there was a further flood of affluent migrants, chiefly from England, to take up posts in industry and commerce in the city. Brain and his colleagues on the County committee, many of whom were in business in the Welsh capital, were not oblivious to these trends and they decided to cash in on the new influx of 'gentlemen' into the area. Many of these well-to-do people were not interested in the run-of-the-mill minor county games that Glamorgan played, but it was a different thing when it came to games with the MCC or, as in the case of the 1902 fixture with the Australians, against touring teams or sides with famous names. Consequently, the Glamorgan committee decided to arrange a cricket week at Cardiff in 1903 with a game against the MCC as its focal point.

Joseph Brain was delighted when he was able to select a full strength Glamorgan XI for the game, while MCC had themselves chosen a strong team. A crowd of over 2,000 attended the match but it failed to be one of Glamorgan's finest hours. They were dismissed for just 61 and 70, as the visitors cruised to victory by 108 runs shortly after lunch on the final day. Brain was naturally upset that his team, considered to be the strongest ever to represent the County, had been swept aside with contemptuous ease by the MCC. His disappointment was slightly eased when the visitors agreed to play an exhibition innings for the rest of the afternoon to entertain the large crowd.

Another special fixture was held a month or so later against the Philadelphians at the Arms Park. However, this too ended in defeat. Glamorgan were dismissed for 92 and 88 and the visitors won by 10 wickets, leaving Brain to accept the fact that his team were still not a match for a touring team. However, it was not for the want of trying, as Brain included for the Philadelphian match his Somerset friend Vernon Hill, and also Arthur Peatfield, a 29-year-old science master from Merthyr County School. Peatfield's performances for Glamorgan were inconspicuous – 56 runs in five innings, with a top score of 22 – and his main claim to fame was that in 1906, when he was living back in the North of England, he played for An England Eleven against the West Indians at Blackpool, despite not having previously appeared in first-class cricket. Because of his links with Glamorgan, he can claim to be the first cricketer to have played for the Welsh county who represented England!

Unfortunately, Brain was injured during the 1903 season, and the Welsh county could finish only in fourth place in the table. Once again the selection committee tried out several new faces in the hope of strengthening the batting, including Dr Teddy Morgan, the Welsh rugby international from Swansea. He played 16 times for Wales between 1902 and 1908, and went on to score the famous match-winning try against the All Blacks in 1905. He was a more than useful club cricketer, but failed to impress in his six innings for Glamorgan.

The Glamorgan committee planned a repeat of the Cardiff week in 1904 to include games between a South Wales XI and the powerful Nottinghamshire team, and also a match between the Gentlemen of South Wales and the Players of South Wales. The latter was an ingenious attempt to emulate the annual Gentlemen versus Players match, and one of the people behind this Welsh version was Vernon Hill, who had moved from Somerset to South Wales and was captaining Cardiff CC. Both he and his close friend Joseph Brain hoped to reap social and financial benefits by arranging an annual Welsh Gents versus Players fixture. Much to their delight it turned out to be a well supported match and was a personal success for George Cording, the 26-year-old Cardiff wicket-keeper. Cording was a popular local schoolmaster and used to invite his pupils down to the Arms Park nets to bowl at him; with the incentive that they would get a penny every time they got 'Sir' out! All this practice paid off because he topscored with 84 in the Gents total of 209 for eight declared, and then produced a fine display of wicket-keeping as the Players were restricted to 165 for six. These 'social' forms of cricket grew in popularity during the early 1900s and a team called the 'Gentlemen of Glamorgan' began playing a number of matches. The first was against the Gentlemen of Essex at The Gnoll in 1905, and the Welsh amateurs included several county regulars including 'Tal' Whittington, Joseph Moore-Gwyn, Stanley Rees and Harry Creber.

It was a much better season for Glamorgan in 1904 as they rose up to third place in the table. A major factor was that both Brain and Riches were restored to full fitness, whilst Vernon Hill was also available on a regular basis. Consequently, the batting was far stronger than the bowling, which relied too heavily on just two or three professionals. Indeed, in the match with Monmouthshire, Phillips and Silverlock put on 284 for the second wicket as Monmouthshire declared at 300 for one! Further ground improvements took place at the Arms Park indicating the growing popularity of cricket and the efforts of Brain and his supporters to provide the spectators with good facilities. A wooden pavilion was erected in the south-west corner of the tree-lined cricket field, which would serve both the cricket and rugby sections of Cardiff Athletic Club. It was a substantial structure containing two turrets and other castellated effects, flanking a raised balcony with a covered seating area below. Also incorporated was a spacious gymnasium (presumably frequented by the burly rugby players rather than the gentlemen cricketers). There was also an adjoining stable for the groundsman's horse, though this was used on occasions as a resting place by those who failed to find accommodation in the town's hotels!

Flushed with these improvements both on and off the field, Brain ambitiously arranged 14 games for 1905. The list included a match in August with the Australians at the Arms Park, though once again it was a combined XI with neighbours Monmouthshire. Arthur Silverlock, Edward Phillips, Edwin Diver (Surrey and Warwicks) and Dick Steeples (Derbyshire) were the guest players, who together with Riches, Bancroft, Russell, Creber, Jack Nash, the Swansea spinner, and the Brain brothers formed a useful team. Indeed, the *South Wales Daily News* believed that the combined team would 'give the visitors a better game than several of the first-class counties have done. Cricket in South Wales needs the fillip a first-class exhibition will give and it will justify the committee's expenditure on more professionals so that Glamorgan may take in the near future her rightful place in the cricket world.'

Brash hyperbole it might be, but here was the first hint that Brain and his colleagues were of the opinion that Glamorgan could aspire to the first-class ranks. After the construction of the pavilion at the Arms Park, they certainly had the facilities for county cricket – a fact which the Australians confirmed when they visited the Cardiff ground the day before the game after sight-seeing at Llandaff Cathedral and the nearby resort of Penarth. Philip Newland, their wicket-keeper, remarked in an interview with a local journalist how 'Cardiff people ought to be proud they had such a ground, and it was incomprehensible there was no first-class team in a centre like this with such a fine ground.' Such comments added weight to the growing claims that now Cardiff was the capital city of Wales, it should stage first-class county cricket too.

A crowd of 8,000 attended the first day's play, with 10,000 on the second, but the performance of the South Wales XI was disappointing, proving that these aspirations of Glamorgan gaining first-class status were somewhat premature. The match began after heavy overnight rain, but the sodden turf did not prevent the tourists amassing a formidable 361, with McLeod scoring an unbeaten 103 and Hopkins 93. However, the conditions were so wet that Steeples, the Newport fast bowler, cut up the pitch so much in his follow through that a new wicket had to be used on the second day, some 18 inches away from the damaged one! The new strip failed to assist the Welsh batsmen, who were bowled out for 132, with only Bancroft, Diver and Creber offering any resistance. The visitors were in an awesome position at 80 for three when rain washed out the final day's play and no doubt saved Brain's XI from an embarrassing defeat.

In fact, 1905 was not a distinguished season for Glamorgan, and they slipped back to ninth place. Bancroft was the only batsman in form and averaged around 51 – it was a feat which brought him a 20-guinea cheque from Sir John Llewelyn, who had always been one of his most ardent admirers and had employed Bancroft's father to coach Willie Llewelyn in the 1880s. Most of the other batsmen struggled, with Herbie Morgan and Joseph Brain showing signs that they were past their best. The lowest point of the season came at Chippenham, when Wiltshire dismissed the Welsh batsmen for just 20 – this remains their lowest-ever total. The only crumb of comfort in a disappointing season came from the bowling of Creber. The Swansea left-armer often had to bowl unchanged throughout a match and through sheer perseverance (and perspiration) he was rewarded with a record haul of 100 wickets.

Brain organised 12 matches in 1906, including away matches with Northumberland and Durham. This involved a long and tiring journey by rail and road, but both games ended in success. The captain-secretary also arranged a fixture for a South Wales XI with the West Indian tourists at Cardiff in early July. Once again, Brain was able to assemble a strong South Wales team, which included Riches, Bancroft, Creber and Nash. But these Glamorgan regulars could not prevent the tourists winning by 278 runs, a result which dashed Brain's hopes of proving the potential of Glamorgan. Just to compound matters, the match attracted few spectators and the Welsh club incurred considerable cost in staging the game.

There was another disappointing season in 1906, and despite Creber's feat of taking 103 wickets, it seemed that the bubble had burst. The team remained in ninth place, which was not an unfair position given the increasing number of grey whiskers in the Glamorgan ranks and the growing absentee list. Sam Lowe announced his retirement at the start of the season and during the summer he was joined by William Russell, Herbie Morgan and Vernon Hill. The latter decided to return to play for Somerset and take over the management of his family's farm near Weston-super-Mare which supplied milk to the buffet cars on the Great Western Railway. Several new faces were introduced, some of whom were not up to minor county standard, so the committee resurrected the colts match, hoping to unearth fresh talent. But it was not a success, with the *Western Mail* saying that 'any talented youngsters were conspicuous by their absence'.

A final blow came at the end of the summer when Joseph Brain announced that he wanted to stand down from the captaincy and retire from minor county cricket. It was the hardest blow the club had so far suffered because Brain had been the driving force behind Glamorgan's almost fairy-tale transformation from the ranks of the third-class counties to one of the leading minor counties. However, he had become disillusioned as support began to dwindle and several of his close colleagues retired from competitive cricket. He indicated that

JOSEPH BRAIN

Joseph Brain was a member of the famous Cardiff brewing family, and was the driving force behind Glamorgan cricket around the turn of the century. He learnt his cricket at Clifton College and Oxford University, and in 1884 was in the varsity side which defeated the touring Australians. He made his county debut for Gloucestershire in 1883, and topped their averages in 1884 above W. G. Grace, after scoring 143 against Surrey. Brain was described as the finest young batsman in England, but unfortunately he failed to live up to this reputation during his career with Gloucestershire during the 1880s.

In 1890 Brain moved to take up a post at the family brewery in Cardiff and in 1891 he made his debut for Glamorgan. He added solidity to the Welsh county's middle order and he became one of their most consistent batsmen in the Minor County Championship. He was elected captain in 1892, and from then on, spearheaded the Club's drive towards recognition as a minor county. He led them until his retirement in 1907, and the fact that the Club survived the cash crisis of the 1890s was due almost entirely to Brain's efforts.

Sadly, his health declined from 1910 and he died in 1914 after a heart attack. The *Western Mail* summed up his immense contribution both on and off the field by saying that 'his prowess at the wicket won him celebrity; his sportsmanship won him friendship; his generous patronage of the game won him gratitude'.

Joseph Brain, the Club's captain during their early days in the minor county championship. (Cardiff Central Library)

he was still willing to assist with the Club's administration, but at the age of 43 and after two lean years with the bat, he believed it was time for someone else to take centre stage in the Club's affairs. Guy Thackeray, a 24-year-old batsman from Cardiff was appointed as Brain's successor. He had played for the club since 1901 and shown himself to be a talented cricketer; he was also a Lieutenant in the Army, and given this military background, he seemed the ideal person to lead the team. However, during the winter of 1906/7 he was posted to America and the Club were left without a captain. Norman Riches was another candidate, but he was still completing his studies to be a dentist, whilst Cardiff's new captain, 'Arthur' Gibson, was unable to be regularly available. So Brain agreed to carry on, realising that there was nobody else to do the job. He also knew that 1907 would be a make or break year for the Club, and after all his efforts in the past few years, the last thing he wanted was to see the winding up of the Club.

THE GROWING DREAMS OF FIRST-CLASS STATUS

A CHANGE TOOK PLACE in 1907 to the format of the two-day minor county competition. The teams were divided into four regional groups, with the top sides in each division playing in an end of season knock-out competition to discover the overall winner. The new system saw a marked improvement in the Club's fortunes and the start of a campaign for Glamorgan to be elevated into the first-class ranks.

They easily won all of their Western group matches in 1907 against Monmouthshire, Cornwall, Dorset and Devon. The zonal matches produced some good batting displays by the Glamorgan batsmen, most notably by Norman Riches, who made an unbeaten 217 against Dorset, and there were useful contributions from some of the younger batsmen including Percy Morris of Swansea and Cardiff's Trevor Preece. The team's finest batting hour came in the game with Devon at Exeter, as they totalled a mammoth 540, which at the time was a record total in the minor county competition and one which still remains the third highest.

After beating Surrey II in the semi-final, they secured home advantage for the final with Lancashire II and a large crowd attended the game, hoping to see the Welshmen take the title outright for the first time. The visitors batted first and totalled 243, with James Heap making 81. The Burnley-born all-rounder then wrecked the Glamorgan batting with his left-arm spin, taking six wickets as the Welshmen totalled just 74. Lancashire made only 121 in their second innings, but this left Glamorgan a stiff target of 291. Despite a fighting 80 by Joseph Brain, it proved well beyond their capabilities, leaving Lancashire the winners, and Minor County Champions, by 108 runs.

There were two new faces in the Glamorgan side of 1908. The first was 31-year-old Stamford Hacker the former Gloucestershire seamer who played on a regular basis following Russell's retirement. Hacker had been playing for Herefordshire, but the possibility of Glamorgan entering the first-class ranks lured him down to South Wales, and he joined the Plymouth Works (Merthyr) club. But Hacker had to wait a further 13 years before he finally achieved his dream of regular county cricket, at the age of 45. The other new face in the Glamorgan side was the 17-year-old Honourable Archer Windsor-Clive from Penarth CC. He was a member of the wealthy landowning family who were involved in the dock development at Penarth, and owned property throughout South Wales. However, it was not these impressive social credentials which earned him a place in the team, because he had played a number of fine innings for Eton, including a century against Winchester and a half-century against Harrow. He was drafted into the Glamorgan side for the match with Monmouthshire in August, and he impressed many judges, looking to be a good prospect for the future.

Glamorgan tied with Monmouthshire for first place in the Western Division and went on to the knock-out stage once again after the intervention of Sir Francis Lacey, the MCC Secretary. He decided in Glamorgan's favour on the slightly dubious grounds that they had won the group the year before. Not surprisingly, there was a lot of dissatisfaction with Lacey's decision, especially when bearing in mind that Monmouthshire had had the better of their drawn game against Glamorgan in August with Silverlock scoring an unbeaten 187. The Welsh team travelled to Chippenham to play Wiltshire in the semi-final, but rain washed out the first two days. Play was possible on the third, and the home team won the toss and elected to bat, hoping to build up a large total. However, Harry Creber had other ideas, and took eight for 18 as Wiltshire collapsed to 41 all out. Glamorgan replied with 172 and were deemed the winners by virtue of their higher first innings score. Staffordshire won the other semi-final and Glamorgan travelled to Stoke for the final. The English team were one of the strongest minor county sides at the time, and included the legendary Sydney Barnes. He virtually won the title for them singlehandedly, taking fifteen for 54 as Glamorgan were dismissed for 60 and 79. Staffordshire won by ten wickets and deservedly became Minor County Champions. Ironically, Barnes became a publican in North Wales after the First World War, and appeared for Wales in their first-class matches in the 1920s.

Season 1908 was Joseph Brain's final one as a player, and during the winter 'Tal' Whittington, the 27-year-old Neath solicitor, was appointed the new captain and secretary. Brain remained on the committee and gave support to Whittington, who shared his desire to see Glamorgan enter the first-class ranks. They were instrumental in arranging a game between a South Wales XI and the Australians at Cardiff in early August 1909. After the off-the-field success of the 1905 game with the tourists, Brain and Whittington assembled a powerful team which they hoped would give a further boost to Glamorgan's claims for higher recognition. The side was led by Ernie Jones, the long-serving Swansea batsman and included Riches, Silverlock, Nash, Creber, Bancroft, Ralph Sweet-Escott, and Whittington himself. The other three members of the side were 25-year-old James Maxwell, who was playing for Swansea after three years with Somerset, Penfold, the wicket-keeper from Plymouth Works (Merthyr) and Albert Whittle, the Neath professional who had played for Warwickshire and Somerset.

The local press quite rightly described it as the strongest South Wales team ever to be assembled. The Australians included their three master batsmen, Syd Gregory, Charlie Macartney and Monty Noble, and a massive crowd attended the game. Over 10,000 people entered the Cardiff ground on the first day, with hundreds more peering over the walls around the ground. With the South Wales score on 150 for three and Silverlock and Sweet-Escott playing some handsome shots, it looked as though the Australians were going to be given a good game.

However, the Welsh team collapsed during the afternoon, and were dismissed for 228. Nevertheless, the tourists found run-scoring difficult against the keen South Wales attack spearheaded by Creber, Maxwell and Nash. Australia finished on 271, and with a first-innings deficit of 43, the Welsh batsmen knew they had to bat carefully and not lose any wickets before the end of the second day's play. However, the Australian bowlers stepped up a gear, removing Riches and Silverlock with only eight runs on the board. Whittington and Bancroft resisted briefly on the final morning, but the Welsh batting was swept aside by the tourists. The Australians were left with a target of 65 which they reached within 55 minutes for the loss of only two wickets. Despite the inevitable result, a crowd of 5,000 had turned up and they were delighted when the Australians generously agreed to bat on, adding a further 118 runs.

The second innings collapse disappointed Brain and Whittington, but they were pleased by the way the batsmen had played in the first innings. They were also heartened by Glamorgan's performance in the Minor County Championship. For the third successive season they won the Western Division and progressed to the semi-final stage to play Nottinghamshire II. Once again, there was rain interference, and Glamorgan progressed to the final by virtue of a higher first innings score. Their opponents were Wiltshire and remembering the previous year's match, the Glamorgan players were optimistic of their chances and a change of luck in the finals. Wiltshire batted first and made a modest 122, with Maxwell taking seven for 43. However, Glamorgan only made 96 and in their second innings the Wiltshire batsmen amassed 297. The Glamorgan batsmen were faced with an unlikely target of 324, and mustered only 159, to give Wiltshire the minor county title.

The Glamorgan players left the Arms Park mortified by the thought that they had lost the final for the third time in a row. But it was not all gloom and despondency within the committee, who believed that the rebuilding programme was over and that a strong new team had emerged. The acquisition of Hacker and Maxwell meant that the club had more depth in the bowling, relieving the burden on Nash and Creber. The county officials also took heart from the performances of Riches and Sweet-Escott with the bat; they each scored over 450 runs and averaged 48 and 45 respectively. In addition, there was a growing pool of professionals in the South Wales and Monmouthshire Leagues whom the committee could call upon, and it was widely believed that Glamorgan had become one of the strongest minor counties, as testified by the divisional and knock-out results. Moreover, Worcestershire and Northamptonshire had recently made a successful transition from the minor county ranks into the County Championship. Whittington and Brain believed the time had come to approach the MCC and the Secretary wrote to Lord's applying for first-class recognition.

The main stumbling block to their aspirations was the absence of capital reserves allowing the club to play 16 fixtures (eight home/eight away), and commit themselves to all the other expenses of regular county cricket. Whittington realised that this was the only obstacle preventing Glamorgan from achieving first-class status. He met with the Earl of Plymouth and drafted a circular with the President's name on it, which was sent to all clubs and businessmen in South Wales. The letter outlined how their quest for first-class status had failed because of the lack of money and the following plea was made for help: 'a strong attempt will be made to justify the County's claim to promotion to the first-class ranks. To succeed in this however, a substantial increase in the Club's membership, and in subscriptions and donations are necessary and an appeal is made for assistance in these directions.' Whittington also organised a fund-raising three-day match at Cardiff between the East of England and the West of England. Players from Essex and Hampshire made up the East XI, whilst Whittington, Bancroft plus amateurs from Somerset and Gloucestershire formed the West team. A fairly large crowd attended the game, and on the final afternoon were treated to a fine display of batting by the West, in particular by Gilbert Jessop, who struck a typically elegant 47 not out in just half an hour as the West successfully chased a target of 208 to win by four wickets.

The format of the Minor County Championship changed once again in 1910; it was now split into two halves with the team at the top of each half meeting at the end of the season to find the overall Champion. The Welsh club fancied their chances of winning the title which would almost certainly generate greater public interest and financial support, which would ensure their promotion into the first-class ranks. However, Glamorgan finished in second place in the Southern Section behind Berkshire, and although they beat Wiltshire in the play-off for third and fourth place, there was great disappointment within the committee ranks. The batting had not been as consistent as in previous years, and the only player in any real sort of form was Riches, but he contracted enteric fever and was unwell for several weeks. The batting was in dire straits when Riches was unavailable because of his illness, and the plight was compounded by the absence of the precociously gifted Windsor-Clive, who had gone up to Cambridge. The low point of the season came in the friendly with Worcestershire at the Arms Park. It had been hoped that this would illustrate the team's strengths – however, it only served to highlight their batting deficiencies as they were dismissed within 55 minutes for just 36, with the Australian John Cuffe taking nine for 5 with his left-arm spin.

The moderate performances resulted in a further deterioration of the club's finances, and by the end of the season, Hugh Ingledew, the Treasurer, reported that the overdraft had risen to £574. This was very worrying because it meant that fewer professionals could be hired, which would weaken the team even further. Some matches had been rain affected, so gate receipts had fallen to under £600, whilst the expenses rose in excess of £1,000 following the staging of several friendlies outside Wales. So all in all it meant that the pursuit of first-class status was competely out of the question.

The only bright note came at the end of the season with the selection of Whittington for the MCC tour to the West Indies. The Glamorgan captain had a fine tour, topping the batting averages with 685 runs at an average of 34, including 154 against British Guiana and 115 not out in the match with All Jamaica. However, he was quickly brought back down to earth on his return to South Wales by the fact that the financial situation of the Club had worsened. It had been brought about by the desperate economic problems in the region, as industry and commerce lost trade and were afflicted by labour problems and strikes. The earlier promises of financial support went out of the window, and Whittington called a crisis meeting with the Club's officials. They studied the depressing balance sheet and after looking at the increase in the expenses in 1910, they realised that the situation had become so grave that it now cast doubts over the Club's continuation in the minor county competition, never mind entering the first-class ranks.

Once again, Whittington met with the Earl of Plymouth to draft another circular to be sent to all of the members and those in the business community in a last ditch attempt to avert the almost unthinkable step of withdrawing from the competition. The letter told how 'there are many gentlemen in the County who are interested in the well-being of our national game, and who would deplore any circumstances which would lead to the winding up of the County Cricket Club owing to want of support. On the other hand, it is manifest that unless some steps can be taken to relieve the Club of their present burden of debt and at the same time broaden the area of support by largely increasing the Members' subscriptions, the county cricket club cannot hope to justify its existence.'

At the Annual Meeting in May, the committee announced that they were opening a shilling fund along similar lines to the one by which Essex had raised £800 a few years before. A public meeting was held at the City Hall, Cardiff, to launch the scheme and gave further publicity to the Club's plight. Support was promised and donations to the fund gradually came in.

Given these financial worries, the Club were fortunate to be allowed to stage a match between a South Wales XI and the All-Indian tourists at the Arms Park. Whittington's contacts within the MCC hierarchy were a great help, and he led a South Wales team which included Silverlock, Phillips and Dr Tresawna from Monmouthshire. The Neath solicitor must have been delighted at the outcome as his team comfortably won by seven wickets. The tourists were bowled out for 53 with Hacker taking six for 17 and Creber four for 27. South Wales made 205 in their first innings with Henry Symonds, a 22-year-old left-hander making an attractive 56. The Indians made 233 the second time around, though Hacker took six wickets again; however, it only left the Welshmen a target of 81. It was appropriate that Riches and Whittington should pave the way to victory and the result gave Glamorgan's funds a well earned boost, with the Shilling Fund looking much healthier only a few weeks later.

Nevertheless, the victory was a deceptive illustration of Glamorgan's form. They finished in only fifth place and suffered two heavy defeats against Staffordshire, proving that they were still not up to first-class standard.

Despite the poor results, 1911 was an exceptional year for Norman Riches, as he scored 1,015 runs at an average of 92.27 to create a new County record. He hit two centuries against Monmouthshire, plus 150 in the game with Carmarthenshire, but his highest and finest innings came at Neath against Buckinghamshire, with the *Western Mail* describing how: 'When the loose ball comes along, he revels in putting the full face of the bat hard against it. Perfect footwork, perfect timing, an elegant flash of the bat and the score-box is ringing up another four.' The results could have been even better if Windsor-Clive had been available. However, he preferred to play instead for St Fagan's during his vacations from Cambridge, alongside his two brothers. The more relaxed atmosphere with his family and the sumptuous St Fagan's luncheons were the obvious attractions for the young batsman.

Financial factors meant that fewer professionals could play for the club in 1911, but fortunately several talented amateurs emerged from

A rare view of the St Helen's Ground, Swansea, around the time of the First World War. Billy Bancroft, the Swansea groundsman and former player, is cutting the outfield with a horse-drawn lawnmower. The wooden pavilion on the far boundary was demolished in 1927. (David Hill)

the local leagues, including 'Jock' Tait from Cardiff and Swansea's Brock Williams.

Tait was a flamboyant amateur with a somewhat cavalier approach to batting, believing that any bowler whom he did not hit for at least three boundaries an over was getting off lightly! The comment was once made that 'according to all the rules of batsmanship, he was not a batsman at all. But he made runs and when he did, the spectators were thrilled and the bowlers demoralised as neither knew what was going to happen next – balls which would normally be driven, he would late cut, and vice versa.' In complete contrast, Brock Williams was a steady middle-order batsman; he was a solicitor in Swansea and was a close friend of Whittington, who persuaded him to turn out for the County. Despite being captain of Swansea, Williams preferred the more casual and social forms of cricket, and agreed to Whittington's approaches only when no-one else was available. He was a member of the Bransby-Williams family of Killay House and organised many games of country house cricket in the grounds of the family home and ran a team called the Public School Nondescripts, who played regularly throughout South Wales.

Williams' association with the County Club, rather than his regular presence on the field, was considered to be important by Whittington for the fact that Williams was a trusted and well-known member of the commercial world in the Swansea area. He had a wide number of contacts, who Whittington believed could be persuaded to lend financial support. During the summer, Williams was drafted onto the committee and he helped Whittington with the fund-raising campaign. They gained the support of the Welsh Rugby Union, Cardiff Athletic Club and Swansea Cricket and Football Club, and a special East *v* West rugby match was arranged. The WRU covered the match expenses and Glamorgan took the gate receipts.

By the start of 1912, the deficit had been lowered to £175, but despite this improvement, Hugh Ingledew felt he could not continue as Treasurer. It came as no surprise when Brock Williams was appointed in his place. His elevation caused a shift in the 'power-balance' within the Club hierarchy towards the West, and as a result strong arguments were put forward in favour of St Helen's staging one of the more attractive fixtures, rather than Cardiff. The Swansea ground was allocated the South Wales game against the South African tourists in June, with the match against the Australians at the end of August being given to the Arms Park. The decision to move one of the prestigious games to Swansea proved to be a fortuitous one, as rain ruined the Australian game at Cardiff.

Whittington was able to assemble a fairly strong XI for the Swansea match, keenly anticipating a repeat of the Indian success and giving further notice of the talented cricketers the Welsh county possessed. The side included Riches, Bancroft, Maxwell, Hacker and Creber, plus Arthur Webb the former Hampshire all-rounder who was playing for Hills Plymouth (Merthyr). However, the tourists gained an easy win by 230 runs, dismissing the Welsh side for 192 and 134. Whittington was the only batsman to offer any resistance, top scoring with 57 in the first innings.

Unfortunately, the team failed to continue its improvement in 1912 and slumped back to a disappointing 10th place in the Minor Counties Championship. Riches failed to recapture his vintage form of the previous year, and in the continued absence of Windsor-Clive, the mantle of leading run-scorer fell onto the captain's shoulders. It was unfortunate because Whittington already had more than enough on his plate with the cash crisis, and he could have done without the added burden of being the only in-form batsman.

An indication of the pressure on Whittington came in the match with Staffordshire in August. As befits a solicitor, he was normally unruffled by peculiar events on the field and he led with a calm assurance. However, near the end of the match, which was moving towards yet another disappointing defeat for the Welsh team,

Whittington got embroiled in a row with the umpires. As the *South Wales Daily News* reported, it all began when 'Creber was the last man in, and after batting right-handed to Bucknell and taking guard in the same manner at the other end, Creber turned round to play Barnes left-handed. The field was changed and Creber played several balls in this way. It seemed to give a rather farcical turn to the game so Barnes, entering into the spirit of it, turned the tables on Creber by skittling the ball down underhand, amidst a roar of laughter. Creber missed the ball and was promptly given out leg-before. As the Staffordshire players departed the field, the Glamorgan captain met the umpires and claimed that notice of the change should have been given to the batsman. A discussion occurred, but the umpires insisted that the decision shoud stand.'

The dispute did not drag on, as Whittington realised that it had been a fairly light hearted incident, without any malice being intended, and that he had acted in the heat of the moment. He apologised and despite widespread newspaper coverage of the incident, it did not harm his 'well-thought-of' position within MCC ranks. Indeed, he was appointed captain of the Minor County team which met the South African tourists at Stoke and at the end of the season, went on the MCC tour to the West Indies. Nevertheless, after his experiences during 1912 and the Staffordshire incident, Whittington felt it was time to stand down as captain, and he handed over the leadership to Norman Riches.

By standing down from the captaincy, Whittington was able to devote more of his time to his duties as Secretary and easing the cash problems. The Club's financial problems had worsened after the moderate season and by the start of 1913, the debts had risen to £450, plus a bank overdraft of £323. Several ideas were put forward at the AGM as to how more money could be raised; in particular, there were calls for a revival of the exhibition matches at Cardiff which Joseph Brain had organised around the turn of the century. Brain was not in very good health, and many people felt that his enforced move to the background of the Club's affairs was one of the causes of the County's severe financial problem. The Club gained support for an exhibition match from Harry Webb, the MP for Llwynarthen, and he assembled a team including leading public figures and cricketers for a two-day game at the Arms Park. On the eve of the game it was agreed that it should be a 12-a-side game so that Webb's team could include George Robey, the well-known comedian, who was appearing at the Cardiff Empire. The match ended in a draw, but it was a successful venture both on and off the field. Riches and Jessop gave a fine display of batsmanship, whilst most of the marquees around the ground were full of the local gentry and prominent personalities.

NORMAN RICHES

Norman Riches was Glamorgan's leading amateur batsman before and after the First World War, and would undoubtedly have been a candidate for Test matches had he played more first-class cricket, and been able to devote his time to the game. However, he opted to follow his father into dentistry after training at Guy's Hospital and played for Glamorgan only on an irregular basis when they finally entered the County Championship. But even though he was then in his late thirties, and had the worries of captaincy, Riches proved himself to be a top-class batsman.

He possessed a sound technique and temperament with a wide range of shots, especially off his legs. He was also a shrewd tactician, and used to push singles to cause a readjustment of the field, and then joyfully smash a boundary through the gap he had cleverly created.

Riches was considered for an MCC tour to the West Indies in the 1920s and a senior Glamorgan official was contacted to see if Riches was available. The reply was: 'It's no good asking him as he wouldn't have the time to go.' But ironically Riches would have jumped at the chance and got time off, had he been approached. His limited appearances for Glamorgan led to claims that he picked his matches and avoided the fastest bowlers, but he completely refuted these by hitting a superb century in 1928 at the age of 45 against the fiery Lancashire attack.

Riches eventually retired in 1934, but maintained close links with the County by serving on the committee and acting as a Trustee.

Norman Riches, one of Glamorgan's finest ever batsmen. (John Riches)

The rise in public support produced a much needed improvement in playing form. Glamorgan won their section of the table in 1913 and played Norfolk to decide the destiny of the title. Norfolk batted first and scored 204, with Glamorgan replying with 168 before rain interrupted proceedings. Play finally got under way again on the final afternoon and Creber fully exploited the wet wicket, taking eight for 38 as Norfolk were dismissed for 61. The Welsh team were left with a target of 98 and seemed to have a reasonable chance of winning their first minor county title outright when rain fell again and prevented them from chasing the target. The outcome was decided by the higher first innings total, so Norfolk were adjudged champions. The Glamorgan players must have rued their luck on the long journey back home, knowing that they had failed in a final for the fourth time, and to make matters worse, they had actually ended the game in a useful position!

Despite their good form, the Club still faced a deficit at the end of the summer. It was reduced to £42 by the end of the year, after several fund-raising events, including a special matinee at Cardiff's Empire Theatre. Once again, Whittington and Brock Williams toiled long and hard during the winter, but unfortunately they did not have any help from Joseph Brain. He had been a willing helper in previous seasons, but during the winter the veteran captain suffered a serious illness. Sadly, he died during June and never saw his dream of Glamorgan entering the first-class ranks come true.

Fortunately, Harry Webb offered to help once again, and arranged for Gilbert Jessop to bring an MCC team to play a fund-raising game at the Arms Park in August 1914. Whittington and Williams also planned a cricket week at St Helen's, after gaining guarantees of support from businessmen and industrialists in West Glamorgan. The focal point of the week was the match with Northamptonshire—this was one of several new fixtures which Whittington had secured; indeed, he hoped that a good performance against the youngest of the first-class counties would strengthen the Welsh county's claims for promotion. He was delighted when Glamorgan had the better of the game, with Riches, who was in outstanding form in 1914, making an unbeaten 95 in their first innings. Northants were set 240 on the final afternoon, but Hacker and Creber bowled well and the visitors never looked like reaching the target.

Despite their form in this match, Glamorgan slipped to sixth place. It was somewhat disappointing because the committee had also taken great pains to strengthen the playing staff. William Bestwick, the 39-year-old former Derbyshire fast-medium bowler, had joined Llanelli as their pro and qualified by residence for the Welsh county. They also acquired the services of Eddie Bates, a stocky batsman and occasional leg-spinner who had played for Yorkshire between 1907 and 1913. Bates had never gained a regular place in the Yorkshire side so he decided to try his luck in the South Wales Leagues and qualify for Glamorgan. He brought with him a toughness gained from the hard school of the Yorkshire Leagues, a quality which many of the impetuous Welsh amateurs lacked. He also came down with a fine wardrobe – he was known as 'The Marquis' because of his sartorial elegance and was once described as being 'not the greatest cricketer Yorkshire ever produced, but easily the most elegantly dressed!'

Glamorgan also improved their links with local clubs in 1914. During the spring a meeting had been held between the County officials and representatives from the leading clubs in South Wales to see how the clubs could help solve the County's financial problems and boost interest in cricket. It was chaired by Thomas Schofield, the well-known rugby player and cricketer who served on the committee for the Bridgend area. Under Schofield's guidance, a match was arranged at The Gnoll between Glamorgan and a combined XI from the Briton Ferry Town and Briton Ferry Steelworks club. Therefore, every attempt was made during 1914 to improve playing standards, stimulate interest and public support, and above all else reduce the debt so that the County could finally gain the main goal of first-class status.

However, events on a wider stage, beyond even the power of Whittington and Williams, intervened to stifle their efforts. War was declared on 3 August 1914 and the last two matches of the season were cancelled. It must have seemed that the fates had conspired once again to thwart the Welsh county's aspirations, just when they were getting back on their feet and clearing the debts. No doubt many of the Glamorgan amateurs went off to do their duty, ruminating on what might have been achieved in the Championship finals, believing that the goal of first-class status would never be secured.

THE DREAM BECOMES A REALITY

THE FIRST WORLD WAR drew to an end during the late summer of 1918, and life began to get back to normal. A new county committee was assembled to pick up the pieces of Glamorgan cricket and continue the drive towards higher recognition. Whittington and Bowden were reappointed as joint-secretaries, and they reassembled much of the pre-war squad. However, there were a few gaps and amongst those who failed to return was Archer Windsor-Clive. The gifted amateur had been one of the earliest fatalities in the war, having died at Landrecies in France on 25 August 1914. The committee and supporters alike felt that they never saw the best of his talents at county level; no doubt the lure of first-class cricket would have seen him more regularly appear for Glamorgan and everyone was left guessing at what he might have achieved if the Club had entered the County Championship.   Other faces were missing as well – William Edwards, a promising middle-order batsman, had been killed in Palestine, Bestwick had been re-engaged by Derbyshire, whilst Bancroft and Creber had decided to retire. Consequently the joint-secretaries sent a circular to all the local clubs with the objective of discovering new players and candidates for trial matches. It seemed like 1888 all over again, but there were important differences. The Club had an established fixture list and cricket had become accepted as a sport in the area, so the officials did not have to worry about publicity. Moreover, there were promises of financial support and there was considerable public support after five long years of war, with people keen to watch cricket again now that life was reverting to normal.

The Glamorgan side returned to the Minor County Championship in 1920 with great optimism for the future and a renewed vigour to set aside the pre-war disappointments. They also played a number of exhibition matches, including a match in July against an eleven raised by Captain J. H. P. Brain, the 24-year-old son of William Brain, who had followed in his father's footsteps by keeping wicket for Cardiff CC. Although it ended in a 104-run defeat for Brain's XI it revived memories of the past and paid handsome tribute to Joseph Brain's contribution to pre-war cricket, besides bringing financial backing from the family's business.

The major friendly in 1920 was against an MCC team at St Helen's. The Glamorgan think-tank, namely Messrs Riches, Williams and Whittington, realised that if the Welsh county were to stake a claim for first-class recognition, it was imperative that they performed well

61

in this match. A strong team was chosen, and Riches led by example, sharing a century partnership with Whittington for the first wicket. Glamorgan eventually totalled 217, but the MCC made only 80 with Swansea's Percy Morris taking nine for 28 with his right-arm seamers. The visitors made 170 in their second innings, but this left Glamorgan with a target of just 34. Riches changed the batting order and asked Colonel Arthur O'Bree from Cardiff and Swansea's Willie Gemmill to open. They saw Glamorgan home by ten wickets, although neither of these amateurs had any strict birthplace qualification for the County. O'Bree had been born in Poona and had spent a lot of his youth in the Indian sub-continent, whilst Gemmill had been born on the island of New Caledonia in the Pacific Ocean and had learnt his cricket at King's School, Taunton. A tropical combination such as this was typical of the characters appearing in minor county cricket at that time, and whatever their background, they were delighted at the boost the victory over the MCC gave to Glamorgan's pursuit of higher recognition.

A fortnight before, Whittington had captained the Minor Counties in their annual game against the MCC. Riches was also selected and he hit a magnificent 147 to confirm that Glamorgan possessed batsmen who were up to first-class standard. Two victories over Surrey II showed that there were several others not far behind. The first win came in the County's opening match of the season. They were set a mammoth target of 371 by the Home County side, believing it to be way out of the Welshman's capabilities. They were proved wrong as Riches and Tait shared a half-century opening partnership. Gwyn Thomas of Pontardawe and Henry Symonds chipped in with 40s, before Whittington (76 not out) and David Reason (90 not out) steered Glamorgan to a dramatic win. The second victory over Surrey II came in August on a damp Cardiff wicket, and this time highlighted the strength of the Welsh bowlers. Rain interfered with the first day's play and on the second morning the visitors were dismissed for 45 with Nash taking four for 8 and Morris three for 17. Glamorgan replied with 139 in the afternoon session with Riches making 53 on what the *Western Mail* called 'a practically unplayable wicket'. The Glamorgan bowlers posed problems for the visitors once again, dismissing them for 78 with Nash claiming five for 20, to leave the Welshmen the victors by an innings and 16 runs. Despite these victories Glamorgan finished in only sixth place. They were handicapped by the unavailability of Percy Morris and Hacker for several matches, which left Nash as the only experienced bowler. Their absence gave an opportunity to a number of promising bowlers from the leagues, including Briton Ferry's Edward James, a 24-year-old left-arm spinner, and 30-year-old Edgar Cooper, a right-arm seamer. Some new batsmen also emerged during the season, including 27-year-old Thomas ('Tubby') Morgan from Swansea, and Frank Pinch, a middle-order batsman from Bodmin in Cornwall, who was a fine back-foot player, with a fierce pull and cut.

The emergence of these new faces and the fair results gave Whittington the encouragement he needed at the end of the 1920 season to continue his pursuit of securing first-class status. Sport as a whole in South Wales had received several boosts at the end of the Second World War. The Football League had been expanded and now included teams from Aberdare, Cardiff, Merthyr, Newport and Swansea. Interest in sport rose and with the local economy picking up, the time seemed right to make a concerted effort at achieving the goal of higher recognition. The previous stumbling block had been the desperate pre-war financial situation. However, the debts had almost been cleared by the end of 1920. Through Whittington and Williams, the Club had gained the backing of the business community in the Swansea and Neath areas, whilst Bowden and Riches obtained assistance in the Cardiff region, especially from Sir Sydney Byass, one of the city's leading businessmen. If Glamorgan were to become first-class, here was the opportunity.

During the autumn of 1920 the committee enthusiastically discussed how to seek the support of the other counties. The requirements for first-class eligibility at the time were home and away fixtures with a minimum of eight first-class counties. Given Whittington's contacts and influence within the MCC and other counties, the committee unanimously agreed that the Neath solicitor should be the person to make the approaches. Whittington was given a free hand by the Club's officials and undertook all of the negotiations singlehandedly. He travelled the length and breadth of England persuading other officials that Glamorgan were suitably equipped, both on and off the field, to enter the first-class ranks. Somerset quickly agreed, not surprisingly given their close links in the early days of the Club. Gloucestershire, Worcestershire, Derbyshire, Leicestershire, North-amptonshire and Lancashire also gave their support, though in some cases Whittington was forced to agree that the Welsh county would guarantee £200. Whittington reported back to the committee in November that he had secured the support of seven counties; they were understandably jubilant at the news and with their target finally in sight, they told him 'to obtain the eighth at any cost whatever'.

However, strong persuasion was not needed because both Sussex and Hampshire readily agreed to Whittington's request for support. At the December committee meeting, the Neath solicitor announced that the required number of fixtures had been obtained. The only shadow on the horizon was that the deficit had risen to £350 and some committee members had cold feet about whether the Club would be able to honour their commitments. After all his hard work at actually gaining 16 provisional fixtures for 1921, Whittington was not going to be defeated at this late stage, and he gained further assurances from businessmen in Cardiff and Swansea that they would write off this debt if Glamorgan gained the MCC's approval in the New Year. Sidney Byass offered to loan the Club around £1,000 over a ten-year period, whilst Daniel Radcliffe of Cardiff and Sir John Llewelyn offered smaller sums. Given these handsome pledges, the committee instructed Whittington to approach Lord's with a request to be recognised as first-class.

All of the Glamorgan officials were jubilant a few weeks later when Whittington received a reply from the MCC endorsing their application. There was plenty of backslapping and wishes of good luck at the 1921 AGM. Praise was heaped upon Whittington, and in recognition of his efforts, he was elected as the first life member of the Club. No doubt there were tears in Sir John's eyes when the 'Grand Old Man of Glamorgan Cricket' was toasted and there were speeches about his involvement and dedication in the early years. His dream of 1888 had finally come true and the only sad thing was that Joseph Brain was not alive to see it and share in the Club's celebrations.

Now that they were a first-class county, the Club had to select at the 1921 AGM the right men both on and off the field. Arthur Gibson, the former Cardiff and Glamorgan batsman was appointed Secretary, with Bowden as his assistant. Brock Williams was elected as Honorary Treasurer, whilst Norman Riches was voted in as captain. After the meeting, Riches discussed with Whittington and the rest of the committee the composition of the playing staff. Hacker, Nash and Bates were hired as professionals at the princely sum of £14 for each away match and £10 for each home game. Whittington also persuaded the 47-year-old Creber to come out of retirement and act as the fourth professional.

Despite the emergence of Pinch and Morgan in 1921, Riches felt that there was still room for another one or two batsmen on the staff. The person he had in mind for one of these places was his 35-year-old Cardiff clubmate Billy Spiller. He was a fine all-round sportsman and played as a centre for Cardiff RFC and Wales, but his duties as a policeman prevented him from turning out for Glamorgan on a regular basis in the Minor County Championship. But now that Riches's team were a first-class county, there was a greater incentive for Spiller and he told Riches that he would play as often as possible. The other vacancy was filled by 34-year-old Herbie Tayler, an all-rounder who had played for Gloucestershire before the war and more recently for St Fagan's and Cardiff.

T. A. L. WHITTINGTON

As J. H. Morgan wrote in 1951, 'the name of "Tal" Whittington will always be identified with the history of Glamorgan CCC as he did more than any other individual to secure Glamorgan's promotion to first-class status'. Whittington was appointed as the honorary secretary in 1909, and after the team's success in the minor county competition, Whittington quickly realised that the dreams of Llewelyn and Brain could achieve reality. Whittington had a solicitor's practice and a wide range of contacts in the commercial world which he used to drum up financial support as he successfully persuaded the MCC to admit Glamorgan into the County Championship.

His father was a doctor in Neath and was a useful sportsman in his own right, having played rugby for Scotland as well as for Llewelyn's Glamorganshire side on several occasions in the 1860s and 1870s. 'Tal' made his Glamorgan debut in 1901 and, after leaving Oxford University, regularly appeared for the County, establishing himself as a top order batsman with a wide range of attractive strokes. He scored over 4,500 runs with a top score of 188 against Carmarthenshire at Llanelli in 1908, and successfully toured the West Indies with the MCC in 1910/11 and 1912/13.

Whittington was a shrewd reader of the game, and after leading the Club and the Minor Counties before the First World War, he took over as captain in 1922 and 1923, though with not as much success as he would have liked. Fortunately, Whittington had a good sense of humour, and as the Club met with problem after problem in the 1920s, he took all the rebuffs and criticism with a wry smile and a cheery word about the future.

'Tal' Whittington – the man who helped secure first-class recognition for Glamorgan. (John Billot)

The Club could not afford to hire many professionals, so they had to rely on the talented amateurs. But most of these were stalwarts from the pre-war era and were nearing, or over, 40. Consequently, a colts trial was held towards the end of the 1920 season, and as a result three young amateurs, all with outstanding public school records, agreed to play for Glamorgan – they were Wyndham Jenkins, a 23-year-old wicket-keeper who had attended Malvern; Trevor Arnott, a 19-year-old batsman and fast medium swing bowler from Wycliffe School, and 23-year-old Johnnie Clay, a fast medium bowler born in Bonvilston, who had gone to Winchester.

The opening match was against Sussex at the Arms Park in mid-May, and great interest was shown during the weeks leading up to the game. But, as in 1889, Glamorgan were unable to take the field at full strength for this first fixture. Both Hacker and Spiller were unavailable, whilst J. H. P. Brain was nursing an injury. In contrast, Sussex were at full strength and their team included such notable cricketers as Maurice Tate, Ted Bowley and the Gilligan brothers, plus Vallance Jupp, the England all-rounder. Norman Riches won the toss and together with Whittington opened the batting, with the ground bathed in glorious sunshine and a crowd in excess of 5,000. It seemed very appropriate that the two people who had played leading roles on and off the field in gaining first-class status should literally set the ball rolling in the opening championship match.

Against an accurate attack, the Welsh batsman did well to score 272 in their first innings, with Henry Symonds top scoring with 58. Edgar Cooper and Jack Nash both bowled well and caused problems for the illustrious visitors; they each claimed four wickets to give Glamorgan a healthy lead of 120. However, the Welsh batsmen found life difficult when they batted on the second day and only the idiosyncratic Tait established himself, finishing on 96 not out at the close of play. With the first ball on the final morning, Tate generously gave his namesake a legside full toss hoping he would reach three figures, but Tait swung and missed. His nerves took over and he was clean bowled by Tate's next delivery, and trudged dejectedly off the ground knowing that he had come within a whisker of being Glamorgan's first centurion in first-class cricket.

Glamorgan were eventually dismissed for 213, leaving Sussex a target of 334. They made a poor start and slumped to 59 for three after some good bowling by Cooper and Creber. But then Ted Bowley and Felix Jenner shared a partnership of 166 for the fourth wicket to tip the balance in Sussex's favour. Riches was forced to recall Cooper and Creber in an attempt to make a breakthrough. It proved to be the turning point as Jenner was caught by Henry Symonds. Further wickets tumbled and despite stubborn resistance by Alfred Gilligan,

*Norman Riches (extreme right) leads out the Glamorgan team for the initial
Championship match in 1921. The rest of the team (left to right): Edgar Cooper,
Jock Tait, Harry Creber, Eddie Bates, Arthur O'Bree, Percy Morris, 'Tal'
Whittington, George Cording (wicket-keeper) and Henry Symonds. Jack Nash is
obscured by Whittington.*

*The delighted crowd congratulate the Glamorgan team after their victory over
Sussex in their first Championship game.*

GLAMORGAN *v.* SUSSEX

Played at Cardiff Arms Park, 18, 19 and 20 May 1921

GLAMORGAN WON BY 23 RUNS

GLAMORGAN	FIRST INNINGS		SECOND INNINGS	
T. A. L. Whittington	c Street b A. E. Gilligan	40	c A. E. Gilligan b Cox	27
*N. V. H. Riches	c A. H. Gilligan b Jupp	16	b Tate	3
W. E. Bates	b A. E. Gilligan	39	lbw b Cox	8
V. L. Morris	b Tate	7	b A. H. Gilligan	13
J. R. Tait	b Cox	31	b Tate	96
†G. E. Cording	c Cox b Roberts	45	c A. H. Gilligan b Roberts	10
Colonel A. O'Bree	b Cox	0	b A. H. Gilligan	8
H. G. Symonds	c Higgs b Bowley	58	b Cox	20
E. Cooper	b Jupp	12	b Cox	0
H. Creber	not out	7	b Cox	7
A. Nash	b Cox	5	not out	5
Extras		12		16
Total		272		213

1st inns: 1-38, 2-78, 3-99, 4-115, 5-169, 6-169, 7-245, 8-252, 9-262
2nd inns: 1-25, 2-41, 3-52, 4-107, 5-120, 6-137, 7-171, 8-171, 9-197

BOWLING	O	M	R	W	O	M	R	W
Tate	26	12	34	1	13.2	4	29	2
A. H. Gilligan	5	0	24	0	7	0	33	2
A. E. Gilligan	21	3	71	2	6	2	17	0
Bowley	5	1	12	1				
Jupp	21	5	52	2	15	4	37	0
Roberts	15	2	31	1	9	0	21	1
Cox	24.5	5	36	3	23	4	60	5

SUSSEX	FIRST INNINGS		SECOND INNINGS	
V. W. C. Jupp	c Cording b Cooper	34	c O'Bree b Cooper	5
E. H. Bowley	lbw b Nash	21	b Nash	146
K. A. Higgs	b Nash	0	lbw b Creber	5
M. W. Tate	b Cooper	11	c Nash b Creber	10
F. D. Jenner	b Nash	6	c Symonds b Cooper	55
*A. E. R. Gilligan	b Cooper	3	c and b Cooper	15
†G. Street	c Bates b Cooper	5	b Nash	11
G. Stannard	c Tait b Nash	41	c Riches b Cooper	4
A. H. H. Gilligan	run out	2	c Tait b Creber	33
G. Cox	not out	7	not out	11
H. E. Roberts	c Cording b Creber	13	c Morris b Creber	0
Extras		9		15
Total		152		310

1st inns: 1-44, 2-48, 3-65, 4-78, 5-80, 6-83, 7-103, 8-131, 9-134
2nd inns: 1-11, 2-45, 3-59, 4-225, 5-249, 6-251, 7-258, 8-289, 9-303

BOWLING	O	M	R	W	O	M	R	W
Creber	17.5	6	25	1	19.2	1	78	4
Morris	4	1	12	0	3	0	20	0
Nash	29	11	45	4	25	1	86	2
Cooper	16	2	61	4	34	3	81	4
Bates					6	0	29	0
Symonds					1	0	1	0

Umpires: T. Flowers and A. E. Street

Sussex were all out for 310, leaving Glamorgan to celebrate a 23-run victory and an almost fairy-tale like start to their first-class history.

The *Western Mail* correspondent was ecstatic, describing how 'it is doubtful whether the oldest follower of the game among the 7,000 or 8,000 people on the ground could recall a parallel to the scene of enthusiasm which followed immediately after the fall of the last Sussex wicket. A wild stampede was made to the pavilion where the captains were overwhelmed with congratulations.'

The two captains stood on the pavilion balcony and made impromptu speeches to the assembled mass. Riches paid handsome tribute to Whittington and Sir John Llewelyn, whilst Arthur Gilligan made some very gracious comments about the way the Welsh team had played. 'You gave us a magnificent game,' he said, 'and we do not mind being beaten in the slightest. We have been down until today, but today we might have won. We did not – Glamorgan did and I congratulate them very much.'

After such a promising start, the County tasted the other side to life as first-class, slumping to eight successive defeats. Gloucestershire, Somerset and Northamptonshire all inflicted innings defeats as the Glamorgan batting showed an air of fragility against top-class bowling. One batting highlight was achieved, however, against Northamptonshire at Northampton in June when Billy Spiller became the County's first centurion in the Championship. He reached three figures with an all-run four on the leg side after batting for 170 minutes. Cording and Pinch also followed his example by making centuries in the next match at Swansea. Glamorgan totalled 405 for seven declared against some indifferent Worcestershire bowling with Cording making 101 and Pinch an unbeaten 138 on his first-class debut. The visitors were then dismissed twice as Glamorgan achieved a victory by an innings and 53 runs. These two matches raised the confidence of the Glamorgan team, but they failed to gain further success during the second half of the season. Hampshire recorded two comfortable wins by an innings and Sussex gained revenge for their earlier demise in the re-match at Hastings.

All in all, Glamorgan did not have an auspicious entry into the first-class ranks, and ended in 17th and last place in the Championship. Their playing record of 14 defeats from 19 matches and only two victories spoke volumes about the difficulties Riches encountered during the season. The main problems were the increased number of

First-class at last, and a splendid start in their opening championship match, with a marvellous win over the powerful Sussex team. The architects of this victory were Edgar Cooper with eight wickets, and Jock Tait with 96, and nobody was more delighted than Norman Riches and 'Tal' Whittington as the team triumphantly left the field, proving that their hard work in gaining first-class recognition had not been in vain.

*A cigarette card of Billy Spiller, Glamorgan's first Championship centurion.
(John Billot)*

days cricket in the Club's calendar and the raised standard of play.
Many of the amateurs still batted with the cavalier attitude which had
been the hallmark of their days in the Minor County Championship.
Riches was the only batsman to display anything like the concentration and discipline needed at the high level, as testified by his unbeaten
177 when carrying his bat against Leicestershire. In stark contrast,
many of the amateurs were hopelessly out of their depth, as testified by
the 55 ducks recorded during the season.

In addition, the team had to be continually changed to meet the
needs and business requirements of the amateurs. Without a settled XI,
no regular close catchers or specialist outfielders emerged and
surprisingly there was not a regular wicket-keeper. J. H. P. Brain,
Cording and Riches himself all did duty behind the stumps at various
times during the season, although he was, in modern parlance, only a
'stopper'. The placing of the field became a major difficulty for the
captain and just to make matters worse, there were always three or
four veterans who had to be hidden in the field. Given these assorted
difficulties, Glamorgan acquitted themselves fairly well and to record
two victories with all these handicaps was a major feat. This view
however was not widely shared outside the principality and *Wisden*
summed up their season by harshly saying that 'Glamorgan's
promotion to first-class cricket was not justified by results as against
two victories there was a heavy set-off of fourteen defeats.'

The committee reflected at length during the winter months on the team's moderate performance. The buoyant optimism which had greeted their entry into the County Championship had quickly been dispelled and just to compound matters the financial support from the business and industrial world had not been as great as expected. The year had started with a £350 deficit and the summer had brought a further loss of £97, despite takings of over £700 at the Sussex game. Fortunately, the Club had the committed backing of buisnessmen like Sir Sidney Byass and loyal patrons such as the elderly Sir John Llewelyn and as the economic position of South Wales deteriorated during the 1920s, the Club became increasingly reliant on these generous benefactors.

The Glamorgan officials were aware of the problems posed by the average age of the 1921 team, which for the Sussex match was 38 years and 2 months. *Wisden* had shrewdly observed how 'one would feel more hopeful of improvement in the immediate future, if the leading bowlers of the team were not so advanced in years . . . It is clear that to hold their own in first-class company, Glamorgan must find young talent, and not depend so much on middle-aged men.' The Club had tried several Welsh youngsters during 1921 but without any success, so it was obvious that the committee would have to bolster the team by hiring professionals from other counties, and bear the financial consequences at a later date.

Agreement was reached with five players, although the registration laws prevented any from appearing on a full-time basis until 1923. Three of the signings were bowlers, one was a batsman and the other two were wicket-keepers, although both were in the twilight of their careers. The first 'keeper was Dennis Sullivan, who had been Herbert Strudwick's understudy at The Oval for many seasons. The 38-year-old was released by Surrey at the end of 1921 and was quick to accept the Welsh county's offer. The other was James Stone, a 45-year-old batsman/wicket-keeper who had spent 15 years on Hampshire's books and had passed 1,000 runs on three occasions. The batsman who was signed was Thomas Abel, the 32-year-old son of Bobby Abel, the England and Surrey opener of the 1880s and 1890s. Thomas Abel had played a dozen games for Surrey after the war, but the hard-hitting opener had not established himself in the side. Without doubt, the main acquisition was Jack Mercer, a 26-year-old medium-fast bowler who had played for Sussex since 1919, where the presence of Maurice Tate limited him to just 12 appearances. He readily joined Glamorgan at £5 per week. Basil Rogers, a 25-year-old seam bowler who had played for Bedfordshire and Oxfordshire was also recruited together with Frank Ryan, a tall slow left-arm bowler who had appeared for Hampshire in 1919 and 1920. Ryan's background was both mysterious and unusual, having been born in New Jersey and educated in the Home Counties, but there was no doubting his abilities as a spinner and he gave the ball a sharp 'tweak'. However, Ryan was something of an eccentric, and he apparently hitch-hiked his way from Hampshire and was penniless when he arrived in South Wales to seek out a new cricketing career.

THE DREAM TURNS INTO A NIGHTMARE

BESIDES STRENGTHENING THE PLAYING STAFF, the committee also spent the winter months attempting to improve the financial situation. They decided to organise a number of fund-raising activities, realising that they could not always go 'cap in hand' to Llewelyn or Byass. During the winter of 1921/2, they contacted the officials of the various Football League clubs in the area regarding the feasibility of a match in aid of Glamorgan's funds. But the two clubs who would have raised most cash, Cardiff City and Swansea Town, both refused to help because of the presence of Thomas Schofield on the Glamorgan committee. Schofield was heavily involved with the Welsh Rugby Union and disliked the activities of the soccer clubs; he had written several attacks on football in the local press which annoyed the representatives from the Cardiff and Swansea clubs.

The cancellation of a fund-raising soccer match was the first blow the club received in 1922. Another came when Riches stood down as captain, because of his increasing involvement in his family's dental practice. However, they were both only mild compared to the untimely death, by his own hand, of Brock Williams in the spring of 1922. Without doubt, it was the most severe jolt the club's administration had ever received. Williams' suicide came as a huge surprise to many of the Club's supporters, but it was less of a shock to his closest friends, especially Whittington who had observed how Williams' character had been shattered by his wartime experiences. Williams had served with the Swansea Battalion of the Welsh Regiment, and was involved in the bloody attack on Mametz Wood in 1916, followed by the Battle of Ypres and the Somme, for which he was awarded the DSO after being wounded in a lung. Although he proudly marched into Swansea in 1919 at the head of his battalion, Lt-Col Williams had been mentally scarred by the horrors of war and was now highly strung with a nervous complaint. Sadly his private life began to fall into turmoil; his solicitor's practice became run down and then he lost a lot of money gambling and by unwise investments. One stroke of good fortune came in 1920 with the success of a boxing promotion with his fellow officer, Major Arnold Wilson.

Williams was also a talented musician, and under the nom-de-plumes of 'Florian' and 'Florian Brock', he wrote the score of several successful songs. Indeed, a new mood of optimism came over him in 1921, as can be seen in the second verse of 'Vagabond Philosophy' which he wrote with his friend Georges Carpentier, the French boxer:

And so in life you'll get
A regular knock-out blow.
Don't lie and grouse, but try to smile
And have the pluck to cry.
The mud and dust will soon rub off
It'll be all right by and by.

Tragically, these turned out to be prophetic words – his mother died in the autumn of 1921 and as a confirmed bachelor, Williams was left feeling lonely and desolate. A further blow came when his business went bankrupt and he was forced to go to London to work for Major Wilson. His friend lent him some money, but Williams began gambling again and visited Belgium to play the casinos. Indeed, he won some money and wrote to Wilson, saying that 'at last I've struck a bit of luck; just when apparently things were hopeless. I shall be able to pay you back what you have let me have.' But he lost it all and by the time Wilson received the letter, Williams had killed himself. Wilson's charlady had gone to clean his London Office, but found the room full of gas and Williams' body slumped on the floor besides two fully turned on gas taps.

None of the new signings was able to play regularly in 1922 and the Glamorgan selectors were still faced with the problems of a team which included too many veterans and changed in composition from match to match. Whittington was reappointed captain, and he tried his best to find the right combination, selecting no less than 43 players in the 23 matches. Another colts trial was held in the hope of discovering new talent, and towards the end of the season several youngsters were selected, including Royston Gabe-Jones, a schoolboy of 15 years and 9 months.

Glamorgan ended the season in 16th place winning just two matches, one of which was against a mediocre Oxbridge XI, and losing 18, including eight by an innings, the heaviest being by an innings and 258 runs against Yorkshire at the Arms Park. In fact the first 12 matches resulted in defeat and there was a horrendous series of low totals – 134, 47, 99, 139, 42 and 99. Bearing in mind their abysmal form, Whittington's team must have surprised even their most ardent supporters at the end of July by registering their first ever away victory in the Championship. Creber fully exploited a turning wicket at Weston-super-Mare as Somerset were beaten by 117 runs. However, there was a quick return to the bad habits in the next match against Northamptonshire. Glamorgan were set a target of 168 and were in a promising position, only for a collapse to occur and transform a seeming victory into a 24-run defeat.

To say that the batting in 1922 was fragile may well be a gross

ROYSTON GABE-JONES

Royston Gabe-Jones can claim to be not only Glamorgan's youngest player, but also the youngest person ever to appear in the County Championship. Even more remarkable was that Gabe-Jones rose from the unknown ranks of schoolboy cricket to make one appearance for Glamorgan and then disappear back into obscurity.

He was born in the Pontypridd area and attended Blundell's School in Devon where he gained a reputation as a talented young sportsman and athlete. He showed promise as right-handed batsman and seam bowler, but it was his outstanding fielding which brought him recognition. Indeed, *The Blundellian* for 1922 commented how he 'was very neat and quick in the field, gathers and returns the ball in very good style, and is almost invariably a safe catcher'.

During 1922 he played several useful innings for Clydach Vale CC, which brought him to the attention of the County's officials who were seeking promising new talent, and in mid-August he was selected to appear in the colts trial match at Cardiff. Despite scoring only six and failing to take a wicket, his fielding greatly impressed Norman Riches and the watching committee. So when the County were without four regulars for the end of season match with Leicestershire at the Arms Park, Gabe-Jones was one of the youngsters called up to make their debuts. Once again he fielded well, and when he batted he patiently occupied the crease for an hour and a half to save the follow-on.

Despite this impressive debut, the County officials never called upon Gabe-Jones again. He returned to Blundell's and captained the school's cricket and rugby teams in 1924 and 1925. After leaving school, he went into business in South Wales and began playing at fly-half for Cardiff RFC, often with Maurice Turnbull as his scrum-half partner. He captained the rugby side in 1933/4, but at the end of the season he retired, and so ended, at the age of 28, an unusual and brief sporting career.

Royston Gabe-Jones (seated), the youngest county cricketer this century. (Blundell's School)

75

understatement. A major factor was that Riches could only play in 11 matches and although he scored 561 runs in these games, his absence at other times was crucial. Bates was the only batsman with an average of over 20, and although Tait, Symonds and Gemmill made runs on occasions, there was still an absence of batsmen up to the demands of regular county cricket, with a staggering 81 ducks being recorded during the summer. The bowlers also struggled during the season, and it was clear that Nash and Creber were well past their best, taking just 42 and 50 wickets respectively. In addition, Hacker was only available for eight matches, though he performed well on his few appearances, taking 34 wickets at 16 apiece.

There were a few rays of optimism in the bowling department. In their sole appearance, Ryan and Mercer made a favourable impact by taking eight wickets each, but without doubt, the most encouraging sign was the emergence of Johnnie Clay, who bowled leg cutters at a brisk pace, besides occasional experiments with leg-spin. The former Winchester schoolboy started the season as a virtual unknown, but he ended it as easily the County's leading wicket-taker, claiming 83 wickets at an average of 22. The committee were heartened by Clay's development, and they made an attempt to secure the services of a coach who would hopefully bring on young Welsh talent. As Clay and Gabe-Jones had shown, the young Glamorgan cricketers were still emerging from the English public schools rather than directly from Welsh clubs. Whittington believed the appointment of a coach to be vital if Glamorgan were going to introduce home-bred talent. This would also reduce the costs of hiring players from other counties and thereby give Glamorgan a chance of surviving as a first-class county. Adverts were placed in several newspapers and eventually Fred Bowley, the Brecon-born former Worcestershire bowler was hired for three years at £400 per annum.

However, the Club finished the season with a loss of £2,800 which inevitably affected Bowley's coaching programme. He wrote to local clubs and schools hoping to find young cricketers who could be properly coached. But the purse strings were kept tight, out of necessity, and Bowley was given little money towards exploiting fully the talent of the youngsters who turned up to his winter sessions. Even if the material were there, the resources and facilities were limited and the County saw little immediate gain from Bowley's employment.

Glamorgan finished in 16th place once again in 1923, winning just three of their 25 matches; 17 ended in defeat, though only five were by an innings. Despite their lowly position, there were some signs of improvement, notably in the bowling, following the full-time availability of Ryan. He showed his worth by claiming 106 wickets, including five in an innings on eight occasions and received useful support from Arnott and Clay, though the latter was handicapped by a back injury. Besides making an impact on the field, Ryan established himself as one of the Welsh county's characters off the field, enjoying life to the full. There are a host of stories about Ryan's activities and habits – one of the best and possibly most apocryphal concerned his late arrival for the match with Somerset at Cardiff. The spinner had stayed on at Blackpool the night before with some Lancastrian friends after their county's win over Glamorgan, whilst the rest of the team returned by train to Cardiff. Apparently Ryan hired a taxi in the early hours of the morning and arrived at the Arms Park at 11.10 the next morning, entering the dressing room with the immortal phrase 'Ryan never lets you down', leaving the speechless Glamorgan treasurer to deal with the tired, and no doubt confused driver and a substantial bill. No doubt the startled official felt that with the County's mounting debts, he could have done without Ryan's night-time escapades.

The season began with heavy defeats in the first two fixtures at Cardiff; further defeats followed against Nottinghamshire and Surrey and by the end of May it was evident that the batting was still weak. The selection committee, which numbered a staggering 32, had heard of a promising young all-rounder in Llanelli called David Davies. Bowley had been impressed by him and there were calls from the representatives of the West Area for Davies' inclusion in the team.

Frank Ryan – one of the most colourful characters ever to play for Glamorgan.

With such a large number of people on the selection panel, an element of confusion was inevitable, and only on the morning of the match with Northants at Swansea in early June did they agree to select Davies. A car was sent on the 25-mile round trip to Llanelli to collect the 26-year-old, but unbeknown to the selectors, he was still fast asleep in bed having worked a double shift at the town's steelworks. His mother had to wake him up and help him get ready for his county debut. But he very nearly didn't make it and was almost refused entry into the ground – Davies recollected: 'I arrived at St Helen's and made for the entrance next to the pavilion, but was stopped by the gateman. "Where do you think you're going?" he asked. "I'm playing", I replied. "Oh no you're not," he said, "get out of it!" I suppose he'd had some experience of people trying to get in for nothing carrying cricket bags. So I held my cricket bag in front of me and charged past him, almost knocking him down in the process. Luckily I spotted Harry Creber, the groundsman and he smoothed things over with the angry gateman!'

It was a truly amazing debut for Davies, because no sooner had he got changed and got onto the pitch than he was asked to bowl by Whittington, who was desperately searching for a breakthrough with the scoreboard reading Northants 57-0. The captain's wishes came true as Davies, with only his fourth ball, knocked out Bellamy's middle stump. He carried on bowling after lunch and took two further wickets to finish with 3-39. But as Dai remembers, he hadn't finished there: 'Glamorgan had about an hour to bat after tea, and I was beginning to feel very tired by now and I was more than thankful to sit on the dressing room bench. Just then Whittington snapped out "Get your pads on Dai, you're first wicket down." I got my pads on, and sat outside trying to summon up strength from somewhere. Thankfully, it wasn't needed because the openers held out until close of play. I went home by train in the evening, very tired and very happy!'

It was hardly a coincidence that this game saw the County's first victory of the summer. In their second innings, Northamptonshire struggled against Ryan's bowling, leaving Glamorgan a target of 191. Davies opened with Tait and the youngster gave the side a sound start, providing the base for a four-wicket win. But it was only a temporary improvement, as in the next match Lancashire bowled out the Welsh team for 96 and 52 to win by an innings. Even worse was to follow against Sussex at Horsham where the Sussex batsmen amassed 447, and won by an innings and 270 runs, and in the next six innings the Glamorgan bowlers conceded 2,523 runs; this meant that the Welsh batsmen, not known for their adhesive qualities, were often chasing high targets.

Dai Davies – one of the stalwarts of the Glamorgan side in the 1920s and 1930s.

By the end of July morale must have been at rock bottom, but once again, just when things were at their worst, the team pulled together and produced two outstanding victories. Firstly, in the match with Gloucestershire, fine bowling by Ryan and Dai Davies dismissed the West Country team for 97 and 123 to give Glamorgan a victory by 232 runs. Then in the following match, the Welsh county registered their first-ever victory over a touring team, defeating the West Indians at Cardiff. Glamorgan were able to select Mercer, and given the fragility of their existing attack, the former Sussex bowler gave an indication in this match of how valuable his services were going to be once he had fully qualified.

After Glamorgan had made 115, there was a fine display of seam bowling by Trevor Arnott, who took seven wickets. Nevertheless, the tourists reached 201 and the Welsh batsmen knew they would have to bat well in their second innings. They rose to the occasion magnificently and in front of a large Bank Holiday crowd totalled 324. The feature of the innings was a partnership of 136 in an hour and a half by Stone and Pinch, with the wicket-keeper going on to make an invaluable 108. The West Indians were left with a target of 239, and

GLAMORGAN *v.* WEST INDIES

Played at Cardiff Arms Park, 4, 6 and 7 August 1923

GLAMORGAN WON BY 43 RUNS

GLAMORGAN	FIRST INNINGS		SECOND INNINGS	
*N. V. H. Riches	lbw b John	5	b John	26
T. R. Morgan	b Browne	29	c Dewhurst b Pascall	12
W. E. Bates	b John	20	c Challenor b John	51
C. F. Walters	b Browne	0	b John	0
J. J. Stone	c Austin b John	19	c and b Constantine	108
F. B. Pinch	b John	4	b Francis	55
D. Davies	b John	0	b Pascall	10
T. Arnott	not out	15	st Dewhurst b Pascall	32
F. P. Ryan	b John	1	b Francis	7
J. Mercer	b John	9	not out	4
†D. Sullivan	run out	1	c Tarilton b Francis	0
Extras		12		19
Total		115		324

1st inns: 1-13, 2-39, 3-46, 4-81, 5-85, 6-87, 7-97, 8-102, 9-114
2nd inns: 1-22, 2-53, 3-53, 4-128, 5-265, 6-267, 7-298, 8-319, 9-324

BOWLING	O	M	R	W	O	M	R	W
John	23	9	52	7	31	5	95	3
Francis	8	2	23	0	30.3	6	77	3
Browne	14	5	28	2	11	4	36	0
Pascall					15	4	37	3
Small					6	1	28	0
Constantine					6	0	32	1

WEST INDIES	FIRST INNINGS		SECOND INNINGS	
G. Challenor	b Arnott	5	lbw b Mercer	110
P. H. Tarilton	c Sullivan b Arnott	75	b Pinch	9
H. W. Ince	b Pinch	21	lbw b Ryan	25
*H. B. G. Austin	lbw b Ryan	40	c Sullivan b Mercer	24
C. R. Browne	c Sullivan b Arnott	0	c Sullivan b Ryan	4
†G. Dewhurst	b Arnott	3	c Davies b Mercer	0
V. Pascall	b Arnott	6	c and b Ryan	0
G. Francis	st Sullivan b Mercer	12	run out	2
J. Small	c Pinch b Arnott	4	c and b Arnott	0
L. Constantine	not out	9	c Sullivan b Mercer	3
G. John	b Arnott	5	not out	2
Extras		21		16
Total		201		195

1st inns: 1-14, 2-83, 3-159, 4-161, 5-162, 6-163, 7-180, 8-184, 9-190
2nd inns: 1-21, 2-100, 3-101, 4-171, 5-184, 6-185, 7-189, 8-190, 9-193

BOWLING	O	M	R	W	O	M	R	W
Arnott	14.2	2	40	7	12	0	49	1
Ryan	9	1	20	1	14.2	0	71	3
Davies	7	0	15	0	3	0	10	0
Pinch	5	1	22	1	3	1	8	1
Bates	4	0	18	0				
Mercer	24	3	65	1	12	1	41	4

Umpires: H. B. Abberley and D. Evans

they began in fine style with George Challenor, their leading batsman, making a faultless century. At 185 for five the tourists were in sight of victory, but Mercer was brought back into the attack and trapped Challenor lbw. This heralded a collapse as Mercer and Arnott ran through the lower order to dismiss the visitors for 195. Glamorgan had finally beaten a touring team and there were great celebrations on the Arms Park ground after the last wicket had fallen. The scale of their success can be gauged from the fact that in their previous match the West Indies had completely outplayed the powerful Surrey team at The Oval and had won by ten wickets.

Whittington and Riches were delighted by the success, believing that it was an indication that Glamorgan had come of age. They were even more pleased by the fact that the Glamorgan team included some promising young Welsh cricketers, including the 17-year-old Cyril Walters from Neath. He had a most impressive schoolboy record in his home town, and had been selected for the County team after a number of outstanding innings, under Whittington's careful eye, for the Neath club. Some of the other young amateurs were making encouraging progress, clearly benefiting from the experience gained in earlier seasons. One of these was T. R. ('Tubby') Morgan, who put together some useful gritty innings and moved up the batting order, opening against the West Indies. The previous year Morgan had scored only 251 runs and was rather unkindly known as 'the stone-wall specialist' after twice carrying his bat for 22 and 14. He grew in confidence during 1923 and amassed 735 runs, though many were still gained by his favourite shot – a deft snick behind the wicket.

Whittington was delighted with the progress of Morgan, Dai Davies and young Walters, but at the age of 42 Whittington's own future as an active county cricketer was clearly limited. He had steadily lost form as a batsman and moved down the order in 1922 and 1923 to give greater opportunities to the youngsters. He averaged only 14 and realised at the end of the 1923 season that it was the right time to retire from cricket. The committee reluctantly accepted his resignation as captain, realising that he had been influenced by both cricketing and personal reasons. The tragic death of Brock Williams had robbed him of a close confidant, who had persuaded their friends in the business world to support the Club. Without his loyal friend, and now without

---

Over the years Glamorgan have recorded many fine wins over touring teams and this game was their first. The West Indies had not been elevated to test match status, but they brought a strong side to Cardiff, including George Challenor and the legendary Learie Constantine. However, they held no fears for Jimmy Stone, who scored a superb century, Trevor Arnott, the Radyr-born all rounder, and new signing Jack Mercer, whose bowling saw Glamorgan to victory.

any cricket, Whittington decided to leave South Wales, and took a teaching post at Lancing College.

The committee appointed Johnnie Clay as the new captain for 1924. At first glance, it seemed a curious decision, selecting a 26-year-old bowler who had missed a number of matches in previous years and had struggled with a back injury. However, during 1923 Clay had experimented with off-cutters and leg breaks, and had some success in this slower style. He therefore decided to concentrate on off-spin in 1924 – it proved to be a wise decision because, as John Arlott said some years later: 'If you look at Johnnie Clay you will see that he looks like an off-break bowler . . . Johnnie Clay was obviously created to bowl it. The fast bowler and the leg-spinner were no more than phases designed to convince him by experience of his natural bent.' His back was not going to be put under so much pressure in this new mode and he was likely to be regularly available, despite his business commitments in the Vale of Glamorgan. All of these factors, plus his amateur status, made Clay the obvious successor to Whittington.

During the winter months, Clay and the committee attempted to strengthen the staff, but they were faced with a worsening financial situation. The poor summer of 1923 produced a £2,951 loss and a fund-raising sub-committee was formed in an attempt to ease the position. A variety of sweepstakes, appeals and competitions were successfully organised, but the Club still faced a total debt in excess of £6,000 at the start of 1924. This meant that they could not afford to lure new professionals with the promise of lucrative salaries. They tried to make a professional post with Glamorgan more attractive in other ways and reached an agreement with the National Oil refinery company, who would provide jobs at their new Llandarcy complex to any big names that joined the Welsh county. In the end only two newcomers arrived – John Bell, the former Yorkshire opener, and Helm Spencer, the Lancashire seamer who had played with success as pro for Llanelli.

The Glamorgan side, under Clay's astute captaincy, continued their steady improvement in 1924, winning five of the 24 matches. They rose up to 13th place, with the new signings and the young Welshmen making valuable contributions. However, the season began in familiar fashion with innings defeats against Surrey and Yorkshire. They were lucky not to lose at Worcester and travelled on to Liverpool, knowing that Lancashire had gained innings victories in the previous two years.

There was no play on the first day and when play began on the second morning the Glamorgan bowlers took full advantage of the damp conditions, dismissing Lancashire before lunch for 49, with Spencer taking five for 9. Many of the Glamorgan supporters who bought an early edition of the evening paper were overjoyed at seeing the lunch score and sent telegrams of congratulations up to Liverpool. But their messages started to arrive just as Glamorgan were going out to field for a second time, having been bowled out by the Lancashire bowlers for 22! Only Bates got into double figures as Ernest Tyldesley with four for 16 and Cecil Parkin with six for 6 wrecked the Welsh batting. The wicket dried out in the afternoon and played easier, allowing Lancashire to declare at 208 for eight, but on the final day Parkin and Tyldesley bowled their team to victory, dismissing Glamorgan for 107.

After this poor start, the team recorded a seven-wicket win at Derby and then defeated Leicestershire by an innings at Swansea. Abel scored a fine 107 and then Ryan claimed eleven for 64 as Glamorgan showed signs of improving form. They achieved the double over Derbyshire a few weeks later at Swansea, winning by an innings after Riches had compiled a superb 170 and Trevor Arnott had made his

Cyril Walters (left) and Maurice Turnbull (right) – the 'bright young things' of Glamorgan cricket in 1924. (Western Mail)

maiden century. Arnott's innings occupied only 75 minutes, and included a number of bold strokes. Indeed, the way he went to his hundred typified his cavalier approach to batting. His score stood at 96, and Riches went down the wicket to give the young all-rounder some advice. 'Now Trevor,' he said, 'don't be rash. Get these four runs in singles.' But Arnott responded by smashing the next ball he faced onto the roof of the rugby grandstand!

A measure of the team's improvement came in the game with Lancashire at Swansea in mid-August. The Northern county were set a target of 146 on the final day, and with their score at 84 for three, they seemed well set for victory. But the Welsh team were playing with confidence, and when Clay brought Ryan into the attack, a collapse set in. Ryan took six wickets in quick succession as the last seven wickets fell for just 23 runs, leaving Glamorgan to celebrate victory by 38 runs. Glamorgan's top scorer was an 18-year-old schoolboy called Maurice Turnbull. His father was a wealthy shipowner in Penarth and together with his seven brothers, Maurice attended Downside School in Somerset. He had a fine record for Downside, averaging 84.7 in 1924, with three centuries, including a school record of 184 inside three hours against King's Bruton. His uncle Bertrand served on the Glamorgan committee and as a result of his outstanding schoolboy record, Clay invited young Turnbull to play for the County during the school holidays. In the handful of innings he played, Turnbull displayed both class and a fine temperament, with the *Western Mail* on one occasion, saying how the youngster 'batted with the assurance, coolness and judgement of a veteran'.

Turnbull's emergence rounded off what was Glamorgan's best season to date, and when coupled with Ryan's haul of 120 wickets, plus the progress made by Arnott and Dai Davies as all-rounders, it gave the County's officials every reason for eagerly looking forward to the next season, believing that the good times were just around the corner.

THE UPS AND DOWNS OF THE LATE 1920s

SEASON 1925 PROVED TO BE one of the worst in the Club's history as the team slumped back to the bottom of the table. The mood of optimism was quickly dispelled as 13 successive matches were lost between 9 May and 17 July. Opposing teams amassed large totals and the Welsh batsmen struggled to build lengthy innings. The failure of the batting was highlighted in the game against Essex at Swansea. Set to score 199 on the final afternoon, Glamorgan seemed well set at lunch for their first victory of the season with their score on 117 for four and Tait and Arnott well set. But after the interval a collapse occurred with the last four wickets falling for just four runs as Essex won by 38 runs. With the emergence of Turnbull and Walters, Riches decided to concentrate on his dentist's practice and played in only seven matches. Without their most experienced batsman, the burden of responsibility fell onto the shoulders of Bates, Abel and Pinch. Only Bates had a good season, scoring over 900 runs as the other two had moderate summers.

The committee were left to reflect on what might have been if the batsmen had produced the goods; their failure was even more disappointing considering that Ryan took 133 wickets and Mercer 96. The only crumbs of comfort for 1926 were that Bell would be available for the first time on a regular basis to bolster the batting and the talented Turnbull would be able to play throughout the second half of the summer after completing his first year studies at Cambridge University. However, the effect of another poor summer had left its mark on the club's finances and the debt stood at over £2,000. The committee had watched the financial situation steadily get worse during the early 1920s, and apart from creating the fund-raising sub-committee, had not taken any drastic action to arrest the decline, believing that things would pick up once Glamorgan started to win. But the events of 1925 showed that the County were still a long way from having a successful side, and despite their faith in the ability of Walters and Turnbull, the Treasurer, E. A. Tyler, and the committee realised it was time to take major steps to reduce the debt.

One of the problems was that Cardiff Athletic Club demanded a sizeable sum for the use of their Arms Park facilities. Through the efforts of Riches, the rent was reduced but it was still a major commitment for the Club to undertake on their shoestring budget. Consequently, the County's officials began to consider whether they could stage matches anywhere else. They knew the fact that matches were played at just the Arms Park or St Helen's annoyed many people in other parts of South Wales, especially those like the miners or steelworkers, who had a limited amount of spare time and did not want the hassle or the cost of a long journey to see the team play. These people felt that Glamorgan wanted their money and subscription fees, but were not interested in rewarding their patronage by staging games outside Cardiff or Swansea.

However, playing matches at club grounds was expensive and Glamorgan needed guarantees of support before committing themselves. Encouraging noises came from Neath, where some of the minor county games had been staged before the war. In addition, Pontypridd CC offered the Club the use of Ynysangharad Park, the town's purpose-built recreational complex which had been opened in 1923 as a tribute to the young men of the area who lost their lives in the First World War. The Glamorgan officials visited the ground and were impressed by the facilities and the standard of the wicket. They were even more delighted when they were given promises of support from people in the Taff and Rhondda Valleys, and the Pontypridd club informed them that they wanted only 10 per cent of the gate receipts. It seemed too good an offer to refuse so the committee allocated the Derbyshire fixture to Ynysangharad Park.

The committee also continued their search for recruits, in particular any players who could strengthen the batting. Once again they looked to the Yorkshire leagues for a suitable replacement and approached 37-year-old Cecil Tyson, the Castleford professional who had played for Yorkshire in 1921 and scored an unbeaten century on his first-class debut. The left-hander had been described by Herbert Sutcliffe as 'an exceptional batsman. No one looked like getting him out during his spell with the county'. However, Tyson's career with Yorkshire had been both brilliant and brief; a disagreement over terms and difficulties with his league engagement had seen him return to club cricket after three first-class appearances. However, he desperately wanted to play at county level and agreed to come down for a trial with Glamorgan. Tyson played in two matches in 1926, and impressed with a top score of 76, but he returned north after finding problems in obtaining a suitable residence and being disappointed with the modest terms of the professional contract which he was offered. Nevertheless, Arnold Dyson, a young opener from Halifax, and Joe Hills, a batsman/wicket-keeper from the Kent staff agreed to join the Club.

But the good news of their acquisition was offset by the further deterioration of the South Wales economy, which hampered the committee's attempts to reduce the debt. Clay realised the gravity of the financial situation and he knew that if the club did not start showing some sign of consistent success, they would be forced to return to the minor county ranks. At their pre-season practices, he coaxed and cajoled the players into giving their utmost, and almost to a man, they responded to the captain's urgings, and put firmly behind them the disappointments of the previous summer.

Clay's team finished in eighth place in the table, and during the first half of the season were even in the race for the title. After three draws, the first victory of the season came at Chesterfield. Mercer posed problems for the Derbyshire batsmen and Glamorgan needed just 142 in their second innings. After the traumas of the previous summer, there were a few flutters in the hearts of the Welshmen, but Bates scored an unbeaten hundred to steer the team to an eight-wicket victory. This was the only fixture in the country in which a result was achieved, and the next day Clay was able to open the morning newspaper and proudly see Glamorgan on top of the table for the first time.

They consolidated their position with victories over Surrey, Gloucestershire and Warwickshire, but their progress was thwarted by a heavy defeat at Trent Bridge. The Nottinghamshire batsmen occupied the crease for over seven hours in amassing 564 for six, and then forced the Welsh county to follow on. Despite a maiden century from Hills, the home team won by an innings. The two counties met at Swansea a week later and this time the Glamorgan bowlers held the upper hand with Ryan taking ten wickets and Mercer eight to see Glamorgan home by two wickets.

The weather badly interfered with the next few matches, including the inaugural match at Pontypridd. Despite the rain clouds, a large crowd turned up and they were treated to a splendid 136 by Riches on one of his rare appearances for the County. The trip to Dudley saw a much needed return to winning form. Worcestershire were bowled out for 98, with Mercer taking seven for 40, and then the Glamorgan batsmen totalled 470 for six declared, with Bell batting nearly five hours for 225 – the first Championship double century for the Welsh team – to set up an innings victory.

It seemed that nothing could go wrong for Clay's team in mid-season, as Walters scored his maiden century against Warwickshire at Swansea, and then Arnott took the first Championship hat-trick for the Welsh team. It came in the match with Somerset as the visitors were dismissed for 59 on a damp Arms Park wicket. After Glamorgan had scored 160, there was a heavy shower which made batting almost impossible against Mercer and Ryan; they bowled out Somerset for 77 to give Glamorgan another innings win. This kept the Club in second place, and interest in cricket within the area was sky high. The Club's next match was against Australia and there was much speculation about whether the Welsh county could defeat the tourists. A record crowd of 25,000 flooded into St Helen's on the second day, with hundreds left on the pavement outside. But they failed to see a Glamorgan victory as Arthur Mailey and Clarrie Grimmett exploited a turning Swansea wicket to set up an Australian victory by 224 runs.

This heavy defeat marked the end of Glamorgan's title challenge, as they failed to win any of their last nine matches, and slipped out of contention. There were a few highlights in these closing matches, in particular Turnbull's long-awaited first century, which came in the match against Worcestershire at the Arms Park. On the bowling front, Mercer finished the season with 129 wickets at 16 apiece; he was rewarded with selection for the Players at the Scarborough Festival and was selected in Arthur Gilligan's MCC team to tour India. Ryan also took over a hundred wickets – it was the fourth consecutive time he had achieved this feat, and he must have come close to selection for the winter tour.

The County's officials had found it difficult, and downright expensive, to attract top class professionals to South Wales, and with limited funds, the Club could not afford to hire any more. Some of the committee felt it was a retrograde step to sign rejects from other teams. It was argued that the money could be better spent on fostering local talent and finding a few more like Walters or Turnbull. No doubt these committee members were delighted by the creation of the South Wales Cricket Association during 1926. The County's officials had casted envious eyes on the highly competitive Yorkshire and Lancashire Leagues which provided a welter of talent for these two counties. They contacted officials of clubs in South Wales once again in an attempt to organise a similar league competition which could act as a nursery for potential Glamorgan cricketers. Friendly matches, not on a league basis, had failed to exploit fully local talent, and there had not been an element of rivalry and competition throughout the region. Successful replies were obtained from Barry, Briton Ferry Steel, Briton Ferry Town, Cardiff, Gowerton, Llanelli, Neath, Newport and Swansea, whilst Daniel Radcliffe put up a handsome sum for a trophy. The new competition proved an immediate success, with crowds of up to 4,000 watching the games between neighbours Neath and Briton Ferry Town. This public support provided the clubs with increased finances which they could put towards coaching, whilst the element of league competition gave them an extra incentive to raise the standard of their play.

During the winter months, the Glamorgan officials also took steps to improve their administrative facilities. They had previously occupied a variety of small premises in Cardiff and Neath, but with the club's organisation expanding, and the team becoming successful, it was clear to Clay and the committee that a purpose-built office suite was needed. Because they did not own the Arms Park or St Helen's, a headquarters at either of these grounds was out of the question. Therefore, they decided to rent a small section of an office block in the High Street at the heart of Cardiff's business district close to the cricket ground.

With all of these off-the-field improvements and developments at club level, further progress was widely expected in 1927. But it proved to be a poor year, with the club slipping back to 15th place. Whilst only eight games were lost, compared with nine the season before, just one victory was recorded and that right at the end of the summer. There were several factors responsible for the sharp decline – the first being the poor weather. Fifteen matches ended in a draw, and two were abandoned without a ball being bowled, including the flag-flying venture to Pontypridd. The second was that the batting was not as effective as before. In particular, Bell had a very disappointing season, scoring just 733 runs compared with 1,547 the year before.

The team were also without their highly rated youngsters. After scoring 303 runs in the first six matches, Cyril Walters dropped a bombshell by deciding to retire temporarily from cricket for business reasons. Turnbull was also absent for all but two games because of an

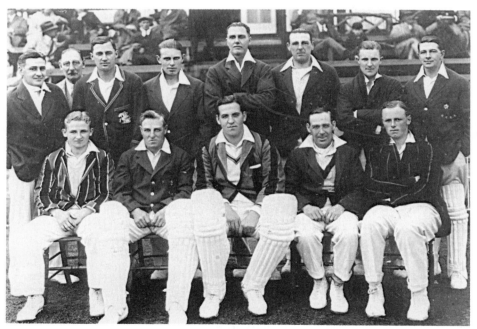

The Glamorgan team which beat Nottinghamshire in 1927. Standing: Dai Davies, C. J. South (scorer), Jack Mercer, Arnold Dyson, Frank Ryan, Joe Hills, Emrys Davies (12th man), John Bell. Seated: Guy Morgan, Eddie Bates, Trevor Arnott (capt), Dennis Sullivan (wkt. keeper), John Morgan.

89

GLAMORGAN *v.* NOTTINGHAMSHIRE

Played at St Helen's, Swansea, 31 August and 1 and 2 September 1927

GLAMORGAN WON BY AN INNINGS AND 81 RUNS

NOTTINGHAMSHIRE	FIRST INNINGS		SECOND INNINGS	
G. Gunn	b Arnott	68	c Arnott b Mercer	2
W. W. Whysall	run out	16	c Arnott b Mercer	10
W. Walker	c and b Davies	11	b Mercer	0
W. R. D. Payton	c Sullivan b Ryan	50	b Mercer	10
†B. Lilley	not out	44	c Arnott b Ryan	1
W. A. Flint	c Hills b Ryan	3	b Mercer	7
S. J. Staples	lbw b Arnott	26	lbw b Ryan	0
*L. Kirk	b Ryan	1	b Mercer	0
F. Barratt	c Arnott b Ryan	0	b Ryan	11
T. L. Richmond	b Mercer	1	c Mercer b Ryan	1
W. Voce	st Sullivan b Ryan	0	not out	7
Extras		13		12
Total		233		61

1st inns: 1-29, 2-45, 3-143, 4-165, 5-178, 6-196, 7-198, 8-226, 9-232
2nd inns: 1-12, 2-14, 3-30, 4-33, 5-34, 6-36, 7-42, 8-43, 9-44

BOWLING	O	M	R	W	O	M	R	W
Mercer	30	9	51	1	14	3	31	6
Arnott	12	2	45	2	2	1	4	0
Ryan	30.2	5	81	5	11.2	4	14	4
Davies	11	4	22	1				
Bates	6	0	21	0				

GLAMORGAN	FIRST INNINGS	
W. E. Bates	lbw b Richmond	163
J. T. Bell	lbw b Staples	57
J. T. Morgan	st Lilley b Richmond	0
*T. Arnott	c Barratt b Richmond	1
D. Davies	c Voce b Richmond	0
W. G. Morgan	b Barratt	7
A. H. Dyson	c Voce b Richmond	27
J. J. Hills	c and b Flint	39
†D. Sullivan	b Flint	31
J. Mercer	b Staples	1
F. P. Ryan	not out	8
Extras		41
Total		375

1st inns: 1-158, 2-159, 3-169, 4-183, 5-226, 6-268, 7-295, 8-351, 9-352

BOWLING	O	M	R	W
Barratt	14	3	45	1
Staples	55	24	104	2
Richmond	42	9	102	5
Voce	24	8	56	0
Flint	9	1	27	2

Umpires: A. Morton and W. R. Parry

injury sustained in the winter playing rugby for Cardiff. A further factor was that the bowling was less effective; although Mercer took 96 wickets, Ryan had a poor season, taking only 71 wickets, whilst Arnott claimed a paltry 35. Spencer was no longer available to provide support, and Clay's business commitments meant that the captain missed 11 games. When he was absent, the pressures of leading the side took its toll on his various replacements and the team's morale gradually slumped.

There was one silver lining amongst the dark clouds of 1927, and that was the contribution of Bates, who by now was in the veteran stage. He produced the best batting of his long career, scoring 1,645 runs at an average of 44. In the first game of the season he hit 105 and 111 against Essex at Leyton to become the first Glamorgan player to score a century in both innings. This was followed later in the season at Kidderminster by a career-best 200 not out against Worcestershire.

Bates also made a vital contribution in the County's final game of the season against Nottinghamshire at Swansea. The visitors arrived at St Helen's needing to secure only a draw to clinch the county title. Taking into account Glamorgan's disastrous season, this seemed a formality and the Mayor of Nottingham had even planned a civic reception to celebrate the winning of the Championship. After Nottinghamshire had made 233, Bates and Bell put on 158 for the first wicket as Glamorgan's batsmen excelled themselves. Bates went on to score 163 as Glamorgan totalled 375. The visitors faced a deficit of 142, but with only a day to go and the poor form of the Welsh bowlers, it seemed likely that their batsmen would safely occupy the crease and secure the county title. However, Mercer and Ryan had other ideas and bowled Nottinghamshire out for just 61 to give Glamorgan their only, and most unlikely, victory of the season. The visiting batsmen departed shell-shocked as Mercer took six wickets and Ryan four, and there are tales of one of the Nottinghamshire tailenders sitting on the pavilion steps with tears flooding down his cheeks as he watched his team–mates return at regular intervals and the title slip from his team's grasp.

The Glamorgan celebrations did not last long, however, as the County were struck by a number of blows towards the end of the season. Firstly, there was the death of Sir John Llewelyn at his home in Penllergaer. He had been responsible for the team's rise out of nothing

---

This was the biggest upset of the 1927 season – Glamorgan, who had not won a game all season and were struggling to raise a strong XI, defeated the mighty Notts team, who were cruising towards the county title. But Bates's dour century, together with the cunning bowling of Ryan and Mercer meant that Notts were deprived of the championship title as Glamorgan won a remarkable game by an innings, proving that 'cricket is a funny game'!

and, although wishing they could be more successful, he must have been proud of the way the club had developed. Secondly, Cyril Walters announced that he would be returning to cricket, but for Worcestershire, and was taking the Secretary's post with the Midlands county. The loss of the young Neath batsman was not fully appreciated until the 1930s when he opened for England alongside Herbert Sutcliffe. Others to depart at the end of the season were Tait and Pinch, and a final blow came when Clay resigned the captaincy because his outside interests prevented him from playing regularly.

It didn't take the committee long to decide who should lead the Club in 1928. Riches was far too old to be considered as a replacement, so the committee appointed Trevor Arnott, the only other amateur, to take over from Clay. Despite all the departures and resignations, Arnott's team won the first game of the season, defeating Worcestershire by 33 runs at the Arms Park. However, only one other match was won during the rest of the summer, and the County remained in 15th place. Ten of the 28 fixtures were lost, including their new match with Oxford University. The students scored 494 and forced Glamorgan to follow on, before gaining an easy win. Later in the season at Huddersfield, Yorkshire amassed 387 for two with Sutcliffe and Leyland scoring centuries and adding 323 for the third wicket, and then just to rub salt into their wounds, Gloucestershire hit the Welsh bowlers for 653 for six, with Wally Hammond scoring a masterly 218 not out and Alf Dipper 188 not out.

These three matches epitomised the Welsh county's problems in 1928, as their bowlers, after three good seasons, failed to take wickets regularly. Arnott played a captain's role by toiling away for long spells, but he lacked penetration, and must have wished that Clay had been available more often to give him support. Ryan ended the season with 86 victims, but this total rather flattered him because he bowled poorly early in the season. Indeed, the committee decided at one stage not to offer him a new contract, but the spinner produced some useful spells later in the year which forced the committee to reverse their decision. Ryan was aptly described by J. H. Morgan as 'an eccentric genius, who on his day, and given the right wicket, would bowl out any side in the country. But as Johnnie Clay once put it, there were times when he did not spin, nor did he toil. Ryan has his little weaknesses – if it had not been for these he would have been an English bowler.' The last sentence was a reference to Ryan's liking for the demon drink, and apparently after one lengthy drinking session after a day's play, he forgot where the team were staying and returned to the ground to sleep under the covers!

The batting was much stronger than the bowling; Dai Davies had by far his best season to date with the bat, scoring three consecutive hundreds, including a career best 165 not out against Sussex. He was rewarded with selection at the end of the season for the Players in their annual fixture against the Gentlemen. Bates had another good season, making 1,515 runs, whilst Bell aggregated 1,500, including over 700 in August alone. There were several new faces in the batting order following the departure of Pinch, Tait and Walters. The most impressive performers were George Lavis, a 20-year-old from Monmouthshire and J. T. Morgan from Charterhouse School and Cambridge University. Morgan also showed promise as a wicket-keeper and played behind the stumps in the end of season matches following Sullivan's surprise decision to quit the game and take up a coaching post at Rossall School.

The moderate season had another adverse effect on the Club's finances. The good year of 1926 had produced a profit of £2,000, but the last two summers had quickly converted this into a sizeable deficit yet again. The business community in South Wales were reeling from the effects of the Depression and promises of substantial support were unlikely. The only comforting thought was that Glamorgan were not alone in their financial troubles. Monmouthshire were also finding it difficult to finance their operations, and were losing promising youngsters like Lavis to Glamorgan, where they could play in a higher standard and make cricket their way of life. At the August committee meeting, Clay told the Glamorgan officials that there was every probability that Monmouthshire would be dropping out of the Minor County Championship, in which they had played since 1901. He felt it would boost Glamorgan if they amalgamated with their neighbours, and ran a second XI in the minor county competition, like several of the other first-class sides. The committee realised that this would give their young cricketers valuable experience, but they knew that it was expensive to run one team, never mind two! These financial considerations held sway and Glamorgan pulled out of the amalgamation negotiations.

During the winter months, the committee made valiant attempts to boost their flimsy finances. Raffles and appeals were launched and an Amateur Boxing Show was held in aid of the Club's funds. Daniel Radcliffe dipped into his generous pocket once again, whilst a number of fund-raising games were planned against local clubs. The committee also took the bold step of allocating the lucrative South African game to Ynysangharad Park. Pontypridd Urban District Council offered their support, and with all the problems over the rent of the Arms Park and St Helen's, the county committee decided to accept the Pontypridd offer, believing that there was nothing to be lost and everything to be gained.

After the difficult season in 1928 Arnott's decision to give up the captaincy came as no surprise. But it left the committee in a difficult position over a replacement; no other amateurs were available on a full-time basis, and it was unheard of for a professional to lead a county team. Consequently, it was agreed that Riches and Clay would share the captain's duties, with the committee hoping that one or the other would be available for every game. It was not to be, however, as Clay appeared in 14 games, whilst Riches could play on only eight occasions. The upshot was that five other people had to take over at various times. It was an extremely unsatisfactory state of affairs, and was a major factor behind the Club slipping to bottom place in the Championship, ending their first decade of top-class cricket in the same position as in their debut season.

The problems were clearly apparent in the opening match against Cambridge University. William Harbinson scored a century in each innings for the students, and together with Middlesex's Edgar Killick added 331 for the second wicket in the second innings. The problems intensified as the season progressed, with 20 of the 31 matches ending in defeat. Mercer bowled his heart out and took 137 wickets, but when Clay was absent, the support bowling was pitifully weak. The middle-order batting also struggled and several mid-innings collapses occurred after Bates and Bell had given them a good start.

Sullivan's hasty departure the season before had left Glamorgan without a specialist wicket-keeper. J. T. Morgan, Hills and James Jones, the former Somerset keeper, were all tried behind the stumps, but without any success. Everyone heaved a huge sigh of relief when Trevor Every, a 19-year-old from Llanelli, emerged as a suitable replacement. He was razor-sharp standing up to Clay and Ryan, and stumped no fewer than ten batsmen in his debut season. Every's athleticism behind the stumps was a far cry from the days of the rotund stoppers, but the fielding in the slips continued to be a problem. Some of the veterans or portly amateurs still had to be hidden in the close-catching positions, leaving the younger members of the side to chase after the ball in the outfield. Sadly, many of the slip fielders' reactions were slow and vital catches were spilled. Jack Mercer vividly remembered how he would often bowl endless spells to the opposing batsmen, desperately trying to dismiss them with an unplayable ball. But when he did produce a lethal delivery to someone like Hobbs or Sutcliffe, they would often get a thick edge to the ball, and see it lob at a comfortable height to first or second slip where one of the veterans would drop it. It speaks volumes of Mercer's patience that he would politely say 'Bad luck, old boy' or 'Well stopped, Sir' to the red-faced fielder and trudge back to his bowling mark, resigned to the fact that he would have to clean bowl the opponents!

TURNBULL TO THE RESCUE

THE 1920S ENDED on a high note with the selection of Maurice Turnbull for the MCC tour of Ceylon, Australia and New Zealand. The 24-year-old had scored over 1,000 runs for Cambridge University, which added to his 373 runs for Glamorgan, made him one of the leading young batsmen in the country. Turnbull's selection pleased his many supporters and everyone connected with the Welsh club were delighted when Turnbull became the first Glamorgan player to appear for England. On 10 January 1930 he was chosen to play in the first Test against New Zealand at Christchurch, though it failed to be a momentous debut. Batting at No 8, Turnbull scored seven and failed to keep his place for the other Tests, despite making a century against New South Wales at Sydney.

Turnbull's spirits must have been boosted by the news that he had been unanimously chosen as Glamorgan's captain for 1930. Although young in terms of years, he was old in playing experience, with six years of county cricket under his belt. It proved to be a momentous decision, because Turnbull threw his heart and soul into the work. He made an immense contribution to the development and the prestige of the club, building up a strong team with talented youngsters and seeing the balance sheet change from showing a large debt to one with a useful cash balance in hand. Not surprisingly, he has been given the accolade of 'the architect of Glamorgan as a first-class county'.

Despite the moderate performances during the late 1920s, Turnbull had at his disposal some promising players. There was a nucleus of seasoned professionals including Bates, Dyson, Mercer, Ryan and Dai Davies, plus experienced amateurs such as Clay and Arnott. The full-time staff also included Cyril Smart, a 28-year-old batsman and leg-spinner who had appeared for Warwickshire in the early 1920s. He had played for Briton Ferry and Maesteg in the SWCA and after a few matches for the Welsh county in the late 1920s, Smart was keen to get back into first-class cricket on a regular basis. Another new face was Richard Duckfield, a 23-year-old batsman who had impressed playing for Maesteg in the local leagues.

This collection of promising youngsters, keen amateurs and wise professionals formed the basis of a sound county XI, and all it needed was astute captaincy to transform them into a successful side. Turnbull fulfilled this role perfectly, and guided the team into 11th place in the table. But it was not an immediate transformation from rags to riches, as five of the opening six games ended in draws. There were signs though that the team were stronger, and more determined in spirit, when they scored 474 against Surrey at The Oval and occupied the crease throughout the last two sessions at Worcester to save the match. Three matches were won in late June and early July, though the inconsistent element was still present as three other games were lost. The victory over Warwickshire at St Helen's was their most convincing, with Bell and Dai Davies scoring centuries as Glamorgan totalled 500. The visitors only just avoided the follow-on and then on the final day collapsed to 73 all out chasing 297, with Mercer and Ryan exploiting another Swansea 'turner'.

Northants were beaten by an innings at Cardiff, but the visitors were injury stricken and failed to turn out a strong team. The highlight of the match was a masterly 160 from Turnbull, who was eager to regain his Test place. He was in fine form in mid-season, passing 50 six times in eight innings, and also came close to leading Glamorgan to victory over the Australians in front of a large Bank Holiday crowd at Swansea. The team's fortunes had improved and over 50,000 people flooded into St Helen's with hopes of a Welsh victory. They were delighted when the tourists were dismissed for just 245, with only McCabe and Bradman offering any resistance as Ryan bowled superbly in front of the massive crowd and took six wickets. However, Glamorgan were unable to come to terms with the spin of Clarrie Grimmett and were bowled out for 99. Vic Richardson, the Australian captain, went for quick runs, setting the Welsh team 218 in 165 minutes. They were given a flying start by a partnership of 93 in just over an hour by Bates and Turnbull. Despite the clatter of quick wickets, the Glamorgan batsmen pressed on and dashed to the crease as each wicket fell in the hunt for runs. They were denied victory only by Richardson's decision to recall his fast bowlers to use up valuable time and not bowl too many deliveries as Glamorgan fell 21 runs short.

This most honourable draw with the tourists indicated that some encouraging progress had been made in Turnbull's first year as captain, and the Welsh captain was delighted to be selected for the MCC tour to South Africa. He played in all five Tests during the winter, making 28 and 61 in the first Test. His best performance was 139 against Western Province and he finished with 541 runs to his name. Whilst the captain was making a favourable impression in the Southern Hemisphere, the County's officials were able to make pleasing reflections on the 1930 summer. The improved form and bumper attendance at the tourist match meant that the Treasurer was able to announce a profit – a rare occurrence in the Club's history.

Nevertheless, the finances were still flimsy and the rental for the use of the Arms Park remained high. The annual venture to Pontypridd showed that there was the existence of large support outside Cardiff and Swansea. The Club were eager to secure this and contacted other clubs in the hope of finding other suitable venues. Clay and Turnbull had links with the Cowbridge and District Athletic Club, and were able to offer their facilities free of charge to Glamorgan. Clay informed the County's officials that a large crowd would certainly attend a first-class game at the Vale of Glamorgan ground, so the committee allocated the Essex and Northants fixtures to Cowbridge.

The match with Northants ended in a row with the MCC after two 'freak' declarations. Rain had prevented any play on the first day, so the two captains, Turnbull and Jupp, got together the next morning and agreed to declare their first innings at 50. The visitors declared at 51 for one, and after an hour's batting, Glamorgan followed suit at 51 for two. However, Turnbull unwittingly broke Law 54 which said that after a declaration in a two-day match the side batting second must occupy the crease for at least 100 minutes. Both captains and the umpires were unaware of the infringement, and their attention was eventually drawn to it by a newspaper reporter after play. The teams, umpires and a posse of pressmen retired to a local hostelry where heated arguments took place over the legality of Turnbull's decision. From the Glamorgan captain's point of view, it turned out to be a profitable move as Northants collapsed on the final morning to the spin of Ryan and Clay, leaving the Welsh county to make just 60. However, both captains and umpires were summoned to Lord's to explain why Law 54 had been broken, and the story goes that when one of the umpires, a cockney called Bill Reeves, was asked about the breaking of the rule, he replied: 'The rule does not apply Sir, it was in a foreign country!'

Nevertheless, Turnbull and Jupp were severely reprimanded for departing from accepted principles, and both umpires were nearly struck off the first-class list. Turnbull accepted the decision, but privately voiced his disagreement with the MCC's view. He was one of a number of county captains who believed that the public wanted results and he felt this justified his declaration. One of his supporters was Percy Fender, the Surrey captain, who was renowned as an adventurous and often controversial captain, and who loved a gamble. Rain washed out the first two days of the game between their two teams at the Arms Park, so on the Friday morning both Turnbull and Fender declared their first innings after one ball. Fender then set Glamorgan a target of 215 in 165 minutes. Bates, Dyson, Turnbull and Viv Jenkins, the Oxford University cricketer and rugby blue, all chipped in with quick runs and the Welsh team won by three wickets. The Surrey captain was not too upset at the defeat because Surrey had come close to winning; Turnbull was naturally delighted at the way his batsmen had risen to the challenge, but the MCC were unhappy once again at the way the captains had reached an agreement, especially after Turnbull's warning for the 'Cowbridge affair'. He fell from favour amongst some of the hierarchy at Lord's and it must have been no coincidence that he failed to gain selection for the MCC winter tour.

Ironically, these were the only two victories in 1931 as the team slipped back to 15th place. The main reason for the decline was that the batting was less effective. Although four batsmen passed 1,000 runs, none had an average over 24, whilst Duckfield failed to make the impact everyone had anticipated. Mercer and Ryan both failed to reach 100 wickets, finishing with 90 and 88 respectively, but had to undertake the brunt of the bowling, with the only real support coming from the two Davies', Dai and Emrys. However, the major headache facing the Club at the end of the season was that the deficit now stood at £4,271. They had taken games to Pontypridd and Cowbridge in search of further support, but this failed to reduce the Club's deficit. The time had come for their costs to be drastically reduced and with a large number of professionals on their payroll it was inevitable that a number of senior players would not be re-engaged for 1932. The axe swung and the heads that rolled were those of Bates, Bell, Hills and Ryan.

The decision to release Bates came as no surprise because he was by now in the veteran category and found regular three-day cricket too demanding. After promising much, Bell had not produced the goods, whilst Hills injured an arm playing football and had difficulty batting and fielding. The hardest decision was the release of Ryan, who had bowled both his heart out and scores of opposing batsmen for nine seasons, but he was now approaching 44 and was not the force he had been in previous years. So not for the last time, a useful player was released because of financial problems. Ryan's departure was not unanimously popular, though it did give greater opportunities to younger bowlers on the staff.

The removal of three 'foreigners' also gave the County more of a Welsh identity which was likely to increase local support and improve the balance sheet. Indeed, the committee agreed to concentrate on local cricketers. Some felt it would lead to the County falling on even harder times, given the standard of club cricket in South Wales, and others predicted a return to the minor counties. But Turnbull and his committee believed that if the support of the South Wales public was to be obtained, and given the balance sheet this was *the* major problem, then the Club would have to be seen as representing South Wales, rather than Yorkshire II as some critics dryly commented.

The committee also realised that the situation would get even worse if they took no fund-raising action. Consequently, they formed a body called the 'Glamorgan Cricket Development Fund' to raise money for the Club. The new body organised a golf competition and raffled a ten-shilling note autographed by Don Bradman. The playing staff also gave a willing hand, realising that their future livelihood as professional cricketers could be in danger. No-one was more helpful than Jack Mercer, who agreed to take a cut of 3 shillings 10 pence (19p) in his weekly salary.

The first year of the home-grown policy saw Glamorgan remain in 15th place; it was not a successful season, though at the same time, the beginning of the end predicted in some quarters did not materialise. The summer began with heavy defeats against Northants, Middlesex, Essex and Kent, the latter having been added to the fixture list in 1932, so that Glamorgan had now played all of the first-class counties. But it was a somewhat dubious honour as Kent rattled up 488 for eight with Frank Woolley making a faultless 146 to set up victory by an innings and 207 runs.

The first win of the season came at Cowbridge, with Leicestershire being defeated by an innings as Mercer and Clay dismissed the visitors for 84 and 68. Three days later the two teams met again at Leicester, with Glamorgan showing their inconsistent streak in losing by 174 runs. The following game at St Helen's undoubtedly provided the highlight of the season for the team's supporters. Gloucestershire set the Welshmen a target of 310 in 270 minutes on the final day, and any thoughts of victory must have evaporated as they collapsed to 36 for three on a Swansea wicket that was crumbling and giving the spinners considerable assistance. But in two hours, Dai Davies and Turnbull counter-attacked the bowling, putting on 183 for the fourth wicket. When the captain was dismissed for 119, it seemed that the run chase might finish, but Trevor Every hit a gallant 46 to see Glamorgan home by two wickets with ten minutes to spare.

Glamorgan achieved victory in only one of the 17 games during the second half of the summer, and that occurred when they returned to Cowbridge. Mercer and Clay once again exploited the wicket, dismissing Somerset for 88 and 40 to set up a victory by an innings and 153 runs. Despite losing eight of the games towards the end of the season, there were some individual highlights, in particular Jack Mercer's hat-trick at The Oval and a superb 208 from Arnold Dyson, plus Trevor Every's maiden century, against Worcestershire at Stourbridge.

The final match of the season saw Nottinghamshire visit the Arms Park, with the memory of their end of season encounter in 1927 still in their minds. Just to add spice to the match, Harold Larwood and Bill Voce had been selected for the MCC's tour to Australia and were likely to experiment with fast 'leg theory' against the Welsh team. The visitors batted first and amassed 386, which gave them enough runs to try out 'bodyline bowling' with its rings of legside catchers. However, the Glamorgan batsmen counteracted the bowling with Dai Davies and Turnbull sharing another large partnership of 220 for the third wicket. Turnbull went on to make a superb 205, slashing high rising balls for boundary after boundary. Glamorgan finished on 502, with J. H. Morgan wryly observing that 'if fast leg theory had been judged on what Maurice Turnbull and Dai Davies did to it at Cardiff in 1932, there would have been no storm in Australia!'

The match ended as a draw with the Nottinghamshire bowlers blaming the feather-bed Arms Park wicket for the failure of their experiment. Controversy over its merit raged deep into the night in one of the taverns near the ground frequented by visiting players. After drowning their sorrows and airing their views, the Nottinghamshire team made their way back to their hotel, but not before some had returned to the ground to 'water' the wicket in an attempt to inject some life into it or to show their contempt of its lethargic qualities. The news of their evening visit quickly spread to some local newsmen and when Trevor Preece, the Cardiff groundsman, arrived the next norning, a dozen or so reporters were waiting to see the wicket. Preece had been tipped off, but although furious at the sight of a number of rusty-coloured patches on the wicket, he refused the offers from the pressmen to reveal the truth and by eleven o'clock the wicket had been restored to its normal state.

On paper, just three wins from thirty matches would hardly warrant any celebration, but there were grounds for optimism in some aspects of the on-field activities. In particular, 1932 saw the birth of an opening partnership which was to serve Glamorgan up to and after the Second World War, as Emrys Davies and Arnold Dyson replaced Bates and Bell as numbers 1 and 2 on the team sheet. Dyson displayed the tenacious qualities of an upbringing in the Yorkshire Leagues, whilst Davies became the first of many solid and pugnacious left-handers to open for Glamorgan. Known as 'The Rock', he had played since 1924 without really establishing himself, and there were some committee members who wanted to dispense with his services. But Clay and Turnbull believed Davies had the ability to make it in county cricket, and their faith was suitably rewarded as he set a string of County records during the 1930s and 1940s.

However, the committee's delight was quickly dispelled as it became apparent that the county's finances had taken another turn for the worse, and this time it looked as if the Club might have reached the end of the road. Despite the reduction in the number of professionals and the fund-raising scheme, the club now had debts in excess of £5,000 and further advances from the bank were unlikely. Glamorgan were not alone in feeling the pinch at this time, as sporting bodies throughout South Wales were being affected by the Depression. So great were the difficulties that Aberdare Athletic and Merthyr Town had to withdraw from the Football League and doubts were cast at committee meetings as to whether Glamorgan could also continue. The situation was sufficiently severe for Tyler and Gibson to resign from their posts of Treasurer and Secretary.

Once again, the players, both amateur and professional, were worried by the financial crisis and wanted to see the club continue, none more so than Johnnie Clay and Maurice Turnbull, who knew of the strenuous efforts made by Riches and Whittington to get the club recognised as first-class. Neither wanted to see all this dissolve, and agreed to take over the Treasurer's and Secretary's posts. They decided to launch a Special Appeal to raise £5,500, which would clear all the liabilities and provide a small working balance to commence the 1933 season. They also realised the gravity of the situation and added that 'all donations will be returned if it is found impossible to continue first-class cricket in 1933'.

Meetings were held at Cardiff, Swansea and Pontypridd to launch the appeal and to Clay and Turnbull's delight they received enthusiastic support. People in all sectors of the community did not like the thought of the Club being disbanded and a variety of fund-raising events were held. Greyhound and athletics meetings were held on the Club's behalf at the Arms Park, whilst donations came in from rugby and golf clubs throughout the area. Efforts were made to make membership more attractive and the Club's officials agreed to produce a yearbook containing a list of all subscribers. Clay also persuaded Sir Sydney Byass to extend the time limit on his £1,000 loan – it should have been paid back, but Byass agreed Glamorgan should wait until they could afford it. Dances and sweepstakes were organised in almost every town and village in the area, and during the winter of 1932/3 it seemed that Turnbull was out every night raising money for the Club, and there were claims that he danced more miles than he had scored runs the previous summer – and he had passed the 1,300 mark.

The captain's efforts were not in vain because by the spring of 1933 the debt had been reduced to £2,677 and the committee unanimously agreed 'to take the risk of carrying on'. At the AGM, Clay summed up the officials' delight by thanking everyone 'for their continued and increased support during a very trying period. The past year may be considered the most crucial your Club has passed in its short history'. As a gesture of thanks to the supporters and a way of tapping new support, the Club's officials allocated a game to Stradey Park, Llanelli in 1933. Tom Jeffreys, a local butcher, had led a campaign to bring first-class cricket to the ground and informed the committee that a large attendance was guaranteed because of the presence of Dai and Emrys Davies, plus Trevor Every in the Glamorgan side. Moreover, the committee knew that the MCC did not consider Cowbridge to be up to county standard, the wicket having deteriorated rapidly after the first day in the four games staged there. Consequently, they allocated the Worcestershire game to Llanelli.

The venture to Stradey Park proved a huge success both on and off the field. A crowd of 4,000 watched on the first day as Glamorgan reached 434 for six with George Lavis making a century, and the two local heroes, Emrys Davies and Trevor Every, scoring 70s. In reply, Worcestershire were dismissed for 114 and 236 to leave the sizeable crowd celebrating an innings victory. However, this was the team's only win during the season as they fell back to 16th place. Despite the poor results, many of the batsmen were in good form, with Dyson making 147 against the West Indies at Cardiff, whilst Duckfield hit his maiden century at Lord's and finished with 1,343 runs at a respectable 37.3. Turnbull was in fine form as well, making a magnificent 200 not out against Northants at Swansea. His outstanding performances resulted in a recall to the England team for the Lord's Test, where he scored 28 as England won by an innings. He was dropped for the next Test, but was recalled for The Oval Test, though he made only four.

The main weakness lay with the bowling, and the Welsh attack frequently failed to capitalise on the advantage gained by the large totals. Mercer's figures deteriorated as he had to bowl for longer periods and he finished with just 79 victims. Clay took only 59 wickets, whilst Emrys Davies, who had been given greater opportunities now that Ryan had gone, took just 31 wickets at 59 apiece. In all, 18 bowlers were tried and many of the supporters wished that Ryan was still available, arguing that his dismissal had been taken by a panic-stricken committee. Despite his release, the bank balance was still in the red and the only ray of comfort was that the match at Llanelli raised £600 in gate receipts. Turnbull and Clay realised that several other areas of similar support still lay untapped and that the staging of a game at them would ease the cash problems even more. One of the possibilities was Neath, where the Town Council had purchased the Gnoll Estate in 1923 and spent a large sum improving the ground. The County's officials were impresssed by the work when they visited the ground, and soon after they confirmed that a match would be allocated to the Gnoll.

The team rose up to 13th place in 1934, showing definite signs of improvement, and the results could have been even better but for two cruel blows early in the season. The first came in the opening match of the summer at Cardiff. The Glamorgan scorebook shows how Trevor Every was bowled by Kent's 'Tich' Freeman in the first innings for nought and was 'absent ill' in the second, but an unfortunate tragedy lay behind these entries. The wicket-keeper had been suffering from eye trouble during the winter and after being bowled by Freeman, Every told Turnbull that he could not see the ball in flight or the bowler's hand. Every was taken to a specialist on the final afternoon of the game, where he was told that he was going blind. Within a year, Every had lost his sight and this match tragically brought an end to a brilliant career. The following week Glamorgan travelled to Gravesend for the return game with Kent. Disaster struck again when Dai Davies was rushed to hospital on the second day with a severe haemorrhage from a stomach ulcer. He remained in hospital for a fortnight and did not play again for the rest of the season.

Turnbull's team did well to pick themselves up after these blows and the loss of such talented players, with Tom Brierley, a 24-year-old Lancastrian who had joined the staff in 1931 as a batsman, taking over behind the stumps. Two more victories were recorded as Northants were beaten at Pontypridd and Somerset were defeated by nine wickets at Swansea. Further success may have been gained had it not been for another spate of injuries – Clay sustained a leg injury against Somerset, whilst Duckfield and Turnbull were hurt during the innings defeat at Lord's. The injury crisis was so severe that the club had to recall the 51-year-old Riches for the match with Gloucestershire at Cardiff. Despite his injury, Turnbull still topped the averages, making over 1,300 runs and remained on the fringe of the England team. He was selected as captain of The Rest in the Test Trial, but he did not make the England team and there was much speculation about how much the MCC had forgotten the events of 1931. Nevertheless, the fact that he scored only 46 and 29 in the Trial and saw his side beaten by ten wickets must have weighed more against him than the 'incidents' at Cowbridge and The Oval. Dyson and Emrys Davies continued to prosper as an opening pair, with Duckfield and Smart emerging as aggressive middle-order batsmen. This platform of runs gave the lower order a confidence it had lacked in previous years, helping the amateurs from the local leagues, such as Claude Haines and Tony Ling, later in the season, when the injury list grew and they had to bat higher in the order.

But once again the bowling was moderate, despite Clay becoming the first amateur to take over a hundred wickets. Mercer had another poor season, taking just 44 wickets, whilst George Reed and Ted Glover, the Cardiff fast bowlers, lacked accuracy and penetration, despite being capable of delivering an unplayable ball. The only bright spot was the emergence of three young bowlers, all under 22 – Harry Dickenson, a fast bowler from Barry, Aubrey Davies, the Swansea leg-spinner, and Closs Jones, an off-spinner from Briton Ferry. Despite their lowly position, the committee believed the Club were making progress, as borne out by the steadily improving financial position. Season 1934 saw the Club emerge with a reasonable profit for the first time, thanks to over £1,000 in gate receipts from the rain-affected match with the Australians and over £1,500 in Test match proceeds. All in all, this produced a profit of £1,401, much to the delight of Turnbull and Clay. It seemed their hard work had paid off and with several promising colts emerging, the future seemed bright enough for the Club to pay back Sir Sidney Byass his £1,000 loan.

THE AMALGAMATION WITH MONMOUTHSHIRE

WHILST 1934 SEEMED TO INDICATE that the worst was over for Glamorgan, it marked the end for Monmouthshire as a minor county. In April their officials contacted Johnnie Clay once again about the question of a merger. The Glamorgan committee welcomed the approach on several counts. Firstly, their own finances were healthier and they could contemplate paying off Monmouthshire's debts. A second reason was that an amalgamation would give the Club a chance to extend their Welsh identity and be representative of the *whole* of South Wales. Thirdly, all of the Monmouthshire players would be qualified for Glamorgan and a new nursery of talent would be available. Lastly, and by no means least, an affiliation would allow Glamorgan to enter a second eleven in the Minor County Championship, where the youngsters could gain further experience.

The proposals though were not greeted with unanimous approval. 'Tip' Williams, the committee member for Cardiff, suggested that too much expenditure would be incurred without any appreciable gain, but he was in the minority, as most of the officials supported the Monmouthshire proposals. An affiliation sub-committee was created and they reached agreement with the Monmouthshire officials subject to the conditions below:

(i) Glamorgan would pay off Monmouthshire's overdraft of £175,

(ii) The Monmouthshire committee would remain in existence and act as a district committee of Glamorgan,

(iii) Monmouthshire would be entitled to arrange matches for a team called 'The Gentlemen of Monmouthshire' provided these games did not interfere with Glamorgan's second eleven fixtures,

(iv) Monmouthshire would guarantee not to enter a team in the Minor County Championship, except by mutual agreement between the two clubs,

(v) Monmouthshire would have representatives on the selection panel for Glamorgan's second team,

(vi) Glamorgan would stage first-class matches in Monmouthshire.

An agreement was reached on 4 July 1934 and the Glamorgan officials planned ahead for their new and increased commitments. J. T. Morgan, the 28-year-old amateur from Cardiff was appointed the second eleven captain, with the brief to help coach and look after the young players who would be playing in his team. In addition, Newport was immediately added to the list of Glamorgan venues, with the Glamorgan officials knowing of the excellent facilities at Rodney Parade which formed part of the Newport Athletic Club's splendid recreational complex.

The results for 1935 showed that Glamorgan benefited from this affiliation, as they rose to 13th place. A settled team emerged with Turnbull, Mercer, Dyson, Smart, Brierley, Duckfield and Emrys Davies playing in all of the Championship matches. This resulted in an improved team spirit and self-belief, as illustrated by the game with the South Africans over the Whitsun Bank Holiday at Cardiff. It proved to be one of the most entertaining for the Welsh supporters in 1935, and one of the most frustrating for the tourists. The visitors batted throughout the first day, amassing 327 for three with Herbert Wade and Athol Rowan making hundreds. They continued batting on the second morning, but conditions were more in favour of the bowlers, and the last seven South Africans fell for just 73 runs. Wickets continued to fall when Glamorgan batted and they were dismissed inside three hours for 142. Even worse was to come when they followed on, losing their first four wickets with only ten runs on the board.

Cyril Smart offered stubborn resistance on the final morning, but wickets steadily fell during the afternoon. The eighth and ninth fell in successive balls after tea, and as Donald Hughes, a 25-year-old schoolmaster making his county debut came out to bat, an embarrassing defeat seemed inevitable. But the young Ebbw Vale fast bowler had other ideas and after surviving the hat-trick ball, he and Smart took the score from 114 for nine to 245 for nine and a draw. To the great delight of an ever-increasing Arms Park crowd, the former Monmouthshire player thrashed the bowling to all corners of the ground in a record partnership of 131 for the last wicket. It was the youngster who took the initiative, as 'Nomad' described: 'Hughes dominated the game to such a degree that even the eager and enterprising Smart was overshadowed . . . as the South African attack was cut to ribbons by some of the most glorious and daring batsmanship which has been my joy to witness.' As the visitors became demoralised and the match was saved, Smart also joined in with the big hitting, and soon after reaching his well deserved century he lofted one ball out of the ground and through the window of the nearby Grand Hotel in Westgate Street! Smart ended unbeaten on 114 with Hughes 70 not out, with four huge sixes and six fours on a memorable debut.

Smart hit the headlines a few weeks later during the match with Hampshire at Cardiff. During their first innings, Smart hit Gerry Hill, the visitors' off-spinner, for 32 in an over, which at the time was a world record. This burst of hitting came on the first day of the match,

Cyril Smart, one of Glamorgan's mightiest hitters, as depicted on a cigarette card.
(John Billot)

which had been quite drab before Smart joined Duckfield and added
130 in the final hour. Hill remembers how Smart was 'going along like
a normal batsman, when he suddenly let loose on me. His six scoring
strokes were from straight to deep square leg; they were all clean hits
and he wasn't dropped once'. Indeed, Smart could easily have scored
five sixes rather than four, had one of the fours not fallen just inside the
ropes on the leg side. His bold hitting saw Glamorgan to 460 for eight;
Hampshire had to follow on, and Glamorgan won by ten wickets.

The good form continued in the next match which was the
inaugural fixture at Newport. Great celebrations were planned by the
Monmouthshire officials and the sumptuous hospitality contributed as
much to the victory as the accurate Glamorgan bowling. The
Leicestershire and Glamorgan teams were presented to the Lord
Mayor of Newport before play began on the Saturday morning, and
after play had finished they were guests of honour at a special civic
reception. On the Sunday, the visitors were taken on a tour of the Wye
Valley; some admired the scenery, though many more preferred the
clear, fresh air as a hangover tonic! After another round of hospitality
on the Monday evening, Glamorgan set the visitors a target of 394.
After all the socialising, they collapsed to 240, leaving Glamorgan and

the Monmouthshire officials to celebrate a successful start to their new arrangements at Newport.

However, the remaining 12 games from 10 July onwards saw Glamorgan slump to eight defeats. Only one more victory was achieved and this was in unexpected circumstances at Hastings. Sussex set the Welsh county a target of 165 in under two hours, but despite the high rate of scoring required, Turnbull instructed his team to go for quick runs. His optimism was rewarded as Lavis hit a rapid 65 to see Glamorgan home by three wickets with only minutes remaining.

The other end-of-season highlight came in the final match at Worcester where Emrys Davies dismissed Frank Warne on the final afternoon to become the first Glamorgan player to achieve the 'double'. In all, Davies made 1,326 runs at 28.21 and took 100 wickets, and his outstanding form was a major factor in the Welsh county's improvement. He provided valuable support to Clay and Mercer, and it must have been no coincidence that Mercer returned to his best form, claiming 109 wickets from nearly 1,100 overs. His yeoman service was rewarded at the end of the season when the committee announced that 1936 would be his Benefit Year. However, the leading bowler in 1935 was Johnnie Clay, who took 65 wickets at a cost of 13 each, and was one of the leading off-spinners in the country. His fine bowling performances were brought to the attention of the England selectors, and he was 12th man for the Tests at Headingley and Old Trafford. He was included for the final Test at The Oval, though his contribution was inauspicious, and he failed to take a wicket in 32 overs, in what proved to be his only appearance for England.

The second team won just one game and finished in 15th place in the minor county table, but these bare statistics hide the real story as several youngsters made encouraging progress under Morgan's captaincy. Glover and Closs Jones improved as bowlers, whilst Willie Jones, a 19-year-old left-hander from Carmarthen impressed with the bat. Behind the stumps, Haydn Davies from Llanelli showed he had the ability to press for a first-team place, and after a promising debut, was offered a contract for 1936. But it wasn't just the youngsters who hit the headlines in the minor county competition – Norman Riches scored 114 on his only appearance, whilst 35-year-old Len Pitchford made 226 against Berkshire at the Arms Park, a performance which brought the Ebbw Vale professional a run in the first team. The committee were delighted by the blend of youth and experience in the second team, and in an attempt to assist further the development of the youngsters, they hired as coach Bill Hitch, the 50-year-old former Surrey and England fast bowler.

The Club slipped back to 16th place in 1936, winning only two of the 28 matches. The batsmen in particular struggled to show their previous consistency, especially in May and June when bad weather confined them to the pavilion for long spells. Dyson, Turnbull and Duckfield all had indifferent seasons, although both of the latter had started the season well. Turnbull registered centuries against Kent and Yorkshire and was selected for the Lord's Test against India. He made a duck in the first innings and shared in a partnership of 108 in the second with Somerset's Harold Gimblett to set up a nine-wicket victory. However, Turnbull failed to gain selection for any other Tests that summer and this proved to be his final Test call. He returned to the Glamorgan side and completely lost form, making just three half-centuries during the rest of the summer.

Duckfield also made a superb start to the season and in the game with Surrey at The Oval he made 280 not out in Glamorgan's total of 550 for six declared. Both of these were the highest-ever scores for the County, and it really looked as if the young batsman from Maesteg had finally turned the corner and established himself on the county circuit. He hit 39 boundaries in his five and a half hour innings, which brought him many tributes. One said how there was 'that indefinable something that registered class. The immaculate flannels, the fastidiously whitened and secured pads, the clotted cream colour of his shirt, the daffodil emblem glowing from his cap – all this allied to his confident stance, with that broad beam which was somewhat disheartening to bowlers.'

But like his captain, Duckfield completely lost form and finished the season with a mere 895 runs to his name. More importantly, he also lost his confidence in the field and started to develop a psychological inability to catch a ball. It preyed on his mind and he began to worry about his future, even more so after turning down a manager's post in a Porthcawl hotel. Duckfield asked to field in any position where his 'problem' would not be exposed; Turnbull tried his best, but there were few places to hide Duckfield and sadly this anxiety over catching was prematurely to finish his career.

Undoubtedly the highlight of the season came in the match at Worcester, where Mercer became the first, and so far the only, Glamorgan bowler to take all ten wickets in an innings. Bowling unchanged, he fully exploited the damp conditions and was aided by some sound fielding, though Mercer showed little emotion when he claimed his record tenth wicket. Even though he was mobbed by the rest of the team, Mercer swung his sweater over his shoulder and walked off the field as if nothing had happened. Despite his nonchalance, there was a standing ovation from the crowd and the players, whilst the bells of Worcester Cathedral, with a remarkable sense of coincidence, rang out with 'The Bells of Aberdovey' to add to the celebrations.

JACK MERCER

Jack Mercer was the mainstay of the Glamorgan seam attack between the wars, bowling over 5,000 overs and taking 1,460 wickets. Indeed, he still remains the only Glamorgan bowler to have taken all ten wickets in a Championship innings. Jack was also a useful lower-order batsman, who loved to smash the bowling to all parts, as testified by his feat of scoring 31 in just nine minutes at Cowbridge in 1931.

Mercer played little cricket as a young man, and spent several years in Czarist Russia, before returning to England when the First World War broke out. He joined Sussex in 1919, but left to join the Welsh county in 1922, and as R. C. Robertson-Glasgow wrote: 'For the next 17 seasons he opened, continued and closed the Glamorgan attack and welcomed with an unfailing humour the reluctance of the batsmen to depart, the umpire to agree and the fieldsmen to bend!'

He was widely acknowledged to have been one of the finest swing bowlers during the inter-war period, yet remarkably he never played in Test cricket. Despite being consistently overlooked, Jack kept his spirits up and lived life to the full, both on and off the field. He was an active member of the Magic Circle, and enjoyed many other pastimes, including horse-racing, and is reputed to have read of his selection on the MCC tour of India in 1926/7 whilst at Longchamp Races!

Mercer joined Northamptonshire when the Second World War finished, and after retiring in 1947 he acted as coach and scorer.

Jack Mercer – the Club's leading seam bowler in the 1920s and 1930s.

WORCESTERSHIRE *v.* GLAMORGAN

Played at Worcester, 29, 30 and 31 July 1936

MATCH DRAWN

WORCESTERSHIRE	FIRST INNINGS		SECOND INNINGS	
R. D. Evers	c Smart b Mercer	3	lbw b Reed	18
*C. H. Bull	c Brierley b Mercer	22	c Turnbull b Reed	66
S. H. Martin	c Turnbull b Mercer	4	b Reed	0
H. H. Gibbons	c Turnbull b Mercer	2	lbw b Mercer	8
†B. W. Quaife	c D. Davies b Mercer	2		
J. Horton	b Mercer	0		
R. H. C. Human	not out	59	c Smart b Reed	42
A. P. Singleton	st Brierley b Mercer	29		
R. Howorth	b Mercer	3	not out	8
R. T. D. Perks	lbw b Mercer	0	not out	14
P. F. Jackson	c Lavis b Mercer	1		
Extras		18		7
Total		143	(for 5 wkts dec)	163

1st inns: 1-14, 2-20, 3-30, 4-40, 5-42, 6-59, 7-113, 8-121, 9-121
2nd inns: 1-58, 2-66, 3-75, 4-129, 5-150

BOWLING	O	M	R	W	O	M	R	W
Mercer	26	10	51	10	21	2	52	1
Reed	12	2	38	0	22	3	55	4
D. Davies	6	1	9	0	6	1	15	0
E. Davies	27	0	27	0	8	3	23	0
Smart					7	1	11	0

GLAMORGAN	FIRST INNINGS		SECOND INNINGS	
A. H. Dyson	c Howorth b Martin	14	c Evers b Martin	6
E. Davies	run out	8	not out	6
D. Davies	b Perks	1		
V. G. J. Jenkins	lbw b Jackson	13		
R. Duckfield	c Human b Howorth	5		
C. C. Smart	c and b Howorth	1	b Perks	0
*M. J. L. Turnbull	c Horton b Howorth	14	c Jackson b Perks	29
G. Lavis	b Perks	34	not out	14
†T. L. Brierley	b Howorth	37		
J. Mercer	c Horton b Perks	12	b Martin	1
G. H. Reed	not out	0		
Extras		12		
Total		151	(for 4 wkts)	56

1st inns: 1-26, 2-27, 3-44, 4-46, 5-49, 6-54, 7-65, 8-127, 9-151
2nd inns: 1-22, 2-25, 3-28, 4-38

BOWLING	O	M	R	W	O	M	R	W
Perks	15	2	38	3	9	1	24	0
Human	1	0	4	0				
Jackson	21	6	38	1	4	0	10	0
Martin	9	2	28	1	6	1	17	2
Howorth	18.1	8	31	4	2	0	5	0

Umpires: J. Newman and E. Cooke

Glamorgan have produced a number of England bowlers over the years, but one record has eluded them and remains with Jack Mercer. This is the feat of taking all ten wickets in an innings which Mercer achieved in this match at Worcester. Remarkably, he never won higher honours despite being considered one of the best swing bowlers of the 1930s.

The combination of bad weather and poor results also hit the Club's finances and gate receipts fell by £3,000 overall. A loss of £1,973 was incurred and the costs of running a second eleven began to mount. The finance committee met at the end of August to debate the situation, and there were calls to cut salaries and scrap the second team. There were even calls for the Club to pull out of the County Championship, but once again Turnbull was not going to be defeated, and he launched another Special Appeal with a target of £1,000. The committee agreed that the minor county fixtures could continue as long as £500 was raised.

Letters were sent to directors on the boards of major firms and shop-owners throughout the region, and public meetings were held at Cardiff and Swansea. The professionals did their bit once again, and Lavis and Duckfield took a cut in their salaries. Turnbull led by example, as he had done before, and travelled all over South Wales seeking support and organising fund-raising activities. He gained the support of the Welsh Rugby Union and Cardiff Athletic Club, who reduced the rent for the use of the Arms Park. Turnbull's efforts were successful and by the end of the year, the target had been achieved, allowing a full second team fixture list to be organised.

The Glamorgan team of 1937 at Edgbaston. Standing: Aubrey Davies, Emrys Davies, Cyril Smart, Tom Brierley, Richard Duckfield, George Davies. Seated: Jack Mercer, Johnnie Clay, Maurice Turnbull (in his MCC blazer), Dai Davies and Arnold Dyson.

The captain and the general public were rewarded by an outstanding team performance in 1937, as the side rose to seventh place in the table, winning 13 of their 30 matches. They made a marvellous advance on the previous season, yet it was basically the same team. The only new face was Austin Matthews, a 33-year-old fast-medium bowler who had been born in Penarth. He had come to the County's attention in the mid-1920s and the committee had contemplated signing him, but instead he joined Northants in 1927. However, Matthews had a difference of opinion with the County's officials at the end of 1936, and he left for coaching appointments at Stowe School and Cambridge University. During the summer, Matthews returned to Penarth and agreed to play for Glamorgan.

Matthews made his debut in July and astonishingly was bowling for England by 14 August. This followed a series of impressive spells with the ball, in particular a return of fourteen for 132 against Sussex on a good batting wicket at Hastings. It caught the attention of the England selectors and he was drafted into the team for the third Test at The Oval, thereby becoming the first Glamorgan professional to play in Tests. In what proved to be his only appearance for England, Matthews took a wicket in each innings, both times dismissing Walter Hadlee, the New Zealand opener.

But Matthews played in only seven matches that summer for Glamorgan and his presence was not the only reason for the team's improvement. The other factor was that Clay could play in 26 games, allowing him to capture a record 176 wickets. Against Worcestershire at Swansea, Clay took nine for 66 in the first innings and eight for 146 in the second, and together with the captain played an important role in a comfortable win. Turnbull made a magnificent 233 in four hours as Glamorgan totalled 417 and eventually won by nine wickets. Many felt that a good performance in the match against Yorkshire would see the spinner return to the England side. The Tykes were reduced to 50 for six as Clay dismissed Sutcliffe, Hutton, Barber and Mitchell, but their lower order rallied and took the score to 255. Rain intervened and the game ended in a draw to dampen any thoughts Clay may have held about regaining a Test place.

Glamorgan registered two victories over the New Zealanders, showing that there were other players worthy of consideration for higher honours. The first win came at Cardiff where Duckfield hit a rare century and Closs Jones took ten for 94 as the tourists were dismissed for 235 and 190 and the Welshmen comfortably won by six wickets. The young off-spinner bowled with such accuracy and consistency on a good batting wicket that all of the batsmen had to play him with extreme caution and could not take liberties with him. On the strength of this performance, Jones was selected for the Rest against the MCC in their 150th Anniversary match at Lord's. Sadly, he was injured during the game and had to miss several weeks, but he was still able to finish with a creditable 61 wickets.

The architect of the second win was Emrys Davies. He provided the backbone of their first innings total of 229 with a steady half-century. The tourists were rocked by a fiery opening spell from Austin Matthews who took three cheap wickets. They recovered to 116 for seven, but on the second morning Emrys Davies snapped up the last three wickets for just one run as Glamorgan gained a first-innings lead of 102. This was extended further as Davies hit 78 and Smart an aggressive 94. New Zealand were set 443, and must have been sick of the sight of Davies as he took a further three wickets in the final session as the tourists slumped to 71 for three. Clay finished off their resistance within three quarters of an hour on the final morning, taking five for 27 as Glamorgan won by 322 runs. Not only was it their largest ever win, it was only the second time between the wars that a county side had achieved the double over a touring team. This was just one of the games in which Davies excelled – he shared in a record opening partnership of 274 with Arnold Dyson at Leicester and then took a hat-trick as Glamorgan won by an innings. Season 1937 was truly memorable for him as he achieved the double again, scoring 2,012 runs and taking 103 wickets.

Nevertheless, the financial situation remained grim, and despite the success on the field, the summer produced a loss of £1,779 because of a sharp fall in membership and the rising costs of staging second team games. The committee realised that the position would be eased by one or two options – either three or four professionals would have to be released, or the club would have to opt out of the minor county competition. Turnbull did not want to see Mercer, Lavis, Dai Davies and Haydn Davies released as an economy measure, but neither did he want the second team to disband after all the hard work in amalgamating with Monmouthshire. However, he realised that the latter option was the better, and to soften the blow to the younger players, it was agreed that the junior members of the staff would be allocated to first division sides in the SWCA.

Both Turnbull and Clay knew that if another loss were incurred, their hard work in raising cash in the past would have been wasted and the club would have to pull out of the County Championship as well. Consequently, a deputation consisting of Major John Bevan, the club's President, Sir William Reardon-Smith, a Vice-President and an influential shipowner in Cardiff, Clay and Turnbull met the Manager of the Midland Bank in Cardiff to discuss the Club's financial position. The manager agreed to ease the situation by giving the Club an unsecured overdraft for nine months, whilst Reardon-Smith, Bevan,

For once, Emrys Davies is dismissed cheaply, caught by King of Surrey during Glamorgan's game at The Oval in 1937. Alf Gover, the successful bowler, leaps in the air with delight, whilst Duckfield is the non-striker.

Clay and Turnbull each gave the club £200 of their own money. The captain also spearheaded a membership drive to find 1,000 new members; the campaign was launched with the claim that 'no stone will be left unturned in an effort to obtain this target before the commencement of the next playing season, and we appeal now in grim earnest for the active assistance of all members in order that this objective shall be reached'. So Turnbull took to the road again, and travelled up and down the valleys, and from the East to the West of the County in search of support, and as before he achieved this target, which spoke volumes of his influence and determination.

Turnbull knew the importance of having a successful season in 1938, but unfortunately, the team failed to maintain their improvement, sinking back to 16th place. Several players were hit by injury, including Clay, Matthews, Hughes and Smart, but the most serious injury was that which Turnbull suffered, though he played several times when not fully fit. His injured knee restricted his movement and he finished with a modest 673 runs at an average of 21.

The poor form of other players also contributed to the slide down the table. Duckfield completely lost his form, making a mere 462 runs and becoming more of a liability in the field.

There were a number of new faces in the team as a result of the injuries and the loss of form by some players. Amongst the newcomers were Wilf Wooller and Phil Clift, both of whom were to give yeoman service to the Club on and off the field. Clift owed his promotion to a series of fine innings for Glamorgan Colts, whilst Wooller was included after some excellent all-round performances for St Fagan's which impressed Jack Mercer, who had seen him play in North Wales and knew that Lancashire had offered him terms. Another interesting newcomer was Sam Silkin, a 20-year-old leg spinner who had been born in Neath. After attending Dulwich School, Silkin had gone to Cambridge and had become good friends with Turnbull's brother. Silkin was hoping to gain a place in the side for the Varsity, so Turnbull invited him to play for Glamorgan against his university colleagues at St Helen's. But he took just one wicket and scored only two runs and failed to secure a place in the University XI. Silkin did not appear again for Glamorgan and concentrated instead on a career in politics and law. In 1964 he became a Labour MP for Camberwell, and in 1974 was appointed Attorney-General, before being elevated to the peerage in March 1985.

Despite the poor playing performances, the Club's finances gradually improved and the £500 debt at the start of the season was converted into a £267 profit. This was the result of an increase in membership fees of over £1,300 due to Turnbull's hard work, whilst over £1,000 was taken at the gate of the rain-affected match with the Australian tourists at Swansea. The committee were delighted by this transformation, but realised that the team still needed improving. They approached Eric Rowan, the 30-year-old South African opener who had made such a big impact on the 1935 tour of England. However, with Mercer in the veteran stage and Matthews available for only half a season, an opening bowler was at the top of their priority list and they snapped up Peter Judge, a 22-year-old fast-medium bowler who had been released by Middlesex, and Allan Watkins, a young all-rounder from Usk.

The signing of Judge was one of the reasons behind the Club's rise up to 13th place. he took 69 wickets and spearheaded a much improved attack, though the major factor in the improvement was a more consistent batting performance. During early June, the side scored 2,152 runs in four matches, at an average of 74 per wicket. The purple patch began at Newport in the match with Gloucestershire which turned into a run feast for both sides. After the Welsh team made 196, Gloucestershire replied with 505 for five declared with Wally Hammond scoring a majestic 302. He hit two sixes and 35 fours to become the highest scorer against Glamorgan; it wasn't just records that were broken during his innings, as he hit a ball through one of the windows of the power station alongside the Rodney Parade ground. It was never repaired and the small round hole remained as a tribute to Hammond's batting prowess until the building was demolished some 25 years later!

Glamorgan needed 309 to avoid an innings defeat, but this awesome task was comfortably achieved as Dyson and Emrys Davies put on 255 for the first wicket, with Davies going on to make a record 287 not out in a $7\frac{1}{2}$-hour stay at the wicket. He might even have surpassed Hammond's score, but the Gloucestershire captain stationed all of his fielders around the boundary during the final stages of the game. One of the reasons was that a well-known bakery had promised a giant-sized Dundee cake to the maker of the highest score of the season, and he wanted to ensure that it didn't travel to Llanelli.

Emrys Davies and Brierley made centuries in the following match against Nottinghamshire, whilst at Tonbridge, the Kent attack was hit for 492 as Turnbull and Closs Jones scored hundreds. The next match produced another high-scoring draw and a second double-century for Glamorgan at Newport. Somerset batted all of the first day, and almost until lunch on the second in making 385, provoking frequent outbursts of protest from the crowd of 4,000. Turnbull was also enraged at their slow play and told the Somerset captain he would keep them in the field for the rest of the match. Turnbull kept his promise and batted on until the close on the third day, by which time Glamorgan had amassed 574 for seven. Dai Davies took the opportunity to show sympathy with the striking miners at the nearby Bedwas Colliery. Before going out on the following morning he asked Emrys Davies to wave to him when the strike finished. News came through at six o'clock that the miners protest was over, so after a sign from Emrys, Dai went down the wicket and was stumped for a career best 216!

The match with Worcestershire at the Arms Park produced another exciting finish. Glamorgan needed to make 228 to avoid an innings defeat on the final day. They lost wickets steadily during the afternoon, and the opponents must have sensed victory when the ninth wicket fell with half-an-hour left and Glamorgan just 11 runs ahead. However, their hopes were dashed as last man Jack Mercer hit a quickfire 41. In one eight-ball over from Dick Howorth he hit 31 (62460661) with the crowd in the new rugby grandstand having to take cover.

GLAMORGAN *v* GLOUCESTERSHIRE

Played at Newport, 31 May and 1 and 2 June 1939

MATCH DRAWN

GLAMORGAN	FIRST INNINGS		SECOND INNINGS	
A. H. Dyson	not out	99	c Wilson b Lambert	120
E. Davies	lbw b Goddard	34	not out	287
T. L. Brierley	b Scott	9	c Hammond b Goddard	5
*M. J. L. Turnbull	c Wilson b Lambert	18	st Wilson b Emmett	77
D. Davies	c Wilson b Scott	1	c Lambert b Sinfield	48
C. C. Smart	b Scott	10	not out	23
W. Wooller	b Goddard	18		
E. C. Jones	c Wilson b Sinfield	0		
†H. G. Davies	c Wilson b Sinfield	0		
P. F. Judge	c Neale b Goddard	3		
J. Mercer	b Goddard	0		
Extras		4		17
Total		196	(for 4 wkts)	577

1st inns: 1-65, 2-74, 3-104, 4-114, 5-132, 6-180, 7-181, 8-181, 9-196
2nd inns: 1-255, 2-265, 3-403, 4-527

BOWLING	O	M	R	W	O	M	R	W
Scott	13	0	52	3	24	1	95	0
Barnett	4	0	18	0	5	0	32	0
Lambert	14	2	50	1	16	0	128	1
Goddard	22.6	7	45	4	38	7	123	1
Sinfield	10	3	16	2	36	5	116	1
Emmett	2	0	6	0	7	0	51	1
Neale	1	0	5	0	1	0	11	0
Hammond					1	0	4	0

GLOUCESTERSHIRE	FIRST INNINGS	
C. J. Barnett	c E. Davies b Mercer	15
R. A. Sinfield	b E. Davies	41
V. Hopkins	c Turnbull b Judge	13
*W. R. Hammond	c H. Davies b E. Davies	302
G. M. Emmet	st H. Davies b Jones	53
J. F. Crapp	not out	60
W. L. Neale	not out	5
†E. A. Wilson		
C. J. Scott		
G. Lambert		
T. W. Goddard		
Extras		16
Total	(for 5 wkts dec)	505

1st inns: 1-24, 2-52, 3-117, 4-285, 5-499

BOWLING	O	M	R	W
Mercer	21	0	105	1
Judge	18	1	83	1
Wooller	23	1	124	0
Jones	9	0	41	1
E. Davies	21	2	91	2
D. Davies	2	0	9	0
Smart	6	1	36	0

Umpires: J. Newman and H. Cruice

The fine run ended in disastrous fashion at Neath as Kent won in two days. This was followed by innings defeats at Bradford and Edgbaston. A return to winning ways occurred at Llanelli, Bristol and Weston-super-Mare, but the season ended on a disappointing note with defeats against Lancashire and Surrey. Both Dai Davies and Jack Mercer announced their retirements at the end of the season. Davies intimated that he wanted to be an umpire, whilst Mercer was offered a post as a coach with the County. The supporters were sad to see the departure of these two stalwarts, but they were cheered by the news that Emrys Davies had been selected for the England tour of India. It was a fitting reward for 'The Rock', but once again, events on the world stage intervened as Adolf Hitler invaded Poland, and war was declared soon after the final games of the summer. The tour was cancelled and no more county games took place for six long years.

Although the 1930s ended on a depressing note, it had been an important and successful decade for Glamorgan, due almost entirely to the hard work of Maurice Turnbull. He had formed a team worthy of first-class status and supervised the easing of the financial worries. The deal with Monmouthshire highlighted his dynamic and go-ahead policies, believing that the County had a bright future. He led from the front and instilled a growing confidence in the young players. The lengths some of the players would go to support the captain reflected their feelings of loyalty for him. For example, in 1935 Glamorgan were one batsman short the night before a game at St Helen's. Turnbull sent a telegram to John Cope, a 27-year-old soccer professional who was playing in Lancashire, but had played well as an amateur for Monmouthshire. Cope caught the midnight train from Manchester which arrived at Swansea at 8 am the next morning. Turnbull lost the toss and Cope spent all day in the field after having little sleep, but he was delighted to have helped his friend and solve Glamorgan's problems.

Turnbull led with an authority which brought out the best from the youngsters, who had the highest respect for him. One of these was Ernie Harris, a 19-year-old leg-spinner from St Fagan's, who made his debut in 1938. He was eager to make his mark in the first-class game, but against Somerset at Newport, Harris dropped a high skier in the deep alongside the beer tent. Some uncomplimentary comments were directed towards the youngster from inside the tent, but what hurt

---

This game produced a series of batting records as the docile Newport wicket became ideal for run scoring. Wally Hammond made the highest score against Glamorgan and Emrys Davies replied with the highest score for the Welsh county. In fact, Davies might also have made a triple century had the Gloucestershire captain not placed most of his fielders around the boundary towards the end of the match.

MAURICE TURNBULL

Without the dynamic presence of Maurice Turnbull, it is doubtful whether Glamorgan would have survived the cash crisis of the 1930s. He masterminded a series of fund raising functions and transformed the Club from a state of near bankruptcy into one with a balance of over a thousand pounds.

But if his efforts off the field were vast, then his presence as a batsman and captain were even greater. He was an inspirational leader, getting the best out of the assortment of players, and their success in 1948 owed much to Turnbull's efforts before the war.

He marked his debut in 1924 by being Glamorgan's top scorer, and repeated the feat with 156 in his last innings in 1939. In between these dates, he amassed over 18,000 runs and his 29 centuries, but these bare statistics hide the full story. Turnbull adopted a cavalier approach and led from the front, being at his best when others were failing or when quick runs were needed, mixing textbook strokes and the unorthodox in an effort to dishearten the bowlers. Off the field he led with a cool authority, insisting that the professionals made an appointment if they wanted to see him, and ensuring that the amateurs always travelled in first-class accommodation and did not mix with the professionals! Nevertheless, he commanded the utmost respect from his players and moulded them into a successful playing unit.

Turnbull played nine times for England and served as a Test Selector in 1938 and 1939. He was a talented sportsman in other fields, having played rugby and hockey for both Cardiff and Wales, and also won the South Wales Squash Championships. One can only guess at what else Turnbull might have achieved had he not given his life to his country in 1944.

Maurice Turnbull – one of the Club's finest captains and the person who saw Glamorgan through their bleak years during the 1930s. (Ron Harries)

more was the hard stare Turnbull gave the young amateur. Harris was keen to appease his captain, and two overs later he redeemed himself by sprinting many yards in front of the sightscreen and diving full length to catch Bill Andrews. In so doing, Harris dislocated a finger and needed first-aid attention, but it was worth it to get back in favour with Turnbull!

Harris made his debut at Maidstone and sat alongside Arnold Dyson in the pavilion watching the Kent bowlers in action. Harris was anxious to learn how to read Doug Wright, the wily leg-spinner, so he asked Dyson for some guidance. His reply was brief, but very true: 'I haven't any idea. I should just play for the pitch of the ball if I were you and hope for the best!' Harris remembered these words when a couple of hours later he was out in the middle, giving solid support to Dai Davies. Harris remembers that 'there were a few darkish clouds in the sky, so Dai appealed against the light to Frank Chester, the famous Test umpire. Chester turned it down with a wry smile, so a few minutes later Dai met me in the middle of the wicket at the end of an over and said "Your turn, lad; you have a go about the light!' Dutifully I obeyed and appealed to the umpire, but Chester typically replied, "Tell Dai, he hasn't got a chance and the shop will be open until 6.30 pm".'

These humorous incidents sum up the atmosphere of Glamorgan cricket in the 1930s. They were a happy band of amateurs and professionals, who through Turnbull's efforts became respected as a team. In the 1920s several English counties had not bothered to play Glamorgan, believing them not to be truly up to first-class standard. This was certainly not the case by 1939 and it is a matter of conjecture what Glamorgan might have achieved during the blank years to 1946. So instead of leading the team to further success, Turnbull went off with the rest of the staff to do his duty on foreign fields. It was hard to believe that he had played his last game for his beloved County.

THE WAR YEARS AND AFTER

ALMOST AS SOON AS war was declared, the grounds at Cardiff and Swansea were taken over by the military. The Arms Park became a military training centre, whilst the ARP took over St Helen's, but both squares were preserved allowing wartime matches to take place. An emergency committee was formed with the purpose of maintaining interest in cricket and raising funds for the war effort. Three matches were planned for a Glamorgan XI in 1940 over the August Bank Holiday, but they had to be cancelled as the government requested continuous work over the holiday period. No matches were arranged in 1941 and 1942, although a match between the Western and Southern Command was held at the Arms Park in August 1942.

There was one anxiety over the whereabouts of some of the Glamorgan players who were in action on foreign fields, in particular Wooller, who was stationed in Java. The Japanese had overrun the Far East and fears grew over Wooller's safety; everyone heaved a huge sigh of relief when it was confirmed in the spring of 1943 that he was in a POW camp. Many of the younger members of the pre-war staff were still stationed in Britain, so the emergency committee arranged four one-day fixtures for a Glamorgan team in 1943. The first, against the Anti-Aircraft Command, was held at Barry in June, and Alf Shea bowled the Welsh XI to victory by taking six for 27. However, his fine bowling meant that the game was over earlier than anticipated, so a time-limit match of 45 minutes batting a side was held to entertain the large crowd. This time the service side won, with Ted Glover smashing 63 in 35 minutes.

The Arms Park was used for two matches over the August Bank Holiday period. The first was against an Army team led by T. N. Pearce, the Essex captain; Lavis made an unbeaten 116 and then Mercer and Clay rekindled memories of old amongst the 2,000 people present by bowling Glamorgan to a 129-run win. There was an ingenious game the following day between 'Glamorgan Past' led by Dai Davies, and 'Glamorgan Future' led by Johnnie Clay. The Past totalled 215 with William Davies, the Briton Ferry pro, making 78; in reply the Future could only make 159, though Gilbert Parkhouse, an 18-year-old from Swansea, made an impressive 37. A fortnight later the RAF were beaten at Barry with Ogwyn Jones, a 21-year-old from Llangennech, and Ernie Carless, the Cardiff City footballer, taking the honours with the bat and ball.

The number of players available gradually rose in 1944 and as the war situation eased, the emergency committee were able to arrange eleven fixtures for a Glamorgan team. After defeats against a British Empire XI and the Western Command, and a draw against the West of England at Bristol, the Welsh team registered a fine win over Learie Constantine's West Indian XI at Barry, with Clay taking five for 33. Wally Hammond scored an excellent century as the RAF won at Cardiff, but 'Glamorgan' were able to win five of the remaining six games. Cyril Smart hit 104 as the West of England were beaten at Barry, whilst Clay took seven for 43 as the Army were beaten at Newport. Other victories were registered over the National Fire Service and the Anti-Aircraft XI, whilst Austin Matthews took four for 21 as the West of England were beaten once again at Briton Ferry.

These games were also successful in maintaining local interest in cricket. Large crowds gathered to see their heroes once again, and for a few hours everyone hoped to forget about the worries of the war. A large crowd had assembled at the Arms Park on 12 August for the game with the National Fire Service, but they were all stunned into silence by the news that Major Maurice Turnbull of the Welsh Guards had been killed whilst undertaking reconnaissance as his company were on the attack near Montchamp in Normandy. Over the next few days, many people reflected on Turnbull's impact on Glamorgan cricket and a host of tributes were paid to him. The most eloquent and surely the most heartfelt came from his close friend and adviser Johnnie Clay. He wrote how 'mere facts and figures do him scant justice. A great player he may have been, but an astute brain made him an even greater captain – the best of his generation who never captained England – and there is little doubt that he would have become one of the game's foremost administrators .... He was indeed a most efficient Secretary; always on the job and his suggestions were based on practical knowledge and experience. He went all out successfully for an increased membership and paid great attention to the comfort of the spectators. In short, by 1939 he converted a shambling, shamefaced, bankrupt into a worthy and respected member of society ... The news of his death came through while Glamorgan were fulfilling one of their wartime fixtures at Cardiff Arms Park, the scene of his first century and many subsequent triumphs. And as the crowd stood in respectful silence, perhaps the more imaginative or sentimental among them may have pictured for a fleeting instant the well-known figure out there on the field and derived some small measure of comfort. For Glamorgan were carrying on and he would have wished that.'

Nine fixtures, including a game in memory of Turnbull, were organised in 1945. However, only three of these matches ended in victory for the 'Glamorgan' team. Clay and Ogwyn Jones each took five wickets as the Western Command were beaten at Briton Ferry.

Sensible batting by Gilbert Parkhouse set up a 17-run win over Learie Constantine's West Indian XI at Barry, whilst good bowling by Ogwyn Jones and Reg Anderson, a 31-year-old policeman from Swansea, saw Glamorgan defeat the National Fire Service at Pontypridd. Although they lost the remaining games, there were some useful performances, notably by Johnnie Clay, who took ten wickets in the game with the RAAF and some promising innings by C. D. Williams, a 20-year-old all-rounder from St Fagan's, who gained a rugby blue at Oxford. Unfortunately, the Maurice Turnbull Memorial match at the Arms Park in mid-August was one of the games which ended in defeat. The West of England XII declared at 219 for eight with Tom Barling of Surrey scoring 99 and Wally Hammond an assured 51. In reply, Glamorgan made only 126, with Haydn Davies top-scoring with a rapid 38, which included three towering sixes. It was a great shame that the Welsh team should produce their worst batting performance of the season in this game in memory of one of their finest batsmen.

These wartime matches kept together the nucleus of the pre-war team and preserved much of the team spirit. This was a great bonus when it came to planning the resumption of the County Championship in 1946. Turnbull's tragic death was a crippling blow, leaving the Club without a captain, but it wasn't a difficult decision to select a replacement and Johnnie Clay, who had been the driving force behind the wartime fixtures, was unanimously elected as the captain for 1946. He agreed to carry on with the duties of Secretary as well, despite the fact that Albert Brown, his right-hand man during the war, had been taken ill, and George Cording, the war-time match secretary, had died. Fortunately, Austin Matthews, Wilf Wooller and Les Spence agreed to act as Assistant Secretaries in order to ease the burden, whilst G. V. Wynne-Jones, the well known broadcaster, lent a hand as Honorary Treasurer.

The representative games during the war had raised over £2,400 so the club started the new era with a clean balance sheet; but their assets stood at only £2,000 and the officials were faced with heavy outlays on reconstructing and re-equipping their grounds because of wartime damage and austerity calls. These measures were a necessity if first-class games were to be staged and the committee once again had to discuss how money might be raised to meet these ends. One of the members of the pre-war committee had been Herbert Merrett, a wealthy Cardiff businessman with a coal-exporting business at Cardiff Docks. Wooller was one of his employees, and together with Clay, he persuaded Merrett to launch a fund to allow Glamorgan to restore their grounds to county standard.

Merrett also hoped that the fund could tackle another of the Club's difficulties, namely the lack of a headquarters. The committee agreed that if sufficient capital could be raised they would contact the Cardiff Arms Park Company Limited about purchasing the ground, or obtaining a plot for an administrative and coaching complex. The Company had taken over the upkeep of the ground in 1922 from the Marquess of Bute on the understanding that the area should be kept for recreational purposes. They had undertaken a few ground improvements, allowing the WRU to erect a stand along the southern boundary of the cricket ground in 1934 and the cricket section of Cardiff Athletic Club to build a new pavilion in 1937, so the Glamorgan officials were optimistic of securing a plot at the Arms Park for their office.

The 'Seating and Nursery Fund', as it became known, also attempted to raise money for proper coaching facilities to be provided 'for all young cricketers and thereby build up a team composed mainly of our own players which will be able to entertain us with cricket of the highest possible class'. In short, it was an attempt to achieve Turnbull's dream of an all-Welsh born XI representing Glamorgan, besides providing adequate seating and amenities for spectators. The aim was to build up a fund of £10,000 and within a few weeks over £1,000 was raised, as Merrett persuaded his friends in the business world to support the club generously.

Clay and his assistants also had the task of reassembling the Glamorgan players from all over Europe and the Far East in readiness for the long awaited return of championship cricket. Willie Jones and Judge returned from the RAF, whilst Haydn Davies was demobilised from the Army. Watkins left the Royal Navy at Portsmouth and Dyson travelled back to Cardiff from a munitions factory and assembled at Cardiff for an intensive net session along with Smart, Ogwyn Jones and Closs Jones. Lavis was re-engaged after his useful wartime performances, together with Arthur Porter, another Monmouthshire player, who had made two appearances back in 1936. There was one new face at the pre-season nets – Maurice Robinson, an Irish-born all-rounder who had played first-class cricket in India during the war and was now stationed at RAF St Athan.

Clift, Parkhouse and Emrys Davies were still on military service and should have been unavailable, but through the influence of Colonel Clay, Private Emrys Davies was posted to Cardiff Barracks and was allowed to join the team. Despite not being demobilised until late July, he managed to play in all of the Championship games, by doing guard duty all night so that he could play during the day in home matches, and 'obtaining' privilege leave to coincide with the away games. The fact that the team had the regular services of a full-time soldier intrigued Field Marshal Montgomery when he was presented to the players in the match at Horsham, but all was explained during a quiet chat with Colonel Clay!

The absence of Parkhouse and Clay meant that the batting was thin, so the committee approached Martin Donnelly, the New Zealand Test batsman who was studying at Oxford University. They hoped he would agree to play for them during his summer vacation, but nothing came of the approach. The officials had also tried to retain the services of Jack Young, who had bowled so well in the wartime matches. The 33-year-old left-arm spinner had been on Middlesex's books since 1933, but had not held down a regular place. He was known to be unsettled and had contemplated joining Leicestershire before the war, so Clay hoped he would agree to join the Welsh club after his success in the friendlies. Young provisionally agreed, and Clay contacted the Middlesex officials to inform them of his intentions, but Sir Pelham Warner did not want to lose Young's services and he persuaded him to return to London. Ironically, Young went on to make his England debut the following year, and made eight Test appearances in all, leaving Glamorgan to rue their luck once again.

A full programme of 26 Championship matches was arranged for 1946, plus two games with the touring Indians. The grounds at Cardiff, Swansea, Newport, Pontypridd and Llanelli had all been cleared of military trappings and were allocated fixtures. However, The Gnoll had suffered severe damage during the war, and was still not ready to stage county cricket. The committee had to decide whether to allocate an extra game to one of the 'fit' venues or to take a match to another ground. Minor county matches had been staged before the war at the Ebbw Vale Association's ground, and their officials persuaded the Glamorgan personnel that the Eugene Cross ground could stage first-class matches. It was allocated the Worcestershire match and over 5,000 people watched the first day's play. Clay was very impressed with the facilities and later in the season the Nottinghamshire match was switched to Ebbw Vale as a result of problems in restoring the wicket at Llanelli.

The results in 1946 must have been beyond the wildest dreams of Clay, as the team finished in sixth place, their highest-ever position. His astute captaincy, drawing on his vast experience, was a key factor and he was rewarded in only the second match of the season, against Lancashire at Old Trafford. This was the Welsh club's first ever win at the ground, even more remarkable considering that Clay's team, operating on a shoestring budget, had arrived at the ground to see rows of nets, numerous coaches and a battery of net bowlers!

Clay's captaincy was the linchpin of the team's success, with the veteran cleverly handling his bowlers and making subtle changes to both the attack and the field. He was not afraid to make interesting challenges either, as in the game with Somerset at Pontypridd. This was badly affected by rain, so on the final morning the two captains agreed to inject some life into proceedings and hopefully entertain the crowd. Ben Barnwell declared the Somerset innings at their overnight score of 51 for one and Clay followed suit when Glamorgan reached the same score against some friendly bowling. The visitors batted again, and with four and a half hours remaining, agreed to set Clay's team a fair target. However, the Somerset batsmen collapsed on the drying wicket and were bowled out inside two hours for just 53. Matthews had eight fielders close to the bat and was virtually unplayable, returning the analysis of 17-9-12-7. Rain interrupted Glamorgan's reply, but there was just enough time for them to reach the target with eight wickets in hand.

The crowd-pleasing side of Clay's captaincy also came to the surface in the match with the Indians at the Arms Park. This was also interrupted by the weather, and play began only in the middle of the first afternoon. The tourists declared at 376 for six but rain again interrupted Glamorgan's reply, so that when play finally got under way at 2.30 on the final day, a dull draw seemed inevitable. But Sarwate and Mankad dismissed the Welshmen for 149, and forced Glamorgan to follow on. With under two hours left, Clay decided to reverse the batting order and treat the crowd to some big hitting. He waived the interval between innings and stayed out in the middle with his last man, Peter Judge. Judge was then bowled with the first delivery of the second innings from the same bowler and departed with the dubious distinction of being dismissed by two successive deliveries within 60 seconds! Clay's slightly eccentric idea nearly backfired on him as the score slumped to 48 for six. The Indians claimed the extra half-hour in search of an unexpected win, but Wooller and Willie Jones staunchly held out.

Another important aspect of the team's success was that for the first time they had a battery of penetrative bowlers and did not have to rely on just two or three as before. Clay, Matthews, Emrys Davies and Judge each took over 50 wickets, with the captain himself topping the averages with 130 wickets at 13 apiece. The batting was more reliable than in the past with Dyson and Emrys Davies continuing their fruitful opening partnership. Willie Jones and Allan Watkins also emerged as top-class batsmen. Jones hit nine half centuries, but strangely no hundreds, yet he still managed to pass a thousand. This had been a personal target for the little left-hander, and as his aggregate approached four figures, he became increasingly anxious and was often in a more jittery state than normal when going out to bat. Apparently the target weighed so heavily on his mind that when asleep at night, he would nudge his wife in bed and say 'run up, there's three here!'

Watkins hit a maiden century against Surrey, after going in with the Arms Park scoreboard reading 82 for five. He counter-attacked the bowling with some fierce drives through the covers on a wicket which was giving the bowlers considerable assistance. The value of his innings can be judged by the fact that only one Surrey batsman passed fifty as Glamorgan made them follow on, before winning by nine wickets. Ironically, Watkins had been a last minute choice for the match, and should have been on pre-season training with Plymouth Argyle FC, for whom he played in the winter. After a series of low scores, Watkins had resigned himself to missing the last few weeks of the season. But after his fine innings, he grew in confidence and the Plymouth manager allowed him to remain with Glamorgan for the rest of the season.

The excellent summer swelled the coffers of the Club and they ended the year with a healthy balance of £4,000. Gate money had soared from £4,000 in 1939 to nearly £15,000 as people flooded into the grounds, glad to see the team playing again and doing so well. The August Bank Holiday match at Swansea against the Indians attracted a crowd of more than 50,000 who paid over £5,000 in entrance money. The gates had to be closed soon after lunch on the Monday with the Club's officials ruefully viewing the long queues outside the ground and wishing that St Helen's could accommodate more people.

The 1946 season was therefore a turning point in the Club's financial history and they finished the year with their healthiest-ever bank balance. The players and officials were freed from the anxiety of financial loss and thoughts that the Club might fold, which had always been in the back of their minds before the war. The Nursery and Development Funds, through Wooller's hard effort and persuasion, brought in £8,000 by June, so the target was raised to £15,000, and by the end of the year they were within £3,000 of achieving this goal. The money allowed much needed ground improvements at Cardiff, Swansea and Neath. Nets and coconut matting were provided at 20 clubs, whilst Wooller began organising a winter coaching scheme with Austin Matthews.

The improved financial position allowed the Club to consider re-entering the Minor County Championship with a second eleven. During the autumn, they contacted the MCC, but were told that their application was too late. Clay was upset at this, especially with a growing number of young colts who could benefit from second team experience. Consequently, he dipped into his pocket once again, and put up the money for a cup competition against the second elevens of Warwickshire, Worcestershire and Derbyshire.

During the winter months Clay realised that his playing days were drawing to a close, and given the improved playing fortunes of the Club, he felt it was time to hand over the captaincy to a younger man. He announced his resignation as captain, and semi-retirement from county cricket saying that 'to be captain of a county side is a full time job and I have many interests and other things to do. There is less need for me to carry on when we have a fully qualified captain in Mr Wooller ready at hand.'

Wooller was an ideal replacement, given his amateur status, playing experience before and after the war, Cambridge education and administrative duties for the Club. The committee agreed and the former Welsh rugby international was appointed captain and honorary secretary for 1947. Wooller had at his disposal the majority of the 1946 staff, apart from Smart and Closs Jones, who had both retired. The partial retirement of Clay meant that there was a vacancy in the spin bowling department. This was filled by the signing from Middlesex of Len Muncer, who could bowl both leg and off-spin. The new captain failed to move Glamorgan any higher in the table, but they managed to finish in a creditable ninth place.

The season began poorly with two heavy defeats against Yorkshire and an innings defeat by the South Africans at Cardiff. However, the side recovered their form in the second half of the season, winning five of their last nine games, and putting up a good fight in their return match with the tourists at Swansea over the August Bank Holiday, which drew a crowd in excess of 50,000. The visitors set Glamorgan a target of 252 on the final afternoon, and at 39 for six another embarrassing defeat seemed likely. But there was a gritty rearguard action led by Watkins, who made a fine 75. He received good support from Robinson, Lavis and Haydn Davies to put the Welshmen in with an outside chance of a remarkable victory. Alan Melville was forced to recall Dawson, his opening bowler to stifle the resistance and secure a hard-earned 40-run victory.

Watkins led a successful run chase against Somerset at Weston-super-Mare later in the season. Glamorgan achieved a target of 290 with six wickets in hand as Watkins struck an aggressive 105, and Lavis made a rapid 87. This was the first of three successive victories as Northants were defeated by an innings at St Helen's, and Muncer took nine for 79 in Surrey's second innings at Cardiff to set up a four-wicket win. The off-spinner had an outstanding year, claiming 107 wickets and forming a fine partnership with Clay in the 13 games in which the veteran appeared. Despite his few appearances, Clay still managed to head the national averages with 65 wickets at 16 apiece. His finest performance came against Leicestershire at the Arms Park when he took six for 5 in an 11-over spell.

The graceful action of Len Muncer, practising before a match at Newport. (David Smith)

There was only one gloomy aspect to the summer, and that was the lack of an effective pair of opening bowlers. Judge lost form and played in just three games, whilst Matthews appeared in only five matches and slipped into retirement. The Club's officials were delighted when Wat Jones, a 29-year-old from Gwauncaegurwen, picked up seven wickets in the victory over Kent. He seemed to be an ideal recruit, but Jones told the club that he did not want to become a county cricketer, and it was back to square one.

The lack of an opening bowler was a blow, but the committee were heartened by the improved coaching facilities, and believed that someone might emerge from the winter coaching scheme. George Lavis was appointed coaching organiser to schools and clubs, and John Riches, the 29-year-old son of Norman, was invited to lead the second team, which had re-entered the minor county competition for 1948. Through the money raised by the Nursery and Development Fund, Lavis was able to undertake coaching in an indoor school along one of the corridors of the North Stand at the Arms Park, attended by a number of promising young players, allowing Lavis to groom them for second team appearances.

The first two seasons after the war had seen a marked rise in Glamorgan's fortunes both on and off the field, with a sound financial base and a crop of talented youngsters. On the field, the batting was solid and apart from the opening bowlers, Wooller had a varied and penetrative attack. There had also been a noticeable improvement in the fielding, especially close to the wicket, with Wooller leading by example, standing fearlessly at forward short-leg. Watkins emerged as an outstanding leg-slip, whilst Clift and Dyson formed an agile leg trap. Wooller, and his mentor Clay, hoped that this determination in the field would provide a launching pad for further success in the future – their dreams materialised quicker than they had expected as 1948 proved to be Glamorgan's year.

THE FIRST CHAMPIONSHIP TITLE

MIDDLESEX WERE WIDELY EXPECTED to retain the Championship title in 1948 after their fine victory the previous year and the batting feats of Compton, Edrich and Robertson, who had each scored over 2,000 runs. Few people fancied Glamorgan's chances of even being in the top six, but Wooller was quietly optimistic, having formed an effective playing unit around him. The captain readily admitted that they 'could not compete with Middlesex in batting or Derbyshire in bowling. But in fielding we gave first to no side. We attempted to make each fielder, be he a deep long-on or a short leg, an integral part of a machine. Each man came off the field with the knowledge that he had fulfilled his part by saving runs in some way or another. If a man failed in batting or bowling, he still knew his part in the game was important.'

It was widely felt that Glamorgan lacked one vital ingredient for success – a good opening bowler. A number of youngsters had been tried in 1947 including William Griffiths, the Cambridge blue and Dennis Good, the former Worcestershire seamer, but they failed to make any impact. Douglas Jardine, the former England captain, drew attention to this in a speech at a cricket dinner at Cardiff in early May. He told the audience, which included virtually all of the committee: 'You cannot win the County Championship unless you have a fast bowler. The Cardiff Police supplies the rugby players, so why does not the National Coal Board supply the fast bowler?' But the Glamorgan officials did not have to shout down a coal mine, because unknown to Jardine, they had signed Norman ('Pete') Hever, a 23-year-old fast-medium bowler from Middlesex. Another Londoner to join the staff was Jim Eaglestone; the left-hander was signed because Arnold Dyson had told the committee he would retire at the end of the season and take up a post at Oundle School. These signings certainly strengthened the staff and with Parkhouse and Clift available on a full-time basis, Wooller was able to choose from a full complement.

The Championship season began in fine fashion as the Welsh batsmen successfully chased a target of 311 in 290 minutes to beat Essex at the Arms Park. The Cardiff wicket was assisting the spinners, and there was ample time for the Essex bowlers to exploit it. However, Glamorgan were given a sound start by Emrys Davies and Clift, their new opening pair, who each made half-centuries. This was followed by some steady strokeplay from Parkhouse and Willie Jones, and Glamorgan coasted home by five wickets. The good batting form was

The 1948 team at Worcester. Standing: Willie Jones, Phil Clift, Jim Pleass, Jim Eaglestone, Gilbert Parkhouse, Norman Hever, George Lavis. Seated: Allan Watkins, Emrys Davies, Wilf Wooller, Haydn Davies, Len Muncer. Inset: Johnnie Clay.

maintained at Worcester where Watkins made a belligerent century; Hever and Wooller then utilised a strong crosswind to bowl out the home team inside three hours on the final day.

The new air of confidence and the superb fielding increasingly became apparent as Glamorgan consolidated their position near the top of the table. At Old Trafford, the Lancashire bowlers got among the Welsh batsmen and on the final morning a defeat seemed likely, but Emrys Davies, drawing on all his experience, occupied the crease for four hours and made 105 to steer Glamorgan to safety. Clay was unavailable for the next game against Somerset at Swansea, so Wooller called up Stan Trick, the left-arm spinner who had made a few appearances in 1946. Trick had been in the services and after being demobbed he joined his family's motor business in Neath. His work commitments prevented him from playing regular county cricket, but he was available for the Somerset match. Trick had been in good form for the Neath club, so Wooller included him, believing that his faster type of spin would be ideally suited to the Swansea wicket. It was an inspired move as Trick took 12 wickets to bowl Glamorgan to a 137-run victory. He was supported by some excellent close to the wicket fielding, particularly by Watkins.

This was the county's 100th Championship win, and it put them at the top of the table ahead of Middlesex and Yorkshire. They maintained this position during June as five of the seven matches ended in resounding victories. The month began with an innings win over Kent at Gravesend, set up by some good bowling by Hever and Muncer, and a career best 207 from Willie Jones. The left-hander never quite believed in his own ability and after this innings he modestly acknowledged the congratulations from his team mates by saying 'I will never do it again.' Yet a fortnight later he was sitting in the Brentwood dressing room after making another double century! Dai Davies was one of the umpires in this match against Essex, and the Glamorgan stalwart took great delight at the way Jones and Emrys Davies shared a record-breaking partnership of 313 for the third wicket. He remembered how 'they just went mad and hit everything in sight. Emrys was playing shots all round the wicket with tremendous vigour and was well into his second hundred, and Willie not far behind. I knew Emrys would keep going like the great fighter he was, but Willie started to complain about feeling tired at about 150. His knees were always giving him trouble, souvenirs of his rugby days with Neath and Gloucester. I knew Willie was thinking of throwing his wicket away. In Welsh he said "I'm tired Dai." I snapped back at him "Keep going or I'll hit you on the head with this wicket!"' Jones took the hint and went on to score 212 not out as Wooller declared at 586 for five, before Muncer bowled Glamorgan to an innings victory.

In between Jones's two double centuries came a pair of comfortable home victories. Hampshire were defeated at the Arms Park after being set 220 on the final day. Jones played a hand in this win too, cleverly flighting his left-arm spinners to take five wickets as the visitors fell 70 runs short. Kent were soundly beaten by 278 runs at Swansea, with Trick and Muncer taking 18 wickets between them on another Swansea 'turner'. The spinners also played an important role in the convincing win over Notts at Swansea later in June. The visitors were set 300 on the final day, but they collapsed to 68, with Muncer taking six for 13.

The following match was against Middlesex at Cardiff, and with Edrich and Compton on Test duty, the Welshmen fancied their chances of recording their first win over the Home County. Hever took five wickets to give Glamorgan a healthy first-innings lead, but then they collapsed to 136 as Jim Sims and Jack Young shared eight wickets with their cunning spin. This left Middlesex with the task of making 275 on the last day. An early breakthrough was badly needed if Glamorgan were going to achieve victory, and Wooller had several lbw appeals against Sydney Brown turned down by umpire Alec Skelding. After his fifth unsuccessful shout, an exasperated Wooller turned to Skelding and said: 'What was wrong with that you blind old bastard?' 'He was not out, Mr. Wooller,' replied the umpire, 'and it is

Willie Jones, who scored two double centuries within a fortnight in 1948, which put the Welsh county on course for their first-ever championship win. (David Smith)

true that my eyesight is not good, that is why I wear these strong glasses, but I can assure you that my mother and father were married, and I'll tell you something else, I don't think you're going to win!' He was right as Brown compiled a watchful 150 and steered Middlesex to victory.

However, Glamorgan's lead was whittled away during July, as Derbyshire won four matches whilst the Welshmen slumped to two defeats and two draws. Many felt that their 'bubble' had burst and the presssure seemed to be telling especially after the game with Leicestershire at the Arms Park, where they were chasing 195 and seemed well set at 120 for three. But they lost seven wickets for 31 runs to the cunning spin of Australians Jack Walsh and Vic Jackson, and plunged to an embarrassing defeat. There was a much needed boost to morale against Warwickshire at Neath, though the leg breaks of Eric

Hollies gave Glamorgan some anxious moments. They were set 104 on a wearing pitch, and lost early wickets to the leg-spinner, who quickly settled into a groove. It seemed that another collapse was going to occur, but Willie Jones stifled his attacking instincts and watchfully played Hollies, content to push singles and accumulate slowly. Haydn Davies lent valuable support and helped steer Glamorgan home, but their delight was short-lived as it was confirmed that Derbyshire had won and had become the new Championship leaders.

The visit of the Australians to Swansea brought welcome relief from the title race, and a crowd of over 20,000 descended upon St Helen's on the first day, hoping to see the Aussies beaten. But Johnson and Ring shared six wickets as Glamorgan were dismissed for 197. Keith Miller made a forceful 84 on the second day, and with the tourists on 216 for three, they seemed poised for a large lead. But in the middle of the afternoon it began to rain, and the rest of the day's play was washed out. It carried on raining right up until lunch on the final day, making it a formality that the match would be drawn. Despite the poor weather, the club's officials were delighted at the large attendance, and more good news came when Derbyshire failed to win their Championship match and extend their lead.

With Surrey and Yorkshire closing the gap behind them, Glamorgan knew that a few victories were vital in August if they were going to sustain their title challenge. But the weather intervened once again to frustrate them, with a mountain mist and a thunderstorm preventing Wooller's team from picking up any bonus points in their match with Gloucestershire at Ebbw Vale. The side travelled over to Weston-super-Mare, hoping for a change of luck, but rain fell on the morning of the match and Glamorgan were dismissed for 70 on a damp wicket. Somerset gained a first innings lead of 96, and by the time the Welshmen batted for a second time, the ball had begun to turn appreciably. Once again, only Willie Jones could come to terms with the bowlers, but when he was dismissed for a gritty half-century, Glamorgan's lead was only 42 with four wickets left. Wooller arrived at the crease, but before he could make any inroads on the bowling, two further wickets fell. It was clearly a case of 'hit or bust', so Wooller launched into some hefty blows. Once again, Haydn Davies lent valiant support, together with Norman Hever, and as a result Somerset were left a target of 105.

Before they went out to bowl, news came through that Derbyshire had been defeated by Nottinghamshire, and Wooller's team realised that they could go back into first place if they could beat Somerset. A mighty task stood in front of them, but Hever rose to the occasion and claimed three early wickets as Somerset got off to the worst possible start. Wooller quickly brought on Muncer to tie down the batsmen. The Glamorgan fielders excelled themselves as the pressure mounted and the batsmen were forced to take risks. Wooller led by example, standing fearlessly at short-leg to take three superb catches, including one from Wellard which lifted him off his feet with the impact – and Wooller was a 15-stone plus rugby player! Wickets fell at regular intervals as none of the home batsmen could build an innings. With the score on 90 for nine, Horace Hazell joined Wally Luckes at the wicket and the tension mounted. But it was the Welshmen who cracked first, as Emrys Davies uncharacteristically spilled a catch. Seven more runs were added and it seemed as if Glamorgan had lost their grip on the game, but then Hazell glanced Muncer once too often, and Watkins dived like a salmon to take the match-winning catch.

Earnest discussions took place during the train journey back home from Weston on how Glamorgan could capitalise on their position at the top of the table. J. B. G. Thomas remembers how 'the twelve players and myself were squeezed into a compartment and my eldest son, then aged five, was put onto the luggage rack for safety by George Lavis, while everyone put forward a theory of how to win the title!' Glamorgan had five games to play, whilst Derbyshire only had four more and Wooller realised that they had to make the most of this advantage. Glamorgan's remaining games were against Middlesex, Northants, Surrey, Hampshire and Leicestershire. Remembering their problems against Walsh's wrist spin, none of the team fancied beating Leicestershire, and given Surrey's improving form, this also seemed a difficult fixture. So it was agreed that they would make the most of the other three games.

But once again, their best laid plans fell foul of the weather as rain caused the match at Lord's to end in a draw. The elements interrupted Derbyshire's match at Scarborough and also prevented a decisive result, but there was fine weather at Weston, where Surrey raced to an eight-wicket win. Not only did this put them into third palce, but they had five more games to play compared with Glamorgan's four. Wooller's team came in for another surprise when it was confirmed that Allan Watkins had been called up to play in the final Test against Australia.

The team arrived back at Cardiff knowing that they badly needed to defeat Northants at the Arms Park, and that if they didn't, they had to hope that Surrey did not win again at Cheltenham. The second day's play finished with Northants 123 runs ahead with six wickets remaining, and it looked as if Glamorgan were going to have to chase runs on the final afternoon. The side were not cheered up when word came through from Cheltenham that Surrey had set Gloucestershire an unlikely target of 291 on a crumbling wicket, and it was confirmed that Derbyshire had won inside two days at Chesterfield.

No doubt many of the team spent a sleepless night realising that their performance on the final day at Cardiff was going to be crucial. Their nerves were not helped when play was halted by drizzle and bad light after just eight balls. Heavy rain fell around lunchtime and in the early afternoon, making it a formality that no more play would be possible. The only comforting thought was that the belt of rain was moving east up the Severn Estuary towards Cheltenham, but would it arrive there in enough time to prevent a Surrey victory? The prayers of Wooller's team were answered when play ended with Gloucestershire precariously placed at 124 for nine. But the sighs of relief were cut short as news arrived from Bradford that Yorkshire had bowled out Worcestershire with just ten minutes to go; this win moved Yorkshire up the table and with four matches to play, they too were in contention for the title. Glamorgan's next match was against Surrey – a game which the players on both sides knew could decide the outcome of the Championship. With Watkins on Test duty and Clift carrying an injury, Wooller was unable to select a full strength team for this vital match. A few eyebrows were raised when the captain recalled the 50-year-old Clay to the side, but it was a move which was to reap rewards beyond even the wildest hopes of Wooller himself.

The Cardiff ground was still wet after heavy overnight rain when Wooller won the toss and he faced a difficult decision. He opted to bat first, believing that the wicket would play less easily later in the game as it became worn. His decision was vindicated as Dyson and Davies put on 91 to launch the innings, but the introduction of Laker into the attack resulted in the fall of three quick wickets. Surrey looked like gaining the initiative, so Wooller moved himself up the order to No 5 and typically counter-attacked the bowling, driving and square-cutting with immense power. However, wickets continued to fall at the other end, and the Welshmen were eventually dismissed for 239 with Wooller top-scoring with 89.

Surrey had to bat for just one hour at the end of the first day, and clearly had their minds on crease occupation rather than quick runs. It seemed like a stalemate situation during the final hour, but Hever and Wooller picked up three wickets with the new ball to wrest the initiative back from the visitors' grasp. This allowed Wooller to introduce Clay, his trump card, knowing the veteran's ability on drying wickets. Muncer was also brought on and Wooller decided to crowd the Surrey batsmen, in anticipation of another wicket. But this change produced a clatter of wickets as Surrey collapsed from 22 for three to 47 for nine by the close. Clay dismissed McIntyre, Bedser and

Laker within one over alone, and the visiting horde of journalists were forced quickly to rewrite their copy as the wickets tumbled, with 'Nomad', who was never lost for the right turn of phrase, writing that 'Clay and Muncer ran through the batsmen like mowers through ripe corn!'

Clay finished off the resistance in the fourth over of the second morning, and Wooller, wreathed in smiles, was able to invite the visitors to follow on. Conditions were slightly easier for batting and Surrey quietly reached 38 without loss before Muncer and Clay were introduced. Again this prompted a collapse as Barton was bowled by Muncer and Clay trapped Squires leg before. Fishlock was smartly stumped trying to drive Muncer and in the next couple of overs Parker and Bedser also made their way back to the pavilion. It seemed that Wooller's team might even achieve victory before lunch, but Constable and McIntyre provided staunch resistance and forced Wooller into making a change. Willie Jones was brought on and five minutes before lunch McIntyre was deceived by Jones's flight and mistimed a drive straight into Clay's hands at mid-off.

There had been a crowd of over 5,000 at the start of the morning, but as news quickly spread around Cardiff that Surrey were on the verge of defeat at 88 for six, the offices and shops emptied, and there were more like 10,000 people watching when play resumed in the afternoon. Wooller brought Clay back on and he soon bowled Laker, before having Clark snapped up at short leg. Surridge and Constable decided to go down fighting, and made a few lusty blows, but it was only a matter of time before they swung once too often. At 144 for

Wilf Wooller triumphantly leads the Glamorgan team off the Arms Park after beating Surrey in 1948.

139

eight Constable was deceived by a slower one from Clay, and soon afterwards McMahon hit Willie Jones to Clay at mid-off, and Glamorgan had won by an innings and 24 runs. The off-spinner had match figures of ten for 65, and he led the team off the field to hearty cheers and a standing ovation from the many office clerks and shop workers, who quickly scurried back to work, hoping that their bosses did not mind their extra-long lunch hour! The following day Derbyshire failed to beat Essex and rain washed out any play in Yorkshire's match at Worcester and at long last it seemed that the gods were smiling on Wooller's team.

But Watkins picked up a shoulder injury on his Test debut after being hit by Ray Lindwall and dismissed for a duck as England were bowled out for 52. He then had to retire to the pavilion after opening the bowling with Alec Bedser, and had to watch as Australia amassed 389 and won by an innings. It was a baptism of fire, but what hurt Watkins even more on the journey back home to Wales was the fact that he would have to miss the game with Hampshire at Bournemouth. He knew that Glamorgan could put the title out of Surrey's reach if they could win this game, and with Derbyshire out of contention, Yorkshire could win only if they won both of their remaining fixtures.

Clay was retained in the team and travelled down to the South Coast with the rest of the side, all of whom hoped that rain would not intervene again. But after just ten minutes on the Saturday morning, the Glamorgan batsmen were forced back into the pavilion, and continuous rain throughout the afternoon washed out play for the day. Bad weather also prevented any play in Yorkshire's game at Taunton, and the Welshmen must have spent much of the Sunday counting the playing time left, and praying that rain would not interfere with any more of the match. Their requests were answered as the match resumed in fine weather on the Monday morning. Eleven and a quarter hours of playing time remained, so Wooller gave his batsmen instructions to get 300 runs quickly so that he could declare in the evening session and have an hour or so at the Hampshire batsmen.

Everything went according to plan, as Emrys Davies, Willie Jones and Arnold Dyson made half-centuries and Glamorgan were bowled out for 315 by 5.30 pm. The situation looked even more promising when news arrived from Taunton that Yorkshire's gamble to put Somerset in and quickly bowl them out had backfired. Somerset had amassed 253 and it looked as if Yorkshire's challenge was faltering. It would be quelled even further if Glamorgan could claim a few wickets during the final hour and repeat what they had done against Surrey. Wooller knew that lightning rarely struck twice, but he told his team: 'we want five of them out tonight – we've got to get after them. I want to hear the ball hit Haydn's gloves every time you return it whether they run or not!'

The Glamorgan team went out and did their captain proud. In Wooller's second over, Rogers played a firm glance off the middle of his bat – it looked like two runs at least, but Parkhouse at short-leg flung himself full length to his right and caught the ball inches from the ground. One of the journalists covering the game was John Arlott and he summed up the importance of the catch by writing that 'with that catch the match was virtually won, because it crystallised Glamorgan's immense psychological advantage which they never lost'. During the final hour, the Hampshire batsmen were crowded and harried into making mistakes. In all, six wickets fell as the Welsh fielders answered their captain's rallying call.

It took only half an hour on the final morning for the Hampshire resistance to end, and Wooller invited them to follow on. Whilst in the Dean Park pavilion, the Glamorgan captain sent a telegram to George Woodhouse, the Somerset captain saying 'Hang on to Yorkshire. We can win here!' He then led the team back out, knowing that they had four hours in which to dismiss Hampshire again and secure the county title. With the score on 22, Hever bowled Rogers, but at the end of the over, he limped off with an injured left foot. Wooller decided that this was the time to introduce Clay and Muncer, and once again, it seemed as if the Welsh captain had the Midas touch, as the spinners quickly took two wickets each. Despite some lusty blows by Desmond Eagar, Hampshire took lunch at 101 for five with Wooller convinced that his side were on the brink of victory. He was even more overjoyed when a telegram arrived from the Somerset captain saying: 'We will beat Yorkshire. Good luck!' The Tykes had been forced to follow on, so the title was almost certain to be Glamorgan's if they could take the last five Hampshire wickets.

In the second over after lunch, Bailey was run out and soon afterwards, Clay dismissed Dawson, Harrison and Herman to put Glamorgan on the brink of the Championship. The umpire standing at Clay's end was Dai Davies, and it was quite fitting that these two stalwarts of the pre-war era should combine, in an amusing way, when the last man, Charlie Knott was dismissed. He was hit on the pads right in front of the wicket. Clay and the rest of the close fielders made a rousing appeal, to which Davies said: 'That's out and we've won the Championship!'

A large number of Welsh supporters had travelled to Bournemouth, or were holidaying in the area, and they mobbed Wooller's team as the players came off the field. It must have felt as if it was the Arms Park or St Helen's as the euphoric Welsh supporters gathered in front of the pavilion and sang 'Mae Hen Wlad Fy Nhadau' and

'Sospan Fach', as it became known that Yorkshire were heading for defeat. The team stood on the pavilion balcony and heartily joined in with the typically Celtic celebrations. Some could hardly believe that they had actually become County Champions, with Emrys Davies apparently refusing to believe it until he heard it on the BBC news!

Wooller had been selected to play for the MCC against the Australians at Lord's, so Johnnie Clay took charge of the team on the journey by train back to Cardiff. It was quite fitting, as he was the sole survivor of the 1921 team, but I doubt if even he could have anticipated the welcome that was to greet the players when they arrived at Cardiff General shortly after 11 pm. Thousands of people had travelled from all over South Wales to share in the triumph and a mighty roar, worthy of an Arms Park rugby international went up as Clay and the team got off the train. The greying veteran gave an impromptu speech, and the players went off to Cardiff Athletic Club for a champagne celebration which went on long into the night.

Two special matches were held in September to celebrate the title success. The first at Swansea was against a South of England XI led by R. W. V. Robins; he sportingly set the Welshmen a target of 251 in 225 minutes, and it was reached with seven minutes to spare, as Allan Watkins hit an unbeaten 111. The following day a game was held at Cardiff against an All England XI which included Len Hutton, Bill Edrich, Maurice Leyland, Douglas Jardine, Johnny Wardle, Norman Yardley and Alf Gover. Jack Hobbs agreed to stand as one of the

Champions at long last! The Glamorgan team receive the congratulations of the crowd from the pavilion balcony at Bournemouth. Left to right: Arnold Dyson, Jim Pleass, Norman Hever, Wilf Wooller, Haydn Davies, Johnnie Clay and Emrys Davies. (David Smith)

HAMPSHIRE *v.* GLAMORGAN

Played at Bournemouth on 21, 23 and 24 August 1948

GLAMORGAN WON BY AN INNINGS AND 115 RUNS

GLAMORGAN	**FIRST INNINGS**	
E. Davies	c Dawson b Shackleton	74
A. H. Dyson	hit wicket b Bailey	51
W. G. A. Parkhouse	c Shackleton b Bailey	2
W. E. Jones	not out	78
*W. Wooller	c and b Knott	29
J. T. Eaglestone	st Harrison b Bailey	2
L. B. Muncer	lbw b Bailey	40
J. E. Pleass	b Knott	0
†H. G. Davies	b Knott	0
N. G. Hever	c and b Bailey	18
J. C. Clay	c Herman b Bailey	2
Extras		19
Total		315

1st inns: 1-95, 2-97, 3-164, 4-210, 5-215, 6-277, 7-278, 8-278, 9-303

BOWLING	O	M	R	W
Herman	14	4	33	0
Shackleton	17	5	45	1
Knott	42	9	133	3
Bailey	41	8	85	6

HAMPSHIRE	**FIRST INNINGS**		**SECOND INNINGS**	
J. Arnold	lbw b Clay	2	c Dyson b Clay	16
N. H. Rogers	c Parkhouse b Wooller	2	b Hever	11
J. R. Bridger	c Parkhouse b Hever	0	b Clay	18
N. McCorkell	c H. Davies b Muncer	34	lbw b Muncer	12
*E. D. R. Eagar	c Wooller b Muncer	0	b Muncer	39
J. Bailey	c E. Davies b Clay	3	run out	3
G. Dawson	c Wooller b Clay	0	lbw b Clay	4
†L. Harrison	st H. Davies b Muncer	10	c Muncer b Clay	5
O. W. Herman	b Muncer	21	b Clay	1
D. Shackleton	c Pleass b Muincer	0	not out	0
C. J. Knott	not out	2	lbw b Clay	4
Extras		10		3
Total		84		116

1st inns: 1-7, 2-8, 3-29, 4-30, 5-47, 6-47, 7-55, 8-81, 9-81
2nd inns: 1-22, 2-39, 3-48, 4-97, 5-100, 6-102, 7-103, 8-111, 9-112

BOWLING	O	M	R	W	O	M	R	W
Wooller	6	4	8	1	6	1	19	0
Hever	6	3	10	1	4	1	9	1
Muncer	11.5	4	25	5	19	9	19	2
Clay	11	0	31	3	20	5	48	6
Jones					6	2	18	0

Umpires: D. Davies and P. T. Mills

This match has a special place in the annals of the Club in that it saw Glamorgan become County Champions for the first time. Solid batting by Emrys Davies, Dyson and Jones gave Wooller a platform from which to attack the Hampshire batsmen. They were forced to follow on as the Welsh bowlers and fielders were on top form, especially veteran Johnnie Clay who shed a few tears when it was confirmed that Glamorgan had won the title.

JOHNNIE CLAY

J. C. Clay made his debut for Glamorgan in 1921, after having played against them for Monmouthshire the previous season. He started as a fast bowler, but soon reverted to off-spin, and became their leading spinner before the Second World War. Clay was a big spinner of the ball as a result of walking around holding a rubber ball and squeezing it to strengthen his fingers. He also commanded superb powers of flight; as Wilf Wooller remembers, it was fascinating to watch a top batsman move forward to play Clay 'and then see the dawning of disbelief as he stretched farther and farther forward to reach a ball whose flight through the air had caused him to misjudge'.

Clay was one of the leading bowlers in the country during the 1930s, yet he played for England only once, in 1935. However, he was not worried by this, and is reputed to have refused an invitation from the selectors, saying: 'I'm much too old. Give the younger players a chance.'

He also acted as Maurice Turnbull's right-hand man during the 1930s as they raised the cash needed for the club to survive. After his close friend's tragic death in 1944, Clay supervised the rebuilding of the Club after the war, and came out of retirement in 1948 to play a crucial role in the final stages of the Championship success. He summed up his feelings of delight by saying: 'It is the greatest thing that has ever happened in my life to see Glamorgan win the Championship.'

Johnnie Clay — a loyal servant to the Club as captain, bowler and administrator. (Cardiff Central Library)

umpires alongside Norman Riches who was delighted to take time off from his dental practice to share in the Club's celebrations. Wooller set the visitors a fair target of 191 in 165 minutes, but they ended nine runs short when stumps were drawn, having been tied down by Clay who conceded just 21 runs from 12 accurate overs, and picked up two wickets.

A host of special functions were held during the autumn to commemorate the Championship success, including a dinner in October attended by all of the 1948 squad, the committee and a host of players from the pre-war and minor county days. Tributes flooded in to Wooller's team and in particular their fine fielding which had proved the old adage of 'take your catches, win your matches'. Watkins finished with 40 catches, Wooller 38, Muncer 31 and Clift 26, whilst Jones, Hever and Eaglestone all earned themselves fine reputations for their alert and keen fielding in the deep. Wooller's captaincy was also widely praised, with many writers citing the way he had welded the squad into a successful team. He may have used strong language and been outspoken in getting the best out of the players, but he clearly recognised their collective effort with ball, bat and in the field by saying 'as captain I can only say to the boys "Thanks to you all".'

The County's finances were in a most healthy state at the end of the season, with a balance in excess of £27,000. Over £18,000 had been taken at the gate, compared with £8,000 the year before, whilst over £7,250 had been raised from membership subscriptions – a rise of nearly £2,500. Some of this cash was put towards the conversion of a corridor in the North Stand of the Arms Park into an Indoor School, whilst money was also spent on a number of improvements at the other grounds. Colonel Bevan summed up the general feeling in his Chairman's comments in the Annual Report, writing: 'Our older members, recalling how some of our earlier reports were pervaded by an atmosphere of defeat and debt, may well marvel at the happy change in our affairs. In thanking them for their past support, we should like to take the opportunity also of recording our appreciation of the services rendered by former players and committee, and especially by the late M. J. Turnbull, whose efforts in troubled times have enabled the club to arrive at its present position.' How sad it was that Turnbull, the architect of the Club's development on and off the field, was not there to witness the team's success.

THE HIGHS AND LOWS OF THE 1950s

TWO GLAMORGAN PLAYERS RECEIVED invitations from the MCC for their winter tour to South Africa in 1948/9. One was Wilf Wooller, but because of his work in Cardiff he declined the invitation. The other was Allan Watkins, and he freed himself of his footballing commitments and established himself in the England team. After half-centuries against Griqualand West and Transvaal, Watkins was chosen for the first Test at Durban. He made only nine and four, and failed to take a wicket, but he impresssed many with his agile fielding and on the strength of this he kept his place for the rest of the series. He proved his worth as a batsman in the fourth Test at Johannesburg in mid-February, where he became Glamorgan's first centurion in Test cricket. He arrived at the crease soon after South Africa had claimed two wickets with the new ball. He saw the score double from 172 for three to 346 for nine, receiving good help from the lower order, and hooking and pulling with great power. He was on 90 when No 11 Jack Young came in. But the spinner gave good support and helped Watkins reach a richly deserved hundred after $3\frac{1}{2}$ hours batting. Watkins set his sights on 150, but he trod on his wicket trying to hook McCarthy and departed to a standing ovation, having helped take the score to 379.

Although Wooller maintained a good team spirit, the Glamorgan players found life at the top tough in 1949. As Champion County they were given few favours, and were expected to bowl sides out rather than be given a sporting declaration. The Welsh public maintained their wild enthusiasm and flocked in their thousands to see the team play, but they failed to see them retain the title. Great faith had been placed on the quartet of all-rounders – Wooller, Watkins, Jones and Muncer – but they were hit by a series of misfortunes and injuries. The worst befell Jones who missed much of the season after being hurt at Gravesend in June. Trick was rarely available, so more demands were made of Muncer. Although he took over a hundred wickets, the spin attack was not as venomous as before, and Wooller had to persuade Clay to come out of retirement for one match at Cardiff.

Emrys Davies had a moderate season, and the bulk of the runs came from Parkhouse and Watkins. Parkhouse established himself at No 3 and batted consistently throughout the summer, whilst Watkins scored four centuries. Despite his good form, and his fighting performances on tour, Watkins played in only one Test during the summer, and then only when Lancashire's Alan Wharton had dropped out of the original side. Watkins gave a reasonable account of himself, scoring 6 and 49 not out, but he failed to gain selection for any other matches. Willie Jones and Norman Hever also came close to national honours, being selected alongside Watkins in the South XI in the Test Trial at Edgbaston, but Jones scored only 26 runs and Hever took just a single wicket.

The greatest advance in the batting came from Phil Clift, who passed 1,000 runs for the first time. He played a remarkable innings in the match at Ebbw Vale after Tom Pearce, the Essex captain, declared and set Wooller's team 177 in just 105 minutes. As the Welsh fielders disappeared into the pavilion Pearce said to Wooller: 'Now let's see what your fast scoring batsmen can do.' They were great rivals and Wooller urged his men to go for the target. Clift responded with an unbeaten 101, hitting Trevor Bailey, the England all-rounder, for six in his opening over, and adding a further 14 boundaries in just 79 minutes at the crease. Glamorgan reached the target in 24 overs for the loss of one wicket, and as the shell-shocked Essex team left the field and climbed up the pavilion steps, Wooller said to Pearce: 'They are pretty bloody quick when they try, aren't they?'

With the retirement of Clay and Lavis' decision to concentrate on coaching, there were a number of new faces in the team during 1949. One of these was 29-year-old Stan Montgomery, the Cardiff City footballer who had previously been on Essex's staff. He made an impressive debut against Derbyshire at the Arms Park. Glamorgan slumped to 38 for eight before Montgomery and Haydn Davies shared a partnership which doubled the score and saw them to a total of 102. They needed 245 on the last day and after his useful performance in the first innings, Montgomery was promoted up the order, and gave useful support to Clift as Wooller's team won by six wickets. He scored a maiden century in the following match at Bournemouth, and shared a partnership of 264 for the fifth wicket record with Maurice Robinson to establish himself in the side for the rest of the season.

The two-day friendly against the RAF at the Maindy Barracks ground in Cardiff gave the selectors a chance to blood several promising youngsters who had been playing well under John Riches in the second team. One of these was Jim Pressdee, a right-hand batsman and slow left-arm spinner from the Mumbles, who at 16 years and 23 days became the Club's youngest post-war cricketer. Another fresh face was Don Shepherd, a 19-year-old fast-medium bowler from Port Eynon, who had spent 1948 on the MCC groundstaff after very nearly joining Worcestershire. Two years before he had been stationed at RAF Defford with the Fleet Air Arm, and played for the station side against Worcestershire II and the Gentlemen of Worcestershire at Pershore. His fiery bowling

Don Shepherd bowls to Laurie Fishlock during the game with Surrey at St Helen's, 1950. Dai Davies is the umpire.

impressed Major Jewell, the former Worcestershire captain, who was acting as umpire, and Shepherd was given a trial and offered a contract by the Midlands county. Word reached the ears of the Glamorgan officials that a young Welsh bowler might be joining Worcestershire, so Lavis had a chat with Shepherd who accepted the Welsh county's offer. Both youngsters had promising debuts, and Pressdee took six for 55 from 25 overs to earn a first-class debut against Nottinghamshire a fortnight later.

During the winter months the Club also acquired the services of Jim McConnon, a 27-year-old from Durham, who Lavis believed was the ideal replacement for Clay. McConnon had played football for Aston Villa, but a knee injury ruined his league career, and he moved to South Wales to play for Lovell's Athletic. He also joined Newport CC and showed promise as a batsman and fast bowler, so the club officials sent him to the Glamorgan Indoor School for further coaching. However, after seeing his tall, flowing bowling action, Lavis believed that McConnon's future lay as a spinner and during the winter

148

sessions, the astute coach successfully transformed him into a useful off-spinner.

The Welsh supporters had accepted the slip down the table in 1949 as a consequence of the injuries and loss of form by some senior players. But with the emergence of these youngsters, plus the new faces of Montgomery and McConnon, they keenly looked forward to further success during the 1950s and a decade of more consistent results. Sadly, their optimism evaporated as the next few seasons turned out to be a series of peaks and troughs, and despite Wooller's strenuous efforts, the team failed to recapture their Championship-winning form. The slide down the table continued in 1950 as they finished in 11th place, with almost every home match interrupted by rain. It was a most infuriating season, as the side were often on top only for the weather to intervene and prevent a positive result. A case was the match against Gloucestershire at Llanelli, where Parkhouse and Emrys Davies shared a magnificent opening partnership of 204 as Glamorgan amassed 405. Rain interrupted the visitors' reply and although they followed on, Glamorgan did not have enough time to press home the advantage.

The most gratifying feature of the season was the rise of Gilbert Parkhouse into the Test team. In 1950 the 24-year-old was described by some as the most gifted batsman to play for the club. He made over 1,700 runs during the season, and established a series of new batting records. He hit seven centuries, including hundreds in each innings against Somerset at Cardiff, and passed 1,000 runs on 17 June – the quickest ever for Glamorgan – during the match with Surrey on a typically slow Swansea wicket which was helping Lock and Laker, the visitors' 'spin twins'. However, Parkhouse showed a complete mastery of their wiles, making a magical 161 out of Glamorgan's total of 448. This innings highlighted Parkhouse's talent against slow bowling, with 'Nomad' writing: 'Tall, upstanding, willowy, with keen eyes and steel wrists, he has much in common with the great Indian cricketers, directing the ball with gentle timing and with strokes which are always correct.'

Parkhouse was called up to play for England in the second Test against the West Indies at Lord's. It was an inauspicious debut with Parkhouse being bowled for nought in his first innings, as the tourists gained their first Test victory in England. He made 48 in the second innings and held his place for the next match at Trent Bridge. He was promoted to No 3 and made 13 and 69, but Ramadhin and Valentine bowled the West Indies to another comfortable victory. Injury and a heavy cold caused him to withdraw from the last of the four-match series at The Oval, but he had done enough to be selected for the touring party to Australia and New Zealand.

A young Gilbert Parkhouse being coached by Billy Bancroft at St Helen's in the 1930s. (Western Mail)

Watkins and Haydn Davies also came close to selection for the tour, and Parkhouse must have wished for a friendly Welsh face or two as he struggled with injury and illness 'down under'. He pulled a leg muscle early in the tour at Perth and after missing several games, he returned to the side for the match at Sydney but received a nasty blow in the abdomen when trying to hook Alan Walker, the left-arm fast bowler. Consequently, he appeared in only two Tests in Australia, plus one against New Zealand, making 99 runs in six innings. The high spot of the tour for Parkhouse came against New South Wales where he shared in a partnership of 228 for the fourth wicket with Reg Simpson. Parkhouse returned home after a difficult tour, with an

GILBERT PARKHOUSE

Gilbert Parkhouse is widely acknowledged to have been the most graceful and elegant batsman ever to wear a Glamorgan cap. Despite being a slightly built and rather frail-looking man, a typical innings from Parkhouse would always contain a series of powerful shots, struck with flawless timing and sheer artistry. He was equally at home against the fastest of bowlers and the most wily of spinners, and rarely let an attack tie him down for any length of time.

He made his first-class debut in 1948, batting at No 3, but soon moved up to open with Emrys Davies and later with Bernard Hedges, with whom he formed an effective partnership during the 1950s. Their running between the wickets was a delight to watch and a model for the many schoolboys who idolised Parkhouse. Gilbert was also an outstanding slip fieldsman, taking over 300 catches and became an important member of the County's close fielding unit.

Parkhouse was chosen for England in 1950 and toured Australia the following winter. But for ill-health and the presence of Hutton, Washbrook, Edrich and Compton, there is no doubt that he would have played far more often for England during the 1950s. There was a belated recall in 1959, but by this time Gilbert was past his best, and one can only wonder at what he might have achieved at Test level. He finally retired in 1964 after scoring over 22,000 runs and ever since has been coach at Stewart's and Melville College in Edinburgh.

Gilbert Parkhouse – the Club's leading batsman during the 1950s. (Western Mail)

arguably unfair reputation of being fallible against the quick bowlers, and it was eight long years before he was selected for England again.

Glamorgan put the disappointments of 1950 behind them as they rose up to fifth place the following year. Just four Championship matches were lost as Wooller rebuilt the team's confidence, and by the end of the summer it was suggested that the team of 1951 were a potential Championship-winning side. This view was put forward after the Welshmen became the only county side to beat South Africa on their tour, inside two days at Swansea. Dudley Nourse put Glamorgan in on a wet St Helen's wicket, and Wooller's side struggled to 111 shortly after lunch. Muncer top-scored with 30, and he continued to be a thorn in the Springboks' side when they batted before tea. The off-spinner took five for 9 as the tourists slumped to 34 for seven by the interval. Mansell and Rowan provided resolute resistance during the final session, but South Africa were eventually dismissed also for 111. The Welsh batsmen fared little better in their second innings, as the top started to come off the wicket, and eventually reached 147 after some lusty blows from Wooller and Pleass. Few people fancied Glamorgan's chances, and at 54 for no wicket the tourists seemed on course for an easy win when they took tea on the second day.

However, they collapsed to 83 all out in the hour or so after tea as Muncer took four for 10 and McConnon six for 10, including a hat-trick, aided by some typically outstanding catching by the close fielders. Wooller led by example, standing so close at silly mid-on he could almost pick the batsmen's pockets. He took one amazing catch in this position, after stopping a firm on-drive from Van Ryneveld and then breathtakingly clutching the rebound inches from the ground. Even Parkhouse, who was nursing a jarred wrist, took two catches whilst substituting on the field for Emrys Davies, including Rowan off a skier, much to the delight of the large crowd, who could hardly believe the turn around in the game after tea. Thousands of people ran onto the field when the last wicket fell, and carried Wooller and his spinners shoulder high from the field. This was followed by scenes reminiscent of Bournemouth in 1948 as the jubilant supporters full of Welsh 'hwyl' massed in front of the pavilion and gleefully sang songs of praise.

The off-spin partnership of Muncer and McConnon was a major influence on Glamorgan's rise back up the table, sharing 234 of the 452 wickets taken in all of the matches. McConnon had started the season as little more than a raw novice, but his length improved during the season and he finished with 136 victims at an average of 16. Another factor behind the return to form of the side was the more consistent batting, highlighted by the record total of 587 for eight declared

GLAMORGAN *v.* SOUTH AFRICA

Played at St Helen's, Swansea, 4 and 6 August 1951

GLAMORGAN WON BY 64 RUNS

GLAMORGAN	FIRST INNINGS		SECOND INNINGS	
E. Davies	c Van Ryneveld b Mansell	19	c Endean b Melle	9
P. B. Clift	c Fullerton b Melle	0	c Melle b Mansell	0
B. L. Muncer	lbw b Rowan	30	b Rowan	8
W. E. Jones	c Tayfield b Mansell	13	c Rowan b Mansell	10
A. J. Watkins	c Mansell b Rowan	26	run out	11
*W. Wooller	c Nourse b Mansell	1	c Mansell b Rowan	46
B. Hedges	c Van Ryneveld b Rowan	6	c Endean b Mansell	10
J. E. Pless	c Van Ryneveld b Mansell	1	c Fullerton b Mansell	29
J. E. McConnon	c McLean b Mansell	4	c Nourse b Rowan	0
†H. G. Davies	b Rowan	1	not out	8
D. J. Shepherd	not out	0	c Van Ryneveld b Rowan	0
Extras		10		16
Total		111		147

1st inns: 1-13, 2-39, 3-63, 4-77, 5-89, 6-105, 7-106, 8-108, 9-110
2nd inns: 1-3, 2-42, 3-48, 4-63, 5-85, 6-107, 7-130, 8-134, 9-147

BOWLING	O	M	R	W	O	M	R	W
Melle	5	0	19	1	9	0	16	1
Mansell	26	11	37	5	36	9	73	4
Rowan	21.4	7	45	4	28	14	42	4

SOUTH AFRICA	FIRST INNINGS		SECOND INNINGS	
†J. H. B. Waite	c Clift b Wooller	1	c H. Davies b McConnon	17
W. R. Endean	c Watkins b Muncer	13	c Watkins b Muncer	35
C. B. Van Ryneveld	c Shepherd b Wooller	4	c Wooller b McConnon	1
*A. D. Nourse	c Watkins b Muncer	6	c Watkins b Muncer	2
J. E. Cheetham	lbw b Muncer	2	c Watkins b McConnon	1
R. A. McLean	c Clift b Muncer	0	lbw b Muncer	10
G. H. Fullerton	b Muncer	2	b McConnon	0
P. N. F. Mansell	b Wooller	21	c sub b McConnon	0
A. M. B. Rowan	not out	49	c sub b Muncer	7
H. Tayfield	c Wooller b Muncer	0	not out	0
M. G. Melle	b Muncer	4	c Clift b McConnon	0
Extras		9		10
Total		111		83

1st inns: 1-1, 2-12, 3-27, 4-27, 5-29, 6-33, 7-34, 8-88, 9-95
2nd inns: 1-54, 2-54, 3-61, 4-61, 5-68, 6-68, 7-68, 8-72, 9-72

BOWLING	O	M	R	W	O	M	R	W
Wooller	15	3	41	3				
Muncer	23.4	12	45	7	8.5	3	16	4
McConnon	9	3	16	0	10	2	27	6
Watkins					6	1	12	0
Shepherd					4	0	18	0

Umpires: H. L. Parkin and L. J. Todd

South Africa were chasing a fourth-innings target of 148, and few people gave Wooller's team a chance of defeating the tourists. But they pulled off a remarkable victory, thanks to fine spin bowling from Muncer and McConnon, and an outstanding display from their ring of close catchers.

153

The famous Glamorgan leg-trap, pictured during the renowned victory over the 1951 South Africans. Left to right: Allan Watkins, Harry Parkin (umpire), Jim McConnon, Phil Clift, Wilf Wooller, Jim Pleass.

against Derbyshire at the Arms Park. Emrys Davies and Parkhouse each scored centuries, followed by half-centuries from Clift, Willie Jones, Watkins and Wooller, to see Glamorgan to a comfortable win.

Allan Watkins finished the season as the County's leading run-scorer with 1,557 runs, besides taking 61 wickets and 37 catches, and he was rewarded with selection as senior professional on the MCC tour to India, Pakistan and Ceylon. He continued his fine form, finishing the tour as leading fielder and performing the unenviable job of stock bowler in the high temperatures, in addition to being the leading run scorer in the Tests. As *Wisden*'s tour correspondent wrote: 'India feared him more than anyone else. His grim determination and fighting spirit were glorious to behold.' This was particularly the case in the first Test at Delhi where Watkins batted for nine hours to save England from defeat. His unbeaten 137 was a model of immense concentration, and he was so tired towards the end of his marathon innings that his knees buckled and he sank to the ground just as one of the Indians was about to bowl.

Wooller and Clay took steps during the winter to strengthen further the Welsh county's finances through the formation of the Glamorgan Supporters Club. This auxilliary association, quite independent of the county club, was created to run a Pools competition, along the lines of the scheme Worcestershire had undertaken, which would raise money to boost county cricket in Glamorgan and the facilities on its major grounds. Once again, it was a successful venture and it raised enough money by 1952 to allow a new terrace with a capacity of 2,600 to be installed at the Arms Park and improvements to be made to the scoreboard at St Helen's.

The strides forward which the Club had made both on and off the field were highlighted as the 1952 season began with Glamorgan's first-ever victory at Lord's. Emrys Davies and Phil Clift shared an opening partnership of 152, but then there was a middle order collapse against Denis Compton's chinamen, and they slumped to 266 all out. However, Shepherd claimed the important wickets of Brown, Edrich and Compton before the close of play on the Saturday and then a

Allan Watkins proudly wearing his English cap and MCC sweater.

heavy period of rain over the weekend compounded Middlesex's problems. Muncer (five for 7) finished them off for 123 on the Monday morning, before Watkins hit a bold 65 as Glamorgan set the Londoners a target of 338. But the England all-rounder had not finished there – he snapped up the wickets of Edrich and Compton within the space of six balls, and after another fine spell of spin bowling from Muncer and McConnon, Glamorgan were able to celebrate a 131-run victory.

A fortnight later Kent were defeated by an innings at Pontypridd and it seemed that the Welshmen could make a sustained bid for the title. But they were dealt another cruel blow during the game with Kent when McConnon aggravated his old knee injury, ironically after a career-best innings of 63 in just 50 minutes. Sadly he was forced to miss the rest of the season, and with Pressdee still on National Service, there was no immediate replacement. McConnon's absence for much of the season stifled the Welshman's title challenge and resulted in their dropping down a couple of places in the table to finish in seventh place.

With the absence of another quality spinner, Muncer had to shoulder the lion's share of the spin bowling, but he typically rose to the occasion and performed the 'double' for the first time. Despite having to bowl over 800 overs, he amassed 1,076 runs, including a career-best 135 against Sussex which justified his promotion up the order to No 4. One of the other pleasing aspects of the season was the further development of Don Shepherd, who took 115 wickets with his fast-medium deliveries. He bowled over 900 overs and was fittingly described by 'Nomad': 'Big, strong and very willing, often bowling himself into the ground and never giving up when the going got tough on good wickets.' Indeed, it was a case of perseverance and lots of perspiration as Shepherd, with a commendable line and length, had his best season to date.

Watkins had a reasonable all-round season, scoring 1,135 runs and taking 84 wickets. He played a leading role in the win by an innings over Leicestershire at Neath, taking five for 16 with his cutters in the visitors first innings and then hitting an aggressive 107. After his excellent performances on the winter tour, Watkins played in the first three Tests of the summer. However, he failed to reproduce his best batting form, and was omitted for the last Test, in favour of the in-form Willie Watson of Yorkshire, though many felt that after his sterling efforts in India, the Welshman was unlucky to be discarded. Clift and Willie Jones also lost form and the heavy burden of batting responsibility fell onto the shoulders of Emrys Davies, who at 48 was one of the oldest players on the county circuit. Nevertheless, he produced a Peter Pan-like performance, to finish the season as leading run-scorer making over 1,700 runs without a century. He was also one of the fittest and nimblest fielders, showing no sign of his age.

The committee were disappointed that the Club registered a £70 loss at the end of the season. Although gate receipts rose to over £17,000, the total expenditure exceeded £25,000 and the Club found it increasingly expensive to take matches to Llanelli, Pontypridd, Neath, Newport and Ebbw Vale. The officials had already raised the admission prices in an attempt to cover these rising costs and a further increase in prices was likely to deter people from coming to watch the team. Consequently, the committee discussed ways of subsidising their expenses in taking matches around the county, and contacted the Steel Company of Wales, who had just financed the construction of a purpose-built sports complex at Margam, close to their successful Port Talbot works. A financial package was agreed and the committee allocated the Whitsun Bank Holiday fixture in 1953 with the Gentlemen of Ireland to the Margam ground. Sadly, the experiment failed as the pitch was not up to first-class standard; a heavy spell of rain washed out the first day's play, and when the game eventually got under way, batting proved to be a nightmare. The highest individual score on either side was 22, and a total of 35 wickets fell for the addition of only 310 runs, as the match ended in a soggy draw.

A few critics had scoffed at Wooller's claims about the 1953 playing staff being as strong as the 1948 squad, but they were forced to eat their words in the first half of the summer as the team occupied a position close to the top of the table. This was the direct result of the restoration to full fitness of McConnon and the return to form of the middle order, especially Willie Jones, who scored over 1,200 runs in his benefit season. The opening game of the season at St Helen's was an early confirmation of Wooller's faith in his team, as Worcestershire were beaten by just one run in one of the most exciting finishes in the Club's history. The visitors had been set 194 in 145 minutes, and after only an hour's batting they had raced to 83 for two. Don Keynon seemed well set, but when on 56 he was bowled by Shepherd, and the Welsh seamers were able to tie down the Worcestershire batsmen. They lost wickets at steady intervals, and entered the final half hour still needing 55 to win, with two wickets remaining. They started to put the shutters up against the quicker bowlers, so Wooller brought on his spinners in a desperate bid to secure the last two wickets. The gamble seemed to have backfired as Whitehead hit McConnon for 31 in three overs to put Worcestershire within four runs of victory, but then he tried to finish the game in the grand manner and was well caught by Parkhouse on the boundary ropes. Wooller brought back Shepherd against the last pair, and the young bowler justified his captain's faith by bowling Hugo Yarnold with the fourth ball of the final over.

A series of large victories in May and June put Glamorgan on top of the table. Kent were beaten by an innings on a green Cardiff wicket, with Ken Lewis taking six wickets and Wooller eleven, whilst Essex were beaten by a similar margin at Llanelli after Watkins had compiled a flawless century and McConnon had claimed eleven wickets. June ended with Glamorgan's sixth victory and their first-ever over Yorkshire. The Tykes looked in a good position at 190 for four, batting first on a slow Arms Park wicket, but they lost their last six wickets for 28 runs as Wooller took the new ball. Glamorgan's early batsmen also struggled and at 85 for five the visitors must have been confident of a useful first-innings lead. But Wooller was in one of his defiant moods with the bat, and he occupied the crease for nearly four hours, and together with Pleass and McConnon guided Glamorgan to a first-innings lead of 59. By now the ball was starting to turn, and McConnon fully exploited the conditions, taking seven for 40 as Yorkshire slumped to 99 all out. Illingworth caused a few flutters in Welsh hearts by sending back both openers with only 11 runs on the board, but some sturdy blows by Willie Jones saw the side home by eight wickets.

A 37-run win at Trent Bridge kept Glamorgan at the top of the table at the start of July and fuelled speculation that the Welshmen could become County Champions. However, these dreams were dashed as they managed only one more victory in the last 15 matches, and finished up in tenth place. This abrupt turnabout in form was partly caused by yet another series of injuries, in particular to Wooller, who damaged tendons in his leg and missed several matches. Not only was he the inspirational driving force behind the team, but he was having by far his best season and with over 1,100 runs and 80 wickets, was in sight of the coveted double. Just to make matters worse, Watkins injured his knee against Sussex and missed the last four games, whilst Muncer suffered a groin strain and missed over a month. Clift, Pleass and Shepherd all lost form towards the end of the season, and the Welshmen looked a shadow of their former selves in the closing games. Indeed, Somerset amassed 458 for eight in the game at Weston-super-Mare in mid-August, after having been dismissed for just 100 and 150 earlier in the season by the Welsh bowlers.

Despite the sharp decline in August, Wooller and Clay were fairly pleased about the way the season had gone. Apart from signing Brian Edrich, from Lancashire, they did not panic into hiring talent from other counties and stuck to their hope of having an all-Welsh XI regularly turning out for the Club. They were delighted when the Supporters Club donated £10,000 towards the creation of a purpose-built Indoor School. The committee discussed where this new complex could be sited – there was no room at either St Helen's or the Arms Park, so the officials accepted the offer from Neath CC of a site at The Gnoll.

The construction of the Indoor School at Neath considerably improved the coaching facilities available in the West, and solved the problems of having to use a corridor in the North Stand at Cardiff. The latter had been a satisfactory stop-gap, but it was draughty and unheated in the winter months, and was not an ideal environment in which a youngster could learn the rudiments of the game. Jim Pleass was one of the coaches who worked there, but as he recollects, the sub-zero temperatures were just one of the hazards: 'This narrow space was some hundred feet in the air, so besides nearly dying of exposure, a coach often suffered from severe vertigo!' The cold air did not help the concentration of the youngsters in Pleass's charge, so in an effort to grab their attention, he would go into the net, without any pads or protection, to show them how it should be done. But one night Pleass was hit in the 'nether regions' by a ball and collapsed in a writhing heap. The youngsters carried their tutor down the six flights of stairs into the rugby physiotherapist's room at the bottom of the stand, hoping to find something which could ease Pleass' pains. But they couldn't see anything suitable and stood around dithering about what to do. Pleass by now had regathered some of his composure, but his pains were not being helped by the youngsters' indecision, so he uttered the infamous words 'Don't rub them, count them!'

The hapless Pleass soon recovered and along with the other 'invalids', reported fully fit for the 1954 season. For once the team was not hit by injuries, and by finishing in fourth place, they showed what could be achieved when everyone was available. McConnon, Wooller and Watkins all took over 100 wickets, with the latter pair achieving the 'double'. The season began with three good victories on Welsh soil. Firstly, Shepherd took a career-best nine for 47 as Northants were beaten by 262 runs at the Arms Park, and then Watkins hit a superb 170 as Leicestershire lost by ten wickets at Swansea. This was followed by a comfortable win over Warwickshire at Stradey Park, as Parkhouse and Bernard Hedges, a young batsman from Pontypridd, both scored centuries and shared a partnership of 219.

However, the best victories were undoubtedly achieved away from home, with the powerful Surrey team being defeated by 110 runs at The Oval. A victory seemed remote on the first day as Tony Lock tore the heart out of the Welsh batting, taking eight for 36 as Glamorgan made 95. However, there was a tenacious fight back and some good bowling by Wooller and Watkins restricted Surrey to a 31-run lead. After some sensible batting by Jones and Pleass, Surrey were left chasing 249 on the final day. However, it was McConnon's turn to exploit the wicket and he took seven for 23 to dismiss Surrey for 76. The strong Derbyshire side were also beaten by ten wickets at Chesterfield. Glamorgan gained a 40-run lead on first innings and then

The Glamorgan team take the field in 1954 for their match with Pakistan at St Helen's. Left to right: Willie Jones, George Shaw, Jim Pressdee, Allan Watkins, Wilf Wooller, Jim McConnon, Haydn Davies, Gilbert Parkhouse, Jim Pleass and Don Shepherd. Bernard Hedges is the 'missing' 11th man!

Watkins took seven for 28 in a fine spell between lunch and tea to settle the outcome, as Derbyshire made just 58, with six of their batsmen failing to score.

Season 1954 saw the retirement of Emrys Davies, some 30 years after his debut. It came in a sudden and dramatic way at Peterborough early in July at a time when Frank Tyson was building up a reputation as one of the fastest bowlers on the county circuit. Northants knew of the form shown by the Welsh spinners, so the Glamorgan team were not surprised to find a green wicket at Peterborough, ideal for 'The Typhoon'. He lived up to this nickname by bowling Davies with a scorching delivery in his opening over; the 50-year-old stalwart quietly returned to the pavilion, took off his gloves and cap, unbuckled his pads and then, with tears in his eyes, told Wooller: 'Skipper, I am finished. I can no longer see the ball.' The rest of the team were speechless, but Davies was true to his word and never batted again for the Club, and at the end of the season became a first-class umpire. Muncer and Hever also left the Club at the end of the year, primarily to give the promising Welsh youngsters like Pressdee greater opportunities in the first team. Muncer's Benefit Year was 1954, and he collected over £3,500 before becoming a coach at Lord's.

That Watkins and Wooller both achieved the 'double' was a major factor in Glamorgan maintaining their good form during the season. It was the first time that the captain had achieved the feat, and he passed both the 1,000 run and 100 wicket mark in the match with Warwickshire at Edgbaston. When Wooller claimed his hundredth victim, the Warwickshire chairman, Alec Hastilow, walked out to the wicket with a tray of vintage champagne and drank a glass with Wooller to celebrate him becoming the first (and only) Glamorgan amateur to achieve this all-round feat.

SHOULD WOOLLER STAY?

THE 1954 SEASON ENDED in encouraging fashion with McConnon's selection for the last two Tests of the summer against Pakistan. He made an encouraging debut, taking three wickets at Old Trafford, and was widely tipped to gain a place on the winter tour to Australia. McConnon did not share this optimism, and when news came through that he had ben selected, McConnon was crossing London to catch a train to Southampton for Glamorgan's end of season game with Hampshire. He arrived at the hotel still unaware of his honour and was utterly speechless when the receptionist congratulated him and passed on some telegrams. The news only sank in when the rest of the team arrived and held an impromptu party to celebrate in the hotel bar!

However, McConnon had little to celebrate on tour and, like Parkhouse before him, met with mixed fortunes in Australia. The spinner failed to play in any of the Tests after some modest performances in the State games were followed by a couple of muscle strains. He got himself fit again shortly after Christmas, but then at Hobart he broke the little finger in his right hand whilst stopping a fierce drive from Neil Harvey. It was a nasty break and McConnon went to see a specialist, who told him that he would not be fit until the closing weeks of the tour at the end of March. Consequently, McConnon opted to fly home, rueing his luck in foreign countries, as he had returned early the previous winter with a leg injury whilst touring India with the Commonwealth XI.

But 1955 did not turn out to be McConnon's year. Although he regained both his place in the Glamorgan team and his confidence, he broke a bone in his left hand after falling heavily in the field on the first day of the game with Essex at Pontypridd in mid-July. He was forced to sit on the sidelines once again, and pondered on his future, doubting whether professional cricket could offer him security. The Club's officials insisted, quite correctly, that he underwent a medical before being offered a new contract. But the spinner's morale after six months of bad luck was at a low ebb and he doubted their motives, and decided instead to go into business in Lancashire and play as the pro for Burnley.

McConnon's absence for half the season was a major factor in the club's fall back to 16th place in 1955, their lowest position since before the war. Emrys Davies' consistency was also missed, and Parkhouse and Jones were the only batsmen in any real form. The team showed a glimpse of their best form during July, when they registered their first-ever win in Yorkshire. It was even more remarkable bearing in mind that the team had just lost to both Hampshire and Leicestershire, had scraped a draw at Derby, and were without the services of Wooller, who had picked up a knee injury. A victory seemed remote as Glamorgan only just avoided the follow on after Yorkshire had amassed 381 for six. The Welshmen were set 333 on the final day, but slumped to 166 for five and a defeat looked the likeliest result. But their fortunes finally took a swing for the better when Pleass was dropped before he had scored. It proved to be a costly mistake as the Cardiff batsman went on to score his maiden century, after nine years of county cricket, and together with McConnon and Pressdee saw Glamorgan home to a famous and unlikely victory by four wickets.

The loss of four experienced players within a short space of time led to the introduction of several fresh faces. The club officials resisted the temptation to hire players from other counties and selected instead several young colts from the second eleven. Don Ward, a 21-year-old batsman and off-spinner was given an extended run in the first team, whilst debuts were given to Alan Rees, a 17-year-old batsman from Port Talbot and Hugh Davies, a promising all-rounder from West Wales. Another person to come into the side late in the season was Tony Lewis, a 17-year-old batsman who had an outstanding batting record while at Neath Grammar School.

A close-knit team spirit had been forged by the Glamorgan players of the early 1950s and their dressing room, full of wise old professionals, must have been a daunting place for the schoolboy amateurs like Lewis to enter. Wooller's team had been their idols and most of the youngsters were in awe of the captain after all he had achieved on and off the field for the County. Lewis had never met the captain and others of the team face-to-face before his debut, so he was not quite sure what to expect when he entered the Arms Park changing room. To his surprise, he found his heroes having a heated debate over what they should do against Leicestershire and the quality of the Cardiff wicket. Tony remembers that 'the shouting ended with a blast from the skipper in my direction "Hello Tony, welcome to the madhouse"'. However, Lewis had an even greater shock when a few hours later he was out first ball to the wily Jack Walsh!

The loss of McConnon and Muncer within the space of a couple of months was a serious blow to the spin attack. Fortunately, Pressdee made excellent progress in his first full season after demobilisation, topping the bowling averages with 72 wickets at a cost of 19 and holding on to 42 catches in the leg trap, a feat which brought him his county cap. His finest performance came in an extraordinary game with Middlesex at the Arms Park. Glamorgan collapsed on the second day against the spin of Titmus and Young on a rough dry wicket and

Middlesex were left a modest target of 145. Nevertheless, they found the going hard against Pressdee and limped slowly towards their target. At 110 for five it still seemed they would win inside two days, but then Watkins took two quick wickets, and Wooller claimed the extra half-hour. His optimism was justified as the young slow left-armer, who had been bowling for nearly 3½ hours, took two further wickets.

The tension mounted as the Middlesex tail edged their way closer to the target, but Wooller had faith in the young spinner and called him up to bowl the final over of the day, with Middlesex needing six to win and Glamorgan just one wicket. But after a marathon spell he was unable to deal the final blow, and Jack Young nudged two two's and a single, and stumps were drawn with the scores level. Five hundred spectators were admitted free of charge the next morning to see the outcome. Play lasted for only 52 seconds as Young hit Watkins's third ball of the morning to the boundary to secure a one-wicket victory. Despite the defeat, Pressdee was able to take great pride from his return of 35-13-47-4, reflecting his control and accuracy.

Towards the end of the summer, Shepherd changed styles and formed a useful spin partnership with Pressdee. Shepherd's decision to become a spinner came about as a result of a 'floppy' wrist which prevented him from hitting the seam regularly. He had taken 79 wickets the previous season, but by August he only had 40 to his credit. Shepherd sought advice from Wooller and Haydn Davies, and spent many hours experimenting in the nets with off-cutters. The change proved a success and he took ten for 85 in the final game of the season against Warwickshire at Neath, much to the delight of the captain, who had played a leading role in the switch.

The brunt of the bowling in 1955 was undertaken by Watkins, an ever-willing workhorse who delivered over 950 overs of either fast left-arm seam or slower cutters, depending on the nature of the wicket. He was rewarded with 113 wickets to achieve the 'double' once again, and many believed that he was a better cricketer than when he had appeared for England. There were calls for his return to the Test team, but despite Wooller's elevation to the selection panel, Watkins was overlooked for the 1955 Test series. However, at the end of the season, he was appointed senior professional on the MCC 'A' team's tour to Pakistan. Watkins appeared in the first two unofficial Tests against Pakistan without success, and failed to keep his place for the final two 'Tests'. In all he scored only two half-centuries and claimed only seven wickets at a cost of over 40 apiece, on what turned out to be an unhappy tour for most of the MCC party.

The committee realised that one of the problems in 1955 had been the lack of experienced batsmen, and they accepted that they would

Jim Pressdee in action during a practice session at the Arms Park.
(Western Mail)

have to strengthen the side by signing players from other teams. They chose Louis Devereux, the former Middlesex and Worcestershire batsman, plus 36-year-old Dick Horsfall from Essex. With a more solid-looking batting line-up on paper, it came as no surprise to see the side rise to 13th place. It could have been an even greater improvement had Horsfall not been forced to return to London midway through the season with a nervous complaint, which caused him to enter hospital and retire from cricket. He was not the only player to leave the staff during 1956, as Jim Pleass, who had made a paltry 99 runs in his 11 innings, finally gave up his bid to gain a regular place in the team and took up a business appointment.

There were other reasons causing the team to remain in the lower half of the table. Parkhouse and Hedges were the only batsmen to show any real semblance of form during the season. Jones and Edrich had disappointing seasons, whilst Watkins failed to pass 1,000 runs for the first time since the war. Clift was still troubled by illness and injury, so Wooller moved up to open with Parkhouse, though the captain failed to establish himself in this position. The bowling was also thin, with Pressdee having a disappointing season with only 31 wickets, losing both form and confidence. Injuries also played a role once again, with Hugh Davies chipping an ankle at Hove, causing him to miss 16 games, whilst Ken Lewis broke down with a serious leg injury.

Several new faces emerged in the bowling attack, including Frank Clarke, a fast bowler from St Fagan's, and Peter Walker, a young left-arm spinner, who had been born in Bristol. His family had emigrated to South Africa, and Walker had impressed Allan Watkins on one of his coaching visits to Johannesburg. Walker had spent a couple of years in the Merchant Navy, before hitch-hiking his way to South Wales in 1952 to see his grandfather who worked for the *Western Mail*. The youngster decided to try his luck in cricket and like his father many years before, joined the Cardiff club. Allan Watkins remembered him, and recommended him to the County officials when Walker walked into the Club's offices and asked for a trial.

The only crumb of comfort as the season went by was the almost miraculous transformation of Don Shepherd into a top-class off-spinner. He was the first bowler in the country to take over a hundred wickets, and finished up with 168 at a cost of only 14, the best seasonal haul for the Club since 1937. His finest performance of the year came at the Arms Park in June, where he bowled Glamorgan to an eight-wicket win over Hampshire, taking twelve for 64. Later in the season, he took ten wickets in the matches against both the Combined Services and Leicestershire. He also played a leading role in Glamorgan's win at Bournemouth which rekindled memories of 1948. Hampshire needed to make 293 in 140 minutes on a damp wicket, but they mustered only 90 as Shepherd returned the remarkable figures of 16-11-6-4.

The problems of the club intensified when George Lavis tragically died at the end of July after a short illness. It was the hardest blow of the summer, as the Club lost their highly rated coach, and the person who had guided the development of many of the youngsters in the first team. J. B. G. Thomas summed up the situation by writing: 'Throughout South Wales and Monmouthshire, young players will feel deeply the loss of a kindly tutor and a helpful adviser. In all my travels, I have never met a more sensitive or kinder sportsman.' A suitable replacement was found when Clift, who himself had been dogged by poor health, decided to retire and take over the duties of coaching organiser with Brian Edrich as his assistant.

Season 1956 proved an unhappy one for the Welsh club, and for the first time there was some criticism in the Press of Wooller's tactics. Some harsh words were written about Glamorgan's approach in the match at Hove, after they had put Sussex in on a well-grassed wicket.

George Lavis, one of the club's finest coaches.

167

PHIL CLIFT

Phil Clift has been one of the most loyal servants of the Club, filling a number of capacities over the past 50 years. He joined the staff in 1936, and the following year made his first-class debut. He quickly established himself as an attractive opener, and so impressed was Don Bradman in 1948 that he described Clift as one of the best prospects in the country. He was also an excellent fielder close to the bat, and was a vital member of the leg trap which steered Glamorgan to their first Championship in 1948.

However, Clift's career was dogged by bouts of illness, and an operation in the 1950s took the edge from his batting. He retired in 1955 with over 6,500 runs to his name, and became the County's coach. During the winter months, he tirelessly ran the indoor schools at Cardiff and Neath, and organised and captained the second eleven and colts team. Almost every young Glamorgan cricketer between the 1950s and 1970s came under Phil's paternal wing, and he established himself as one of the best coaches in the country.

Phil also assisted his great friend Wilf Wooller with the administration and was appointed Assistant Secretary in 1972. It was inevitable that Phil would eventually succeed Wooller as Secretary, and he held that office between 1978 and 1983. He has maintained his links with the club after his retirement, by scoring for the first and second elevens, besides helping to manage the Glamorgan Under-19 team.

Phil Clift, who has given a lifetime of service to Glamorgan cricket both on and off the field.

Contrary to Wooller's expectations, the home team were able to amass 379 for seven and then bowled out Glamorgan for just 64 after a rainstorm on the second morning had livened up the wicket. They followed on 315 behind, but batting was easier a second time around, with Wooller and Parkhouse occupying the crease for five hours in an opening stand of 135. Glamorgan eventually made 200 for one to save the game, with Wooller 79 not out after batting for 400 minutes. Robin Marlar, the Sussex captain tried everything he could to dislodge the Welsh captain, delivering lobs and using all of his team as bowlers. Wooller's stoic defiance was not greatly appreciated by the Sussex supporters and was slow handclapped by the crowd. He was booed off the ground, but in the face of such a deficit, his obvious approach was to save the game rather than set Sussex a target.

Sadly, the incident did not end there, as the Sussex committee lodged a protest with the MCC, remembering that the previous year Glamorgan had taken 123 overs to score 256. There were also some articles in the cricketing press criticising Wooller's reluctance to press on for runs and declaring once the deficit had been erased. These claims of unsporting behaviour rose to the surface once again in the game with Essex at the Arms Park. The Welsh captain warned Gordon Barker, the Essex opener, three times for backing up too far and on the fourth occasion, Wooller removed the bails as he was about to bowl. Nevertheless, Glamorgan were set a sporting target of 180 in 108 minutes on the final day. Wooller told his team to go for quick runs and at 162-4 a rare Glamorgan victory seemed imminent. But Watkins, Ward, Haydn Davies and Shepherd were all dismissed in quick succession, and five runs were still needed when Ken Lewis came to the wicket in the penultimate over. Pressdee scraped a single and then with two balls left, a delivery from Preston went for four byes and Glamorgan had won by one wicket.

Glamorgan's fortunes took a turn for the better when McConnon agreed to rejoin the club. He had helped Burnley to win the Lancashire League, taking 52 wickets at an average of just 6.8. This success rekindled his enthusiasm for the game and he was approached by Warwickshire about a return to the county circuit. But Glamorgan had retained his registration, and after hearing of his success, they offered him a new contract, plus a guarantee of a benefit. He accepted these terms and took 99 wickets to show that he had lost little of his skill. He formed a fine partnership with Shepherd, and the spinners were instrumental in the defeat of Lancashire at Old Trafford, and the comprehensive win over Somerset at St Helen's.

These were two of four successive victories at the end of May and early June which renewed the team's belief in their abilities after a difficult couple of years. This became apparent at Trent Bridge at the end of June when they won by 27 runs after having to follow on. Half centuries from Willie Jones, Devereux and McConnon saw Glamorgan to 295 and then Notts were dismissed for 75 as Wooller and Hugh Davies ran through their batting. They proved that it was not a fluke by beating Notts a fortnight later at Llanelli with Hedges making a fine century.

Another batch of promising youngsters made their debuts during the season, including Alan Jones, a 20-year-old left-hander from Velindre in the Swansea Valley. He had made a favourable impression with the second eleven, but like Tony Lewis, he began his county career with a duck at Bristol. But professional cricket is a hard game, and these promising young colts had a tough baptism as the club slipped down the table after a promising start to the season. Northants and Somerset both won by ten wickets, whilst Middlesex won by seven wickets and Gloucestershire by 266 runs. There was also an embarrassing defeat against Yorkshire at Cardiff; set 173, they appeared to be cruising at 156 for five, but Illingworth, Trueman and Pickles ran through the lower order and Yorkshire scraped home by four runs.

Morale in the dressing room dropped as the team slid down the table in the second half of the season, and not for the last time, off-the-field events and rumours captured as many headlines in the local press as the team's playing performance. The first involved the question of Glamorgan finally acquiring a ground of their own. Wooller and Clay had dreamed of a Welsh Lord's where Glamorgan could have a proper HQ, an Indoor School to help bring on the youngsters and a clubhouse to show off their mementos. The officials of Swansea Corporation had been sounded out, but they were not willing to sell St Helen's, whilst there was no chance of buying the Arms Park. Some of the Glamorgan committee had become disillusioned with the Cardiff ground, feeling that the rental was too high and complaining about the lack of space for new stands to the south or east of the cricket ground, because of the tennis courts and bowling green belonging to Cardiff Athletic Club. It was a case of too many large eggs being forced into a small basket, and just to add spice to the debate, there were dark mutterings about the quality of the wicket. Five of the six matches played there in 1957 ended inside two days, with an estimated loss of £500 in gate receipts.

During the summer, a sub-committee was formed to discuss the feasibility of acquiring a site a mile or so to the north of the city centre on land in Sophia Gardens which belonged to Cardiff Corporation. The Welsh capital was due to stage the Commonwealth Games in 1958 and had considered a recreational complex in the Gardens and a racecourse in the surrounding fields. The sub-committee's approach

An aerial view of the Arms Park in the centre of Cardiff, with the rugby stadium and the cricket ground beyond the North Stand. In the top left-hand corner is the Castle which belonged to the Marquess of Bute, the Club's first President. (Western Mail)

was successful and a provisional agreement was reached on a 50-year lease at £300 pa for a practice ground at Sophia Gardens, with possibilities of further developments once a suitable wicket had been created. It seemed a good offer, when the club were paying around £500 each year for the use of the Arms Park, but the West Area of the county committee opposed the scheme, fearing that it would mean fewer matches at Swansea, or even playing all games at Cardiff.

The matter was hotly debated during the autumn and winter, and a special committee meeting was held at Bridgend at the end of January to try to resolve the issue. Johnnie Clay summed up the feelings of many members by telling the meeting that 'all we want is a good cricket side and the object in going to Sophia Gardens would be for that purpose. It would be invaluable as a nursery ground; it could be considered as a county ground later.' Feelings were running high, so Colonel Bevan, the Chairman, quelled the fears of the West by saying that they 'could be absolutely certain there would be no change in the allocation of fixtures. The debate should be dispassionate and the distribution of matches should be ruled out of the argument.' His comments were persuasive and the committee agreed to proceed with the negotiations to obtain a ground at Sophia Gardens.

However, it wasn't just the West-East friction that caused heated debate. Wooller did not exactly see eye to eye with some of the committee who had close affiliations with Cardiff Athletic Club. They did not like the thought of a move from the Arms Park, and it upset many of the Athletic Club's senior members who knew about what their organisation had done in the past for Glamorgan. A delegation from the Athletic Club met with the Lord Mayor of Cardiff, who used his casting vote at the Cardiff Corporation's meeting to terminate the Sophia Gardens scheme. It was a severe blow to both Wooller and the club – the one opportunity to acquire and develop a major ground and club headquarters during the first hundred years.

This was not the only matter under discussion during the winter months. Wooller was considering his playing future, realising that at the age of 44 his best years were behind him and that he was increasingly becoming prone to niggling injuries. With a host of talented youngsters emerging, he told the committee during 1957 that he would stand down if a suitable replacement could be found to lead the side. Some officials believed that one of the professionals could take over; Haydn Davies had done a good job as a deputy, but he too was nearing the end of his career. With Watkins also getting on in years, it was suggested that one of the younger pros could be groomed for the job during 1958. However, the senior committee members felt that the club should stick to the traditional policy of an amateur captain. But the only other amateur registered by the club was Tony Lewis and he was still on National Service. To get an amateur captain, the Club were going to have to look outside their boundaries, so they placed adverts in newspapers and magazines. Some of the students at Oxford and Cambridge were considered, including Ted Dexter, the Cambridge captain for 1958, John Pretlove and Dennis Silk, but there was little response.

The committee had increasingly become populated by successful club cricketers, businessmen and industrialists, few of whom had any first-class experience. Many were more familiar to the ways of commerce and some had fallen out with Wooller over his forthright view that the Club's purse strings should be kept as tight as possible and that the finances should not be gambled with. The Hove 'incident' in 1956 and the flurry of letters from Sussex had embarrassed some of the committee and they were upset by another storm in a teacup in the game at The Oval in 1957. It came when Peter May drove the ball to mid-on where Hedges dived and appeared to catch the ball. May began to walk back to the pavilion, but then realised that Hedges had not caught the ball; by the time he realised his mistake, the ball had been quickly returned to Wooller, who whipped off the bails with May well out of his ground. The Surrey supporters booed Wooller but May exonerated the Welsh captain by saying that under similar circumstances he would have done the same thing. Nevertheless, there was a torrent of criticism from the London Press with renewed claims of bad sportsmanship, whilst E. M. Wellings claimed in the London *Evening News* that: 'Glamorgan have become the most unpopular county team in my memory.'

Wooller's critics also alleged that his presence was not conducive to the development of the youngsters, many of whom were afraid of him, and it was argued in some quarters that through nerves or fear, the colts failed to play at their best or were simply not interested in playing for the first eleven. Wooller had also lost some friends over the abortive attempts to secure a nursery at Sophia Gardens, so his announcement to stand down was seen by the anti-Wooller faction as an opportunity to ease him out of the limelight. It was also hoped in some quarters that he would give up his duties as the Club Secretary, with some people feeling that Wooller was not prepared to devote himself full time to the Secretary's job if he carried on in just this capacity because of his interests in journalism and broadcasting. These people conveniently forgot that Wooller had undertaken these outside jobs for some time whilst captaining the team, without ever impairing his efficiency on the field!

Wooller knew of these feelings against him and the search for a replacement, so in March 1958 he wrote to the committee saying that 'the real issue is whether the County wants me to remain on a permanent basis – it must be permanent (subject to cash resources, of course) – or whether they think it unnecessary.' Not everyone on the committee had an axe to grind with Wooller, and there were several who felt it would be a great shame if his 20 years of playing experience and knowledge were lost, particularly when there was no obvious successor. But they were in the minority and at their meeting at the end of June, the committee offered Wooller a post of part-time consultant/adviser at a salary of £500.

In short, they wanted Wooller's advice and guidance, but cut his salary in half and stripped him of his authority. Naturally after all his efforts after the war and in 1948, Wooller was deeply upset and tendered his resignation as captain-secretary with effect from the end of the 1958 season. Soon afterwards, Johnnie Clay, his fervent supporter, followed suit, saying: 'I regard this decision about Wooller as a tragic blunder, made by a committee out of a combination of ignorance and personal prejudice.'

Whilst all this was going on, Norman Riches, the chairman of the selection committee, had continued to contact several people about the captaincy in 1959. One of the people approached was A. C. 'Tolly' Burnett, a 33-year-old science master at Eton who had won a blue at Cambridge back in 1949. Despite the fact that he had not played first-class cricket for nine years, the committee announced on 23 July that Burnett would be joining the club during August. Wooller had agreed to continue as captain until the end of the season in order to help groom his replacement and ensure a smooth change-over rather than leave the Club high and dry without a leader. But, despite still holding the post of Secretary, he had not been told of the negotiations with Burnett, and was upset that the Club had gone behind his back. He was even more angry when Burnett told him, other members of the team and even Edgar Truran, their faithful scorer, that he had been offered the captaincy for 1959 and it was merely up to him to decide whether to accept the offer.

It became abundantly clear that some of the officials were hoping that they could dispense with Wooller's services if Burnett gained a sabbatical from Eton. But the captain was not the only member of the playing staff whose future was in question. Others became worried by the behind-the-scenes manoeuvres as Burnett sent secret reports on the team to senior club officials. Some quite naturally found this unnerving and unsettling, and both Willie Jones and Haydn Davies announced their retirements. It was a great pity that these loyal servants should decide to leave, especially Haydn Davies who had appeared in 254 consecutive Championship games between 1947 and 1957. But with all the arguments going on and rumours flying around, both felt it was an apt time to finish their careers.

However, Burnett did not have a happy return to the first-class game. He made nine on his debut against the New Zealanders and made a mere 62 runs in his other ten innings to finish with an average of just 6.4. He led the team on two occasions, but without success, and decided to return to Eton at the end of the season. Despite all the rows, Wooller offered to stay on for one more season, a move which spoke volumes for his commitment to the Club, but the committee rejected the offer, and remained adamant that a replacement would eventually be sought.

So at the end of the season the Club were left without a captain for 1959, plus a lot of intrigue about the future, and acrimony over the parlous state of affairs. Wooller had built up a successful playing unit, but now the off-the-field situation had brought about a deterioration in events on the field. The season had begun with victories in May over Notts, Kent and Northants, but as the rumours and controversy grew, the team went to pieces, winning just one match between 31 May and 12 August, to finish in a disappointing 15th place. Injuries to Wooller

*Haydn Davies takes a fine catch off Allan Watkins' bowling to dismiss Pretlove of Kent in the game at Gravesend in 1957. Gilbert Parkhouse is the jubilant slip fielder. (*Western Mail*)*

and McConnon did not help, neither did the loss of form of Parkhouse or the lack of progress by Don Ward or Billy Davies, a young bowler from Barry.

There were a few bright spots, notably the form of Walker and Pressdee with the bat, and the emergence of 22-year-old Brian Evans as an opening bowler. But these were small rays of hope as 1958 turned into a summer of discontent. Many members were unhappy with what was happening, and their feelings of displeasure rose to the surface in August after the game with Lancashire at the Arms Park. Wooller put the visitors in on a damp green wicket, and then stood back and saw them amass 351. Even worse was to come when Glamorgan batted, as they were quickly dismissed by Statham and Tattersall for just 26! To their relief, rain washed out the rest of the match, but soon afterwards, Ken Prickett, a member from Llanelli, began collecting the signatures of over 50 members needed to call a special meeting and sort the matter out.

On 31 October 1958 the first ever Special General Meeting of the Club was held at Bridgend Town Hall with over 350 members present, and it clearly showed the groundswell of public opinion behind Wooller and the opposition to the committee's proposals. Johnnie Clay was one of the first to address the meeting, and he began by asking a simple question: 'How is the County going to fare without Wilf Wooller? This County has been wet-nursed first by Mr Turnbull and then by Mr Wooller. They have nursed the committee, who have been fairly complacent on the whole . . . the Club is going to be a ship without a rudder if Wilf Wooller goes. Who is going to look after the coaching of all the various teams? Someone who knows something about it has to be in charge . . . Mr Riches may be your answer, but what is coming is "wait until we get our new secretary-captain". But you will not get one. There is nobody suitable to step into Wooller's shoes . . . It is an absolute disaster for you to let Wilf Wooller go!'

No decisions were made at the meeting and there was a rejection by the Club's officials for a vote of no confidence in the committee. However, the evening clearly illustrated the belief amongst the rank and file members that Wooller should continue as captain-secretary, and act as an administrator when he eventually retired. After several unofficial meetings and a lot of hard thought, the committee agreed to hold a members' referendum to settle the issue once and for all. During late November and early December, the following notice was circulated to all of the members:

1. We have to inform you that a difference of opinion has arisen in the General Committee and following several meetings, a substantial majority were not in favour of retaining the services of Wilf Wooller after 31st December, 1958 as Secretary on a permanent basis at his existing remuneration of £1,000 p.a.
2. Wilf Wooller was offered alternative terms by the committee which he declined.
3. Members are asked to answer 'YES' or 'NO' to the following question:
   'Do you agree with the decision of the committee?'

The ballot papers were collected and it transpired that there was a majority of 333 against the committee, with 1,098 voting 'NO' and 765 'YES'. On hearing the result, Colonel Bevan resigned as Chairman together with ten other committee members. Wooller and Clay withdrew their resignations, and it was agreed to leave it to the new committee to be elected at the 1959 AGM to decide whether Wooller should continue as captain.

WOOLLER RETIRES AND WHEATLEY TAKES OVER

THE REAPPOINTMENT OF WOOLLER as captain-secretary for 1959 was a formality at the annual meeting in 1959. The meeting elected 23 new committee members, and Judge Rowe Harding, the former Welsh rugby international and Cambridge blue, as the new Chairman. The first task for the new body of officials was to heal the wounds that had been opened, so they publicly thanked all of the long-serving committee men who had resigned and made them life members.

The atmosphere within the Club was much healthier during the spring of 1959 and not surprisingly there was an all-round return to form. The side rose back up to sixth place in the table, and could have finished even in second place if the game with Middlesex had not ended in a draw. Parkhouse's fine batting was one reason behind the much needed rise back up the table. In all, he hit six centuries and formed a solid opening partnership with Bernard Hedges, who had moved up the order and himself made over 1,500 runs. Parkhouse's outstanding form brought him to the attention of the selectors and he was called up for the third Test against India at Headingley. He opened with Lancashire's 'Noddy' Pullar and they put on what was a record 146 for the first wicket against India. Parkhouse was eventually dismissed for 78 and kept his place for the fourth Test, when he made 17 and 49. The selectors were thinking of an opening pair for the winter tour to the Caribbean, and despite his fine reputation against the quicker bowlers, they were unsure whether or not to take him. Consequently, they tried out Raman Subba Row in place of the Welshman for the final Test. The Northamptonshire batsman made a stylish 94 and secured a place on the tour, leaving Parkhouse to muse over the winter months about playing for an unfashionable county.

Another reason behind the County's improvement was that McConnon and Shepherd each claimed over 100 wickets. They were instrumental in several comfortable wins, in particular the victory over Worcestershire at Swansea. They shared six wickets in the visitors' first innings, and then McConnon took eight for 62 in the second as Worcestershire were dismissed for 186. This was the first of 13 victories during the season – as many as in their Championship year. The second win came against the Indians at Cardiff in the middle of May and was most encouraging because Glamorgan fielded an inexperienced side because of injuries. Pressdee was promoted to No 3, but he fully justified it as he scored his maiden century. Wooller was amongst those on the injured list, so Watkins led the team and he set the tourists a target of 293 on the final day. When Datta Gaekwad and Chandra Borde were at the wicket an Indian victory seemed likely, but Gaekwad was run-out after a fine piece of fielding by Deveraux, and a collapse set in. Don Ward picked up two wickets and the Indian tail quickly folded, leaving the young Glamorgan team to celebrate a well deserved win by 51 runs.

Peter Walker also made an important contribution, maturing as an all-rounder and finishing with 79 wickets and 1,540 runs to his name, including a maiden century at Cheltenham. He also took 64 catches to beat Turnbull's County record, and ended the summer as the leading fielder in the country. He pulled off many breathtaking catches at leg slip, several of which proved to be match-winning efforts. One was against Middlesex at Swansea where the visitors were chasing 158 on the last afternoon. At 130 for nine Glamorgan seemed assured of victory, but Tilly and Hurst shared a stubborn last-wicket partnership, taking the score to 155 for nine to put Middlesex on the brink of an amazing victory. Tilly then leg-glanced McConnon for what seemed like the winning runs, but Walker took off at leg-slip and held a stunning left-hand catch at full stretch in mid air. He clung on to the ball when he hit the ground, and Glamorgan had won by three runs.

It was catches like this that brought Walker the accolade of 'the safest pair of hands in the country'. He readily admits to having developed this art whilst in the middle of the Atlantic and Pacific Oceans, rather than in the new Indoor School. As a 16-year-old he had served as a galley boy on board a ship travelling between the Persian Gulf and Los Angeles. The ship's crew, who were predominantly Finnish, used to wile away the hours on the long journey by having potato-catching competitions. Walker remembers how 'it became a matter of national pride not to miss anything that was remotely catchable. Inevitably, potatoes kept disappearing over the side until a week from port we'd run out completely, much to the annoyance of the less sporting members of the crew!'

A final factor in Glamorgan's better fortunes was that most of the players stayed fit throughout the season. A few picked up niggling injuries early on, but the only two to have major ailments were Clarke and Brian Evans, the young seamer from Clydach. This meant that Watkins and Wooller were pressed into service as opening bowlers towards the end of the season. They typically rose to the occasion, with the captain himself not being afraid to bowl long spells of fast-medium at the age of 45. One of these came at Cheltenham, where he had selected an extra batsman rather than another seamer in anticipation of a typically slow wicket at the College ground. However, when it was Glamorgan's turn to bowl, the humid weather favoured the seamers rather than the spinners. Wooller was suffering from a damaged hamstring and a sore arm, but he nevertheless was prepared to undertake the brunt of the bowling. He even soldiered on when the home team were forced to follow on, limping in to bowl off a shortened run, and hobbling off in between overs for pain killing injections and strapping for his leg. Despite all these ailments, he took four wickets in the second innings, as Glamorgan won by an innings. It was a remarkable performance by Wooller, and his courage was aptly summed up by John Evans, the team's masseur, who said: 'If he took off the strapping his leg would fall off!'

These herculean efforts took their toll however, and during the winter months Wooller realised that his playing days were finally drawing to a close, and he informed the committee that he would definitely retire at the end of the 1960 season. Those who anticipated that the Welsh captain would go out in a blaze of glory were proved wrong as he missed 12 matches due to a variety of injuries, compounded by his efforts in 1959. In all, he claimed only a dozen wickets and scored just over 600 runs, with only one half-century. During the season, the papers were full of tributes to the Glamorgan captain, with once again the best coming from John Arlott, who wrote: 'None of his friends – and few of his enemies – can quite believe they will not see him in action again. It is hard not to feel that one day when some match or other has become bogged down, there will be an explosion from the Glamorgan secretary's observation post and we shall see that towering figure plunging down the steps once more, head and shoulders thrown aggressively forward, lumbering out to take the game by the scruff of the neck, and by example and unminced words, instil urgent, combative life into it.'

Wooller's final season in charge saw Glamorgan finish in a slightly disappointing 11th place. This was mainly the result of the loss of form with the bat by Pressdee and Walker, who together managed some 2,000 runs less than in the previous year. Ironically, Walker had made a promising start to the season, enhancing his reputation as an all-rounder and outstanding fielder with a series of useful performances. A fighting fifty against Middlesex at Lord's impressed the selectors, and with Wooller's glowing comments, it came as no surprise when Walker was chosen for the first Test against South Africa at Edgbaston. He made only nine in the first innings, but top-scored in the second, with a well composed 37, and was retained for the second Test at Lord's, where he hit an attractive half-century. He made 30 in the third Test, but he had been chosen primarily for his spin bowling, and had failed to take wickets. Consequently, he was omitted to make way for new faces. He returned to the Glamorgan side, but completely lost form, making just one half-century in the remaining 20 innings and claiming only 17 wickets.

WILF WOOLLER

Wilf Wooller learnt his cricket in North Wales, playing first for Rydal School, then Denbighshire and then winning two Blues at Cambridge. He moved to work in South Wales, but found little time at first for cricket, until Maurice Turnbull, his former rugby team-mate for Cardiff, persuaded him to play for the County in 1938 and 1939. Ever since, he has lived and breathed Glamorgan cricket.

It was to Wooller whom Clay turned when the Club were rebuilding after the war, and within a couple of years, he was leading them to their first Championship success. Over the next 12 years, he was a ruthless captain, always leading from the front and never afraid to ask anyone to do a thing which he himself would not think twice about; indeed, he was ready to do anything in the side's best interest, whether it was opening the batting or the bowling, or fielding at short-leg. By sheer application, he made himself into an excellent all-rounder and a measure of both his ability and durability can be gauged from the fact that he achieved the 'double' in 1954 at the age of 41!

Wilf continued to play a leading role in the Club's affairs after retiring in 1960, acting as Secretary until 1978. However, as the Club struggled during the 1970s, his forthright views were heavily criticised and his last few years in office were filled with controversy. Nevertheless, as J. H. Morgan wrote in the 1978 *Wisden*: 'even if Wilf strolled through the corridors of cricket power with an almost arrogant air, few would question his well-informed background of the game he loves'.

Wilf Wooller — Club captain from 1947 until 1960, and a major force behind the modern development of the Welsh club.

Pressdee also lost form and confidence, especially as a bowler, and took only two wickets all season. McConnon picked up several small injuries, with the net result that Shepherd had to shoulder the brunt of the bowling, delivering almost twice as many overs as anyone else on the staff. Nevertheless, 'Shep' thrived on hard work and had a truly magnificent season in his well earned benefit year, claiming 142 wickets at 17 apiece. It was quite fitting that he should produce his best performances on his 'home' ground at St Helen's, taking eleven wickets against Warwickshire and eight for 45 against the South Africans.

Shepherd also played a leading role in the excellent win at Swansea over Yorkshire, as Glamorgan won by 72 runs to show a rare glimpse of their true form. He took five for 52 as the County Champions slumped to 177, and then combined with Don Ward to dismiss them for 144 as they unsuccessfully chased a target on the final afternoon. This was a worthy reward for Wooller's team because they had come within a hair's breadth of defeating Yorkshire a fortnight earlier at Bradford. The game had been finely poised with Yorkshire two runs short of their target and the last pair at the crease when Shepherd produced a superb delivery which completely baffled Mick Cowan, the No 11, and shaved the off stump, but the bails did not drop. The Welshmen were left to consider their bad luck as Ray Illingworth hit the winning runs in the next over.

The most pleasing aspect about the second half of the summer was the continued development of Alan Jones and Tony Lewis. Jones moved up the order to No 3 and showed he had both the temperament and technique required to bat in this position. Lewis had spent May and June as a Freshman at Cambridge, where he scored 1,307 runs, including a maiden century at Taunton. He continued in fine form on coming down, making over 600 runs in 14 appearances to earn his county cap.

The loss of form by Walker and Pressdee gave Don Ward a greater opportunity to display his talents as an off-spinner. One of his lengthier spells came in the game with Surrey at Cardiff. Harry Baldwin, the former Surrey cricketer, was standing at square-leg and just after Ward had completed a delivery he called: 'No ball'. It completely baffled the young player why Baldwin had called out because he had a perfectly legitimate action. Wooller was also puzzled, so he went over the umpire and asked why. 'Six fielders on the leg-side', he said, to which Wooller replied: 'Nonsense – we'll count them.' The umpire started counting: 'One, two, three, four, five and number six on the long-on boundary.' Wooller by now was creased up in laughter. 'Harry, you clot,' he said, 'that person on the ropes is a bloke with a white coat selling scorecards!'

The behind-the-scenes discussion over Wooller's replacement as captain was more rational than in 1958, even though the committee stuck to the principle that the new captain should not be a professional, which ruled out Allan Watkins, who had acted as captain when Wooller had been injured. Once again, the only amateur was Tony Lewis, and with his studies at Cambridge, it was out of the question for him to take over the captaincy. Consequently, the club contacted a variety of individuals and eventually agreed terms with Ossie Wheatley, the 26-year-old fast bowler from Warwickshire. A former Cambridge blue, he had impressed the Glamorgan officials by taking nine wickets against them in the match at Edgbaston, and he agreed to accept a business appointment in South Wales.

Wheatley's acquisiton marked not only the end of the 'Wooller era', but he also became the first person from outside the principality to lead the Welsh side in the Championship on a regular basis. He had an extremely hard act to follow, and only had a limited amount of captaincy experience. However, he had the support of Wooller, who agreed to remain with the Club as their Secretary. Nevertheless, Wheatley had a difficult first year in charge, with another round of injury and illness causing the team to remain in the bottom half of the table. The first blow came before the season had even started when Tony Lewis was injured playing rugby for Cambridge and had to miss the entire cricket season.

The second blow came when Allan Watkins announced his retirement at the beginning of June after 23 years of county cricket. He had been increasingly troubled by asthma and a stomach complaint, and after the Kent match at Gravesend, he decided to take a warder's post at Usk Borstal. Soon afterwards, the Club met with another setback when McConnon damaged his knee during the game with Hampshire at Swansea. Once again he sat on the sidelines and pondered on his future with the Club. It was his benefit year, and at the age of 39 he knew his best years were behind him. He was anxious to gain security for his family, and at the end of the season he also announced his retirement.

Wheatley had every reason to be satisfied that his young and often inexperienced side actually gained nine victories, including a first ever double over Surrey. Sound batting by Hedges and Parkhouse set up a five-wicket win at Ebbw Vale, whilst some penetrative bowling by Brian Evans and Peter Walker created a nine-wicket victory at The Oval. Just as encouraging were the team's performances against the Australians. The tourists enforced the follow-on in the game at the Arms Park, but a century from Pressdee, supported by Ward and young wicket-keeper David Evans, saved Glamorgan. In the match at Swansea, Shepherd and Walker bowled out the visitors for 192, but then Glamorgan collapsed to 94 for eight. In came Shepherd, and in the space of 15 minutes he hit 51, with six sixes, three fours, a two and a single. This handsomely reduced the Aussies' lead, and they eventually set Glamorgan 306 in 280 minutes. Alan Jones gave them a flying start with a fluent 70 but then heavy rain washed out the rest of the game with Glamorgan on 124 for two.

Wheatley's first season in charge had seen the start of the rebuilding process, and there was great optimism for 1962. However, they remained in 14th place as it proved to be yet another transitional year in the Club's history. They were given a great boost when Tony Lewis reported fully fit at the start of the season. He had another magnificent season, making over 1,300 runs for Cambridge University, and scoring two good centuries for Glamorgan against Notts and Sussex. Pressdee and Hedges both passed the 1,800 run mark and their good form was responsible for the handful of victories that the team recorded, including two in one week at Cardiff. First of all, they defeated Yorkshire, the eventual champions, by five wickets after Pressdee had struck an aggressive 80 not out. Later in the week, they defeated the touring Pakistanis by seven wickets; young Alwyn Harris hit a century in their first innings, and then after some hostile bowling by Wheatley and Pressdee steered Glamorgan to victory.

However, the team were still plagued by injury and loss of form; Parkhouse struggled during the early part of the season, and was hampered by a back injury. He moved down the order to No 5 but still failed to produce his best form, and in mid-July was dropped from the team for the first time in his long career. Many of the youngsters, including Euros Lewis and Billy Slade, failed to make the progress that had been anticipated, so when Wheatley, Walker and Tony Lewis were called up for the Gents and Players match, Wooller came out of retirement to play against Middlesex. Although he scored just seven runs and took a single wicket, the veteran captain typically bowed out with a final verbal blast. It was directed at Bob Gale who had scored 200 out of Middlesex's total of 434-6; as Gale departed back to the pavilion, Wooller told him: 'That's the worst bloody two hundred I've ever seen!'

The Club were dealt a couple of severe blows at the end of the season. Firstly, the Treasurer reported a fall in gate receipts to just over £5,500, the lowest since the war. The Club's expenditure had risen to over £36,000, so a sub-committee was created to find means of economising and a new membership drive was started. However, by far the hardest setback came when Peter Walker informed the club he was quitting county cricket and returning to take up a business appointment in South Africa. It was a huge shock to both the officials and the supporters, and resulted from Walker's feelings of insecurity in professional cricket which had heightened after his recent marriage.

The question of Sophia Gardens also rose to the surface again during the autumn. In November, the officials of Cardiff Athletic Club met with representatives of the Glamorgan committee to discuss the future of Cardiff Arms Park. There were problems with the quality of the playing surface at the rugby ground, and the WRU, who had long treasured the idea of a National Stadium of their own, devised a plan for a new arena near Bridgend. The news that international rugby would leave the capital city came as a bombshell to Cardiff Athletic Club. Besides a severe loss of prestige for the club, the city's shopping centre would lose thousands of pounds which were spent on international and big match days. Consequently, the Athletic Club, together with the council officials, devised an alternative scheme whereby the existing rugby stadium would be enlarged and reserved for major matches, whilst a smaller ground for other games would be built on the cricket pitch. To compensate the cricket section, the City Corporation agreed to make a ten-acre site available at Sophia Gardens, which could also be used by the tennis and hockey sections of the Athletic Club. The Glamorgan officials agreed with the proposals because at long last it would solve the problems of the shortage of space at the Arms Park, and they would be able to move to a much larger and purpose-built cricket ground, with the WRU and Athletic Club subsidising the removal costs!

The loss of Walker's services and the retirement of Ward did not augur well for the immediate future, but to everyone's delight the wheel of fortune turned the right way in 1963 and the team enjoyed their most successful year since 1948, to finish in second place behind Yorkshire. The factors behind this were Tony Lewis's availability on a full-time basis for the first time, Alan Jones's emergence as a top-class opening batsman and Pressdee's rediscovery of his bowling ability. It had been claimed that the loss of the latter's bowling had been due to over-coaching or mishandling by the Club. Whatever the cause, two winters of playing club cricket in South Africa allowed Pressdee to regain the belief in himself as a bowler, and he returned to take 104 wickets and achieve the 'double'.

The Glamorgan spinners played an important part in the rise up the table, with Shepherd, now the senior pro, and Pressdee proving to be almost unplayable on the turning wickets at Swansea. Not surprisingly there were claims from some quarters that the Welsh club were preparing their wickets especially for 'Shep' and 'Pres', and that the spinners were ineffective away from St Helen's. These views were totally disproved as the Welsh spin twins shared 19 wickets on a perfect batting wicket at Bournemouth to steer Glamorgan to a win.

Their fortunes really picked up at the end of June when Peter

Walker rejoined the Club. He had missed the competitive thrust of county cricket and his wife missed life in general in South Wales, so they returned with Walker taking up a journalist's post with a television company in Cardiff. It was just the boost the Club needed, and they responded with a purple patch in the few weeks leading up to the beginning of August. Five of the ten matches were won in convincing fashion, beginning with a comprehensive win over Worcestershire. Wheatley took ten wickets in the victory over Gloucestershire at Pontypridd, and then, at Colchester, a disciplined century by Tony Lewis coupled with fine spin bowling by Shepherd and Euros Lewis saw the Welshmen to a 23-run win over Essex.

The good run was temporarily halted by an innings defeat against Somerset on a raid-sodden wicket at Neath, but there was a welcome return to form at Glastonbury, led by Alan Jones, who scored a magnificent 187 not out in the first innings and an unbeaten 105 in the second. He continued this fine form in the tourist match at Swansea, hooking Wes Hall time and again for four after four, and his brave innings of 92 saw Glamorgan to an honourable draw.

The match with Notts at Ebbw Vale at the end of August showed that Wheatley's team had regained their confidence and the will to win. The visitors batted first on the slow wicket, and were reduced to 110 for nine as Pressdee ran through their batting with the remarkable figures of 15-12-5-6. But 'Bomber' Wells and Keith Gillhouley shared a last-wicket partnership of 60 and then the Notts spinners tied down the Glamorgan batsmen to give Notts a first innings lead of 18. Rain intervened to liven up the wicket, making Shepherd, Pressdee and Wheatley virtually unplayable. The visitors were dismissed for 44, leaving Glamorgan to score 63 for victory. A bold partnership by Alan Jones and Tony Lewis saw Glamorgan to the brink of victory, and despite the clatter of wickets, Pressdee kept a cool head to see them home by three wickets. The spinners also held the upper hand in the final game of the season as Glamorgan beat Lancashire to rise into second place in the table. Euros Lewis took six for 10 in the Lancashire first innings and Shepherd six for 35 in the second as the Welshmen won by an innings. They were aided by some excellent wicket-keeping by David Evans, who broke the County record with 89 victims and became the leading keeper in the country.

Season 1963 also saw two other landmarks in the Club's history. The first was the acquisition of their first West Indian professional, a fast bowler by the name of Tony Cordle. The 23-year-old had emigrated from Barbados to London two years before but after ten noisy and hectic days with London Transport he moved to join his brother and sister in the quieter Welsh capital. Cordle did not have a job for several weeks after moving to Cardiff, and regularly went

Alan Jones hooks against the West Indies at St. Helen's.

down to the Labour Exchange in Westgate Street, alongside the Arms
Park ground. As he climbed the stairs one day, Cordle remembers
looking out of the window and seeing 'the green turf and the cricket
scoreboard – the first friendly sight I had seen in Britain!' He joined
the Cardiff club and within a few weeks had earned the nickname of
'Speedy'. He impressed the County officials in a few second eleven
matches at the end of 1962 and joined the County on a regular basis in
1963. Sadly, Brian Evans broke down again and was forced to retire,
but it gave Cordle an opportunity to break into county cricket.

The second milestone was the club's inaugural one-day game
against Somerset at Cardiff in May. A solid century by Bernard
Hedges saw Glamorgan reach 207 for eight after their 65 overs, and

then some accurate bowling by Jeff Jones, the young left arm quick bowler, and Pressdee saw Glamorgan home by ten runs. They were drawn at home again in the second round – this time against Worcestershire at Neath, but Tom Graveney halted their progress, making a magnificent 93 as Glamorgan went down by 46 runs.

The season ended on a high note with the selection of 22-year-old Jeff Jones for the MCC tour to East Africa and India. It came as a surprise to some, but those who saw the left-armer take 58 wickets during 1963 were left in no doubt that here was a potential England fast bowler. In fact, Jones won his England cap before his county cap, by playing in the Second Test against India at Bombay, a match which earned the title the 'Cripples Test', because four of the party were injured and everyone who was fit was automatically chosen. Jones failed to take a wicket but, as *Wisden*'s correspondent remarked: 'The venture was valuable experience. He showed the will to improve and had the run-up and action necessary for success as a fast bowler.'

There was a widespread feeling that Wheatley's team had finally

Jeff Jones. (Fleet Street News Agency Ltd)

turned the corner. Alan Jones had come of age as a graceful opener, making the imminent retirement of Parkhouse more bearable. Tony Lewis had made an encouraging start to his first season as a full-time county cricketer, and Jeff Jones was on the verge of the England team. They also boasted one of the best spin partnerships in the country, and the fielding, led by David Evans and Peter Walker, was razor sharp. At long last, it looked as if the transitional years were over.

THE AUSTRALIAN YEARS

THE SUMMER OF 1964 will always be remembered in South Wales as the year when Glamorgan beat Australia at St Helen's. Rain had interrupted their encounter three years before with the match finely balanced, and many arguments had taken place as to whether the Welshmen would have won. With the improvement of Wheatley's team, there was great optimism that Glamorgan could finally defeat the Aussies for the first time in 1964. They achieved this, much to the delight of the enormous Bank Holiday crowd, yet the side had an unfamiliar look about it. Euros Lewis was brought in as an opener, Slade came into the middle order, Eifion Jones played behind the stumps and Cordle opened the bowling. I doubt if even the most ardent of supporters would have dared to predict the manner in which victory would be gained with such a young team.

Wheatley won the toss and elected to bat, but none of the Glamorgan batsmen came to terms with the Australian attack, and they slumped to a modest 197. It seemed a disappointing total, but a shower in mid-afternoon dampened the wicket, just to the liking of the Welsh spinners. 'Shep' and 'Pres' were almost unplayable, and by the close the tourists had collapsed to 39 for six. Over 25,000 people poured into St Helen's on the second day and right from the first ball, there was an air of expectancy that, at long last, the Aussies were going to be beaten. However, the left-handed Tom Veivers had other ideas, and he made a stubborn half-century, cleverly selecting which ball to hit. Nevertheless, wickets continued to fall at the other end, and the tourists were dismissed for 101.

The weather was set fair and with a lead of 96, Wheatley's team seemed destined for a big lead. But the wicket was still responding to spin and only Lewis and Alan Rees played with any confidence, especially against the well flighted leg spin of Bobby Simpson, the Australian captain. From 62 for two Glamorgan steadily lost wickets and were eventually bowled out for 172 soon after tea. The target for the visitors was 268, and with an hour and a half of play remaining and all of the last day, they could afford to take their time and make sure that they did not collapse again. The Aussies comfortably achieved these aims in the evening, and they ended the second day on 75 for one.

The final day dawned clear and bright, and another bumper crowd filled St Helen's, knowing that there would be a result one way or the other. The balance had tipped in the visitors' favour the night before, and the Welsh team knew they would have to take early wickets in order to get back into the game. Their morale was lifted as three quick wickets fell, including Norman O'Neill to a superb running catch by Tony Lewis. At 92 for four Glamorgan had regained the initiative, but once again Tom Veivers counter-attacked the bowling, hitting Shepherd and Pressdee for two gigantic sixes. However, he went for one shot too many against Pressdee and was bowled for 54, to the accompaniment of an enormous roar from the crowd. The scoreboard stood at 169 for five, and Lawry was the only front-line batsman left. He found a worthy partner in Barry Jarman and they added a further 38 to put the Aussies back within sight of the target. The obdurate opener had batted for nearly five hours without making a mistake, but then he hit a long hop from Pressdee straight into Rees's hands at mid-wicket. The crestfallen tourist made his way back up the 70-odd steps into the Swansea pavilion, and a buzz went around the ground as the Glamorgan spinners went in for the kill.

The tension mounted as 'Shep' and 'Pres' tied down the Aussies, waiting for the lower order batsmen to make a mistake. They did not have to wait too long as Martin gave a caught and bowled chance to Pressdee, and Jarman was caught by his opposite number, Eifion Jones. Slade then took a fine diving catch to dismiss Sellers, and a minute or two later, Hawke was caught at the wicket, and Glamorgan had won by 36 runs. With the National Eisteddfod just down the road, it seemed as if half the population of the Principality surged onto the field and were there to join in with the celebrations. The champagne corks popped, and speeches were made, and as the songs grew louder, it became clear that it wasn't just Glamorgan that had won, it was Wales too!

This famous victory was sadly the only high-spot during another moderate season. The summer had begun with Shepherd and Pressdee bowling the Welshmen to a 117-run victory at Hove. There were two narrow victories over Worcestershire and Essex in the Gillette Cup, and Gwyn Hughes, the young Cambridge blue scored a promising 92 against the Australians at Cardiff. However, there were only two other victories in the 14 Championship matches before the historic win over the tourists at Swansea, and Glamorgan heavily lost the quarter-final of the Gillette Cup at Old Trafford. Nevertheless, the victory over the Aussies restored the team's confidence and the season ended on a high note with wins over Somerset, Gloucestershire, Kent and Nottinghamshire. However, they finished in a disappointing 11th place and were handicapped by injuries to Jeff Jones and David Evans.

There was a welcome return to form in 1965 and it was no coincidence that most of the staff stayed fit throughout the season. Consequently, Wheatley could select a full-strength team on many more occasions than he had previously done, and the Welshmen were able to make a sustained bid in the title race. They registered only three

GLAMORGAN *v.* AUSTRALIA

Played at St Helen's, Swansea, 1, 3 and 4 August 1964

GLAMORGAN WON BY 36 RUNS

GLAMORGAN	FIRST INNINGS		SECOND INNINGS	
A. Jones	c Simpson b Martin	33	c Connolly b Martin	15
E. Lewis	c Simpson b Veivers	7	b Hawke	11
A. R. Lewis	c Hawke b Veivers	0	c Connolly b Veivers	36
P. M. Walker	b Hawke	41	c and b Veivers	9
J. S. Pressdee	b Martin	6	st Jarman b Simpson	24
A. Rees	c Simpson b Hawke	48	c Jarman b Simpson	47
W. D. Slade	not out	14	c Connolly b Simpson	9
†E. W. Jones	c Connolly b Veivers	0	b Veivers	4
A. E. Cordle	c Sellers b Veivers	6	c Potter b Simpson	6
D. J. Shepherd	c Martin b Veivers	24	not out	9
★O. S. Wheatley	c Redpath b Hawke	11	c O'Neill b Simpson	1
Extras		7		1
Total		197		172

1st inns: 1-42, 2-46, 3-50, 4-62, 5-130, 6-147, 7-150, 8-156, 9-182
2nd inns: 1-13, 2-49, 3-67, 4-74, 5-126, 6-152, 7-152, 8-162, 9-171

BOWLING	O	M	R	W	O	M	R	W
Connolly	6	1	22	0	3	2	6	0
Hawke	26.1	8	51	3	15	3	30	1
Veivers	28	11	85	5	28	6	65	3
Martin	7	0	31	2	8	2	25	1
Simpson	1	0	1	0	14.1	4	33	5
Sellers					13	6	12	0

AUSTRALIA	FIRST INNINGS		SECOND INNINGS	
W. M. Lawry	c Slade b Shepherd	7	c Rees b Pressdee	64
I. R. Redpath	c Walker b Pressdee	6	lbw b Shepherd	5
N. C. O'Neill	st E. Jones b Pressdee	0	c A. Lewis b E. Lewis	14
J. Potter	c E. Jones b Pressdee	2	b Shepherd	0
★R. B. Simpson	b Pressdee	2	c Walker b Shepherd	32
†B. N. Jarman	c Slade b Shepherd	4	c E. Jones b Pressdee	34
T. R. Veivers	c E. Lewis b Pressdee	51	b Pressdee	54
J. W. Martin	b Shepherd	12	c Pressdee b Shepherd	6
R. H. D. Sellers	lbw b Shepherd	4	c Slade b Shepherd	4
N. J. N. Hawke	c E. Jones b Pressdee	0	c E. Jones b Pressdee	1
A. N. Connolly	not out	0	not out	0
Extras		13		18
Total		101		232

1st inns: 1-15, 2-15, 3-17, 4-21, 5-21, 6-39, 7-65, 8-90, 9-95
2nd inns: 1-59, 2-80, 3-88, 4-92, 5-169, 6-207, 7-217, 8-228, 9-232

BOWLING	O	M	R	W	O	M	R	W
Wheatley	4	3	1	0	5	1	11	0
Cordle	5	1	7	0	7	1	14	0
Shepherd	17	12	22	4	52	29	71	5
Pressdee	15.2	5	58	6	28.1	6	65	4
E. Lewis					26	13	51	1
Slade					1	0	2	0

Umpires: W. H. Copson and F. Jakeman

This was one of Glamorgan's finest hours and the architects of the victory were their 'spin twins' Don Shepherd and Jim Pressdee, who tied down the Australian batsmen as they struggled to reach a target of 268. Once again, the Glamorgan fielders excelled themselves and this win was celebrated in the Celtic style by the massive Welsh crowd.

victories in the first 11 games, but no team built up a lead in the early part of the season, so when Glamorgan defeated Sussex in mid-June, it put them on top of the table. A ten-wicket defeat by Middlesex saw them fall back to third place, but two victories over Lancashire kept them in the title race. Rain interfered with the game against Leicestershire at Ebbw Vale, but it did not prevent a positive outcome to keep Wheatley's team in contention. He was never afraid to set a sporting declaration and he challenged Leicestershire to make 149 in 110 minutes on the damp wicket. Conditions were ideal for Don Shepherd and in the space of eighty minutes, the visitors were dismissed for 33, with the wily off-spinner finishing with the remarkable analysis of 10-8-2-5.

Leicestershire could do little right against Glamorgan in 1965, because a month or so later, they went down by an innings at Grace Road. Rain had again interrupted play on the first two days and a tame draw seemed inevitable when Leicestershire began their second innings on the final morning, just 68 runs behind. However, the overnight rain had freshened up the wicket, and Jeff Jones bowled fast and straight on the damp surface to reduce the home team to 3 for five, with all five victims to Jones without the left-armer conceding a run. A partial recovery took place, but Leicestershire were eventually dismissed before lunch for 40, with Jones returning his career best figures of 13-9-11-8.

*'c Walker b Shepherd'. Colin Bland of South Africa is about to fall to that famous combination. (*Western Mail*)*

This amazing victory meant that the county title would return to Wales if Wheatley's team could secure maximum points in their last three games. However, rain intervened in the match with Derbyshire at Cardiff and the Welshmen were caught on a wet wicket against the fiery Harold Rhodes. He took nine wickets and the visitors won by 91 runs. Morale was temporarily raised by a fine win over Surrey at St Helen's, set up by Wheatley's bowling, but the elements had the final say as rain dampened the wicket for the match with Essex at Llanelli. The conditions were fully exploited by leg-spinner Robin Hobbs, who took 12 wickets, and he was assisted by some outstanding close catching and more than a few nervous shots by the Welsh batsmen. Essex won by five wickets inside two days and Glamorgan had to be content with third place.

The game at Llanelli was an anti-climax, and all concerned were understandably disgruntled at the way the season had ended. Emotions were running high, and events were marred by an unfortunate incident after the match between Pressdee and Wooller. The all-rounder tried to leave the pavilion by going through a small back room which the administrative staff used as a temporary office. There were a lot of valuables and money lying around the room, and Wooller was anxious that the exit was kept closed to prevent any pilfering from outside. The two individuals had never seen eye to eye over many matters and a heated argument took place as Pressdee thrust his way through. Strong words were exchanged and Pressdee stormed off towards the Press tent. He had already decided to emigrate to South Africa, so he told the journalists that one of the reasons for his leaving was that he could not get on with the Secretary.

There had been earlier clashes between the players and the administration with some resenting comments that Wooller, as a professional servant of the Club, had made whilst commentating on TV, criticising the performance of his players. There were allegations that Pressdee had deliberately tried to bait the Secretary, so the committee inquired into team discipline and Wheatley's authority both on and off the field. Spurious allegations were made, as for example at Colchester, when Ossie Wheatley arrived in a dinner jacket. Some newspapers carried stories of the captain attending an all-night party, but in fact all that had happened was that he and Tony Lewis had attended the Hawks Club Dinner in London the evening before and did not have any other casual clothes apart from their whites!

These were not the only worries for the committee during the winter months. The Treasurer reported a deficit of around £6,700, despite an increase in membership and gate receipts. The cause was the high level of expenditure and some cost-cutting measures were inevitable unless a new source of income could be found. A lucrative offer came from Colwyn Bay CC in Denbighshire, who had been founded in 1924 by Wooller's father. The Secretary knew of the success of the Club's festival and testimonial matches, which were held on a regular basis at the height of the holiday season at the popular coastal resort. Impressive ground improvements had taken place, so the committee allocated the Derbyshire fixture to the Rhos ground. But they could not afford having an extra venue, especially one some 200 kilometres away from the Club office. Some of the established venues would have to make way, and Llanelli and Newport were dropped from the fixture list, despite the fact that a trek up north was virtually an away game!

The loss of Pressdee and the rising expenditure worried the Club's officials, but it was not all bad news at the end of the summer. Glamorgan II had won the Second Eleven Championship under Phil Clift's guidance, and there were a host of young players, including Brian Lewis, Ian Morris, Len Hill, Malcolm Nash, Kevin Lyons, and brothers John and Roger Davis, who all showed great promise for the future. The committee were also heartened during the winter months by the good form shown by Jeff Jones on the MCC tour of Australia and New Zealand. Things had not looked good when he was barred by the umpire from bowling against New South Wales after running down the wicket. Jones carefully worked at his follow-through and he was rewarded with a place in the England team for the second Test at Melbourne. His work in the nets paid off, and he captured the wickets of four top order batsmen and kept his place for the rest of the series, plus the three-match rubber against New Zealand. Overall, the left-armer finished the tour as the leading wicket-taker with 48 victims, and much to the delight of the Welsh officials, it looked as if he had made the grade as an international cricketer.

Further successes were keenly anticipated in 1966 after the success of the second team, and the first team's brave effort in the title race the previous year. But as so often in the Club's history, they failed to maintain this progress and fell back to 14th place. It would be easy to attribute this to Pressdee's departure, but in fact there were other factors including the poor weather. Six matches at Swansea were rain-affected, and in the past the Welshmen had relied on several victories on the notorious St Helen's 'turners'. Even so, the loss of Pressdee was a major blow; it upset the balance of the side, and his experience in the middle order was missed. It was particularly frustrating as Tony Lewis and Alan Jones frequently laid a solid foundation, only for a collapse to take place once they were parted. Lewis had a vintage season, passing 2,000 for the first time and hitting five centuries, including a career best 223 against Kent at Gravesend. Jones scored over 1,800 and made a brave century against the West Indians at Swansea and their ferocious attack of Wes Hall and Charlie Griffith.

But all too often the batting relied on Lewis and Jones. Of the other batsmen, Walker, Hedges and Rees all had moderate seasons, and none of the youngsters made any impact. It was a similar story in the bowling, where Wheatley and Shepherd both took over a hundred wickets. But they lacked support, especially when Jeff Jones was on England duty. It was a disappointing summer for the left-armer, who failed to capitalise on the progress he had made during the winter and lost form at both county and Test level. Admittedly he was unlucky with dropped catches in the first Test, but he took only one wicket in 46 overs in the second, and lost his place to the in-form John Snow for the rest of the series. He returned to the Championship circuit, but failed to reproduce his best form and finished the season with only 52 wickets to his credit.

The season ended with the final county game at the Arms Park, though Glamorgan failed to mark the occasion with a win. Somerset set them 223 in 180 minutes and their run chase epitomised their batting failures that season. Alan Jones gave them a flying start with a rapid 50 in the first hour, but the middle order collapsed yet again, and they ended 71 runs short of their target. During the autumn of 1966

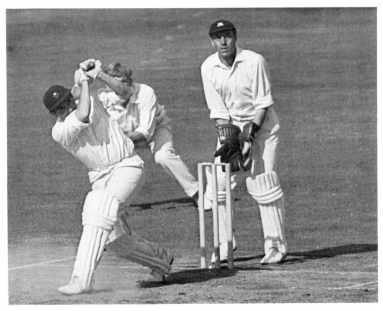

Tony Lewis sweeps Fred Titmus for a boundary at Lord's in the game with Middlesex in 1965. John Murray is the wicket-keeper and Clive Radley is at first slip. (Sport and General)

the rest of the pitch was ploughed up and the contractors began demolishing the old stands, and transferring some of the seating to the new ground at Sophia Gardens. But the move was not entirely trouble free, and there were difficulties with the installation of the drains under the new pitch; indeed, there have been claims that the drainage system was laid the wrong way round. One of the channels ran across the square and soon after the inaugural match against the Indians in May, a ridge started to appear half-way down the wicket. This led to several complaints as well as more than a few cuts and bruises as the quick bowlers regularly hit the ridge, much to the discomfort of the batsmen. Problems arose in the first Championship match at the ground against Northants, with complaints of an irregular bounce. The MCC Inspector of Pitches visited the new wicket, and soon after, remedial work was taken to settle the new surface down. This was finished by mid-August, when Glamorgan registered their first victory at Sophia Gardens, defeating Kent by an innings after some hostile bowling by Jeff Jones and Cordle.

This was one of only four Championship victories, as the Welsh county spent most of the summer rebuilding their team as well as their new ground. Wheatley had intimated that 1966 was his last year as captain and that he wished to play instead on a part-time basis in order to concentrate on his business commitments. The committee did not take long to find a replacement, appointing Tony Lewis and restoring the 'tradition' of a Welsh leader. Although many felt Lewis was destined to become the Glamorgan captain, he was being asked to take over at a difficult time. However, his transition into the job was made easier by the presence of Shepherd, who was the perfect senior professional with a vast knowledge about opposing players and away grounds.

Nevertheless, Lewis had a difficult first season in charge as the team remained in 14th place. The loss of Wheatley's experience as an opening bowler was a major blow, though Cordle made steady improvement and formed a useful partnership with Jeff Jones. The left-armer had a much better season, taking 91 wickets, and regaining his confidence. Several youngsters also made encouraging progress including off-spinner Roger Davis and seamer Malcolm Nash. The major problem area once again was the batting, and the situation was not helped when Rees and Lewis himself lost form, and Hedges announced his retirement. A number of young batsmen also got their chance, but unlike the bowlers, some of them were not quite ready for the higher grade of cricket, and their inexperience was often cruelly exposed.

The County's officials were worried by the lack of experience in the middle order and once again they discussed how this could be solved.

The 1960s had seen the introduction of overseas players into County teams and it was argued that Gamorgan could not afford to ignore this trend, and that a Test batsman from another country could solve their problems. It was against the long held dream of an all-Welsh team, but the committee agreed to consider an overseas replacement. They were highly impressed when Majid Khan made a superb 147 in the space of just 89 minutes for Pakistan in their game at St Helen's, hitting no fewer than 13 sixes, including five in an over from Roger Davis. The young Pakistani was the son of Jehangir Khan, who had been up at Cambridge with Wooller, and the Glamorgan Secretary was delighted when his old friend's son accepted the offer of a contract with the Welsh county. There were few restrictions at the time on the number of overseas players, so the Club also agreed terms with Bryan Davis, the 27-year-old Trinidadian batsman, who agreed to spend the 1968 summer in South Wales qualifying to appear for Glamorgan in their Championship games in 1969.

Despite the signing of these overseas stars, the committee were not in an entirely buoyant mood at the end of the summer. There was depression over the continued lack of support and another fall in revenue, compounded by the costs, in excess of £25,000, which had been spent in the transfer to Sophia Gardens. They had also received an adverse report from the MCC regarding the state of the wicket at Eugene Cross park, and Ebbw Vale had to be dropped as a first-class venue. On the other hand, there was delight with the selection of Jeff Jones on England's winter tour to the Caribbean. He had re-established himself as one of the country's leading fast bowlers, and played in all of the five tests against the West Indies. His overall return of 25 wickets at 36 apiece was an untrue reflection of how well he bowled, often on unresponsive wickets and in long spells in the high temperatures.

Jeff Jones returned home, optimistic of keeping his place in the England side for the Ashes series against Australia. However, 1968 turned out to be a sorry year for the 26-year-old, as he damaged ligaments in his shoulder and elbow at Ilford in early June, and had to sit on the sidelines for the rest of the summer. Even worse was to come when a specialist found a mild arthritic condition in the elbow joint, plus a wearing of the bone structure. Jones tried to make a comeback, but the injury had affected his smooth action and he was unable to bowl properly. After a long chat with Tony Lewis, Jones was forced to give up his fight and had to retire prematurely from county cricket.

The omens for 1968 looked to be bad when Jones broke down, but every cloud has a silver lining, and the loss of the left-arm quickie resulted in Wheatley playing on a more regular basis. He took 82 wickets, and his presence gave a much-needed boost to the attack.

Majid's acquisition also had a major impact on the side. The gifted Pakistani hit over 1,300 runs, and helped Glamorgan to a number of victories. His most impressive contribution came on a difficult wicket at Neath against Surrey. His magical touch brought him 85 runs as he became the only batsman on either side to pass fifty, and set up a ten-wicket victory. Majid's presence gave confidence to the younger players who followed in the middle order. They were able to flourish and score runs more quickly, with even Cordle and Nash making useful contributions. One of the young batsmen to benefit was Eifion Jones, and he became the first Glamorgan wicket-keeper since Tom Brierley to score over 800 runs. The stocky keeper also made a maiden century against Sussex at Hove, during a partnership of 230 with his brother Alan as Glamorgan batted through the final day. This was yet another incident-packed game with Sussex, with one of their batsmen failing to walk after being caught by Euros Lewis, and complaints by Tony Lewis that one of the boundaries was only 36 paces away from the square. Some people were upset that Glamorgan failed to set Sussex a target on the last day, but with one short boundary, how could Lewis declare, and in any case, they had been put in by Sussex who had hoped to bowl Glamorgan out twice.

The team had a purple patch between the beginning of July and the end of August during which they won ten of their 13 matches, and rose to a creditable third place in the table behind Yorkshire and Kent. The fine run ironically began with a 103-run win over the eventual Champions at Sheffield. Lewis challenged them to make 205 in 155 minutes, but they were dismissed for just 101, as Shepherd made up for earlier disappointments on Yorkshire soil by taking six for 40. However, Geoff Cope restored Yorkshire pride the following week in the return match at Sophia Gardens, taking 12 wickets as the white rose county comfortably won by ten wickets. But this was only a temporary hiccough to the Welshmen's morale, and they recorded consecutive victories over Northants, Warwickshire, Sussex and Somerset. The latter was one of the most comprehensive of all their wins in 1968, as Nash, the young left-arm seamer took seven for 15 to skittle Somerset out for 40, before Alan Jones raced to a fine century to set up a nine-wicket win. They reinforced their superiority a few weeks later at Taunton, with Majid hitting a graceful century. Lewis set the home team 299 on the final day, but they ended 53 runs short after some accurate bowling by Shepherd and Walker.

The end of season encounter with Notts at Swansea saw a remarkable, and record-breaking innings from Garry Sobers, the visitors' captain. He had given instructions to his team to go for quick runs on the second afternoon, but some of his batsmen decided to play for their average and try to remain not out when the declaration came.

The West Indian became increasingly frustrated as they blocked up rather than hit out, and when he arrived at the crease just before tea, he still had the prospect of a declaration in his mind. This would require an explosive burst of hitting, but if ever there was a man to achieve this, Sobers was one of the few to fit the bill. Lewis knew that the visitors were contemplating a declaration, so he brought on Malcolm Nash at the pavilion end, who was experimenting with left-arm spin around the wicket, in the style of Derek Underwood. The rest is history, as Sobers hit six sixes in an over from the young bowler.

The first two balls disappeared high over the heads of the mid-wicket fielders and into the crowd sitting in the stands in front of The Cricketers Inn. Nash pushed his third delivery a little wider into the off-side, but Sobers went down the wicket and drove it into the pavilion enclosure beyond the long-off boundary. Nash tried another variation by dropping the fourth ball a little shorter but Sobers rocked onto his back foot, and pulled it high over the scoreboard. The young bowler was still not disconcerted, even if the fielders seemed to be spreading further and further out, and he put the next delivery on a good length on the off stump. Sobers for once made a mistake and the ball travelled straight to Roger Davis on the long off boundary. He caught it, but in so doing fell over the ropes, and after a consultation between the umpires, another six was signalled.

By now the crowd and the players alike were aware that the great West Indian all-rounder was on the verge of becoming the first player to hit six sixes in an over. As Nash regathered the ball and pondered on where to put the last delivery, Eifion Jones jokingly said to Sobers: 'Bet you can't hit this one for six as well.' The West Indian simply turned around and grinned, took guard and despatched the ball like a rocket out of the ground and down St Helen's Avenue. So hard did Sobers hit it, that the ball was not found until the next day. Despite the fact that he was within sight of making the fastest century on record, Sobers stuck to his decision and declared after hitting the final six and walked off to an appreciative ovation from the large crowd. Nash typically offered his warm congratulations to the West Indian, and philosophically summed up his ignominious achievement by saying 'some have fame thrust upon them!'

However, 1968 will always be remembered as the year when Glamorgan achieved the 'double' over the Australians, winning for the second time within four years at Swansea. Ironically, the Welshmen were once again not at full strength. Tony Lewis had a throat infection, so Bryan Davis came into the side and Don Shepherd took over the captaincy. He won the toss and elected to bat first on a dry, easy paced wicket, that was likely to assist the spinners on the third day. Alan Jones was in scintillating form and time and again he pierced

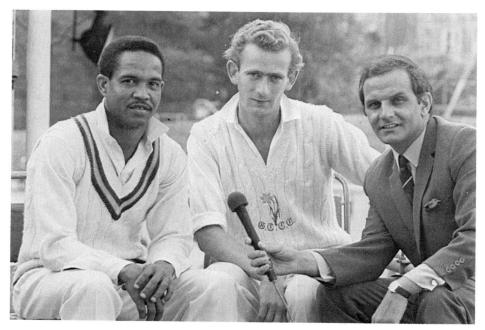

Garry Sobers and Malcolm Nash are interviewed by Brian Hoey of the BBC after Sobers' six sixes at Swansea in 1968. (BBC)

the field with exquisitely timed shots. He had made 99 and was on the verge of a memorable hundred, when he was lured down the wicket by Ashley Mallett and holed out on the mid-on boundary.

Glamorgan were eventually dismissed for 224 at tea on the first day, and as the tourists went back into their dressing room, some of them recalled their encounter back in 1964 when they had collapsed after tea. Surely it couldn't happen again, but they had reckoned without the controlled left-arm swing of Nash and the superb fielding of the Welshmen. The events after tea were an almost copybook repeat of their previous encounter as the Aussies slumped to 77 for six. Glamorgan firmly held the upper hand on the second morning, and by midday, the ground was full of Welshmen, keenly anticipating further Australian wickets. They were not disappointed as some smart wicket-keeping by Eifion Jones, plus a fine caught and bowled by Brian Lewis saw Australia all out for 110. Glamorgan had a first innings lead of 114, so Shepherd told the batsmen to go for quick runs in their second innings. The two Davises, Bryan and Roger, responded perfectly and shared a rousing stand of a hundred inside an hour. Cordle and Shepherd added a few lusty blows later in the afternoon, and the acting

GLAMORGAN *v* AUSTRALIA

Played at St Helen's, Swansea, 3, 4 and 5 August 1968

GLAMORGAN WON BY 79 RUNS

GLAMORGAN	FIRST INNINGS		SECOND INNINGS	
A. Jones	c Hawke b Mallett	99	c Sheahan b Mallett	10
R. C. Davis	b Connolly	24	c Gleeson b Hawke	59
B. A. Davis	c Cowper b Gleeson	1	c and b Cowper	66
P. M. Walker	c Inverarity b Cowper	19	lbw b Gleeson	13
M. J. Khan	st Jarman b Mallett	55	c Sheahan b Hawke	13
A. Rees	c Inverarity b Gleeson	0	not out	33
†E. W. Jones	c Sheahan b Mallett	3		
A. E. Cordle	st Jarman b Gleeson	1	c Redpath b Gleeson	17
M. A. Nash	c Inverarity b Mallett	0	c Cowper b Gleeson	7
B. Lewis	not out	6	st Jarman b Gleeson	4
*D. J. Shepherd	c Redpath b Gleeson	10	c Connolly b Mallett	14
Extras		6		14
Total		224	(for 9 wkts dec)	250

1st inns: 1-50, 2-51, 3-110, 4-194, 5-203, 6-203, 7-204, 8-207, 9-211
2nd inns: 1-15, 2-115, 3-148, 4-157, 5-165, 6-193, 7-209, 8-227, 9-250

BOWLING	O	M	R	W	O	M	R	W
Renneberg	11	2	35	0	8	2	25	0
Hawke	3	0	10	0	14	4	27	2
Connolly	14	4	21	1	5	0	17	0
Gleeson	23.3	9	73	4	17	3	56	4
Mallett	12	3	46	4	16.2	1	85	2
Cowper	9	2	33	1	8	0	26	1

AUSTRALIA	FIRST INNINGS		SECOND INNINGS	
R. J. Inverarity	c R. Davis b Lewis	31	b Nash	28
*†B. N. Jarman	run out	1	c R. Davis b Shepherd	13
I. R. Redpath	b Nash	13	run out	13
R. M. Cowper	c Walker b Nash	0	c E. Jones b Lewis	42
A. P. Sheahan	b Lewis	12	c and b Walker	137
L. R. Joslin	c Khan b Lewis	19	c and b Lewis	7
N. J. Hawke	c and b Lewis	6	c Khan b Shepherd	6
A. A. Mallett	c E. Jones b Nash	11	run out	4
J. W. Gleeson	c E. Jones b Nash	11	c R. Davis b Lewis	0
A. N. Connolly	lbw b Nash	1	not out	22
D. A. Renneberg	not out	0	c Khan b Walker	3
Extras		5		10
Total		110		285

1st inns: 1-3, 2-20, 3-22, 4-36, 5-77, 6-80, 7-91, 8-105, 9-109
2nd inns: 1-35, 2-45, 3-116, 4-128, 5-173, 6-195, 7-196, 8-219, 9-259

BOWLING	O	M	R	W	O	M	R	W
Nash	15.3	6	28	5	10	2	22	1
Cordle	3	2	1	0	8	1	34	0
Shepherd	16	9	11	0	27	9	63	2
Lewis	20	6	51	4	32	4	131	3
Walker	8	3	14	0	8.2	2	25	2

Umpires: C. G. Pepper and J. F. Crapp

Glamorgan entered the record books as they became the first county to defeat Australia on consecutive tours. It was almost a repeat of their 1964 victory as the tourists found life difficult against the accurate Welsh spinners. The game was a triumph for Don Shepherd, leading in place of the indisposed Tony Lewis, and a tribute to his subtle tactics and clever bowling changes.

captain was able to declare at the close, leaving the Aussies a target of 365 in 390 minutes on the final day.

The weather stayed fine and the ground quickly filled up with another large crowd, bubbling with excitement at the thought of another famous Welsh sporting victory. Once again, the Glamorgan fielders rose to the occasion and were on top form, with Alan Rees swooping at cover to run out Ian Redpath, whilst Nash produced a superb 'nip-backer' to bowl Inverarity. However, Sheahan and Cowper started to build a useful stand against the seamers; Shepherd realised they were at ease against the quicker bowlers, so he brought himself and Brian Lewis on in an attempt to frustrate the batsmen. At first the runs continued to flow, but gradually the spinners settled into the groove and tied down the batsmen. The scoring rate dropped and Cowper was forced to swing across the line against Lewis, giving Eifion Jones a straightforward catch – Shepherd had won the first battle.

Lewis quickly disposed of Joslin, so Barry Jarman came in with the specific intention of hitting the spinners off their length. He made a few firm blows, but then Shepherd's flight deceived him and Roger Davis held on to a sharp chance at short leg. The Welsh fielders really excelled themselves as Majid ran out Mallett when Sheahan tried to scamper a single which would have brought up his century, and then Roger Davis took another good catch to send Gleeson back to the pavilion. Australia had lost eight wickets and with barely 200 runs on the board, Glamorgan were heading for victory.

The only man standing in their way was Paul Sheahan, and he was determined to go down fighting, hoisting the Glamorgan spinners high into the members enclosure. He gave a sharp chance to Lewis when he had made 120, but a few overs later he repeated the shot against Walker, and the lanky spinner clung onto the sizzling drive. Connolly and Renneberg continued the big hitting, but it was only a matter of time before Glamorgan would win. With the scoreboard on 285 for nine Renneberg swung at Walker and Majid took a fine catch at cover. Once again, the crowd swarmed onto the field to congratulate their heroes, who had become the first county to defeat Australia on consecutive tours. The jubilant supporters gathered in front of the pavilion, once again singing Welsh hymns, and even a rendition of 'Waltzing Matilda' echoed around the ground. Shepherd addressed them from the players' balcony and he was greeted with a mighty roar and sustained applause in recognition of his shrewd captaincy. Jarman also spoke to the crowd and praised the Welsh team for their fine efforts, finishing with the apt comment: 'What's new about being beaten by Glamorgan?'

THE YEAR OF THE WELSH

THE YEAR OF 1969 was a proud one for all Welshmen, both home and overseas. Prince Charles, now the Club's Patron, was invested as Prince of Wales at Caernarvon Castle, whilst the national rugby team had another successful year. It was also the year when Glamorgan won the Championship for the second time, exactly 100 years after the first attempt to form a county side. It had become increasingly obvious in 1968 that Lewis's team were finally fulfilling their potential after several years of rebuilding, and there was a growing belief that a Championship-winning team was taking shape. Few believed that they would achieve this without being beaten, a feat not achieved since Lancashire were Champions in 1930.

During the winter months, Wooller and Tony Lewis carefully discussed how the title might be won. The bonus points situation at that time favoured quick scoring in the first innings. For bowling there was one point for every two wickets taken, making a maximum of 5, but the batting points were limitless with 1 point for every 25 runs over 150. It was agreed that Roger Davis should open with Alan Jones, with Majid at No 3, Tony Lewis at No 4 and Bryan Davis at No 5, followed by Walker, Eifion Jones, Cordle, Nash and Shepherd. The loss of Jeff Jones had caused some anxiety about the bowling, but the club had acquired the services of Lawrence Williams, a young opening bowler from Tonna. It was hoped he would be the perfect foil to Nash, allowing Cordle to concentrate on being a reliable stock bowler.

All of this was fine on paper, but the officials knew the effect injuries had made in previous seasons. However, for once luck was on their side and all of the regular eleven stayed free from injury and no one was called up to play for England. Indeed, the only others to be called up to play in Championship matches were Ossie Wheatley, Kevin Lyons and David Lewis, the Cardiff leg-spinner. As in 1948 Glamorgan fielded a settled team, which generated a good team spirit. The healthy morale emanated from Tony Lewis's approach to the team. Roger Davis remembers: 'Tony treated all players as equals – a stark contrast to the game of ten years before when junior amateurs and senior professionals occupied different changing rooms, and as long as the players gave of their best on the field, he encouraged them to enjoy themselves when at rest. Off the field we laughed and laughed, and this enjoyment and vitality showed through in our play on the field. There was a willingness to take chances and our confidence that luck would favour the brave.'

There were other similarities with 1948, such as the close fielding being of the highest quality. Bryan Davis at first slip, Majid at second, Roger Davis at short square-leg and Peter Walker at backward short-leg formed a safe ring of close catchers, whilst Eifion Jones emerged as one of the leading keepers in the country.

There were important differences though to 1948 too. In particular the fact that Lewis's squad also had to adjust their game to the demands of the new John Player Sunday League competition. They won their inaugural game at Northampton by seven runs, with Shepherd taking five wickets, and a few weeks later defeated Derbyshire at Ebbw Vale with young seamer Graham Kingston taking six for 36. Their most impressive win came in mid-June on their first visit to Llandudno. The Glamorgan committee allocated the Leicestershire fixture to the ground because it had the reputation of having the best crowd-pulling potential in North Wales. They were not disappointed as several thousand holidaymakers crowded into The Oval ground. Leicestershire made a slow start, before rain fell and interrupted their innings. This presented the Welshmen with the comfortable task of making 73 in just 27 overs, which they achieved without loss.

Nevertheless, Glamorgan won only a further five games in the new Sunday competition and they ended in tenth place. Overall, the team found it difficult to adapt to the shorter games, and the fielders, so brilliant close to the wicket, were rather cumbersome in the wide open spaces. Instead, they all concentrated their efforts on the three-day

Eifion Jones, one of Glamorgan's finest keepers, clings onto a low edge from Middlesex's Harry Latchman at Lord's in 1968 off the bowling of Don Shepherd. Ian Morris is at short-leg and Majid Khan is at slip. (Sport and General)

games, and were handsomely rewarded, though a Championship success looked unlikely, as the season began with bad weather and a series of drawn matches. In fact, they nearly lost the opening game of the season against Yorkshire at St Helen's, and Nash and Shepherd had to bat throughout the last 20 minutes to stave off defeat. Rain washed out the next two matches, and the first victory of the season did not come until early June when Somerset were beaten inside two days at Cardiff.

Lewis's team were still in a mid-table position when they travelled to Bournemouth to play Hampshire, who were in sparkling form and had Barry Richards, one of the finest opening batsmen at that time. Not surprisingly, the game was played on a good batting wicket, and the home team quickly raced to 337 for five before declaring. Majid and Eifion Jones then shared a useful partnership, and Lewis was able to declare 67 runs behind. Hampshire began batting on the final morning with the prospect of a Welsh run chase later in the afternoon, but rain fell with their score on 28 for one and the players were forced to leave the field. It continued to drizzle after lunch and the prospect of further play seemed unlikely.

In mid-afternoon, Lewis went to see Roy Marshall, the Hampshire captain, and they agreed to call off the game if it was still raining after tea. The Welsh captain reported back to the Glamorgan dressing room and told his team to get changed, but Shepherd, the wise senior pro, urged him to seek confirmation from the umpires, Lloyd Budd and Peter Wight, before leaving the ground. Lewis walked over to their hut, a few yards away from the pavilion, and said 'I suppose it is all off?' But Wight replied: 'There are more than two hours to go, the rain is not heavy, the wicket will be playable almost as soon as it stops. It is far too early to abandon the match.' Lewis returned to the pavilion and told his men to stay, but by this time the Hampshire team had got changed and departed for their next match. A message was sent out for them to return, but they could not be found.

About an hour later, the rain stopped and the umpires decided that play could restart. So at 5.30, in front of no more than half a dozen people, out trooped the Glamorgan players. Tony Cordle marked out his run, and Lewis adjusted an imaginary field, before Lloyd Budd called 'Play'. The umpires waited the statutory two minutes and then without a Hampshire player in sight, they awarded the game to Glamorgan. Not surprisingly, a heated debate took place in the following weeks over the legality of the decision. The Welsh officials admitted that they did not particularly relish the points under the circumstances, but as Peter Wight said: 'It's the law'. The MCC held a meeting and upheld the decision, but Hampshire appealed. By the time of the second meeting, Glamorgan were in the title race and they did not want to be remembered as the side that won the Championship by virtue of some obscure regulation. So when Lewis went to Lord's for the hearing he told the MCC that they would not object to Hampshire's appeal, and the match was declared a draw.

The Glamorgan team were undeterred by the farcical incident at Dean Park, and in the next three weeks they beat Sussex twice and defeated Worcestershire by 29 runs to move up into second place in the table, some 50 points behind Gloucestershire. The West Country team were in good form and looked to be on course for their first Championship title this century. In mid-July they travelled to Sophia Gardens knowing that another three or four victories would virtually guarantee them the title. The game however proved to be the turning point in Gloucestershire's fortunes and they crashed to a demoralising defeat. After Glamorgan had made 337, Nash and Cordle ripped the heart out of the visitors' batting as they slumped to 117. Lewis opted to bat again rather than enforce the follow-on, as the weather was set fair, and his bowlers needed a rest. He left the visitors a target of 364, but they were never in the hunt as Williams and Nash shared seven wickets to steer Glamorgan to an emphatic victory by 208 runs.

The gap behind the leaders was closed during the end of July and early August as Lewis' team continued in their winning vein. At Derby, Roger Davis and Alan Jones put on 224 for the first wicket and then Williams and Nash bowled them to an innings win. The following week at Northampton Alan Jones and Majid put on 179 for the second wicket in the first innings, and then in the second, when Glamorgan were chasing 218 in just two and a half hours, they had another magnificent stand of 132 in 77 minutes to see the team to a seven-wicket victory.

These splendid wins boosted the Glamorgan morale, and a week later they travelled to Cheltenham to meet Gloucestershire, who were still leading the Championship, but were playing with less confidence. This became clear as Nash took six for 37 to bowl them out for 73 on a green wicket. The Gloucestershire bowlers also found conditions initially to their liking, but Majid and Bryan Davis batted skilfully and drew on all of their Test experience to give Glamorgan a lead of 210. The pressure was on the home batsmen and their early order played nervous shots against Nash and Williams. The Welsh fielders held their catches and Gloucestershire were quickly reduced to 7 for three. The wicket was starting to crumble, so Lewis brought on his spinners. The Gloucestershire batsmen found life just as uncomfortable against them, and Glamorgan coasted home by an innings and 50 runs.

For the first time, the London press started to realise that the Gloucestershire bubble had burst, and with Glamorgan on a crest of a wave in second place, the journalists flocked to St Helen's the following week for the Welsh county's game with Middlesex. They were treated to a game of fluctuating fortunes, with the outcome in doubt right until the final over. The visitors batted first, but Nash sent back Russell and Parfitt without a run on the board. Clive Radley restored their fortunes with a fine century, and with help from the tail, saw Middlesex to 301. Glamorgan replied with 310 for six, with Majid playing another quite brilliant innings in quick time to allow Lewis to declare soon after tea on the second afternoon.

The visiting batsmen fared better in their second innings, and were 150 runs on by the next morning with Featherstone and Smith well set. But a collapse took place after Lewis brought back Nash and Cordle, and Glamorgan were left with a target of 196. It seemed a reasonable one, with plenty of time available, but Roger Davis and Majid were soon back in the pavilion as Middlesex regained the initiative. A useful partnership between Alan Jones and Tony Lewis steadied the ship before the opener was caught off Ron Hooker. Bryan Davis and Walker quickly followed, but Eifion Jones remained firm with Lewis to put Glamorgan back on course for victory. Then Price dismissed Lewis and Cordle was well taken by John Murray to put Middlesex back on top, with the Glamorgan tailenders at the wicket. However, Eifion Jones was a gritty fighter and in the closing overs he received good support from Nash as Glamorgan inched closer to the target. The outcome was settled in the final over as the stocky wicket-keeper hit Hooker for six and Glamorgan had won by three wickets to go to the top of the table.

Heavy rain at Chelmsford prevented Lewis's team from consolidating their position, but they had a game in hand over Gloucestershire and they knew that wins in two of the last three matches would be enough to secure the title. Most important of all, the Essex and Worcestershire games were in Wales and the side returned to St Helen's to play Essex over the August Bank Holiday period fully aware of the immeasurable effect this home advantage would give them, especially since most of the team were Welsh and responded to the fervent Celtic support. A massive crowd turned up and they witnessed yet another enthralling game, with fortunes seesawing throughout the match. Lewis won the toss and opted to bat first knowing that the Swansea wicket would be crumbling towards the end of the game. However, they mustered only 241, and then the Welsh attack faltered as Lee Irvine hit a sparkling century to give the visitors a lead of 95. Lever and Turner sent back Roger Davis, Majid and Lewis before the Welsh reply had got into full swing and Glamorgan ended the second day on 123 for four.

The ground was nearly full by the start of the final day's play, with the Welsh supporters knowing that the first hour could decide the

The 1969 Championship squad at Swansea:
Back row:: David Lewis, Roger Davis, Malcolm Nash, Lawrence Williams,
Bryan Davis, Eifion Jones, Kevin Lyons
Front row: Alan Jones, Don Shepherd, Tony Lewis (capt.), Tony Cordle and
Majid Khan. (BBC Wales)

outcome of the match and the destiny of the title. It was a dour battle as
Alan Jones and Peter Walker stubbornly defended; they saw off the
Essex attack and prevented their seamers from making further inroads.
The bowlers began to tire, and with the early threat behind them, the
batsmen began to open out and go for quick runs. Although they both
fell after steady half-centuries, the later batsmen carried on with the
quick scoring and Lewis was able to set Essex a fair target of 190 in two
hours.

   Essex got off to a shaky start as Wheatley sent back both openers,
but then Barker and Fletcher shared a useful partnership to put their
side on the road to victory. Shepherd and Roger Davis were
conceding runs, but Lewis had faith in his spinners. His belief was
justified as Davis tempted Barker down the wicket to be stumped by
Eifion Jones. The young spinner also had Fletcher smartly caught by
Bryan Davis, before Shepherd produced a beauty to bowl Irvine to
swing the balance back in Glamorgan's favour. Boyce and Taylor
soon followed, but there was a plucky partnership between Robin

Hobbs and Ray East and Essex agonisingly came closer and closer to the target. Shepherd eventually dismissed Hobbs in the penultimate over, and last man John Lever came in with Essex needing eight runs and Glamorgan just one more wicket. Amidst great tension, Lever and East scampered a few furtive singles, but they still needed three off the last ball. However, East deftly cut the final ball down towards the third man boundary and it looked as if the Essex tailender had made a match-winning stroke. But Ossie Wheatley, on one of his rare appearances, sprinted around the ropes and returned an arrow-like throw over the top of the stumps, Eifion Jones didn't have to move an inch and he triumphantly removed the bails with Lever well out of his ground and Glamorgan had won by one run.

This nerve-tingling win put Glamorgan in a virtually unassailable position, and a win over either Worcestershire or Surrey would guarantee the title. A crowd of over 10,000 flocked into Sophia Gardens for the Worcestershire match and they were able to witness one of the finest innings of the summer. The Cardiff wicket was still unpredictable and most of the Welsh batsmen found batting difficult against Holder, Brain and Gifford. The exception was Majid; the graceful Pakistani remained unruffled and used his magical charm to make 156 out of the total of 265. Hugh Jeffreys, the Glamorgan scorer, summed up Majid's breathtaking mastery of the Worcestershire attack by saying: 'It was an innings which defied description; suffice to say that the next highest scorer was Alan Jones with a mere 37.'

Worcestershire could muster only 183 against the accurate Welsh bowlers, with only Ron Headley and captain Tom Graveney looking comfortable against Nash, Wheatley and Shepherd. Glamorgan had a useful lead of 82, so once again Lewis told his batsmen to go for quick runs. Walker responded with an aggressive 63 and Eifion Jones made a breezy 39 before being hit on the head by Holder. He was helped into the Glamorgan dressing room in a dazed condition; the medical opinion was that he should rest, but the loyal keeper was not going to miss out on the kill, and despite still feeling giddy, he took his place on the field as Lewis challenged the visitors to make 255.

Nash and Cordle got in amongst the early Worcestershire batsmen, with the Barbadian sending back Cass, Ormrod, D'Oliveira and Graveney with less than 50 runs on the board. Lewis brought on Shepherd and the veteran spinner steadily worked his way through the lower order, and in the process took his 2,000th first-class wicket. He finished proceedings by getting Brian Brain caught at slip off bat and box and Glamorgan had won by 147 runs to become County Champions once again. It was a moment of sheer delight for Lewis and he remembers how as 'the crowds gathered I looked for Don Shepherd and he for me. We hugged each other briefly and walked off

GLAMORGAN *v.* ESSEX

Played at Swansea, 30 August and 1 and 2 September 1969

GLAMORGAN WON BY 1 RUN

GLAMORGAN	FIRST INNINGS		SECOND INNINGS	
A. Jones	c Boyce b Turner	75	c Taylor b Lever	69
R. C. Davis	lbw b Boyce	2	b Lever	2
M. J. Khan	c Turner b East	23	b Turner	28
*A. R. Lewis	c Taylor b Turner	1	c Irvine b Lever	21
B. A. Davis	c Ward b East	78	c Irvine b Hobbs	5
P. M. Walker	c Barker b Hobbs	14	c Ward b Boyce	50
†E. W. Jones	c Fletcher b East	0	st Taylor b Hobbs	28
A. E. Cordle	c Taylor b Boyce	20	b Hobbs	30
M. A. Nash	c Edmeades b Lever	14	not out	36
D. J. Shepherd	not out	2	not out	2
O. S. Wheatley	c and b Hobbs	0		
Extras		12		13
Total		241	(for 8 wkts dec)	284

1st inns: 1-5, 2-58, 3-65, 4-156, 5-196, 6-210, 7-210, 8-230, 9-239
2nd inns: 1-8, 2-50, 3-90, 4-109, 5-144, 6-181, 7-227, 8-272

BOWLING	O	M	R	W	O	M	R	W
Boyce	18	3	52	2	25	5	79	1
Lever	15	5	38	1	22	4	64	3
East	19	3	63	3	9	3	19	0
Turner	20	8	44	2	11	1	31	1
Hobbs	11.1	2	32	2	36	16	78	3
Fletcher					1	1	0	0

ESSEX	FIRST INNINGS		SECOND INNINGS	
B. Ward	c R. Davis b Wheatley	31	c R. Davis b Wheatley	21
B. Edmeades	lbw b Nash	4	c Lewis b Wheatley	10
G. Barker	lbw b Wheatley	17	st E. Jones b R. Davis	28
K. W. R. Fletcher	lbw b Wheatley	49	c B. Davis b R. Davis	44
L. Irvine	b R. Davis	109	b Shepherd	29
K. Boyce	c B. Davis b Shepherd	16	c Lewis b R. Davis	11
*†B. Taylor	c Cordle b R. Davis	70	c Lewis b Wheatley	5
S. Turner	not out	23	c R. Davis b Shepherd	2
R. N. S. Hobbs	not out	8	c E. Jones b Shepherd	17
R. E. East			not out	14
J. K. Lever			run out	2
Extras		9		5
Total	(for 7 wkts dec)	336		188

1st inns: 1-5, 2-48, 3-63, 4-139, 5-165, 6-294, 7-304
2nd inns: 1-29, 2-36, 3-43, 4-109, 5-123, 6-125, 7-131, 8-163, 9-185

BOWLING	O	M	R	W	O	M	R	W
Nash	24	5	84	1	3	0	16	0
Wheatley	26	3	77	3	10	0	40	3
Cordle	8	2	32	0	4	0	33	0
Shepherd	28	10	78	1	11	0	56	3
Walker	3	0	20	0				
R. Davis	10	1	36	2	9	0	38	3

Umpires: D. J. Constant and G. H. Pope

This was a nail-biting win which put Glamorgan on course for the title. Essex were set a fair fourth-innings target, but they struggled against the accurate Glamorgan bowlers and the superb outfielding, especially by Wheatley, who ran out Lever off the final ball.

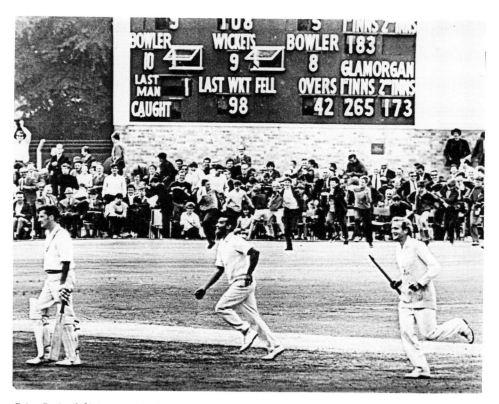

Brian Brain (left) is out, and Glamorgan have won. Bryan Davis and Malcolm Nash quickly grab mementoes before the crowd invades the pitch. (Western Mail)

together. We had hit near perfection – his caution, control and devoted professionalism, and my own musketeering instincts with a team of many skills and adaptability, and without too many egos getting in the way of an overall design which called for unselfishness.'

Congratulations flooded in from all over the country and Welsh exiles overseas who had been eagerly following the team's progress in the newspapers and on the BBC World Service. Telegrams arrived by the sackload, proving the extent of support for the Welsh county, and even Prince Charles sent a message: 'I am delighted by your splendid win, especially in this particular year. Many congratulations – do it again next year!' Lewis's team had won several awards from national newspapers and they stored up the crates of champagne for the Championship-winning party on the evening of the victory over Worcestershire. The small pavilion bar at Cardiff rang out as the team and their elated followers celebrated with songs of every description.

TONY LEWIS

Although born in Swansea, Tony Lewis was brought up in Neath, close to the Gnoll ground. Like so many youngsters in South Wales, he soon developed an interest in sport, and emerged as a talented rugby player and cricketer at Neath Grammar School. He also showed promise as a violinist and was preparing to go on the Welsh National Youth Orchestra's summer tour in 1955 when he was called up to make his County debut for Glamorgan.

After his National Service, Tony went up to Cambridge University to read history, and became a double Blue by representing the university at both cricket and rugby. After coming down, he established a regular place in the Glamorgan team and became one of the mainstays of their batting in the 1960s. During the winter he continued to play rugby and began a career in journalism and broadcasting, into which he went after retiring in 1974.

Back in the late 1950s, Lewis came under the wing of Wilf Wooller, who believed even then that the young amateur would one day captain the Welsh county. This prophecy came true in 1967, and Tony quickly established himself as one of the most astute leaders on the county cricuit, and in 1972/3 led England on their winter tour of India, Pakistan and Sri Lanka.

Tony's finest hour as a cricketer came in 1969 when he led Glamorgan to the Championship. Their success was based upon the excellent team spirit which he had forged and everyone made an important contribution at one time or another. No one was more delighted than Tony at the team's success, and at the end of the season, he went to a host of functions to celebrate their win. In fact, the story goes that so often did he make a speech during the autumn that when his young daughter banged with her spoon on the table at home he automatically rose to say a few words!

Tony Lewis – the man who led Glamorgan to their second Championship title.

The Welsh members sang their traditional melodies, whilst Bryan Davis and Cordle chipped in with Caribbean calypsos.

At the end of the season, Glamorgan were honoured by the appointment of Lewis as captain of MCC's touring team to the Far East. Alan Jones and Don Shepherd were also selected and 'The Three Musketeers' played with distinction at some exotic locations in Ceylon, Malaysia, Singapore and Hong Kong. Jones struck centuries at Colombo and Bangkok, whilst Shepherd took five for 16 against the Royal Bangkok Sports Club. Lewis also led the Welsh county on their celebratory three-week tour of the West Indies in April 1970 which Peter Walker had arranged with the help of Rizla, the cigarette paper manufacturers.

The Glamorgan team performed reasonably well on what remains their only overseas venture outside the UK in the Club's history. They lost the opening match against St George's CC in Bermuda, but they drew the next three games against St Kitts, Windward Islands and Grenada. The party then flew to Trinidad for the final two fixtures of the tour. The first, a 40-over match with Trinidad Colts, was won by 25 runs with Roger Davis taking three for 19, but the second, the 'mini-test' at Port of Spain against Trinidad, ended in a five-wicket defeat, despite a graceful century from Alan Jones.

These games in the Caribbean proved to be useful match practice and the Glamorgan team returned to Britain hoping to obey the royal request they had received after the Worcestershire match and retain the title in 1970. After their rousing Championship success, many commentators were predicting that the 1970s would see Glamorgan achieve greater consistency and further success. However, it was not to be, as things went from bad to worse in the next ten years or so, with the 1970s proving to be the most turbulent decade in the Club's history.

THE SORRY SEVENTIES

FEW COULD HAVE PREDICTED the worries ahead as Glamorgan had another good summer in 1970 and finished in second place. It soon became evident that the side had benefited from the Caribbean tour as Kent were beaten in the opening game of the season. Other wins in May and June kept them in the top three in the table; the air of confidence within the Welsh camp can be gauged from the way they defeated Somerset at Glastonbury, although everything did not go according to plan at first. Somerset declared at 323 for nine and then Tom Cartwright ran through the Welsh batting, leaving Shepherd and Williams desperately saving the follow on. Somerset went for quick runs and left the Welshmen a formidable target of 331 on the final day. Majid and Lewis made breezy half-centuries, followed by a superb 91 from Bryan Davis, to put Glamorgan on course for a five-wicket victory with time in hand.

Lewis' team entered August knowing that a further three or four victories would see them retain the title. They travelled to Cheltenham with high hopes of repeating the victory the year before, but their optimism was dispelled as the home team made 324 and rain dampened the wicket just as Glamorgan were about to commence their reply. They lost two wickets with 15 runs on the board, and then David Allen joined the attack and began to turn the ball prodigiously bowling to Tony Lewis and Majid. At the end of an over from the spinner, Lewis walked down the wicket to his partner and glumly said: 'We are going to get stuffed here if we are not careful', to which the Pakistani curiously replied: 'Not if you're buying ice-creams again!' Cheltenham is famous for its delicious Cotswold Dairy ice creams and the Pakistani had a liking for them. The previous year Lewis had struck a 'bet' with him and had bought the Pakistani two ices for his innings of 69. So Lewis said 'Of course I'll buy you an ice-cream', and Majid replied: 'Last year I make mistake – this year I shall have lots and lots of ice-cream.' And he did, 'winning' six ices in all for a majestic innings of 157. Together with Lewis, the Pakistani put on 176 inside two hours and saw Glamorgan to a 32-run lead. Shepherd and Walker then exploited the turning wicket and the Welshmen were left chasing a target of 121. The openers went cheaply once again, but watchful batting by Majid and his captain saw them to a five-wicket win.

Another amusing incident came after the game with Warwickshire at Edgbaston as the team made their way on to Middlesbrough to play Yorkshire. Kevin Lyons and Lawrence Williams were in charge of the team van, and they had a truly epic journey. They initially got lost and then broke down in the middle of the Yorkshire moors, and had to get a tow from a lorry. But as they were going over a hill the towrope broke and the lorry disappeared. Lyons and Williams eventually got the van repaired in the middle of the night, and arrived at Middlesbrough with the team's kit with barely half-an-hour to spare, much to the relief of the rest of the side. But as fate would cruelly have it, Glamorgan lost the toss and the two weary travellers had to go out to field. Lewis tossed the ball to Williams and asked him to open the bowling, to which the 'Tonna Terror' replied: 'Not a wink of sleep, stuck on the Yorkshire moors, and then straight out of the van to bowl at Yorkshire. Where's the glamour in playing county cricket?'

Glamorgan went to the top of the table ahead of Lancashire in mid-August after an amazing victory over Sussex at St Helen's. It was brought about by another display of gifted batting from the overseas stars and a sporting declaration by Lewis. Rain caused the loss of eight hours on the first two days, so after a delayed start on the last afternoon, Lewis declared with Glamorgan 148 runs behind. Jim Parks optimistically declared the Sussex second innings after three overs, and left Glamorgan 154 in ninety minutes plus the final twenty overs. Lewis crossed his fingers and hoped his batsmen would achieve the target on the damp wicket. He need not have worried as Bryan Davis and Majid nonchalantly stroked the ball all around the ground to set up a nine-wicket victory.

Kent were closing the gap in third place, so Glamorgan desperately needed to defeat Northants in their next game. Rain curtailed play once again on the first two days, but Roger Prideaux, the visitors' captain, was more wary with his declaration on the last day, knowing of the way Davis and Majid had made a mockery of the target in the Sussex match. He set the Welshmen 241 in 150 minutes, but they never looked like making it, despite a brave 88 from Lewis. However, their morale was boosted in the next match as Don Shepherd took 12 Derbyshire wickets to set up a four-wicket victory, meaning that the outcome of the Championship would not be decided until after the final round of matches.

Glamorgan were playing Lancashire at Sophia Gardens, whilst Kent were playing at Folkestone and a victory for any of the three would almost guarantee the title. However, rain intervened yet again at Cardiff after Lancashire had declared on 303 for five, and Glamorgan were trapped on a damp wicket and forced to follow on. A bold 114 from Walker saw them to safety in the second innings, but news came through from Folkestone that Kent were on the verge of an innings victory over Leicestershire. Lewis realised he had to bowl Lancashire out again if Glamorgan were to retain the title, so he set them 137 in the final session. They lost early wickets but never looked like being bowled out and the game petered out into a damp draw. The title went to Kent and the Welshmen were left to ponder on the vagaries of the British climate, though the weather was not entirely to blame, as there had been several instances where victory had agonisingly slipped from the team's grasp. None of these was more infuriating than against Essex, whose last pair, East and Lever, held out throughout the last hour to save the match.

The team were also troubled by injuries – Nash damaged his hip, whilst Alan Jones, the cornerstone of the batting, suffered from back trouble. Ironically Jones started the season in blistering form, and after centuries against Hampshire and Worcestershire, was close to making 1,000 runs in May. His outstanding form earned him a well deserved, and long overdue, place in the England side against the Rest of the World in the first 'Test' at Lord's. However, he made 5 and 0, both times caught behind the wicket by Farokh Engineer off Mike Procter's bowling. Cowdrey and Edrich were restored to the England team for the second match of the series, and after his disappointing debut, Jones was one of the batsmen to make way for them. Soon afterwards, the left-hander ricked his back, which had been aching for some time, and he was forced to miss the last six weeks of the season.

Despite the misfortune of Alan Jones, the Welsh supporters were able to take some consolation from the performances of Don Shepherd and Eifion Jones. 'Shep' topped the national bowling averages with 106 wickets, whilst Jones created a new County record with 90 victims to become the country's leading wicket-keeper, and came close to selection for the MCC's winter tour of Australia. However, their delight was tempered by the news that Bryan Davis was quitting county cricket. The Trinidadian's family had not settled down in Cardiff, and he wanted to return with them to the West Indies and commute to play for Glamorgan in the summer months. But he was unable to find any work in Trinidad which would allow him to do this, and he reluctantly had to leave the Club. The committee spent the winter months seeking a replacement, and amongst the names considered were Alvin Kallicharran, Norbert Philip, Abid Ali and Hedley Howarth. However, the eventual choice was Roy Fredericks, the 29-year-old opener from Guyana.

The departure of Davis was the first misfortune to hit the club and 1970 marked the end of their table-topping era. They sank to 15th place in 1971 after a number of key players were injured early in the season. Fredericks broke a bone in his forearm in only the third match, and was not fit until July, whilst Lewis and Walker both picked up niggling strains in the early weeks and were handicapped for much of the summer. However, the most serious, and almost the most tragic in the Club's history, came in the match with Warwickshire at Sophia Gardens at the end of May. Roger Davis had emerged as a fearless and quite brilliant short-leg, and was crouching in his customary position (and remember these were the days before shin-pads or helmets were introduced). Neal Abberley, the Warwickshire opener, middled a leg glance off Nash which hit Davis a sickening blow on the temple. The stricken fielder collapsed in a macabre silence and went into violent convulsions with legs twitching and jerking.

Some of the shocked Glamorgan fielders ran to the pavilion to summon medical help, but fortunately there was a doctor in the members' enclosure and seeing the situation, he sprinted out to give help. As Davis's face took on a dark blue tint, the doctor announced that the player had stopped breathing and he began mouth-to-mouth resuscitation. Thankfully, he started to breath again and after a seemingly endless 20 minutes, Davis was carried off the field and taken to hospital. The shaken Glamorgan team continued the match, but they had been unnerved by what had happened. They lost the game by eight wickets, and Tony Cordle took over at short-leg wearing a white boxing helmet. The immediate news from the hospital was not good – Davis at first could not speak coherently and there were fears that he was suffering from brain damage. Davis dispelled these by making a full recovery and he was able to return to the team in mid-August, though he was wise enough never to field at short-leg again.

A second factor in the slide down the table was the loss of form by several senior players. Alan Jones was still hampered by injury and was not at his best, whilst Shepherd only took 70 wickets and Walker 38. Fredericks also failed to show any consistency with the bat and his adventurous style brought heavy criticism from some writers, who felt that a county opener should push straight down the line in the early overs, rather than attempt the unorthodox. He silenced some critics with a blistering 84 against Yorkshire in their Sunday League encounter at Swansea, but the overall feeling was that his cavalier approach was not suited to the needs of the three-day games.

As a result of the crop of injuries, the Glamorgan side included a number of young colts, including Maesteg's Gwyn Richards and Clive Davies, a young spinner from the MCC groundstaff. Others to get their chances were Mike Llewellyn, an all-rounder from Clydach, Stuart Harrison, a seamer from Cwmbran and Robert Hadley, the Neath-born Cambridge blue. When 17-year-old John Hopkins made 88 on his debut at Colwyn Bay, there were wide smiles on the faces of the County's officials, but one swallow does not make a summer and many of the young players found life hard in county cricket. Some of the batsmen were nervous starters and only showed fleeting glances of their true potential when they were fortunate to survive their opening

A smiling Roger Davis after fully recovering from his near-fatal accident.
(Sport and General)

overs. There were disappointments too from a financial point of view, with the Treasurer reporting a cash loss of £12,000 to bring back memories of the inter-war period.

Overall, 1971 was not a happy 50th year of first-class cricket for the Welsh club, and the committee realised that the Championship-winning unit was starting to break up. Their greatest fear lay in the bowling; Cordle and Williams had disappointing seasons and none of the youngsters made any impact. Consequently, the officials considered various players released by other clubs, including Bob Willis, Bob Cottam and Mike Selvey. In addition, Phil Edmonds, the Cambridge blue and future Test player, travelled to Cardiff to discuss terms with Wooller, but the young spinner declined the Welsh county's offer and joined Middlesex. Eventually, 'Butch' White, the

37-year-old former Test bowler joined the club from Hampshire, together with John Solanky, a 30-year-old Tanzanian who had a good record playing for Devon.

Despite the signings, the decline continued in 1972, when just one County Championship game was won, and for the first time since 1922 they failed to win a home Championship match. Once again, they failed to make any impact either in the one-day competitions, finishing bottom of the Sunday League, only getting as far as the third round of the Gillette Cup and losing to Warwickshire in the quarter-final of the Benson and Hedges Cup. The team seemed to lose confidence in their ability and all too frequently hit the self-destruct button after getting into promising positions. An example was the match with Northants at Swansea; after the visitors had made 300, Alan Jones and Roy Fredericks shared a record opening stand of 330, with the West Indian making a career best 228 not out. His five-hour stay at the wicket confounded his critics who believed he was not capable of a long innings. The visitors set Glamorgan a fair target of 248 in 145 minutes, and at 211 for three with over half an hour to go, a Glamorgan victory seemed on the cards. But they lost their last seven wickets to Bedi and Cottam for the addition of just seven runs and Northants gained a surprise win.

Another disappointing display occurred in the end-of-season Sunday League game against Worcestershire at Colwyn Bay. The visitors were put in and lost three early wickets against Nash. They were struggling at 42 for four, but then some slack fielding let them off the hook and they were able to recover and set Glamorgan a target of 178. Jones and Fredericks gave them a steady start, before Majid accelerated the tempo with a rapid half century. They seemed well on course at 160 for three with plenty of overs in hand, but there was another startling collapse as five wickets were lost against Holder and Brain, including three in the last over when just three more runs were needed. They finished on 175 for eight to give Worcestershire a two-run win, and once again the journalists were able to attach the cliché 'snatching defeat from the jaws of victory' to the way the Welshmen played. This match was Don Shepherd's last for Glamorgan, as the veteran spinner decided to retire at the end of the season. The North Waleans were the last to see him perform in Glamorgan's colours, and he hung up his well-worn bowling boots with more first-class wickets to his credit than any other cricketer not to play in Tests.

The behind-the-scenes bickerings began to reach the surface during the summer, and sadly they were to mar events throughout the decade. There was the start of some friction between players and senior officials, together with a breakdown in communciation between the committee and the team. In addition, Tony Lewis did not

DON SHEPHERD

For 24 years Don Shepherd bowled with his classical high action and commanded respect from all of the leading batsmen on the county circuit. His reward was a record 2,174 wickets, yet despite numerous appearances for the MCC and the Players, he never played in Tests, for reasons that still remain a mystery.

He changed styles in the 1950s from fast bowling and became one of the finest off-spinners in the country, taking over 100 wickets on 12 occasions. He was quicker than the average spinner, and had the priceless ability to undercut the ball and make it move in the air to deceive a batsman, making him think it was an off-break, only to edge it into the slips or to the wicket-keeper, who would often stand back to Shepherd.

'Shep' was virtually unplayable on helpful wickets, as testified by a series of truly remarkable analyses, including six for 5 against Nottinghamshire in 1961, five for 2 against Leicestershire in 1965 and seven for 7 against Hampshire in 1966. He was also an aggressive lower-order batsman, who frequently launched a series of furious assaults on the bowling, the most spectacular being in 1961 when he scored a half-century against the Australians in just 15 minutes. Shepherd was a model senior professional to Tony Lewis during the 1960s, and his wise counsel was an important factor behind the Championship success in 1969. His experience has not been lost to the Club since 'Shep' now combines his duties as a radio commentator with a role as the County's bowling adviser.

Don Shepherd and colleagues celebrate the 1969 Championship win.
(Western Mail)

enjoy the role of hatchet man, and this bad feeling within the Club was affecting his own form, and he told the committee that he wanted to step down from the captaincy at the end of the season. He candidly remembers that there was 'a feeling of mistrust which had grown up between players and the Club, the captain inevitably squeezed in the middle of the sandwich placating neither side and both parties trying to eat him for breakfast. If I had been fully fit to play regularly, I would have fought on. As it was my painful knee injury, following an endless shoulder injury, persuaded me to resign.'

Despite these injuries, Lewis was appointed as the England captain on the MCC winter tour to India and Pakistan, and on 20 December 1972, Lewis became the first Glamorgan player to captain England in Test cricket by leading out the team for the first Test at the Feroz Shah Kotla ground in Delhi. Despite a duck in his first innings, Lewis shared in an unbroken partnership of 101 with Tony Greig to steer England to a six-wicket win shortly after lunch on Christmas Day. Later, in the fourth Test at Kanpur, Lewis scored his maiden Test century, making 125 in brilliant style against the canny Indian spinners. His effort was even more remarkable considering that the touring party had received written threats, allegedly from the Black September terrorist movement, saying that one of them would be killed. The threats came to nothing, but with all the worry, it was not surprising that India won the series 2-1.

Whilst the England team worried over their safety, the Glamorgan committee spent the winter months deciding who should replace Lewis as captain. Don Shepherd would have made an ideal replacement had he not retired, and the officials were left with a difficult decision. Peter Walker was one of the candidates, having led the team when Lewis had been absent, but the 1972 season had ended on a sour note for the all-rounder. He had been out of form and was dropped for the match at Worcester to make way for some of the younger players. The all-rounder did not like the decision, and the way some of the senior players were being handled, feeling that the Club's officials were making decisions without consulting the players. Walker began to ponder on his future and was reluctant to sign a new contract while there was friction between the dressing room and the committee room. His uncertain mood was not helped by the offer of a match contract only for 1973, without a retainer. Walker admits that: 'I became a source of some irritation to the committee, so it was obviously useful to remove me . . . The way out was to offer me terms that were both insulting financially and degrading professionally, leaving me, as probably intended, no option but to decline.' Despite these contractual difficulties, Walker was one of the people tipped to be the new Glamorgan captain when the cricket committee met to resolve the situation in early February. Nash and Roger Davis also had their supporters, but the eventual choice was Majid, with Alan Jones as his senior professional. It was clear to Walker that his future lay in journalism and on 2 March the committee received a letter from him formally resigning from the Club.

Glamorgan often had an inexperienced line-up in 1973 with young spinner Barry Lloyd, Arthur Francis, a batsman from Clydach and 16-year-old Alan Lewis Jones from Alltwen, as the officials hastily undertook a rebuilding programme. But once again, there was no substitute for experience, and the youthful side won only four games and finished in the lower half of the table. The only things the Welsh supporters had to cheer were Tony Lewis's selection for the first Test at Trent Bridge, and the allocation of a one-day international to St Helen's in July. A crowd in excess of 10,000 turned up and saw England comfortably defeat New Zealand by seven wickets with Dennis Amiss making a workmanlike century. But by now Ray Illingworth had resumed his duties as England captain, and after Lewis's failure with the bat at Nottingham, and his withdrawl from the second Test through injury, there was no Welsh presence in the England team. Lewis continued to struggle with his knee for most of the season, and was understandably out of form and unable to reclaim his Test place. Alan Jones and Majid also had indifferent spells, and the Glamorgan batting became even more thin when Roy Fredericks left in mid-June to join the West Indian touring party.

Even before his departure to join his fellow countrymen, there were some doubts over Fredericks' future with the Club. The Welsh attack was struggling, with only Nash regularly troubling the opposition batsmen, and it became clear that an overseas fast bowler was needed. A number of Test bowlers, including Imran Khan, were mentioned as possible replacements, but the TCCB were tightening up the rules on overseas players in county cricket and under their regulations another foreign player could be signed only if Majid or Fredericks was released. Wilf Wooller was one of the Pakistani's leading supporters, so it was clearly a case of whether or not Fredericks would stay. Even before the start of the season, the committee considered releasing the West Indian in order to sign a bowler, but no decision was taken because Majid, who ironically supported Fredericks' retention, was likely to be touring England with the Pakistan team in 1974. This meant that the Welsh county could sign another overseas player and they contacted Lord's to get the TCCB's blessing. However, complications had arisen over Solanky's status and despite his qualification with Devon, the Registration Committee deemed that Solanky would be considered as an overseas player until the end of the 1974 season. In short, this meant that the Club could not sign another overseas player immediately.

There was another twist in the Fredericks saga during the summer as some of the young Welsh batsmen began to make encouraging progress in the first team. It soon became clear that if Fredericks was given another contact for 1974, there would be room only for one of the young colts, and the committee's dilemma now became a matter of principle – whether the Club should engage and give priority to overseas players such as Fredericks, or whether they should continue to develop home-grown players as had been the practice since the days of Turnbull and Clay. Strong arguments were raised to support both views. On the one hand, Roger Davis had flourished as an opener in Fredericks's absence, whilst Hopkins, Llewellyn, Richards and Ellis, a young batsman from Llandudno, were all making sound progress and had been waiting in the wings long enough. On the other hand, there was a school of thought that overseas players should be hired, especially if they brought a winning team, whilst others argued that Fredericks's experience would be invaluable in Majid's absence and if Tony Lewis continued to be hampered by his knee injury.

The committee spent a long time reviewing both of these arguments and eventually a vote was taken at the general committee meeting at the Bridgend Police Club on 18 December. The voting went 11–10 in favour of not retaining Fredericks and it was agreed that the West Indian should be released. It brought a torrent of objections and at the 1974 AGM Peter Walker criticised the Club officials 'not only for their general approach to Fredericks, but to star players and their naïve faith in local talent which is not, in my view, of a high enough standard to compete in the modern first-class game.'

Negotiations began for an overseas fast bowler who could appear in 1975 when Solanky had completed his residence qualification. Amongst the names considered was Sarfraz Nawaz, the Pakistani opening bowler, but he decided the rejoin Northants. Majid recommended Jeff Thomson or Dennis Lillee, but the Club were seeking a long term replacement, and members of the cricket committee believed that neither Australian was likely to give lengthy service. So instead the chairman of the cricket committee, Bill Edwards, contacted officials in the West Indies about any likely recruits. At that time there were a number of young bowlers on the fringe of the West Indies team who were keen to get into county cricket, including Michael Holding, Uton Dowe and Greg Armstrong, and eventually it was the latter who was invited to South Wales in the second half of the season for an extended trial.

The 1974 season turned out to be yet another bleak one, as the Club ended in 16th place in the Championship with just two wins to their credit. They fared little better in the Sunday League or the Benson and Hedges Cup, whilst there was an embarrassing defeat against Lincolnshire in the Gillette Cup. The Welshmen were put in by the

Greg Armstrong, the Club's somewhat erratic West Indian fast bowler of the mid-1970s. (Universal Pictorial)

minor county on a damp Swansea wicket, and in the humid atmosphere they collapsed to 59 for eight, before a brave partnership between Nash and Cordle took the score to 155. The wicket had dried out by the afternoon, and as the tide went out, conditions became easier for batting, allowing the visitors to coast to a six-wicket win.

This defeat was a great blow to the morale of the young Glamorgan side, but without a doubt, the biggest setback came towards the end of July when Tony Lewis sadly had to announce his retirement, despite having fully recovered from his injuries. As with Peter Walker, Lewis's decision was due in part to the committee's refusal to offer him a full contract. Though his presence in an inexperienced side would have been invaluable, the officials would only offer him a match fee. Lewis was naturally upset, but he realized that the youthful side needed his experience, and played in all the early games. However, by mid-season he could manage no longer the day-to-day demands of county cricket and decided to retire. Just to add to the Club's worries, Majid was absent from mid-June, so Alan Jones took over the captaincy. He tried his best with the raw talent that was available, and the only Championship win under his leadership that year proved that the young team did have high potential. This came in unlikely circumstances at Sophia Gardens against County Champions Hampshire. Nevertheless, Glamorgan won, and they did so after nearly having to follow on! Hampshire made 234 in their first innings, and then their ferocious West Indian paceman, Andy Roberts, reduced Glamorgan to 43 for seven by the close of the first day, with Roberts having claimed all seven wickets. On the Monday morning, Roger Davis bravely guided the team past the follow-on, but Hampshire still had a useful first innings lead of 144 and their opening pair, Barry Richards and Gordon Greenidge, was amongst the best in the world. However, Nash and Cordle were undaunted by this and they used the new ball wisely, taking four early wickets. Young Barry Lloyd spun his way through the middle order and removed the dangerous Richards, and Glamorgan were left with a target of 284. It seemed a daunting prospect after the way Roberts had wrecked their first innings, but they had plenty of time in which to seee him off, and they bravely knuckled down and applied themselves. No more so than Len Hill, the Newport County footballer, who had been playing for the Club ever since 1964, but had never had the opportunity really to establish himself. He was struck several painful blows by the quicker bowlers, but he bravely soldiered on to make 90, and together with Eifion Jones steered Glamorgan to a heart-warming win by five wickets.

This fine win lifted the morale of the young colts and a further boost came with Armstrong's promising debut against the Pakistani tourists. The West Indian dismissed both Majid and Mushtaq in a fiery opening burst on an easy paced wicket and it looked as if the Glamorgan batsmen would not have to put up with a torrent of short-pitched bowling any more because they did not have anyone to dish it back. The committee were also delighted at the prospect of the Club having an overseas quick bowler at long last, but their delight was tempered by yet another gloomy financial report. The lack of success had caused membership levels to plummet down, and a number of cost-saving measures had to be introduced, including the dropping of Neath and Colwyn Bay from the fixture list.

It was believed that Armstrong's signing could be the turning point the club so badly needed, but the West Indian failed to make a major impact and was plagued by a run-up problem which resulted in a spate of no-balls in 1975. Wooller and the coaching staff made an attempt to rectify these faults, but Armstrong still finished the summer with a modest haul of 45 wickets at a cost of 31. Despite Armstrong's difficulties, the team made some improvement and rose to ninth place. The batsmen were in good form, with Roger Davis making a career best 1,243 runs, whilst both Majid and Alan Jones passed 1,300 runs.

GLAMORGAN *v.* HAMPSHIRE

Played at Sophia Gardens, Cardiff, 17, 19 and 20 August 1974

GLAMORGAN WON BY FIVE WICKETS

HAMPSHIRE	FIRST INNINGS		SECOND INNINGS	
B. A. Richards	b Nash	42	b Lloyd	60
C. G. Greenidge	lbw b Nash	15	c and b Nash	1
D. R. Turner	b Nash	13	lbw b Nash	5
*R. M. C. Gilliat	c A. Jones b Davis	65	lbw b Cordle	11
T. E. Jesty	b Nash	8	b Cordle	3
P. J. Sainsbury	lbw b Solanky	9	c Richards b Lloyd	6
N. G. Cowley	c and b Solanky	6	b Lloyd	6
M. N. S. Taylor	c Lloyd b Nash	23	c Cordle b Davis	8
†G. R. Stephenson	not out	32	c Hill b Nash	19
R. S. Herman	b Davis	0	c Lloyd b Nash	10
A. M. E. Roberts	b Cordle	12	not out	2
Extras		9		6
Total		234		137

1st inns: 1-43, 2-60, 3-81, 4-100, 5-129, 6-165, 7-166, 8-216, 9-218
2nd inns: 1-7, 2-20, 3-41, 4-45, 5-89, 6-90, 7-101, 8-107, 9-135

BOWLING	O	M	R	W	O	M	R	W
Nash	29	5	73	5	11.5	4	35	4
Williams	11	4	36	0	5	0	11	0
Davis	26	6	35	2	16	6	24	1
Lloyd	2	0	12	0	14	7	26	3
Cordle	11.1	1	24	1	11	2	23	2
Solanky	19	6	45	2	3	0	12	0

GLAMORGAN	FIRST INNINGS		SECOND INNINGS	
*A. Jones	c Richards b Roberts	15	run out	33
G. P. Ellis	c Sainsbury b Roberts	8	c Gilliat b Cowley	11
R. C. Davis	not out	33	not out	32
L. W. Hill	lbw b Roberts	1	c Greenidge b Cowley	90
J. W. Solanky	b Roberts	0		
G. Richards	b Roberts	0	lbw b Roberts	10
†E. W. Jones	lbw b Roberts	0	c Herman b Sainsbury	67
A. E. Cordle	c Richards b Roberts	16	not out	28
B. J. Lloyd	c Stephenson b Roberts	0		
M. A. Nash	c and b Sainsbury	2		
D. L. Williams	run out	3		
Extras		12		13
Total		90	(for 5 wkts)	284

1st inns: 1-16, 2-29, 3-39, 4-41, 5-41, 6-41, 7-41, 8-63, 9-72
2nd inns: 1-19, 2-60, 3-118, 4-224, 5-248

BOWLING	O	M	R	W	O	M	R	W
Roberts	22	6	47	8	31	5	91	1
Herman	7	2	21	0	15	2	29	0
Taylor	5	2	4	0	5	2	7	0
Sainsbury	10.2	7	6	1	63	38	73	1
Cowley	1	1	0	0	21.1	7	43	2
Richards					12	5	25	0
Jesty					5	4	3	0

Umpires: D. J. Constant and D. G. L. Evans

Hopkins and Francis both showed they had the temperament to succeed, whilst A. L. Jones hit a sparkling 55 opening the innings against Australia. There was still a Jekyll and Hyde aspect to the batting – on their day, the batsmen could be extremely good, yet at others they could be bad – but overall the good days outnumbered the bad.

The best batting displays came at Wellingborough in the Sunday match with Northants as Majid scored one of the fastest ever fifties in the competition, despite arriving late at the ground after getting lost en route from London. The Northants fielders must have wished that he had never got there, as the Glamorgan captain raced to 50 off only 22 balls and ended with 75 in 27 minutes, with five sixes and seven fours. Ellis chipped in with 66 and Davis 75 as Glamorgan finished on 266 for six. Nash and Davis soon got amongst the home batting, which slumped to 68 for seven. Resistance was finally ended by Alan Jones, who took the last three wickets with his well flighted off-breaks, bowling in tandem with brother Eifion.

Nash and Solanky took the bowling honours during the season, with the left-armer claiming 85 victims, including 14 wickets in the victory over Hampshire at Basingstoke, with a career best nine for 56 in the first innings. He also returned his best figures in the Sunday League in the end of season game at Worcester, claiming six for 29, including five wickets in his last seven balls. On the debit side, however, Cordle took only 49 wickets and Williams played in just three games and began considering a job outside cricket. The team were also without a top-class left-arm spinner, though there was a glimmer of hope when 22-year-old Tony Allin from Devon agreed to join the Club for 1976. He had produced a number of good performances for the minor county and the Welsh county had high hopes of him. They also acquired the services of 19-year-old Rodney Ontong, an all-rounder from South Africa who had been on the MCC groundstaff and had played for the second eleven on the recommendation of Len Muncer.

The results in 1975 had proved that the youngsters had the ability to succeed at first-class level and the acquisition of Allin and Ontong further strengthened the staff. It was widely believed that Glamorgan had turned the corner – how wrong this proved as the Club entered into one of its darkest hours and became notable more for events in the committee room than on the field of play.

Glamorgan's largely inexperienced side struggled in the early stages of this game against the talented Hampshire team, in particular Andy Roberts whose bowling almost forced Jones's team to follow on. However, they tenaciously fought back and thanks to determined contributions from Len Hill and Eifion Jones, they ended up the worthy winners.

THE 'MAJID AFFAIR' AND A LORD'S FINAL

THE LONG, HOT SUMMER of 1976 turned out to be one of the most troublesome in the Club's history, as the team finished bottom of the Championship for the first time since 1929 and occupied 16th place in the Sunday League. The first-class season began with heavy defeats against Somerset, Lancashire and Northants, and the first Championship win eventually came at the end of June, when Warwickshire were defeated by three wickets after Cordle and a revitalised Williams shared 15 victims. The main problem was that a number of batsmen were sadly out of form, including Majid, who averaged under 16 by mid-June. In addition, Armstrong took just 16 wickets in the first six games and was still as erratic as ever, delivering over 60 no-balls.

There was deep concern within the committee room about the poor results, especially after the progress which had been made in 1975. There was also a mounting loss of money, with the Club having already had a deficit of over £10,000 during the previous summer. The costs of staging first-class cricket were still high, but the bad form meant that gate receipts were still moderate, and little money was coming into the Club's coffers. There was growing criticism from the members about both the lack of results and the worrying financial situation, so the Club's officials had to be seen to be taking action. An economy sub-committee was created to study ways of further reducing expenditure and they made several recommendations, including cuts in administration costs and playing staff. The release of players had become a thorny issue and the legal department of the TCCB had advised all the county clubs on labour relations, in particular giving written warnings to anyone whose future was uncertain. Consequently letters were sent to six players at the end of June informing them that 'the officials are deeply concerned at the quality and standard of play', and 'are not happy about your personal performance. The Committee therefore felt it only right and proper that you should be advised at the earliest possible date of their opinion.' In short, they would not be re-engaged if their form did not improve.

Few eyebrows were raised when it was revealed that three of the six recipients of these letters were members of the second team – seamer Rupert Hill, wicket-keeper Kim Davies and batsman Tyrone Powell. None had hit the headlines or had staked a claim for inclusion in the first eleven, and could hardly have been surprised when the letters arrived. Powell eventually got a call-up, but few envied him when he was asked to make his debut against the West Indies at Swansea. He opened with Alan Jones in the first innings, but was clean bowled by Daniel for a duck. It wasn't surprising that soon after this traumatic start, Powell developed a stomach upset – who wouldn't have butterflies at the prospect of facing Holding, Daniel and Julien on a hard, fast wicket knowing that your future as a professional cricketer depended on it – he batted lower in the order in the second innings, but had the misfortune to go in to face Holding with his tail up and was dismissed without scoring again, a victim of highly questionable man management.

However, it was a huge surprise to discover that the other people who received the letters were Roger Davis, Lawrence Williams and Len Hill. The feelings of remoteness between players and committee had steadily grown worse, and with few senior players around to give wise council, the letters to these three intensified the difficulties. This had been the first bad patch Davis had encountered during his career and he was deeply shocked to receive a warning. A few days later he resigned in protest, and when Len Hill was axed at short notice for the match at Bournemouth, he also tendered his resignation. Many of the members were also surprised at the treatment of Davis and Hill, not to mention the unlucky Powell, and John Thomson, a member from Cardiff, began a protest campaign and called for an extraordinary general meeting where members could be told about what was happening.

Sophia Gardens and St Helen's were alive with rumour and speculation about other departures and as the team continued to struggle, there was growing criticism of Majid's captaincy. There had already been talk for several years about dissatisfaction in some quarters over the Pakistani's style of leadership. There were claims as well that he was not interested in the run of the mill, one-day matches after a diet of all-year-round cricket. An example of his relaxed attitude and apparent indifference to limited-over games came in the John Player League match at Portsmouth. Richard Gilliat, the Hampshire captain, walked into the Welsh dressing room looking for the Pakistani so that they could go out and toss. But Majid replied: 'Just throw up the coin where you are standing.' Fortune favours the brave and Glamorgan won the toss, but Majid had not gone out to look at the wicket and to the surprise of his team he said: 'Well, Richard, you can bat.' Even though Glamorgan managed to win, events like this were misconstrued by the team, many of whom were playing for their professional futures, and a feeling of resentment towards the Pakistani started to build up. It was unfortunate that they were not brought out into the open and amicably settled at an earlier date. Once again, one can only speculate at what might have taken place had a few more wise heads, like Shepherd and Lewis, been around; instead the situation was allowed to drift and feelings became magnified out of all proportion to the original source of complaint.

To compound matters, the young Muslim found it increasingly difficult both to communicate and relax with the young Welshmen and the rest of the team. Indeed one player said: 'I think we would have felt he was more human if he could have thumped the table with a pint glass and told us what he thought of us with a few good Anglo-Saxon expressions!' But there was little mixing between Majid's Eastern thinking and the down to earth attitude of some of the young Welshmen. Local papers claimed Majid would sit in the pavilion reading or having a quiet snooze, rather than sit on the balcony and be seen to be taking an active interest in the events on the field. Sadly, the Pakistani became increasingly isolated from the rest of the team as the criticism of his leadership and the team mounted. As Tony Lewis wrote a few years later: 'As criticism heaped up and the disloyalty both of the players and of the Glamorgan administration which once wooed him could be heard paraded on all home grounds, Majid returned to his introverted self. On the field he thrust his hands deeply

Majid Khan, the Club's captain from 1973 until the trouble-torn season of 1976. (Universal Pictorial)

into his pockets, used his shirt collar as blinkers and carried on as best he could . . . the public which had crowned him in 1969 were now prepared to crucify.'

With the team still failing to make any headway, several senior Club officials began criticising Majid. Some of them, such as Wilf Wooller, had been amongst the Pakistani's most vehement supporters in his early years with the Club, but it was a different story by July 1976. The Secretary was particularly annoyed at the way the Gillette Cup match with Warwickshire at the end of June had been lost after Glamorgan had made 283 for three, and he believed it illustrated an apparent lack of appreciation of the basic tactics in one-day cricket. The following week, there was an incident between the captain and the Secretary during the match at Swansea with Nottinghamshire, over whether Gwyn Richards was fit to act as 12th man. Even worse was to come at a meeting of the cricket committee in the Cardiff office on 19 July, when Wooller and several committee members told Majid of their grievances, with one senior official saying that five players had approached him during June and July making criticisms of the captain.

The tensions which had been simmering over the past few weeks had come to boiling point, and soon after the meeting the Pakistani wrote to the Club claiming interference by Club administrators and he tendered his resignation from the captaincy, though he agreed to carry on playing until the end of the season. However, Majid was a sensitive and proud man, and the whole situation had become too much for him. A fortnight later, at his own request, he was omitted from the team to play Somerset at Weston and he quit the county scene amidst widespread public confusion and deep private sadness. Views were expressed in the media that the Pakistani should never have been appointed captain in the first place, and some critics went as far as suggesting that the Club were now paying the price for getting rid of Peter Walker at the start of the 1973 season, arguing that none of these problems would have arisen had Walker taken over the captaincy.

However, the members' organisation led by John Thomson were sad to see the departure of Majid, who through his genius with the bat had given many hours of delight to the cricketing public of Wales. There were widespread claims of a players' conspiracy, fuelled by rumours of a team meeting in 1973 which discussed Majid's unsuitability for the job of captain. As far as Thomson's group were concerned it had been the administrators' fault that Glamorgan, and Majid, had failed to achieve any success and the targets of their complaints were Wooller and the Club officials. Their cause was aided by Majid's comments on his departure from Wales at the end of the summer. He said: 'The committee were well aware that the senior players were strongly criticising my captaincy. These committeemen, if they had been genuine well-wishers of the club, would have come to me and said: "Let's sort it out". Instead, I felt I had to resign . . . Wilf Wooller has been a great man for Glamorgan cricket for 40 years but he would not accept the fact that he was no longer captain of the side. Although his duties were just those of Secretary and he was not on the selection committee, indirectly he influenced people who were selectors to pick the team he wanted . . . Glamorgan need to hold a thorough investigation into the whole situation. No matter if a man is a great Glamorgan cricketer or a top official, he should go if he is found not to be doing his job in the best interests of Glamorgan cricket.'

Soon after these strong words had been splashed all over the back pages of the local newspapers, Thomson's rebel members' group held a meeting at which there was a call for the mass resignation of the Club's management committee, with Thomson himself saying: 'There is club and player friction which could be avoided and which is a management problem. The old brigade have got to go, lock, stock and barrel, leaving no skeletons behind!' In the face of such vehement public protest, the Club set up a special sub-committee to examine the allegations of internal trouble, and after several meetings, some changes were made amongst the administration. Quite independently, Judge Rowe Harding decided to stand down as Chairman because of poor health and old age. Ossie Wheatley, who by now was a successful businessman in South Wales was appointed the new Chairman, whilst the structure of the committee was reduced from 36 to 24, with an even split in members between West and East. There was also talk of appointing a manager, in an attempt to improve the communication between the dressing room and the officials, but no action was taken.

Whilst all these changes were taking place, there were encouraging signs out in the middle for the future as a new (and united) team spirit was forged under the captaincy of Alan Jones. This was clearly in evidence in the final Sunday League game of an eventful season, as Somerset travelled to Cardiff needing to win to secure their first-ever title. The game was played in front of a massive crowd in excess of 7,000, many of whom had entered the ground early in the morning before the gatemen had arrived! One of the decisive incidents in the outcome of the match came in the early overs after Brian Close had put Glamorgan in, when Close himself dropped Alan Jones at square leg. It was a costly miss, as Jones went on to score 70 in a Glamorgan total of 191 for six. Nash dismissed Denning, Close and Botham in his first five overs, but then Burgess and Kitchen played sensibly and the visitors steadily edged closer to the target. Nash came back for his last three overs, and at 171 he bowled Breakwell. Taylor was run out with the score on 180, and a further eight agonising runs were added before

Jennings was dismissed in similar fashion. The tension mounted as Burgess faced the last ball from Nash, needing three runs to tie the game and secure the Sunday trophy. He hit the ball back over Nash's head down towards the sight screen, and the Somerset supporters began cheering. But Alan Jones ran in from his boundary and hurled the ball back to Nash as Burgess and Dredge completed their second run. They needed another and set off in desperation, but Nash calmly lobbed the ball to Eifion Jones, who removed the bails with Dredge well out of his ground.

Several of the youngsters continued to make progress during 1976, justifying the officials' faith in their ability. Hopkins and Richards both made maiden centuries, whilst Francis made several useful innings at No 3 and A. L. Jones played for Young England. The biggest boost came in the bowling, however, where Tony Allin topped the averages with 44 wickets at 22 apiece. His finest spell came at Sophia Gardens against Tony Greig's Sussex team. Allin completely baffled the visitors and took eight for 63 as Glamorgan won by five wickets. His name was suggested for the MCC tour to India and Pakistan, but in September he told the County's officials that he did not want a career in professional cricket. With all the public and private rows taking place, it was not surprising that the quietly spoken farmer's son should decide to quit county cricket – had he joined the Club in any other year, the story might have been very different.

Allin was one of several players to leave at the end of the summer. Geoff Ellis turned down the offer of a one-year contract, feeling aggrieved that he had not been offered terms for two years like all the other young batsmen. Solanky, Williams, Powell and Rupert Hill were also released, together with the enigmatic Armstrong, who had finished with a disappointing 25 wickets at a cost of over 37. His signing had not been a success, and the club were left to rue the fact that Michael Holding, who had been on their short list, was now making a name for himself as one of the fastest bowlers in Test cricket.

With the aid of hindsight, it was clear the committee had opted for the wrong man, so when it came to finding a replacement, they were determined to get it right. A host of names were mentioned, with Kevin Lyons, the Assistant-Coach, recommending Peter Kirsten, Garth Le Roux and Allan Lamb as the officials debated whether to go for a batsman or a bowler. However, the officials believed they could get the best of both worlds by signing a world-class all-rounder, and once again Bill Edwards' West Indian contacts were used to hire the Barbadian Collis King.

The internal wranglings had also left the Club without any experienced middle-order batsmen, and a number of possible

Tony Allin – a left arm spinner who had a successful, but brief, career with the Welsh county. (Western Mail)

replacements were discussed including John Jameson, Mike Denness and Roland Butcher. However, the officials decided that after all the rows over the selection of young Welsh players, it was not in the best interests of the Club to hire a batsman from another club. The bowling, however, did need strengthening as there were few home-

234

grown replacements waiting in the wings. Don Wilson, the Yorkshire bowler, was one possibility, but the Club eventually agreed terms with Tom Cartwright, the former Somerset and Warwickshire bowler. Although Cartwright was 42, the Club signed him in the hope that he would also be able to undertake some of the coaching duties which Phil Clift had relinquished and groom some new Welsh bowlers.

By the time Christmas came, the dust had finally settled on a year full of turmoil and public debate. It had been a sad 1976 in many ways, with a lot of blood-letting in public, some arguably for the better and some undoubtedly for the worse. Everyone connected with the Club vowed to put their grievances behind them and get down to the task of restoring the team's pride and standing on the county circuit. They did so with almost unbelievable results and what happened in 1977 seemed almost too good to be true. Even a Hollywood scriptwriter could not have anticipated the improvements which actually took place, culminating with Glamorgan playing in a one-day final at Lord's for the first time.

It was even more remarkable considering that the Club had made little, if any, impact in limited-over cricket; only twice had they reached the Benson and Hedges quarter-finals and had progressed little further in the Gillette Cup, whilst their highest position in the Sunday League had been tenth. So what caused the sudden transformation? The change of leadership certainly helped, if only to restore the players' faith and improve the feeling within the team. However, more fundamental developments had taken place by the time the 1977 season got under way. Rodney Ontong was now recognised as an English qualified player, following a successful appeal by the Club to the TCCB that the talented all-rounder had learnt his cricket in this country, and the acquisition of King and Cartwright gave the Club a stronger and more experienced squad for the limited overs games.

There was evidence of these improvements during the one-day games in May and June. After a defeat at Ilkeston, Jones' side recorded three victories in the next four John Player League games. Some tight bowling by Nash and Richards, plus an aggressive 79 not out from Llewellyn steered Glamorgan to a three wicket win at Bristol. Ontong was the match-winner in the following game against Yorkshire at Cardiff, taking three wickets in seven balls. Warwickshire were also defeated at Swansea by just one run, after Nash had fielded brilliantly on the boundary to run out Kanhai who was going for a second run to tie the match. They also won their group in the Benson and Hedges Cup, defeating Warwickshire by a comfortable margin, and beating the Minor Counties (West) after a courageous innings by Eifion Jones on a difficult wicket at Amersham.

The 1977 Gillette Cup squad at Swansea:
Back row: Alan Lewis Jones, John Hopkins, Tom Cartwright, Collis King,
Rodney Ontong, Mike Llewellyn, Alan Wilkins, Frank Culverwell (scorer)
Front row: Malcolm Nash, Eifion Jones, Alan Jones (capt.), Tony Cordle,
*Gwyn Richards, Arthur Francis. (*Western Mail*)*

Although they lost the quarter-final against Hampshire, Alan Jones was pleased by the way the team had gelled into a useful one-day unit. Despite the long odds offered by the bookmakers, he was sure they would do well in the Gillette Cup. They had a first-round bye, so the team travelled to Worcester in mid-July for the second-round match. Ironically, the two teams had met at New Road the previous week in a Championship match, and Glamorgan had won by eight wickets after John Hopkins had made a magnificent 230. The Maesteg-born opener hit 26 fours in an innings lasting $6\frac{3}{4}$ hours to register the highest post-war score for the County. His record-breaking feat gave the team the lift it required and they returned to Worcester hopeful of registering their first win in the Gillette Cup since 1972. Their confidence was not misplaced, as the battery of Glamorgan seamers restricted Worcestershire to 213 for nine, and a solid innings of 62 not out by Arthur Francis saw the Welshmen home by five wickets.

They were drawn against Surrey in the quarter-final at Sophia Gardens and after the defeat in the 55-overs competition by Hampshire, they were determined not to go out at this stage again. Surrey batted first and ominously passed 50 without loss, but then their experienced opener, John Edrich, damaged a calf muscle and had to call for a runner. Richards picked up two wickets and then the middle of the Surrey innings faltered against the left-arm seam of Alan Wilkins, a 24-year-old from Cardiff who was in his first year on the full-time staff. Glamorgan were left with a target of 200, but Hopkins and Francis went cheaply and Surrey regained the initiative. However, a gritty partnership of 101 between Alan Jones and Collis King steadied the Welsh ship, before a belligerent 37 from Llewellyn saw them home by four wickets.

Leicestershire were the opponents in the semi-final at St Helen's, but the game was spread over three days because of rain. With a bad weather forecast, the toss was always going to be crucial and much to the delight of the large crowd, Alan Jones won it and put Leicestershire in. They were restricted to 172 for seven after some tight fielding and good bowling, with once again Wilkins and Richards taking the honours, though the visitors were also hampered by frequent interruptions by rain. Glamorgan were given a flying start with an opening stand of 108 between Alan Jones and Hopkins, but then there was the flurry of three quick wickets. A recovery took place through Eifion Jones and Gwyn Richards and Glamorgan approached their target. A chorus of 'Mae Hen Wlad Fy Nhadau' drifted out from the packed pavilion and spurred on the two Welsh batsmen, and the winning run was hit with 15 balls to go. An enormous cheer went up and the two batsmen hugged each other in the middle, with the normally reserved Richards shouting 'We've done it Eif, we've done it!'

The sound of delirious Welsh voices and champagne corks popping must have sounded like a dream to the young players who had tasted the less glamorous side to professional cricket in the previous few seasons. One of these was Rodney Ontong, and he remembers: 'It was an unbelievable feeling, sitting in the dressing room taking it all in, whilst the crowd carried on singing outside. We didn't even know who we were going to be playing at Lord's for a week, as Middlesex spent six days struggling against Somerset. But to be quite honest, we weren't really interested in who our opponents were going to be – we would have played anyone!'

The team were on a crest of a wave and morale within the area was sky high. In the three weeks between the victory at St Helen's and the final at Lord's, almost every pub and club in South Wales was alive with cricket fever. Doubts had been cast previously over the depth of support, but here was clear evidence, as so often had been the case in the past, that the Welsh public would support a successful side. At the start of the season, the Treasurer had been gloomily looking ahead to the future, but now he had a happy smile on his face as money and membership subscriptions flooded in. Jones's team also showed in this period leading up to the final that their place at Lord's was no fluke. There was a gallant batting display in the Sunday League game against Essex, held at Aberystwyth as part of the town's 900th anniversary celebrations, with Glamorgan ending 15 runs short of the target set by the powerful Essex team. This was followed by three successive Sunday wins, as the team went through August without defeat in this competition. Notts and Lancashire were comfortably defeated and most important of all, Middlesex, their opponents at Lord's, were beaten by 35 runs at Cardiff after another fine bowling display by the Welshmen.

This series of victories was just what the team needed as it travelled to Lord's on the night before the final. They were followed from Wales the next morning by trains, coaches and cars by the score, and on the morning of the match Lord's was alive with Welsh voices, making it seem more like Cardiff Arms Park on the day of a rugby international. Sadly, the weather was more in keeping with a winter's day, and the pitch was only just fit for play after heavy overnight rain. Once again, the toss was going to be crucial, but this time luck was not on Jones's side and Mike Brearley had no hesitation in asking Glamorgan to bat first after winning the toss.

The early Welsh batsmen found it difficult to score quickly and they did not get the full benefit of powerful strokes, as the ball travelled slowly over the wet outfield. It was left to Mike Llewellyn at No 5 to give the innings a much needed impetus. His first three scoring strokes were 4, 6, 4 off Gatting, and later he struck a colossal six, hitting Emburey high over long on and into the gutter on the top tier of the famous pavilion. But once Llewellyn was out for 62, the innings rather fell away and Middlesex were left to make 178.

The Middlesex side was brimful of class batsmen and with conditions improving all the time, it did not appear too daunting a target. However, they got off to a dreadful start as Nash drifted the first ball of the innings across Brearley and had the Middlesex captain caught behind for nought. Brearley quietly walked off as the Welsh national anthem echoed around the famous ground. Another quick wicket would really have put the cat amongst the pigeons, but in the next over Clive Radley was dropped in the slips by King. This proved to be the turning point of the match, as the Welsh bowlers found little assistance once the shine had gone off the ball. The gritty and determined Radley did not look back after this escape, and in his unflappable style, he steered Middlesex to a five-wicket win. As Alan Jones reflected: 'Lady Luck had been with us in the early rounds, but in the final she left us to fend for ourselves. At several stages in the game, had things gone in our favour, I may have held the trophy aloft as

Mike Llewellyn hits John Emburey for six on to the roof of the Lord's pavilion during the 1977 Gillette Cup Final.

winning captain. As it happened, however, Middlesex won and won well.'

At the end of the match you could have been excused for thinking that Glamorgan had won, as Welsh supporters jubilantly gathered in front of the historic pavilion, sang their hearts out and waved their banners. They were not downhearted by the defeat, because the match had shown that Glamorgan were a force to be reckoned with, and possessed some very promising players, who most important of all,

239

GILLETTE CUP FINAL
GLAMORGAN *v.* MIDDLESEX

Played at Lord's, 3 September 1977

MIDDLESEX WON BY FIVE WICKETS

GLAMORGAN

*A. Jones	lbw b Selvey	18
J. A. Hopkins	b Edmonds	47
C. L. King	c Barlow b Selvey	8
R. C. Ontong	c Gould b Gatting	0
M. J. Llewellyn	c Gatting b Featherstone	62
G. Richards	b Edmonds	3
†E. W. Jones	run out	11
M. A. Nash	c Gatting b Featherstone	3
A. E. Cordle	not out	8
T. W. Cartwright	st Gould b Featherstone	3
A. H. Wilkins		
Extras		14
Total	(for 9 wkts)	177

Fall: 1-21, 2-47, 3-50, 4-115, 5-129, 6-163, 7-163, 8-171, 9-177

BOWLING	O	M	R	W
Daniel	11	0	41	0
Selvey	12	4	22	2
Gatting	7	1	28	1
Edmonds	12	3	23	2
Emburey	12	2	32	0
Featherstone	6	0	17	3

MIDDLESEX

*J. M. Brearley	c E. Jones b Nash	0
M. J. Smith	lbw b Cartwright	22
C. T. Radley	not out	85
M. W. Gatting	c Hopkins b King	15
G. D. Barlow	lbw b Richards	27
N. G. Featherstone	b Nash	3
P. H. Edmonds	not out	9
†I. J. Gould		
J. E. Emburey		
M. W. W. Selvey		
W. W. Daniel		
Extras		17
Total	(for 5 wkts)	178

Fall: 1-0, 2-45, 3-72, 4-146, 5-153

BOWLING	O	M	R	W
Nash	12	3	31	2
Cordle	8.4	1	29	0
Cartwright	12	3	32	1
King	5	1	19	1
Richards	12	2	23	1
Wilkins	6	0	27	0

Umpires: D. J. Constant and T. W. Spencer

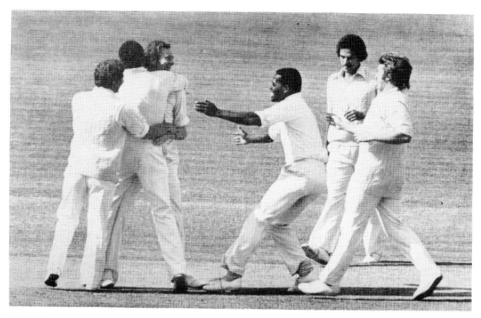

Malcolm Nash dismisses Mike Brearley with his first ball in the 1977 Final and is mobbed by his happy team-mates. Left to right: Richards, Cordle, King, Ontong and Llewellyn.

were Welsh. All of those who assembled in front of the team's dressing room at Lord's, plus all of the many exiles who had loyally gathered around their radio sets in far-flung places, fervently believed that this match marked a new era in the Club's history, and hoped that Jones's young team would have a decade of further success in the 1980s. However, they have had little to cheer in the last few years and are still waiting for Glamorgan to secure another major title.

This was the Club's first appearance in a one-day final and despite losing, they put up a good fight after being asked to bat in damp conditions. In particular, Mike Llewellyn launched a furious assault on the Middlesex spinners, hoisting Emburey on to the pavilion roof, whilst the wily combination of Eifion Jones and Malcolm Nash dismissed Middlesex skipper Mike Brearley with the first ball of his team's innings.

HOPES OF A NEW ERA OF SUCCESS

JUST AS IT SEEMED that a new era in the Club's history was about to unfold, there was the end of another, with the retirement in November 1977 of Wilf Wooller. He had served the Club for almost 40 years and had been much maligned in recent years as quarrels behind the scenes spilled onto the playing arena and personality clashes got into the newspapers.

Phil Clift was appointed as the new Secretary, and another change saw Tom Cartwright become the Club's first Manager. There were changes as well to the playing staff – Collis King had proved inconsistent with both bat and ball, and was carrying a niggling injury, making it difficult for him to endure the day in, day out demands of the county circuit. The committee decided to release him at the end of the 1977 season, and replaced him with another all-rounder, Peter Swart, a 31-year-old Rhodesian, who had played with much success for Haslingden in the Lancashire League.

Despite everyone's hopes and dreams, the new era failed to materialise and 1978 proved to be yet another frustrating season. Somerset put paid to any thoughts of another Gillette Final at Lord's with a comfortable 70-run victory in their second round encounter at Cardiff, and the team finished 13th in the Championship, an improvement of just one place. In several games, Jones's team got themselves into promising positions and then let things slip. A case in point was the Middlesex match at Swansea. Glamorgan did well to bowl them out for 200, but then they collapsed on the second day for just 162. They fought back to have Middlesex on 114 for five, but then a partnership between Butcher and Gould saw the visitors to 264. The target of 303 on the final day was within Glamorgan's capabilities, but they collapsed to the spin of Emburey, and lost by 176 runs.

The major weakness was in the bowling which once again lacked any real fire power. The release of King had given the committee an opportunity to hire a quick bowler, and all of the teams in the challenge for the Championship had one or at least two fast bowlers on their staff. But the committee decided to hire Swart, who only bowled at a brisk medium pace and by no stretch of the imagination was a fast bowler. It was like backing a pony to race against thoroughbreds and win the Derby, and sadly the Club paid the price for this decision. But in their defence, the rumblings of the Packer Affair meant that few overseas players of any quality were on the market. For the first time in the Club's history, no bowler took over 50 wickets; Nash picked up just 42 in his benefit year and Swart claimed a mere 43. The only faint ray of hope in the bowling came from the performances in the second eleven of a young South African called Neal Radford, who was playing in the SWCA, and Andy Mack, a left-arm seamer signed from Surrey, who took 16 wickets at 12 apiece in his few first-team appearances and on the strength of this topped the national bowling averages. However, Mack was unable to play more often because of several minor injuries, whilst Radford was restricted to the second team because of his overseas registration.

Further changes to the personnel were inevitable after this indifferent season, but the only player to leave the staff was young batsmen Peter Crowther, and this at his own request. Crowther was suffering from poor health and his mental attitude was not helped by his dismissal on 99 on his debut against Cambridge University.

Several steps were taken to try to improve matters; at the time they were made in good faith, but once again, by virtue of hindsight, some were highly questionable. One of the first changes took place in the captaincy. Jones had done a reasonable job, and had the confidence and support of the rest of the team, but the committee thought otherwise and opted for a new leader, preferably one with experience of playing for England. As Alan Jones relates below, it was yet another decision made by the administration without confiding in the players. He believed that 1978 'hadn't been a bad season; there was still a lot of work to do, but the team was willing to learn. I was therefore disappointed to hear rumours that the Club was actively searching for a new captain in 1979. I packed my bags for South Africa hoping that this was just idle gossip. It was only when I was 4,000 miles away, that the decision was made not to retain me as captain.' If Jones was not so loyal to the Welsh club, he could easily have stayed put out in South Africa or have joined another county.

The man appointed to take over was Robin Hobbs, the 37-year-old former Essex and England leg-spinner who had retired from playing county cricket back in 1975. Not surprisingly, he found the task of returning to first-class cricket a considerable one, and he ended the season with just 22 wickets at a cost of 36, averaged 8 with the bat, and saw the side finish at the bottom of the Championship without a win for the first time in the Club's history. Things reached rock bottom in the Sunday League match with Derbyshire at Swansea at the end of August. The visitors scored 202 for six and then dismissed Glamorgan for just 42. It was too much for some of the supporters to bear, and when the Swansea scoreboard read 42 for eight two patrons from Fred's Bar, on the Mumbles Road side of the ground, came out onto the pitch and took guard with children's bats! Trust the Welsh to find something to laugh about in the darkest hours.

As the season progressed without any detectable sign of improvement, the team came in for a lot of criticism and the committee came

Robin Hobbs, the captain for 1979, giving the ball a 'tweak' in the Sophia Gardens nets. (Western Mail)

under fire for recalling the veteran Hobbs. In all fairness to the officials, the spin attack needed strengthening, but the bone of contention was that in the modern era of fast bowlers and one-day cricket, could an old-fashioned leg-spinner be the answer? They held high hopes of Neil Perry, a 21-year-old slow left-armer who had joined the staff from Surrey, and had turned in some promising performances for the

244

second eleven. But he too failed to make an immediate impact at first-class level, claiming just 13 wickets at a cost of 43.

There were many other disappointments, with Mack only picking up 14 wickets and Wilkins a modest 30. Just to compound matters, Nash was badly affected by injury and made only nine appearances. In his absence, the 39-year-old Cordle bravely shouldered the brunt of the bowling and deservedly finished the season as leading wicket-taker with 58 victims. There were difficulties in the batting too, with Richards and Llewellyn losing both form and confidence, whilst A. L. Jones opted to finish his college studies rather than enter professional cricket on a full-time basis. The only young batsman to make any progress was Geoff Holmes, a 21-year-old Geordie, who scored a maiden century against Gloucestershire.

The disappointments of 1979 were succinctly summed up in *Wisden* by J. B. G. Thomas, who wrote: 'The senior players were getting older, the younger players lost form and the coach was unable to arrest the decline, whilst the atmosphere lacked the traditional gaiety of Glamorgan cricket. In the later stages of the season, few spectators attended matches and interest appeared to be fast fading. It was not a summer to remember. Welsh followers were left extremely disappointed. Much hard work has to be done on and off the field.' The last few words indirectly relate to rumours of friction between the Manager and the players which began to surface towards the end of the season. There was talk of some of the youngsters resenting being told what they could or could not do off the field, and a series of small incidents occurred.

At the end of the season, Alan Wilkins decided to join Gloucestershire, whilst Richards left the staff, and it looked like being another winter of discontent. But Wheatley and his committee did not shy away from the criticism or the huge task which confronted them, and they made a number of changes. Hobbs stood down as captain for 1980 and was replaced by Nash who was happily restored to full fitness. Peter Swart did not seek a renewal of his contract, so the officials opted to replace him with a pace bowler from overseas. A number of Australians were considered, whilst an attempt was made to contact Kapil Dev. Eventually, the Club reached agreement with Vintcent van der Bijl, the highly rated Springbok quick bowler, but at a late date, his employers in South Africa withdrew their permission for him to have time off to play in county cricket.

Australian Alan Hurst was considered as a replacement, but he then developed a back injury, and it looked as if the fates were conspiring against the Club. However, they eventually signed 22-year-old Ezra Moseley, a little-known Barbadian pace bowler who had been recommended to the Club by Reg Simpson and Trevor Bailey. The regulations on overseas cricketers allowed the Club to hire another player, so the committee decided to hire an overseas batsman as well. One of the people considered was Parvez Mir, a Pakistani who played for Norfolk, and had appeared for Glamorgan against the Sri Lankan tourists at Swansea. However, the eventual choice was his fellow countryman, Javed Miandad, who had failed to secure a regular place in the Sussex team.

Despite the signing of Moseley and Miandad, there were still a few gaps in both the batting and the bowling. The names of Clive Radley and Barry Wood were mentioned in the Press as possible replacements, but the Club turned to 31-year-old Norman Featherstone from Middlesex and Allan Jones, the former Sussex, Somerset and Middlesex seamer. They were wise signings, but it was infuriating for the Club to have to look outside its boundaries for replacements, and the officials were left to ponder on the reasons why so few of the young colts of the early 1970s had been able to establish themselves in county cricket, and if their coaching and practice facilities were adequate for a first-class county.

These gloomy thoughts were quickly cast aside as Nash's team made an excellent start to the new season. It was soon evident that the team was greatly benefiting from the winter changes, as Miandad struck an unbeaten 140 in the opening Championship match and Moseley bowled fast and straight to claim seven wickets. Their first victory since August 1978 came in the following match at Bristol. Nash played a captain's role by taking 11 wickets, before Miandad scored another century to steer the Welsh county to a seven wicket victory, which was celebrated in the dressing room by champagne, bought at his own cost by the happy Nash! His team also made a good start in the limited-over competitions. There were victories in the Benson and Hedges Cup over Gloucestershire and the Minor Counties, whilst there were three successive victories in the John Player League, and it seemed as if the new era had finally arrived.

Unfortunately, these improvements were short-lived and the team failed to maintain their early form in the Championship and finished in 12th place. Only three other matches were won and there were heavy defeats against Surrey and Sussex. They also lost form in the Sunday League, winning just one other game and they sadly finished at the bottom of the table. The second half of the season was like so many before them, as the team suffered a series of draws and defeats, and team morale began to sink. The only thing they had to smile about was the outstanding performance of Alan Jones in the game with Hampshire at Basingstoke. The veteran left-hander hit an unbeaten 204, his first double-century and the fiftieth three-figure innings in his long career.

The slip down the table was frustrating after the excellent start, but the team showed an indication of their true form by winning the Tilcon Trophy at the Harrogate Cricket Festival under the shrewd captaincy of Barry Lloyd. The semi-final game with Yorkshire was rain affected, but Alan Jones and John Hopkins saw the Welsh county to a win on a faster scoring rate. Kent were the opponents in the final, but they found run-scoring difficult against the accurate bowling of Moseley and Holmes, who each took four wickets as Kent were dismissed for 222. Holmes played a leading role when Glamorgan chased the target, and scored an unbeaten 87 to see them home by six wickets and deservedly win the Man-of-the-Match Award.

Glamorgan's two West Indian fast bowlers of the 1980s: Winston Davis and Ezra Moseley. (Western Mail)

Holmes was just one of the youngsters who made steady improvement in 1980, and with the first team's slide down the table, it was a great source of comfort to see the second team win the second eleven championship with a number of talented young players making significant contributions to the team's success. They included 16-year-old Hugh Morris, a product of Blundell's School and the England Schools team, and Greg Thomas, a young pace bowler from Trebanos, who had made his first-class debut the year before against Sri Lanka. However, Thomas sustained a back injury, and had to undergo surgery at the end of the season for a stress fracture. The youngsters confirmed this promise by winning the under-25 title in 1981, but unfortunately few of them reproduced this form when they were selected for the first team.

Many people had high hopes for the Club in 1981, but these were dispelled as the side slipped down to 14th place in the table. Apart from Ontong, few of the young batsmen made any impression, whilst Simon Daniels, a young seamer from Durham who had been signed following Tony Cordle's retirement, took only eight wickets. The only crumb of comfort was the marvellous batting of Javed, who amassed a Club record 2,083 runs and finished with an average of 69.43, the best-ever by a Glamorgan batsman. He hit eight centuries in all, including two double-centuries, with the one at Colchester being described by some of his team-mates at the finest innings they had ever seen. Essex had set the Welsh county 325 in 323 minutes, and when Alan Jones departed without a run on the board, and was quickly followed by Ontong and Featherstone, the Essex supporters must have anticipated a comfortable win. But Miandad displayed an almost magical variety of shots on a wicket that was giving the spinners considerable assistance, combining watchful defence with wristy strokeplay, and hit 22 boundaries to take Glamorgan to the verge of victory. But no-one else could follow his example and wickets steadily fell at the other end, leaving Glamorgan 14 runs short and Javed 200 not out.

The Pakistani's quick-scoring abilities were of great value in the one-day competitions, and his consistent batting was a factor behind the team's rise up to 10th place in the Sunday League. In particular, he scored 107 not out to set up a comfortable victory at Leicester, but when the Pakistani failed, it was often a case of a Glamorgan defeat. An example came in the Club's first-ever visit to the delightful Abergavenny ground in Gwent. Javed was dismissed for a duck by the wily Jack Birkenshaw, and Worcestershire won by 18 runs, though a different story may have occurred if the Pakistani had stayed at the crease for a little longer.

The County's rebuilding programme was dealt a cruel blow when

Moseley broke down with a severe back injury at the beginning of August, and had to miss the rest of the season. Although Greg Thomas was making steady progress after his own back injury, the loss of Moseley's fire power was a major handicap to the attack, where only Nash and Lloyd took over 50 wickets. Another blow occurred in the spring of 1982 when Norman Featherstone informed the Club that he was staying in South Africa. The former Middlesex batsman had added a solidity to the middle order, and had also been tipped as a future Glamorgan captain. Indeed, at the end of the season Malcolm Nash resigned from the leadership for personal reasons, and a senior Club official told Featherstone that he might be appointed captain in 1982. However, Featherstone heard nothing more whilst out in South Africa, where a lucrative business offer was made to him. He must have thought the matter of the captaincy had been dropped, so he accepted the offer and retired from first-class cricket.

The officials came in for some criticism over the way they let things drift, and they surprised some people again when they appointed Javed as the captain, with Barry Lloyd as vice-captain despite the fact that Miandad was available only for the first half of the summer because of the Pakistani tour. There were other changes for 1982 as well, with Cartwright becoming chief coach and Hobbs and Perry being released, whilst A. A. Jones decided to retire. One newcomer to the staff was Charles Rowe, the 31-year-old batsman who had been in and out of the Kent side for the last few seasons. It was hoped that Rowe could take over Featherstone's role of stabilising the middle order, but Rowe took time to settle and the batting once again was rather inconsistent. This was compounded when Javed left to join his countrymen in mid-season, and his absence was crucial when the side were chasing targets.

The loss of Miandad's run-scoring talents was a contributory factor behind the team finishing in 16th place in the table. Moseley's back problem was equally as important a factor behind this lowly position. The West Indian broke down with a recurrence of the injury after a couple of second team games, and the problems with the bowling intensified when Nash was also injured early in the season. Despite the progress that Thomas and Steve Barwick, a 22-year-old seamer from Briton Ferry were making, it was obvious that the attack needed a spearhead and someone who could snuff out tail-end resistance.

The medical reports on Moseley's long term fitness were not encouraging, so the Club decided in mid-season to seek a replacement. Franklyn Stephenson, Terry Alderman and Steve Jefferies were all contacted but for a variety of reasons they were not available, whilst Neal Radford, who had been playing in the SWCA had moved north to join Lancashire. However, Winston Davis, a 24-year-old from St

Vincent, who had broken several bowling records in the Shell Shield, was available and the Club hired his services. Davis made his debut in mid-July, and although he finished with 42 wickets, he was troubled with run-up problems which resulted in a spate of no-balls. There were claims that the Club had signed 'another Greg Armstrong', but Davis showed that he had more control than the previous West Indian quickie, and when he got his run-up and rhythm he could be genuinely fast and trouble the top order batsmen.

The fact that the side once again had a hostile fast bowler raised morale and their performance improved towards the end of the season, in particular in the Sunday League, where it had been felt that they were most handicapped by the absence of Javed. There was some steady batting by the home grown batsmen, and the side won six of their last eight games to rise to 10th place. Glamorgan had also failed to win a three-day game in the first half of the season when Miandad was available, and they had to wait until early September for their first victory of the season. They were set 315 by Gloucestershire, and after half-centuries by Alan Jones, Arthur Francis and Charles Rowe, Eifion Jones saw the Welshmen home with a huge six over mid-wicket.

There were several changes amongst the Club's hierarchy at the end of the 1982 season. Phil Clift announced his retirement after over

Younis Ahmed glances Eldine Baptiste and is superbly caught by Alan Knott in the Benson and Hedges Cup game with Kent at Sophia Gardens. Javed Miandad is the non-striker. (Western Mail)

40 years with Glamorgan as player, coach and administrator, and was richly rewarded with a Testimonial in recognition of his service. The post of Glamorgan Secretary attracted over 200 applications, including one from Japan, though it was Philip Carling, the former Nottinghamshire chief executive, who was eventually selected as Clift's replacement. Ossie Wheatley also stood down as Chairman, happy in the knowledge that an experienced administrator had taken over from the loyal Clift, and he was replaced as Chairman by Gwyn Craven, a Swansea businessman.

There was also yet another change in the captaincy of the Club, with the committee realising the problems encountered in 1982 by having two captains. Many felt that Barry Lloyd had deserved a chance to take over the captaincy on a full-time basis, but the officials decided to seek a replacement from another county. Many players were considered, including Vic Marks, the Somerset spinner, but the eventual choice was Mike Selvey, the former England and Middlesex seamer. Selvey became the County's seventh leader in the space of eight years as the committee desperately tried to find both the best combination of players and the right captain, but Selvey's appointment only heightened accusations that the Club had more chiefs than Indians – claims that increased in intensity as the Welsh county continued to occupy the lower half of the table during the 1980s.

THE JAVED-WINSTON DEBATE

EZRA MOSELEY'S BACK INJURY was important as the Club's new decision makers sat down to discuss the strategy for the 1983 season and beyond. Under the TCCB's new regulations on overseas players, they could theoretically play both Moseley and Miandad because both had been signed back in 1981, yet they could not play Javed and Winston Davis together in the same side. It was a major headache trying to sort out which combination should play and it quickly became a straight choice between Miandad or Davis as doctors reported that Moseley was unlikely to regain full fitness after his injury.

Many arguments were voiced in support of either the Pakistani batsman or the West Indian quick bowler. There was no doubting Javed's ability as a match-winning batsman in one-day games, but was he the right choice in three-day games? Many of the home-grown batsman had flourished towards the end of the 1982 season and the last few County Champions had won the title because of their world-class fast bowling attack. In addition, it was pointed out that Javed had won few three-day games for the Welshmen, and that several county captains had become cautious in setting declarations when the Pakistani had been playing, especially after his amazing innings at Colchester, and they were more reasonable in their declarations when Davis was chosen instead. However, the slow nature of the Welsh wickets rather nullified Davis's pace, and few of the spectators at Cardiff or Swansea had seen him in full steam on the quicker type of wickets encountered elsewhere on the county circuit.

It was a tricky decision, and many of the committeemen favoured a 'horses for courses' policy, making a decision on which of the two should play once the wicket on which the match would be staged had been inspected. In the end, Davis appeared in 15 of the 24 Championship games, whilst Miandad played in just four of the three-day games and some of the limited-over games. However, Davis was somewhat erratic, claiming 52 wickets at 27 apiece and delivering around 250 no-balls as his run-up problem persisted. At the same time, several of the batsmen failed to find their touch, and the selection of the lanky West Indian ahead of Miandad annoyed a faction of the Club's members who had been thrilled by the Pakistani's batting, and they felt that his batting talents were being wasted. Their feelings of disillusionment and resentment heightened as the Club continued to struggle during the season, winning just two Championship matches to finish in a disappointing 15th place.

Three matches at the end of the season were a microcosm of the mixture of problems and bad luck which the club faced in 1983. Firstly, Mike Selvey withdrew from the side to play Northants at Cardiff due to injury and then saw Rodney Ontong put the visitors in on a fine batting wicket to amass 529 for eight, with Wayne Larkins making a superb 252 which included a century before lunch. Even worse was to follow in the next match at Edgbaston, despite the fact that Selvey was restored to full fitness. Glamorgan made 389 for five on the first day and after rain interruption on the second, Selvey set Warwickshire a target of 414 on the last day. To his horror, they reached this target with over an hour to spare and eight wickets in hand, as Alvin Kallicharran and Andy Lloyd shared a partnership of 308. On such a placid surface, Ontong correctly fancied his team's chances of a run chase on the last day; but the large Northants total brought criticism from the Press and, more importantly, exposed the weakness of the Welsh bowlers.

The team then travelled to Hampshire for the final round of matches and their spirits were hardly boosted when some of the team were the innocent victims of a 'hit and run' accident as they made their way towards Southampton on the Friday evening. Happily, the team took the field in one piece for the last Championship match and the final Sunday League match of the season at Bournemouth. Dean Park had so often been a lucky ground for the Welsh team, and it looked as if it would be the case again as Hampshire's score slumped to 145 for nine, chasing the Glamorgan score of 159. However, storm clouds were gathering in the English Channel, and the umpires told Selvey that they would take the batsmen off if he recalled Winston Davis to bowl the final overs. It would have meant that Hampshire would have won on a faster scoring rate, so Selvey had to stay out in the middle if he wanted to win the game. However, the Welsh captain had to call up Charles Rowe and recent signing Stephen Henderson, the former Worcestershire and Cambridge University batsman, to bowl the final overs, and then watch helplessly as Steve Malone, the Hampshire No 11, who had more wickets than runs to his credit, hit two boundaries to win the match. Alan Wilkins, who had rejoined the Club at the start of the season, summed up their feelings by saying: 'That's the first time I've ever seen Malone actually hit the ball, never mind score any runs!'

These matches highlighted the problems which the Glamorgan attack faced in 1983. Selvey ended the season as leading wicket-taker with 62 victims, but he was one of six bowlers to average over 30. They often found it difficult to contain opposing batsmen, with Essex's mammoth 310 for five in the Sunday League match at Southend serving as a macabre example of their shortcomings. To an extent, the attack was handicapped by injuries to key personnel; Nash struggled to maintain fitness, Barwick suffered from various back and side ailments, whilst Thomas broke down again with a leg injury. The only bright spot in the bowling department came from Ontong, who showed signs of promise as an off-spinner after changing styles from medium pace.

Overall, it was yet another disappointing season, with the chatter around the home grounds being concerned more with off the field events than on. Many supporters did not like the watering down of the Club's Welsh identity, in particular amongst the hierarchy, even though Secretary Philip Carling had taken a course in Welsh. The feelings of an Anglicisation were increased when Stephen Henderson arrived midway through the season, followed by Alan Jones's retirement, and the release of Malcolm Nash at the end of the season. Many of the Club's loyal followers were sad to see Jones and Nash finish their careers, but there was no doubting that their best years were behind them. Jones retired with a record 34,056 runs to his name and a testimony to his consistency over the years was that he had scored over a thousand runs on 23 consecutive occasions since 1961. His services were not totally lost, as he took over the position of Club coach and second team captain, as Cartwright became national cricket coach for Wales.

Eifion Jones also effectively finished his first-class career in 1983. He was given a one-year contract and a Testimonial, but he was told that Terry Davies, the 23-year-old from St Albans, was likely to be the regular first-team keeper. This was one element of the rebuilding process which took place over the winter months. Season 1983 had shown that the spin attack was not penetrative enough – Rowe's 37 wickets cost 41 apiece, whilst Lloyd finished with 18 wickets at over 46 – and they badly needed a slow left-armer. Consequently John Steele, the 37-year-old spinner from Leicestershire and Mark Price, a young Lancastrian, were signed, whilst the batting was strengthened by the acquisition of the well travelled Pakistani Younis Ahmed. There was one other 'signing' as well, this time off the field, as the Club teamed up with Peter Llewellyn Photocopying Ltd, a Swansea-based office equipment company, who agreed to become the County's first major sponsor.

These new signings and departures, however, also increased the claims of a loss in the essential Welshness of the team, and an undercurrent of disapproval was evident amongst some of the members. The allegations of an English-Welsh split within the dressing room were not helped by a practice match before the start of the 1984 season between the Welsh-born members of the playing staff and those born elsewhere, which the Welsh XI won, much to the displeasure of many of the Englishmen.

ALAN JONES

Alan Jones is surely the finest batsman never to have played Test cricket for England. He scored over 36,000 runs in his 27-year career. It had been argued that a shoulder injury, which restricted his fielding, was the reason for the selectors ignoring him, but his record of 1,000 runs in 23 successive seasons suggests that their decision was wrong.

He made his debut in 1957 and moved up to open the batting on a regular basis in the early 1960s. Right up until his retirement in 1983, he acted as the side's sheet anchor. He shared many fine opening stands with a variety of partners including Bernard Hedges, Gilbert Parkhouse, Roger Davis, Roy Fredericks and John Hopkins. He combined a fine technique with admirable powers of concentration, and time and again proved himself to be among the best and most consistent opening batsmen in the country.

National recognition eventually came his way in 1970 with selection for the series with The Rest of The World, but it seemed like a token gesture as Jones only played in the opening match, and just to rub salt into his wounds, the bureaucrats at Lord's later stripped the series of Test status.

Despite his sadness at never playing in Test cricket, Jones was wholly professional throughout his long career, and was highly respected by players and committee alike. He was a model for the youngsters in the Welsh team, and for the players in the second eleven, whom he coached after his retirement, and he was justifiably rewarded with an MBE in the 1982 honours list for his services to Glamorgan cricket.

Alan Jones, who has scored more runs than any other batsman not to have played for England.

Despite the strengthened playing staff, the side rose only to 13th place in the Championship and once again several key players were handicapped by injury. The most serious were the shoulder and knee problems which hampered Mike Selvey. He struggled to stay fit, and as a result of his ailments, Winston Davis was regularly chosen as the overseas player. However, the West Indian was still erratic and took just 48 wickets, often lacking the fire-power which Selvey had hoped he could produce. Javed was also injured during the early weeks of the season after being hit on the head by a bouncer from his old adversary, Dennis Lillee, during Bishen Bedi's benefit match in India. The Pakistani felt giddy and ill after this blow and he was not fully fit until the start of June.

Despite Javed's return to fitness, Davis was still chosen as the overseas player. It was a decision which continued to annoy many of the supporters, as the West Indian still struggled with no-balls and run-up problems, and was generally ineffective on the slow Welsh wickets. Their displeasure was further fuelled by claims from some quarters that Miandad's non-selection was because of a personality clash between him and the captain. Whatever the reasons, Javed was left very disgruntled in the wings, and during June asked for ratification of his position with Glamorgan. Some of the Club's earlier difficulties with overseas stars had been caused by the players consulting with a committee man, rather than going directly to the chief decision-makers, so Miandad had a meeting with Club Chairman, Gwyn Craven to discuss his future with the Club. Miandad did not like the situation and he brought up the possibility of being released from his contract if the Club were prepared to pay a settlement fee. After the meeting he wrote to the committee asking for their long-term commitment to him, but the situation soon changed in his favour as Winston Davis was called up to join the West Indies tour of England after an injury to Milton Small, and the Pakistani finally got a first-team call-up. He wasn't going to miss the chance of making several points and he made over 800 runs in his seven Championship games, including 212 against Leicestershire in front of his many fans at St Helen's.

Selvey's problems had steadily mounted as the team once again failed to find their winning touch in the Championship during the first half of the summer. Morale was lifted by a thrilling two-wicket win over Somerset at Cardiff, after Greg Thomas had achieved his first ten-wicket haul. Chasing 272 on the final afternoon, A. L. Jones set them on their way with a rapid 85 and was supported by an unbeaten 72 from Ontong to put Glamorgan in sight of their first Championship success. Three wickets quickly fell and the outcome was left in the balance, but Selvey strode purposefully out to the wicket and hit the winning runs. Nevertheless, the delight was short-lived; Selvey's own bowling had lacked consistency and several of the committee felt that as a result of his injuries, Selvey's contribution was below what was expected. He was 'rested' for the games which followed the victory over Somerset, and then at the end of July announced his retirement from county cricket. As Ron Jones wrote in the 1985 Yearbook: 'Selvey's decision to retire surprised some with its timing, but clearly he was finding it more difficult to take wickets with any sort of regularity. His captaincy had been refreshing to some – puzzling to others – he may though, as his contribution, have seen Glamorgan over a difficult period and at least pointed them towards better things in the future.'

Ontong had been appointed vice-captain at the start of the season, so he took over in a caretaker capacity for the rest of the season. Coincidentally or not, the change of captaincy produced a change of fortune, as the South African led the team to consecutive victories over Northants at Swansea and Warwickshire at Edgbaston in mid-August. John Steele's left-arm spin played a crucial role in both of these victories. The slow St Helen's wicket gave the slower bowlers considerable assistance, with both Ontong and Steele claiming eight victims as Glamorgan won by six wickets. The jubilant team travelled on to Birmingham, where Steele once again picked up eight wickets. Warwickshire were set 350 to win, but they struggled against the accurate Welsh spinners, plus their revitalised fielders, and were dismissed for 182.

These victories resulted in a new mood of optimism by the end of the season. Although Glamorgan had only won four games, it was the most in a season since 1975, and for the first time since 1969 they were unbeaten at home in the Championship. The new spin combination of Ontong and Steele had played a crucial role in this improvement, and for the first time since 1970, two Glamorgan spinners took over 50 wickets, with Ontong claiming 74 and Steele 68. There were other encouraging signs as Greg Thomas began to bowl with sustained pace and hostility, showing that he had fully recovered from the assortment of injuries which had affected him earlier in his career. There were pleasing signs in the batting as well, especially from A. L. Jones. The left-hander had moved up to open on a regular basis with Hopkins and never looked back after scoring at long last his maiden first-class hundred against Gloucestershire at Sophia Gardens in May. Four centuries followed and he ended the season with a career best 1,811 runs. Hopkins also reached the 1,500 mark for the first time, whilst Holmes benefited from a move up to No 3 and played a number of solid innings. Younis hit a century at Oxford on his debut and continued to produce some delightful stroke play, adding a touch of

257

class to the middle order. Henderson and 21-year-old John Derrick from Aberdare also made useful contributions, whilst Hugh Morris scored a maiden century against Yorkshire.

At the end of the season, Eifion Jones, Arthur Francis, Charles Rowe and Barry Lloyd were all released as the committee made several cost-cutting measures after yet another poor financial summer. It was accepted that the playing staff would have to be pruned, but there was some criticism of the scale of the exercise. Many felt that Barry Lloyd could have made a useful captain, whilst others argued that Rowe had not been given enough chances and that he would have regained his confidence under Ontong's captaincy. A lot of eyebrows were also raised when Kevin Lyons was sacked as second team captain and coach. Lyons had helped in the development of many players in the 1984 team, and his sacking came as a surprise to both the youngsters and supporters alike.

At the end of the season, the committee discussed who should lead the team in 1985. Ontong had done a good job after Selvey's departure, but the South African had a lot on his plate. He was still learning the trade as an off-spinner and had moved down the order from No 3 in order to have more time to relax. But if Ontong was not going to captain the side, there were no obvious candidates within the team, and the committee were wary of importing another captain from outside Wales. They were also keen to have stability after another topsy-turvy period in the leadership and eventually decided to offer the job to Ontong.

Towards the end of September some of the Club's officials met with Ontong to discuss the offer and the County's future strategy. He accepted the post, but expressed concern at the Miandad-Davis situation. Ontong believed that the Club desperately needed to play an overseas fast bowler on a regular basis, but several of the committee-men believed that Davis was not the answer. They considered that the West Indian was still inexperienced in terms of seven days a week county cricket, and that he appeared somewhat casual at times, giving the impression he was not trying his best. In contrast, they felt that Javed was a top-class cricketer who always gave his best and inspired the young batsmen, whilst Greg Thomas and Steve Barwick were making enough progress as a new ball pair to warrant Davis's release.

During the autumn, the committee, under the guidance of cricket chairman David Lewis, the former leg-spinner, began considering other English qualified fast bowlers to support Thomas and Barwick, and provide cover if either broke down again, with Javed filling the overseas spot. Les McFarlane, the former Lancashire and Northants pace bowler and Steve Malone, the former Essex and Hampshire bowler were contacted and in the spring of 1985 they agreed terms with Glamorgan and Davis was released. So like Roy Fredericks some

12 years earlier, a West Indian Test cricketer left the Club in order to allow the promising home-bred youngsters to have greater opportunities and restore the Welsh identity of the Club.

Many of the supporters were delighted that the overseas player debate had been resolved in Javed's favour, and the Pakistani responded by scoring a century in the opening Championship match of the season at The Oval, and guiding Glamorgan to a seven-wicket win. This was followed by a nine-wicket victory over Somerset with Javed playing another leading role with a quickfire 86 as Ontong declared at 387 for seven and forced Somerset to follow on. Javed also made a major personal contribution in the Sunday League, scoring a record 573 runs at an average of 63.37, although the side managed to win only four games and finished in 14th place.

Javed's finest moment of the season came in the match with the Australians, which saw the return of first-class cricket to The Gnoll following a substantial sponsorship deal of around £20,000 with the Neath Development Partnership. There was a festive air to the match with a host of gaily coloured tents and marquees lining the boundary boards, and the Pakistani rose to the occasion with a superb display of strokeplay, reaching a faultless double-century with a mighty six onto the Mayor of Neath's marquee alongside the pavilion. Together with Younis Ahmed, he almost rewrote the Club's batting records as they shared a partnership of 306, the highest by any English county for the fourth wicket against Australia. It was a truly memorable display of high-class batting from the two Pakistanis and at the end of the season they presented their bats to the Neath club, where they hang today in the pavilion alongside the one used by W. G. Grace when he played at Neath in 1868 and bagged a pair!

Unfortunately, both of these master batsmen were hampered by injury during the season. Javed picked up a mystery back injury, whilst Younis missed several weeks after being hit on the jaw by a ball from David Lawrence, the Gloucestershire fast bowler. Indeed, the Club's progress was once again halted by a catalogue of misfortune. The victories over Surrey and Somerset had put them on top of the table, but they slipped down to 12th place after serious injuries to John Steele and A. L. Jones. Steele badly shattered a bone in his hand against Somerset whilst stopping a drive off his own bowling by Nigel Popplewell, and Jones dislocated his shoulder as he dived to stop a ball in the opening Sunday League game of the season. Both attempted comebacks, but neither fully recovered; although these blows ended their first-class playing careers with the club, both are still attached to Glamorgan – Steele is now the second team captain, whilst Jones leads the recently formed Glamorgan Colts team in the SWCA.

Despite their slide down the Championship table, Ontong's team showed signs of considerable improvement on recent seasons by reaching the quarter-finals of the Nat West Trophy. They began with an eight-wicket victory over Scotland, and then in the next round, Greg Thomas demolished Sussex taking five for 17 in a fiery opening blast as they collapsed to 136. Worcestershire were the opponents in the quarter-final at St Helen's, as many pundits began suggesting a repeat of their 1977 run in the competition. However, for the second year in succession, Javed was injured on the eve of an important NatWest game, and together with Thomas, he failed a fitness test on the morning of the match. The elements were also conspired against Glamorgan as heavy rain fell up until lunch and delayed the start. News that the Club were desperately trying to contact Ezra Moseley, who was now playing in the Lancashire Leagues and whose registration the Club had kept, prompted Worcestershire to make an effort to start the match as soon as the rain stopped. The umpires made an inspection over the soggy outfield after lunch, and Phil Neale, the visitors' skipper, got all of his team out of the dressing room to assist with the mopping up operations. The umpires decided to start the game at six o'clock, and after being put in, Glamorgan slumped to 51 for four. Despite stubborn resistance the next morning from Ontong

*Rodney Ontong shakes the hand of Matthew Maynard after his debut century against Yorkshire. Terry Davies (left) and Phil North pass on their congratulations, whilst Mark Price relaxes in the background. (*Western Mail*)*

*Greg Thomas, 'the fastest white man in county cricket', in full flight at Sophia
Gardens. (*Western Mail*)*

and Morris, this evening session virtually decided the result of the match, and Worcestershire ran out the winners by four wickets.

The team's progress in the competition gave evidence of the restored self-belief in the Welsh camp. Ontong steadfastly never allowed the team to be intimidated and few of the other counties considered them to be a push-over any more. The team played with a lot more confidence, and this rubbed off on the youngsters who came into the team towards the end of the summer. One of these was Matthew Maynard, and he enjoyed a remarkable debut against Yorkshire at Swansea, hitting a superb century to become the first Glamorgan batsman since Frank Pinch in 1921 to score a hundred in his first Championship innings. Glamorgan were chasing a target of 272 on the final afternoon, and this must have been remote as Maynard arrived at the crease with the Swansea scoreboard reading 120 for four and the Yorkshire spinners extracting spin and bounce from the worn wicket. Soon afterwards a further three wickets fell but Maynard was undeterred and he launched a lone assault on the bowling, advancing time and again down the wicket and striking a series of crisp boundaries. By the time he had reached 84, most spectators believed he would quieten down and carefully look for ones and twos, but he continued in his cavalier style and hit three successive straight sixes off Phil Carrick to reach a truly amazing century. Although the scoreboard read 237 for nine a famous victory seemed a possibility if Maynard could stay at the crease for a few more minutes, but two balls later he was caught at point and a relieved Yorkshire team had won.

Despite Maynard's quite brilliant debut, the Club's management still had a few headaches at the end of the season. In particular, they were still searching for an opening bowler to support Thomas, as neither Malone or McFarlane established themselves. An indication of these difficulties came in the Sunday League game with Nottinghamshire at Swansea, as the visitors' lower order batsmen smashed 37 in the final two overs against the quick bowlers to achieve an improbable victory. Whilst their signing of these two recruits had not met with success, the performance of Greg Thomas justified the committee's faith in him as a genuine fast bowler. He produced a series of hostile spells in May and June to earn the tag of the 'fastest white bowler' on the county circuit.

One of Thomas's fastest spells came against Hampshire at Southampton in front of Test selector A. C. Smith. Thomas worried all the front line Hampshire batsmen with his pace and lift off a relatively easy paced wicket, and he hurried Gordon Greenidge into an injudicious hook shot. Mark Nicholas was also in trouble against Thomas' pace and the Hampshire captain came in for some teasing from the fiery Welshman. When Glamorgan had been batting

Matthew Maynard, the Club's latest England batsman, drives forcibly in the
Sunday League match against Worcestershire at Swansea in 1987.
(Morton Davies)

Nicholas had been fielding as usual in the slips and had regularly spurred on Malcolm Marshall, his West Indian pace bowler. So when the Hampshire captain came in to bat Thomas sent a series of balls whistling past Nicholas's face, and after one ferocious lifter, he glared down the wicket and mockingly said: 'Come on Marshy, come on Marshy, you don't like it when it's up your nose do you!'

However, from mid-June onwards the 25-year-old faced one niggling injury after another, and didn't bowl a ball in the Championship after the Kent match in early August and finished with a modest haul of 34 wickets. Nevertheless, he had shown enough promise as a fast bowler and had clearly impressed A. C. Smith, and was chosen for England's winter tour to the West Indies. The only worries were his minor injuries, so from September until Christmas, Thomas worked at building up his fitness by running in the hills around his home in the Swansea Valley, training with his local rugby team, and bowling at the Indoor School at Neath. He didn't let his many supporters down and vindicated his selection with a series of hostile spells in the Test series. In fact there was an almost fairy-tale start to his England career as Desmond Haynes edged Thomas's first ball in Test cricket head high between first and second slip, and was dropped by Willey in the gully off Thomas's second. He gained revenge by having Haynes caught behind in his second spell, and he took a further seven wickets in the next couple of Tests, though a poor performance in the fourth Test cost him his place for the last match of the series.

The West Indian tour was a difficult one for the English party, with a 5-0 'blackwash' in the Test series, and allegations about the off-the-field affairs of some of the tourists. However, Thomas returned home with a glowing reputation and many of the Glamorgan supporters predicted a bright future for the Welsh team at long last, hoping that Thomas's bowling coupled with the developing talents of Hugh Morris and the precocious abilities of Maynard would see the team achieve success in one of the major competitions. But like so many times in the past, the optimism was quickly dispelled and the Club went through yet another crisis period.

CHAPTER TWENTY-ONE

WHERE IS JAVED?

THE CLUB WAS PLAGUED by further internal wranglings in 1986, with worries over both the captaincy and the overseas player situation. It all began at the end of the previous summer when Ontong departed to South Africa for the winter after telling the cricket sub-committee that he was not prepared to lead the side in 1986 if they did not have an overseas fast bowler. The officials sympathised with him because even with Javed's outstanding batting, Glamorgan had only won a handful of games and had frequently failed to bowl sides out. Thomas had made significant progress, but he had not yet played a full season, and now with his England selection, there was every likelihood he would miss several Championship games.

The officials had been impressed by the way Ontong had led the side once again, and they desperately wanted to stabilise the team by keeping his services. So at the end of the season, McFarlane and Malone were released, along with Price and Henderson, and attempts were made to hire a high-quality strike bowler. Bruce Reid and Craig McDermott were amongst the names considered, but eventually Ezra Moseley was re-signed on a part-time basis with the intention of his playing in certain midweek Championship games, and Javed playing in the rest, and all of the Sunday matches. The officials considered this to be the best solution to their problem and after Carling had flown out to South Africa to talk to him, Ontong agreed to lead the side in 1986.

But Moseley's re-engagement upset Javed, who was unhappy at the thought of playing once again on a rota basis. His contract was due for renewal at the end of the next season, so during the autumn he sought confirmation of his future with the Welsh club. He asked the Club for a new three-year contract, and added that if he was not going to be offered this, he would prefer not to play for the Club at all in 1986 as he felt his heart would not be in it. The Club's officials could not realistically meet these requests or give such long-term assurances when knowing Ontong's views about an overseas quick bowler. They were worried by the Pakistani's threat that he would not fulfil his contractual obligations, and they informed him that they expected him to be available for 1986, during which a review would be made of his future with the Club.

But the matter did not end there, as Miandad hit a six off the last ball to win a lucrative tournament for Pakistan in Sharjah during April, and then failed to return to South Wales for Glamorgan's opening matches of the new season. He had been due to report back at the end of April, but he remained in Pakistan, telling the Club that he had to resolve a few domestic matters and that he would return later in May. However, the Club's officials took a dim view of his absence and felt aggrieved that he had not been available for the zonal games in the Benson and Hedges competition, when his quick scoring abilities were badly needed. It didn't take them long to agree that the Pakistani was in breach of his contract by not returning in April, and they asked Philip Carling to contact Javed and tell him to return immediately. However, Javed still remained in Pakistan and eventually in a telephone call from Lahore, the Pakistani told the Secretary he would not be returning, and said: 'It seems that I am only required to play for part of the season. My future does not rest with Glamorgan. It is here in Pakistan.'

The Club accepted his resignation, but the matter still dragged on. In mid-season, the Pakistani returned to Swansea to collect his belongings from his home in South Wales and sell the house. During the surprise visit, he met with Gwyn Craven and made an attempt to be reinstated, asking for a new contract, based on either two or three years with a benefit in 1990. A faction of the membership felt that a reconciliation might be possible, but his team-mates had been deeply hurt by Javed's non-arrival at the start of the season, feeling that the Pakistani had let them down. The committee were of a similar mind, especially since the Club had been kind to Miandad in the past by paying him when he was touring with Pakistan and had not been available to play for Glamorgan. Not surprisingly, they turned down his request and Javed returned to Pakistan.

Ezra Moseley was committed to play at the weekends for Littleborough in the Lancashire League, so Javed's resignation left the Welsh club in need of yet another overseas player for their weekend matches. They attempted to get special dispensation to sign a replacement on a short-term basis, and amongst the batsmen considered was Richie Richardson, who had played for the second eleven a few years before whilst attached to the Neath club. However, the TCCB refused Glamorgan's request, saying that they should stick to the regulations that overseas players were to be signed for a minimum of two years. Although the Club's officials felt that they had extenuating circumstances, they accepted the ruling and realised that the matter now was not the question of just a short-term replacement, but the Club's longer-term strategy. On the one hand, they did not want to be rushed into a hasty signing until they had given proper consideration to the matter, but on the other, there was the need for having someone to share the overseas duties with Moseley in 1986. Fortunately, Denis Hickey, a young Australian quick bowler had been attached to the Club on an Esso Scholarship and registered with the

TCCB with the intention of playing second team cricket. The Club's officials realised his selection for midweek Championship matches would give them the breathing space they needed whilst they deliberated over who should replace Javed.

It seemed like a repeat of the 1970s all over again as the Club's management debated whether the overseas player should be a batsman or a bowler. Eventually, they decided to sign a top-class spinner who would be most effective on the slow Welsh wickets, and a strike bowler who could give extra pace to the attack when necessary, but to stop a repeat of the Javed episode, the officials stressed that both of the signings would have to agree to share the overseas duties. This was in their favour as many of the foreign stars did not want to play county cricket on a seven-days-a-week basis. They hoped that Ezra Moseley could fill the fast bowling berth, but in his few appearances in 1986 he showed that he had lost some of his pace and was struggling to recapture his form at county level. Consequently, others players were approached and Corrie Van Zyl, the Springbok quick bowler was signed, together with Ravi Shastri, the talented Indian spinner.

It had been a sorry start to the 1986 season, as the whereabouts and future of Javed hung over the Club, and for the first time, they failed to win a zonal match in the Benson and Hedges Cup. They also failed to

Sophia Gardens, Cardiff: Glamorgan's home in the Welsh Capital since 1967. (Gerard Elias)

find their winning touch in the Championship, and after five draws they crashed to heavy defeats against Essex and Warwickshire. Ontong increasingly found his role as captain during times of stress both on and off the field was putting severe pressure on his own game. He had thought hard over whether to continue in the first place, and now that there were public and private rows affecting his form, he felt it wise not to continue.

He told David Lewis during July that he did not want to lead the team in 1987, and after a lot of quiet discussion, Ontong realised it would benefit his successor if he stood down immediately and allowed the next captain to gain valuable experience during the second half of the summer. It was a decision which spoke volumes for Ontong's commitment to Glamorgan, and he was the first to pledge his support to 22-year-old Hugh Morris who took over and became the Club's youngest ever captain.

Morris could hardly have taken over the job at a more difficult time. The side were entrenched at the foot of the Championship table, without any wins, and they were out of contention for any of the one-day honours. A few critics believed that Morris's elevation was another poor management decision, as he was only in his first full season after completing his college studies, and that his relative inexperience at county level would count against him. But they were made to eat their words as Morris led Glamorgan to victory against Leicestershire in his first game in charge and then hit his first century in the Sunday League the following weekend at Ebbw Vale.

Glamorgan ended the season at the bottom of the Championship table, but it was widely believed that this was an untrue reflection of their real ability. The team had weathered several difficult weeks early in the season, and there had been yet another change in captaincy, but they had improved sufficiently in the second half of the season to defeat County Champions Essex in the last game of the summer. In addition Greg Thomas and Matthew Maynard had continued their development, with Maynard passing 1,000 runs for the first time and Thomas building on his success in the West Indies. The fast bowler was still affected by minor injuries and was increasingly frustrated by the lifeless Welsh wickets, both of which hampered his claims for a regular Test place, and finished with only 39 Championship wickets.

When Thomas was at peak form and bowling on a responsive surface, he showed that he was still able to worry some of the best batsmen on the county circuit. An example of this came in the match with Somerset at Taunton, though for once the batsman had the last laugh. The player in question was Viv Richards, and several times Thomas sent some balls whizzing past the great batsman's nose, causing him to sway out of the way. After one particularly quick ball,

Thomas glared down the wicket at Richards and said: 'It's red, it's round and it's fast.' The master batsman was rather taken aback by the Welshman's hostility, both verbally and with the ball, and he decided to counter-attack. A few overs later, he stepped away to leg and smashed a ball from Thomas straight back over the bowler's head, over the stands and into the nearby River Tone. This time Thomas stood disbelievingly at the end of his follow-through as the ball sailed out of the ground, and Richards nonchalantly leaned on his bat and said: 'Hey man, you know what it looks like, you go and find it!'

There were several important changes in personnel over the winter months, starting with the release of Younis. Although he remained a batsman capable of scoring runs, he was now approaching 40 and the committee believed he lacked mobility in the field, especially in the limited-overs games. An experienced batsman was nevertheless needed in the middle order, so the club signed Alan Butcher, the Surrey and England batsman, who had fallen out with the management (or more accurately the manager) at The Oval. There was also a change of wicket-keeper as Terry Davies decided to settle with his wife in Australia and retire from county cricket. His decision came as a surprise to many, but the Club were lucky enough to sign Colin Metson, who had acted as Paul Downton's understudy at Middlesex.

All in all the Club entered 1987 with one of its strongest staffs for many years, and coupled with the quiet development of Holmes, Derrick and Barwick, there seemed every chance that the team would rise up the Championship table. This they achieved, with a final position of 13th, but they could have risen even further had it not been for another spate of injuries. Ontong missed over a month after having to undergo a knee operation, Van Zyl sustained a stress fracture in his foot and Barwick damaged some muscles in his rib cage. Thomas also broke down again, with an ankle injury, infuriatingly after regaining his place in the England team for the one-day series with Pakistan.

The most serious injury in the batting department came in the Sunday League match against Yorkshire in May, when Alan Butcher badly damaged a calf muscle whilst turning for a second run. Butcher's absence for eight weeks weakened the batting, and with John Hopkins out of form, there were calls for remedial action. Things came to a head when Glamorgan suffered a heavy defeat at the hands of the Minor Counties in the Benson and Hedges Cup, and soon afterwards the Club's officials met to discuss the situation. Tony Cottey, the young Swansea batsman, and former Gloucestershire player Paul Roebuck were both scoring heavily for the second team and had their supporters for promotion into the first team, but the committee decided to offer a contract to 34-year-old Paul Todd, the former

Nottinghamshire batsman who had single-handedly steered the Minor Counties to their victory over Glamorgan.

Although Todd's signing did not meet with unanimous approval from everyone in the Welsh club's hierarchy, he showed his value by hitting a typically aggressive 90 against Pakistan and compiling a more sober century at Worcester in August to save Glamorgan from defeat. By this time, Butcher had returned to the team, and he gave an illustration of his return to top form by scoring centuries against Leicestershire, Worcestershire and Derbyshire. The latter typified his professional approach because he had to retire midway through his innings after being hit on the arm. However, he returned to face the fiery Derbyshire attack and unselfishly protected the lower order. His score remained on 99 for several overs as he refused a number of singles so that last man Steve Barwick would not have to face Michael Holding. Butcher eventually reached three figures and deservedly finished the season with over a thousand runs and a county cap to his name.

But the batting star of 1987 was undoubtedly the irrepressible Matthew Maynard. During the season, he blossomed into a batsman capable of regularly making large scores rather than a fancy twenty or thirty plus the odd fifty. He deservedly won the Apex Packaging Award for Glamorgan Player of the Year after finishing the season as the side's leading run scorer with over 1,600 runs, at an average of over 40, besides being the leading fielder in the country. The 21-year-old hit the headlines with an ebullient century before lunch against Somerset at Weston, followed the next day by the fastest televised Sunday League fifty against the same bowlers. Both innings illustrated his refreshingly uncomplicated approach to batting, and wide range of forcing shots off both the front and back foot. Technically speaking, however, his finest innings came later in the season against Derbyshire at Cardiff, where he remained unflustered against their battery of pace bowlers, and carefully saw them off one by one with an audacious display of batting.

Hugh Morris also produced some good innings, and despite a moderate second half of the season, he still amassed over 1,300 runs, averaging just over 28. He hit a hundred in each innings of the match with Warwickshire, and shared a record partnership of 249 for the second wicket with young Stephen James against Oxford University. A particularly gratifying aspect of the season was Shastri's promising start, showing that the Club had at long last acquired a successful overseas bowler. The young Indian proved to be an enthusiastic and popular member of the side, scoring nearly 800 runs and taking 34 wickets in his 12 appearances. He formed an effective partnership with Ontong, and the new 'spin twins' were instrumental in the innings victory at Swansea over Lancashire, who ended as runners up in the Championship. Their bowling in tandem at St Helen's rekindled memories of 'Shep' and 'Pres' some 20 years before. Indeed, much of the Club's success in the past has been based on a pair of high-class spinners, supported by keen fielding, and at the end of 1987, many people were suggesting that the Club were finally on the verge of a new era of success.

So the Club's 99th year ended like so many before it, with a mood of optimism for the immediate future. Perhaps this is because the Welsh are a supremely optimistic breed, never wanting to lie down for long and refusing to accept the worst. But now that they had the spin partnership of Shastri and Ontong, plus the steady and sometimes exciting batting of Maynard, Morris and Butcher, there were signs that the club were not too far from a successful run in one of the major competitions — maybe it would come, fittingly, in Centenary Year.

CHAPTER TWENTY-TWO

THE CENTENARY SEASON

THE WELSH CLUB CELEBRATED their 100th birthday by having their best ever season in one-day cricket. They finished in their highest ever position in the Sunday League, and reached the quarter-finals of the Nat West Trophy and the semi-finals of the Benson and Hedges Cup. And if luck, that most capricious ingredient of limited-overs cricket, had been on their side, this history could have had a fairytale ending, with the Welsh county reaching the finals of one of these competitions.

Yet during the winter months, the omens for 1988 were not looking good, and it seemed unlikely that they would have a successful season. Firstly, Greg Thomas has become so disillusioned at having to bowl on slow Welsh wickets that at the end of the 1987 season he asked for a release from his contract, which still had a year to run. But the committee did not want to lose the fast bowler, or make a precedent of releasing a talented player before his contract expired, so they refused to let Thomas join another county for the 1988 season. Around Christmas, news came through from the Southern Hemisphere that Simon Base, the 27 year old seamer, had decided to join Derbyshire, whilst both Ontong and Metson had broken their arms. Then in the spring, the Treasurer reported at the A.G.M. that the club had entered Centenary Year with a loss in excess of £27,000 from the previous season.

On the field events began with defeats at Bristol, and a ten-wicket loss at Southampton, and the critics began to write off Morris's team for yet another season. But a dramatic transformation took place in the space of a week in mid-May. They defeated Somerset, the Combined Services and Gloucestershire in the Benson and Hedges Cup, and finished narrowly on top of their zonal group, thereby securing a home draw with Nottinghamshire in the quarter-finals. The match saw a remarkable batting performance by Matthew Maynard, who a week before had chipped a bone in his left index finger, and was doubtful for the big match right up until the very morning of the game. He took a brave decision to play, and Glamorgan were very grateful indeed. He arrived at the crease with their score on 32-2 chasing a daunting 221, but he soon launched into a ferocious assault on the Notts bowlers, without any apparent pain from his damaged finger. Together with John Hopkins, he shared an unbeaten partnership of 187 and was eventually out when Glamorgan were on the verge of victory, making 107 off just 117 balls to see them to a place in the semi-finals for the first time ever.

Fortune still seemed to be on their side when they were drawn at home to Derbyshire and, on the morning of the game, Morris won the toss and invited the visitors to have first use of the Swansea wicket. They found run scoring difficult against the accurate Glamorgan attack, and were tied down to 140-4 off 45 overs; but some loose bowling and bold hitting by the Derbyshire lower order saw them plunder 77 runs in the final ten overs, and Glamorgan were left with a target of 218. Butcher and Hopkins provided a solid platform for the run chase, and after tea Maynard and Shastri began to reel off a salvo of handsome drives. It looked as if the dream of a Lord's final in Centenary Year might come true, but in the space of a few overs these hopes evaporated. Kim Barnett opted to bring back Michael Holding in an attempt to stem the flow of runs. His decision was justified in bizarre fashion as Maynard knocked of his strapless helmet with his left forearm as he drove against the West Indian, and then, to the horror of the young batsman and the crowd of 8,000, the falling helmet knocked off a bail.

Things went from bad to worse as the light deteriorated and, in the gloom, Shastri was caught in the slips. Soon afterwards, the umpires called off play with the Welsh county on 130-5 after 43 overs, but rain prevented a prompt resumption the next day, and the game eventually got underway again midway through the last afternoon. Sadly, the task of making 88 runs in 12 overs proved to be too much for the Glamorgan batsmen, despite some lusty blows from Ontong and Holmes, every time a ball went into the air, it was caught by a Derbyshire fielder. Morris's team ended 14 runs short and, not for the last time in 1988, his team agonised on their bad luck. The tale of the missing helmet strap passed into the folklore of Glamorgan cricket, and left their supporters talking about yet another 'might-have-been'.

Glamorgan had by far their best year in the Sunday League during 1988, and were in the top half of the table for virtually all of the season. Ironically, the year had begun with a heavy defeat at Bristol, but it was followed by victories at home over Somerset and Derbyshire, and three impressive away wins at Edgbaston, Trent Bridge and Chelmsford. Their position in the top six was maintained by a nail-biting win over Yorkshire at Cardiff. The visitors appeared to be cruising to victory, needing 41 off the final seven overs with eight wickets in hand, but they dramatically lost five wickets in as many overs to John Derrick and Steve Watkin, the young Maesteg seamer, who was only playing because Greg Thomas was injured. Their steady bowling and a few rash strokes turned the game around and Glamorgan won by 15 runs. Thomas soon regained fitness, and a few weeks later produced a match-winning spell against Surrey at Ebbw Vale. The visitors were chasing a target of 198 and their cause looked a forlorn one at 116-6, with only 11 overs left. But once again their lower order took full advantage of some loose bowling and as the target was reduced to 16 off the last four overs, many of the Welsh supporters turned their minds back to the semi-final a few weeks before. But Thomas, bowling at speed and to a full length, settled the outcome, taking the last three wickets in the space of six balls to leave Surrey eight runs adrift of their target.

A place in the top four and the newly inaugurated Refuge Assurance Cup now looked a distinct possibility, but their luck cruelly ran out again during the match with second place (and eventual champions) Worcestershire at Swansea. The match was reduced to a 22-over contest because of rain, and despite being put in, Glamorgan made a flying start, with John Hopkins hitting three mighty sixes. Maynard was just starting to unleash some powerful drives when a heavy shower rolled in from Swansea Bay and forced the players off the field with the Glamorgan score on a handsome 73-1 after just 9.3 overs. But the drizzle hung around long enough for this original game to be abandoned, and a new 11-overs-a-side match was started. Glamorgan were put in yet again as Morris lost the toss, and the young skipper disconsolately trudged up the 50-odd steps to the dressing room knowing that the side batting second in a Sunday slog has an enormous advantage. To compound matters, his batsmen failed to regain their touch after the break, and never looked likely to set the visitors as high a target as before the stoppage; 82 in 11 overs was easily within Worcestershire's range and they cruised to a hollow win.

Surely nothing else could go wrong after this harsh twist of fortunes; but it did, as Rodney Ontong and Steve Barwick were involved in a serious car crash en route from Colchester to Wellingborough. Both were badly shaken and Ontong severely damaged ligaments in his knee, causing him to enter hospital for another operation and miss the rest of the season. The unlucky defeat against Worcestershire meant that Glamorgan had to win both of their remaining Sunday games and rely on Gloucestershire losing one of their matches. It was a stiff task at the best of times, and was even harder following the accident to two of their best Sunday bowlers. Even so, the Welsh county managed to defeat Northamptonshire by five wickets with Phil North, the young spinner from Newport, taking 3-20 in only his third Sunday outing. But the team's delight was short-lived as it was confirmed that Gloucestershire had convincingly beaten Kent.

The following week, the Glamorgan side travelled to Llanelli knowing that a place in the top four depended on them defeating Leicestershire and Gloucestershire failing to win at Chelmsford. Once again, the elements intervened, with heavy overnight rain seeping

One of Glamorgan's leading all-rounders, Rodney Ontong, bowling against Worcestershire at Neath in 1987.

under the protective sheets and on to the Stradey Park wicket. The start was delayed, ironically in glorious sunshine, and eventually a 13-over-a-side contest commenced. But it proved to be academic as news came through that Gloucestershire had won by five wickets, and Glamorgan had to be content with 6th place. Had they secured another six points it might have been a different story, and the team left Llanelli knowing that they might have had them if the match at Pontypridd against Lancashire had not been abandoned with the Welsh team in a strong position, and if the match at Eastbourne had not been tied with Sussex scoring ten vital runs in the final over.

Despite this success in the limited-over contests, Glamorgan finished in 17th place in the county championship, winning just one four-day match, and, for only the second time in their history, failing to win a three-day game. Their sole championship victory came at Edgbaston as Warwickshire chased 194 on the final day. They slumped to 107-9, before Small and Gifford shared a stubborn tenth wicket partnership as Warwickshire, in nail-biting circumstances, inched closer to their target. They had put on 82 in bizarre fashion when Thomas trapped Small leg before and, much to the relief of the Welshmen, they had registered their first win.

Many factors contributed to their lack of success in the championship, the most important being the lack of penetration in the bowling and despite some promising spells by young Watkin, Glamorgan failed to bowl out sides twice. An example was the game with Surrey at St. Helen's where the visitors were in a precarious position shortly after lunch on the final day with a lead of just 134 with only four wickets standing. However, with the aid of several dropped catches, they managed to hold out until tea and the match ended in a disappointing draw. Other factors were the appalling weather, causing the loss of around 20 per cent of playing time in home matches, the spate of injuries, with virtually all of the front-line bowlers being sidelined at some stage of the summer, whilst midway through the season Corrie Van Zyl decided to return to South Africa earlier than anticipated to take up a job.

The Welsh county came agonisingly close to winning several games, none more so than at Chelmsford as Essex pursued 273 on the final afternoon. A typically aggressive 72 from Graham Gooch seemed to have put his side on course for a comfortable win, but a spell of 5-38 by Geoff Holmes revived Glamorgan's hopes, and Essex needed two off the last ball with their ninth-wicket pair at the wicket. Derek Pringle guided the ball down to fine leg, but Maynard returned a fine throw straight to Colin Metson and Pringle was run out going for the second run, leaving the Essex score on 272-9. There was some doubt over whether the game had been drawn or tied, because of the absence of Geoff Miller with a back strain since the first day. The scorers were prepared to enter him as 'absent hurt' and declare the match a tie, but the umpires ruled that the game should end in a draw because there was not another delivery to prove whether or not Miller was absent!

So Glamorgan finished their Centenary Year at the foot of the championship table – the same position as in their first year in the competition some 67 years before. In between these times, the club has passed through many bleak years, with only a few high points along the way. But the signs are that the club is finally emerging from the doldrums and despite their lowly position in the championship, the Welsh county appear to be moving in the right direction both on and off the field. A well-balanced side has been assembled, with a blend of youth and experience, whilst a host of talented youngsters quietly develop in the wings. Over the past few years a successful marketing campaign has boosted the club's finances, and a coaching programme for young Welsh cricketers has been devised with the support of Allied Steel and Wire. The success of this scheme, the coaching framework devised by national coach Tom Cartwright and the success of Alan

Jones' Glamorgan Colts team in the SWCA all augur well for the future of the club and a continuation of the all-important Welsh identity.

The Glamorgan side of the 21st century could also be playing at a new venue in Cardiff, with the club's officials discussing the possibilities of acquiring land in the redeveloped Cardiff Docks which, most important of all, would mean that Glamorgan would have a ground and headquarters of its own – the absence of which has been a major stumbling block in the club's development. The future, therefore, offers much hope, as testified by the emergence of Matthew Maynard into the England team in Centenary Year, and together with Greg Thomas and Colin Metson, was considered for a place in the England party for the winter tour in India. And the evidence of the one-day games in 1988 would also suggest that Hugh Morris could soon be leading Glamorgan to their first-ever major limited overs title. The days of despair may at last be over!

STATISTICAL SECTION

BIOGRAPHICAL DETAILS
OF GLAMORGAN PLAYERS

The following played in inter-county and major representative games, 1889–1988

NAME AND EXTENT OF CAREER (Other counties and clubs in brackets)	BIRTHPLACE	DATE OF BIRTH	DATE OF DEATH
Thomas Ernest Abel *1922–1925* (Surrey)	Kennington	10. 9.1890	23. 1.1937
Hubert Griffiths Alexander *1898*	Pontypridd	9. 9.1873	unknown
Anthony William Allin *1976* (Devon, Minor Counties)	Bideford	20. 4.1954	
Reginald Mervyn Bulford Anderson *1946*	Swansea	25. 4.1914	12. 8.1972
T. M. Arkell *1898*	unknown	unknown	unknown
Gregory DeLisle Armstrong *1974–1976* (Barbados)	Bank Hall, Barbados	11. 5.1950	
Trevor Arnott *1921–1930* (Wales, Monmouthshire, MCC)	Radyr	16. 2.1902	2. 2.1975
Harry Arundale *1914–1920*	unknown	unknown	unknown
H. Bainton *1911*	unknown	unknown	unknown
John ('Jack') Bancroft *1908–1922*	Swansea	1879	7. 1.1942
William John ('Billy') Bancroft *1889–1914* (South Wales, West of England)	Swansea	2. 3.1871	3. 3.1959
Thomas Marriott Barlow *1894–1897*	Salford	12.1864	27. 1.1942
Ian Barry *1900*	unknown	unknown	unknown
Stephen Royston Barwick *1981–*	Neath	6. 9.1960	
Simon John Base *1986–*	Maidstone	2. 1.1960	
Steven Bastien	Mile End	13. 3.1963	
William Ederick Bates *1920–1931* (Yorkshire, Wales, Cheshire)	Kirkheaton, Yorks	5. 3.1884	17. 1.1957
A. M. Batty *1891*	unknown	unknown	unknown
Herbert Wood Baxter *1920–1921*	Stockport	1883	25. 4.1962
Sir Horace Owen Compton Beasley *1899*	Brentford	2. 7.1877	1. 1.1960
John Thomson Bell *1924–1931* (Yorkshire, Wales)	Batley	16. 6.1895	14. 8.1974
Frank Bennett *1914*	unknown	unknown	unknown
William Bestwick *1914–1920* (Derbyshire)	Heanor	24. 2.1875	2. 5.1938
Col John Maybery Bevan *1920*	Llanelli	1886	24. 6.1970
Cecil F. Biggs *1906*	unknown	unknown	unknown
Selwyn Hanam Biggs *1891–1899*	Cardiff	6.1872	unknown
Edgar A. Billings *1911–1914*	unknown	unknown	unknown
Frank Binch *1894–1895*	Lancashire	1864	unknown
David Blackmore *1934*	Swansea	3. 1910	unknown
Ronald Winston Boon *1931–1932*	Barry	11. 6.1909	
Elvyn Bowen *1928–1933*	Llanelli	1907	24. 8.1965
George E. Bowen *1891–1892*	unknown	unknown	unknown
Joseph Hugh Brain *1891–1908* (Oxford University, Gloucestershire)	Kingswood, Bristol	11. 9.1863	26. 6.1914
John Henry Patrick Brain *1920–1928*	Cardiff	17. 3.1896	11.12.1945
Michael Benjamin Brain *1930*	Cardiff	13. 4.1910	24. 8.1971

Name	Place	Born	Died
William Henry Brain 1891–1907 (Oxford University, Gloucestershire)	Clifton, Bristol	21. 7.1870	20.11.1934
Thomas Leslie Brierley 1931–1939	Southampton	15. 6.1910	
Anthony Compton Burnett (later Compton-Burnett) 1958 (Cambridge University)	Chipstead, Surrey	26.10.1923	
Burton 1891	unknown	unknown	unknown
Percy Frank Bush 1902–1903	Cardiff	23. 6.1879	19. 5.1955
Alan Raymond Butcher 1987– (Surrey, England)	Croydon	7. 1.1954	
John Philip Cadogan 1897–1900	Neath	1866	29. 6.1918
Dr Alexander W. Cameron 1900–1913	unknown	unknown	unknown
Michael James Cann 1986–	Cardiff	4. 7.1965	
Ernest Francis Carless 1934–1946	Barry	9. 9.1912	26. 9.1987
Harry Lascelles Carr 1934	Lambeth	8.10.1907	18. 8.1943
Carrington 1896 (substitute from Surrey groundstaff)	Herne Hill	16. 5.1880	
Thomas William Cartwright 1977 (Warwickshire, Somerset, England)	Coventry	22. 7.1935	
John Chandless 1911–1927	Cardiff	21. 8.1884	1. 6.1968
Frank Clarke 1956–1960	St Fagan's	8.10.1936	
John Gowan Clarke 1889–1903	unknown	unknown	unknown
John Charles Clay 1921–1949 (Wales, England, Monmouthshire)	Bonvilston	18. 3.1898	11. 8.1973
Phil Brittain Clift 1937–1955	Usk	3. 9.1918	
H. Clough 1909	unknown	unknown	unknown
Robert Henry Colley 1899	unknown	unknown	unknown
Edgar Cooper 1912–1921	Briton Ferry	16.11.1891	15. 3.1959
John James Cope 1935 (Monmouthshire)	Ellesmere Port	1. 8.1908	
George Ernest Cording 1900–1923	Tredegar	1. 1.1878	2. 2.1946
Anthony Elton Cordle 1963–1980	Bridgetown, Barbados	21. 9.1940	
Phillip Anthony Cottey 1986–	Swansea	2. 6.1966	
Arthur Brynley Creber 1929 (Scotland)	Sketty	11.10.1909	10. 8.1966
Harry Creber 1898–1922 (South Wales)	Birkenhead	30. 4.1872	27. 3.1939
Peter Gwynne Crowther 1977–1978	Neath	26. 4.1952	
James S. Cullen 1893	unknown	unknown	unknown
Simon Anthony Brewis Daniels 1981–1982 (Durham)	Darlington	23. 8.1958	
John Gilbert Dauncey 1957	Ystalyfera	9. 4.1936	
Alexander Charles Robert David 1913	Cardiff	5.11.1889	unknown
Edmund Usher David 1889–1898	St. Fagan's	24. 4.1860	26. 6.1942
Rodney Felix Armine David 1925–1929	Cardiff	19. 6.1907	2. 7.1969
C. B. Davies 1913	unknown	unknown	unknown
David ('Dai') Davies 1923–1939 (Wales)	Llanelli	26. 8.1896	16. 7.1976
David Aubrey Davies 1934–1938	Swansea	11. 7.1915	
D. E. Davies 1892	unknown	unknown	unknown
David Emrys Davies 1924–1954 (Wales)	Sandy, Llanelli	27. 6.1904	10.11.1975

David Roy Davies *1950*	Llanelli	12. 8.1928	
Gwynfor Davies *1932*	Sandy, Llanelli	12. 8.1908	10. 3.1972
Gwynfor Davies *1947–1948*	Cardiff	10. 6.1919	
Hugh Daniel Davies *1955–1960*	Pembrey	23. 7.1932	
Haydn George Davies *1935–1958*	Llanelli	23. 4.1912	
John Anthony Davies *1952*	Pontypridd	3. 2.1926	
Morean Kimsley Davies *1975–1976*	Clydach	13.10.1954	
Mark Nicholas Davies *1982*	Maesteg	28.12.1959	
Terry Davies *1979–1986*	St Albans	25.10.1960	
Thomas Clive Davies *1971–1972*	Pontrhydyfen	7.11.1951	
W. A. Davies *1893*	unknown	unknown	unknown
William David E. Davies *1932–1935*	Briton Ferry	28. 6.1906	1.10.1971
William George Davies *1954–1960*	Barry	3. 7.1936	
William Henry Davies *1922–1927*	Briton Ferry	7. 8.1901	
Bryan Allan Davis *1968–1970* (Trinidad, West Indies)	Belmont, Port of Spain	2. 5.1940	
Francis John Davis *1959–1967* (Oxford University)	Cardiff	23. 3.1939	
John Darelan David Davis *1911*	Cardiff	1879	27.11.1950
Roger Clive Davis *1964–1976*	Cardiff	1. 1.1946	
Winston Walter Davis *1982–1984* (Windward Islands, West Indies, Northamptonshire, Tasmania)	Kingstown, St Vincent	18. 9.1958	
John Derrick *1983–*	Cwmamman	15. 1.1963	
Louis Norman Devereux *1956–1960*	Heavitree, Exeter	20.10.1931	
Harold J. Dickinson *1934–1935*	Barry	1912	
Charles W. Donnelly *1890*	unknown	unknown	unknown
John Donovan *1891–1895*	Cardiff	1864	20. 8.1921
Michael Donovan *1891*	unknown	unknown	unknown
John Downey *1891*	unknown	unknown	unknown
Richard George Duckfield *1930–1938*	Maesteg	2. 7.1907	30.12.1959
Robert David Louis Dudley-Jones *1972–1973*	Bridgend	26. 5.1952	
Anthony Arthur Duncan *1934* (Oxford University)	Cardiff	10.12.1914	
William B. Dunford *1895*	unknown	unknown	unknown
Frederick William Dunn *1911*	unknown	unknown	unknown
Arnold Herbert Dyson *1926–1948*	Halifax	10. 7.1905	7. 6.1978
James Thomas Eaglestone *1948–1949*	Paddington	24. 7.1923	
Brian Robert Edrich *1954–1956* (Kent, Oxfordshire, Minor Counties)	Cantley, Norfolk	18. 8.1922	
Aubrey Mansel Edward Edwards *1947*	Penycraig, Pontypridd	4. 7.1918	
J. P. Edwards *1895*	unknown	unknown	unknown
William Armine Edwards *1913*	—	1891	1.11.1917
Alfred George Eldridge *1891–1896* (Wiltshire)	Greenwich	21.11.1863	unknown
Charles George Carew Elers *1910–1911* (Devon, West of England)	Lyme Regis	2. 1.1867	11.12.1927
Geoffrey Phillip Ellis *1970–1976*	Llandudno	24. 5.1950	
Henry Augustus Ellis *1904–1906*	unknown	unknown	unknown
William Emery *1922* (Wales)	Merthyr Tydfil	1897	1962

Name	Place	Born	Died
David Gwilym Lloyd Evans *1956–1969*	Lambeth	27. 7.1933	
Sir David William Evans *1891*	Dowlais	4.11.1866	17. 3.1926
Gwynn Evans *1939* (Oxford University, Leicestershire)	Bala	13. 8.1915	
Herbert Price Evans *1920–1922*	Llandaff	30. 8.1894	19.11.1982
John Brian Evans *1958–1963* (Lincolnshire, Minor Counties)	Clydach	9.11.1936	
Talfryn Evans *1934*	Sandy, Llanelli	10. 6.1914	3.1944
William H. Evans *1891*	unknown	unknown	unknown
Trevor Every *1929–1934*	Llanelli	19.12.1909	
C. Farr *1892*	unknown	unknown	unknown
Norman George Featherstone *1980–1981* (Middlesex, Transvaal, N. Transvaal)	Que Que, Rhodesia	20. 8.1949	
L. Fenwick	1920	unknown	unknown
Edwin V. Fletcher *1906*	unknown	unknown	unknown
David Arthur Francis *1973–1984*	Clydach	29.11.1953	
Roy Clifton Fredericks *1971–1973* (Guyana, West Indies)	Blairmont, Guyana	11.11.1942	
Albert Edwin Freethy *1908–1921*	Swansea	27. 4.1885	1966
Arthur Royston Gabe-Jones *1922*	Clydach Vale	25.11.1906	26. 2.1965
Henry F. Gage *1892–1893*	unknown	unknown	unknown
Peter Warlow Gatehouse *1957–1962*	Caerphilly	3. 5.1936	
Frederick William Geary *1923*	Hinckley	9.12.1887	8. 1.1980
William Neilson Gemmill *1920–1926*	Thio, New Caledonia	14.6.1900	18. 9.1987
John P. A. Geoghegan *1891–1898*		1867	15. 4.1916
Reginald Arthur Gibbs *1902–1914*	Cardiff	6.1882	28.11.1938
Arthur Gibson *1902–1909*	unknown	1873	unknown
William D. Gibson *1904*	unknown	unknown	unknown
Edward Robert Kenneth Glover *1932–1938*	Worcester	19. 7.1911	23. 3.1967
Dennis Cunliffe Good *1947* (Worcestershire)	Leeds	29. 8.1926	
Russell Christopher Green *1984* (Suffolk)	St Albans	30. 7.1959	
Sir William Hugh Griffiths *1946–1948* (Cambridge University)	Marylebone	26. 9.1923	
William Henry Gwynn *1890*	Swansea	1856	1. 4.1897
David Graham Pugsley Gwynn *1922–1923*	Swansea	8.12.1904	11.12.1934
William Stamford Hacker *1908–1923* (Gloucestershire, Herefordshire, South Wales)	Chipping Sodbury	8.12.1876	8.12.1925
Robert John Hadley *1971* (Cambridge University)	Neath	22.10.1951	
Claude Vincent Godby Haines *1933–1934* (Devon)	Bristol	17. 1.1906	28. 1.1965
Gordon Hansford *1920*	unknown	unknown	unknown
Alwyn Harris *1960–1964*	Aberdulais	31. 1.1936	
George Joseph Harris *1932*	Underwood, Notts	22.11.1904	
Kenrick Henry Harris *1913* (Monmouthshire, Wales)	Newport	1888	
Leslie John Harris *1947*	Cardiff	20. 7.1915	28.10.1985
Wilfred Ernest Harris *1938–1947*	Cardiff	24. 4.1919	
George Benjamin Harrison *1924–1925*	Askam, Lancs	1895	

Stuart Charles Harrison *1971–1977*	Cwmbran	21. 9.1951	
Bernard Hedges *1950–1967*	Pontypridd	10.11.1927	
Stephen Peter Henderson *1983–1985*	Oxford	24. 9.1958	
(Worcestershire, Cambridge Univ., MCC)			
Norman George Hever *1948–1953*	Marylebone	17.12.1924	11. 9.1987
(Middlesex)			
Denis Jon Hickey *1986*	Mooropana,	31.12.1964	
(Victoria)	Victoria		
Victor Allen Hickley *1894–1898*	Bridgwater	1874	5. 1.1956
Rev Lyonel D'Arcy Hildyard *1891*	Bury	5. 2.1861	22. 4.1931
(Somerset, Oxford Univ., Lancashire)			
Ernest Edward Hill *1911*	unknown	unknown	unknown
Leonard Winston Hill *1964–1976*	Caerleon	14. 4.1941	
Mervyn Llewellyn Hill *1923*	Cardiff	23. 6.1902	28. 2.1948
(Cambridge University, Somerset, Devon)			
Percy Montgomery Tickell Hill *1898*	Llandaff	1877	27. 4.1944
Rupert Knight Hill *1975*	Jamaica	14. 8.1954	
Vernon Tickell Hill *1894–1905*	Llandaff	30. 1.1871	29. 9.1932
(Somerset, Oxford University)			
Joseph John Hills *1926–1931*	Plumstead, Kent	14.10.1897	21. 9.1969
John William James Hinwood *1923*	Wilton, Wilts	8. 4.1894	14. 5.1971
Joseph Owen Hirst *1907*	Leeds	1868	12. 3.1948
Walter Robertson Hoare *1901*	Marlow	27.10.1867	1. 7.1941
(Norfolk)	Bucking,		
	Hampshire		
Robin Nicholas Stuart Hobbs *1979–1981*	Chippenham	8. 5.1942	
(Essex, Suffolk, England)			
Albert Edward Hodges *1936*	Newport	29. 1.1905	
(Wales)			
Geoffrey Clark Holmes *1978–*	Newcastle-on-		
	Tyne	16. 9.1958	
T. Holmes *1894*	unknown	unknown	unknown
John Anthony Hopkins *1970–1988*	Maesteg	16. 6.1953	
(Eastern Province, MCC)			
Thomas Joseph Hordley *1892–1894*	unknown	unknown	unknown
Richard Horsfall *1956*	Todmorden,	26. 6.1920	25. 8.1981
(Essex)	Yorks		
James J. Horspool *1905–1913*	unknown	unknown	unknown
Alan Raymond Howard *1928–1933*	Leicester	11.12.1909	
(Wales)			
Percy Howells *1900*	unknown	unknown	unknown
Donald Wynn Hughes *1935–1936*	Colwyn Bay	1911	12. 8.1967
Wilfred D. Hughes *1937–1938*	Monmouth	12. 7.1910	
Gwyn Hughes *1962–1964*	Cardiff	26. 3.1941	
(Cambridge University)			
T. E. Hughes *1893*	unknown	unknown	unknown
Hugh Murray Ingledew *1891*	Cardiff	26.10.1865	1. 2.1937
Norman Ernest Jacob *1920–1922*	Neath	9. 7.1901	12. 3.1970
David Harry James *1948*	Briton Ferry	3. 3.1921	
Edward Hugh James *1920–1922*	Briton Ferry	14. 4.1896	15. 3.1975
Evan Llewellyn James *1946–1947*	Barry	10. 5.1918	
Stephen Peter James *1985–*	Lydney	7. 9.1967	

Harold Harvey Jarrett *1938* (Warwickshire)	Johannesburg	23. 9.1907	17. 3.1983
Keith Stanley Jarrett *1967*	Newport	18. 5.1948	
Javed Miandad *1980–1986* (Sussex, Pakistan)	Karachi	12. 6.1957	
Huw Jenkins *1970*	Swansea	24.10.1944	
Lewis Jenkins *1889*	unknown	unknown	unknown
Vivian Gordon James Jenkins *1931–1937* (Oxford University)	Port Talbot	2.11.1911	
Wyndham Leslie Trevor Jenkins *1921*	Newport	26. 8.1898	1971
Jack Johns *1920–1922*	Briton Ferry	15.10.1885	10. 1.1956
Thomas S. Johns *1920*	Briton Ferry		
Charles R. H. Johnson *1896–1908*	unknown	unknown	unknown
Alan Jones *1957–1983* (Western Australia, Northern Transvaal, Natal, Combined Services, MCC, England)	Velindre	4.11.1938	
Allan Arthur Jones *1980–1981* (Sussex, Somerset, Northern Transvaal, Middlesex, Orange Free State)	Horley, Surrey	9.12.1947	
Alan Lewis Jones *1973–1986*	Alltwen	1. 6.1957	
David Alfred Jones *1938*	Aberkenfig	9. 3.1920	
Daniel E. Jones *1889–1890*	unknown	unknown	unknown
Emrys Closs Jones *1934–1946*	Briton Ferry	14.12.1911	
Edward Cyril Jones *1926*	Cardiff	11. 3.1896	23.12.1978
Ernest William Jones *1890–1912* (South Wales)	Swansea	12.1870	17. 9.1941
Eifion Wyn Jones *1961–1983*	Velindre	25. 6.1942	
Frederick N. Jones *1890–1893*	unknown	unknown	unknown
Hugh Jones *1920* (Gloucestershire)	Lydney	1889	10.11.1918
Harry Ogwyn Jones *1946*	Llangennech	6.10.1922	
Ivor Jeffrey Jones *1960–1968* (England)	Dafen	10.12.1941	
James M. Jones *1928–1929* (Somerset, Wales)	unknown	unknown	unknown
John Walter Jones *1910–1914*	unknown	unknown	unknown
Rev Owen Jones *1891–1897*	unknown	1862	1924
R. G. Jones *1891–1893*	unknown	unknown	unknown
Thomas Charles Jones *1925–1928*	Pontypool	1. 4.1901	19. 7.1935
Watkin Edward Jones *1946–1947*	Gwauncaegurwen	6. 7.1917	
Wilfred Edward Jones *1929–1933*	Pontardawe	2. 2.1912	
William Edward Jones *1937–1958*	Carmarthen	31.10.1916	
William Maxwell Jones *1933–1938*	Alltwen	11. 2.1911	12.1941
Arthur Frederick Joseph *1946*	Neath	13. 3.1919	
Peter Francis Judge *1939–1947* (Middlesex, Buckinghamshire)	Cricklewood	23. 5.1916	
Rev Cyril Edwin Kindersley *1891*	Dorchester	13. 9.1865	12. 1.1938
Collis Llewellyn King *1977* (Barbados, Worcestershire, Natal, West Indies)	Fairview, Barbados	11. 6.1951	
Graham Charles Kingston *1967–1971*	Newport	1.11.1950	
William Lambert *1897–1898* (Middlesex, Hertfordshire, Northumberland)	Hatfield	19. 4.1843	4. 3.1927

285

E. Landers *1890*	unknown	unknown	unknown
George Lavis *1928–1949*	Sebastopol	17. 8.1908	29. 7.1956
Peter John Lawlor *1981*	Gowerton	8. 5.1960	
Harold Bertie Letcher *1890–1908*	unknown	1871	15. 6.1942
Anthony Robert Lewis *1955–1974*	Swansea	6. 7.1938	
(Cambridge University, England)			
Brian Lewis *1965–1968*	Maesteg	18. 7.1945	
David Wyndham Lewis *1960–1969*	Cardiff	18.12.1940	
(Transvaal, MCC)			
Euros John Lewis *1961–1966*	Llanelli	31. 1.1942	
(Sussex)			
Harry T. Lewis *1903*	unknown	unknown	unknown
Kenneth Humphrey Lewis *1950–1956*	Penygladdfa	10.11.1928	
Robert Ajax Lewis *1890–1892*	Pontypridd	1868	1913
S. A. Lewis *1906*	unknown	unknown	unknown
William Edgar Lewis *1889–1890*	Bridgend	26. 9.1862	26.12.1930
James Lindley *1889–1890*	Nottingham	18. 7.1844	15.10.1911
Anthony John Patrick Ling *1934–1936*	Skewen	10. 8.1910	12. 1.1987
(Somerset, Wiltshire)			
James Edward Fryer Linton *1932*	Llandaff	7. 5.1909	
Michael John Llewellyn *1970–1982*	Clydach	27.11.1953	
(Wiltshire)			
Sir John Talbot Dillwyn Llewelyn *1896*	Penllergaer	26. 5.1836	6. 7.1927
William Dillwyn Llewelyn *1889–1893*	Ynysygerwn	1. 4.1868	24. 8.1893
(Oxford University, MCC)			
Barry John Lloyd *1972–2983*	Neath	6. 9.1953	
John P. Long *1891–1893*	unknown	unknown	unknown
Richard Lowe *1896–1901*	Kirkby-in-	18. 6.1869	3. 7.1946
(Nottinghamshire, Sussex)	Ashfield		
Samuel Lowe *1895–1902*	Kirkby-in-	1867	3.1947
(Nottinghamshire)	Ashfield		
Kevin James Lyons *1967–1977*	Cardiff	18.12.1946	
James Edward McConnon *1950–1961*	Burnopfield,	21. 6.1922	
(England, Cheshire)	Durham		
Leslie Leopold McFarlane *1985*	Portland,	19. 8.1952	
(Northamptonshire, Lancashire, Bedfordshire)	Jamaica		
Andrew James Mack *1978–1980*	Aylsham,	14. 1.1956	
(Surrey)	Norfolk		
John Frederick Mackay *1895*	unknown	unknown	unknown
John Charles Pengelly Madden-Gaskell *1922*	Pontypool	1. 3.1896	4. 2.1975
Majid Khan *1968–1976*	Ludhiana, India	28. 9.1946	
(Cambridge University, Pakistan)			
Steven John Malone *1985*	Chelmsford	19.10.1953	
(Essex, Hampshire, Durham, Minor Counties, Wiltshire)			
A. H. Mann *1896*	unknown	unknown	unknown
Kenneth Ramsden Marley *1894*	Darlington	1865	1915
William Edward Marsh *1947*	Newbridge	10. 9.1917	6. 2.1978
E. G. Martin *1913–1921*	unknown	unknown	unknown
Orlando Bridgman Martyn *1891*	Broughton,	1855	10.12.1943
(MCC)	Middlesex		
Frederick William Mathias *1922–1930*	Abercynon	7. 8.1898	19. 4.1955
(Wales)			

Austin David George Matthews *1937–1949* (Northamptonshire, England)	Penarth	3. 5.1904	29. 7.1977
James Maxwell *1909–1914* (Somerset, South Wales)	Taunton	13. 1.1884	27.12.1967
Matthew Peter Maynard *1985–* (MCC, England)	Oldham	21. 3.1966	
Frank Claxton Meggitt *1923*	Barry	17. 2.1901	9.10.1945
William Mendelson *1896*	unknown	unknown	unknown

John ('Jack') Mercer *1922–1929*
  (Sussex, Wales, Northamptonshire)
	Southwick,
	  Sussex
		22. 4.1895	31. 8.1987

Colin Peter Metson *1987–*
  (Middlesex)
	Goff's Oak,
	  Herts
		2. 7.1963	

Hamish David Sneddon Miller *1963–1966* (Western Province, Orange Free State)	Blackpool	20. 4.1943	

Parvez Jamil Mir *1979*
  (Derbyshire, Norfolk, Pakistan)
	Sutrapur,
	  Pakistan
		24. 9.1953	

Charles A. Mizen *1891*	unknown	unknown	unknown
Steven Monkhouse *1987–1988* (Warwickshire)	Bury	24.11.1962	
Stanley William Montgomery *1949–1953*	West Ham	7. 7.1920	
Howell Gwyn Moore-Gwyn *1903–1912*	Neath	7. 7.1886	31. 7.1956
Joseph Gwyn Moore-Gwyn *1906*	unknown	unknown	unknown
Aubrey Neil Morgan *1928–1929* (Wales)	Llandaff	30. 1.1904	14. 9.1985
Dr Edward Morgan *1903–1913*	Abernant	22. 5.1880	1. 9.1949
Edward Noel Morgan *1934*	Garnant, Carms	22.12.1905	27. 8.1975
Frederick W. Morgan *1896*	unknown	unknown	unknown
Herbert E. Morgan *1889–1905*	Penarth	1870	1933
Howard William Morgan *1958*	Maesteg	29. 6.1931	
John Trevail Morgan *1925–1934* (Cambridge University, Wales)	Llandaff	7. 5.1907	18.12.1976
Thomas R. Morgan *1913–1925*	unknown	1892	unknown
William Morgan *1889–1901*	unknown	1862	22.10.1914

William Guy Morgan (later Stewart-Morgan)
  1927–1938
  (Cambridge University, Wales)
	Garnant, Carms	26.12.1907	29. 7.1975

William Percival Morgan *1925*	Abercrave	1. 1.1905	3. 3.1983
Alec W. Morris *1889–1897*	unknown	unknown	unknown
F. H. Morris *1893–1896*	unknown	unknown	unknown
Hugh Morris *1981–*	Cardiff	5.10.1963	
Ian Morris *1966–1968*	Maesteg	27. 6.1946	
Vernon Leslie Morris *1921–1929*	Briton Ferry	13. 6.1894	11. 1.1973
William Percy Morris *1906–1925* (South Wales)	Swansea	19. 6.1881	30. 7.1975

Ezra Alphonsa Moseley *1980–1986*
  (Barbados, Eastern Province)
	Waldrons
	  Village,
	  Barbados
		5. 1.1958	

Ernest Moss *1923*	unknown	unknown	unknown
Dr William A. Moynihan *1898*	unknown	unknown	unknown
David Mullens *1896*	unknown	unknown	unknown
A. Mullins *1890*	unknown	unknown	unknown
Bernard Leonard Muncer *1947–1954* (Middlesex)	Hampstead	23.10.1913	18. 1.1982

287

Name	Place	Born	Died
J. F. Murray *1911*	unknown	unknown	unknown
Albert ('Jack') Nash *1902–1922*	Blean, Kent	18. 9.1873	6.12.1956
Malcolm Andrew Nash *1966–1983*	Abergavenny	9. 5.1945	
Lewis Dillwyn Nicholl *1891–1895*	Merthyr Mawr	25. 9.1864	5. 1.1956
Patrick John Easthope Needham *1975*	Cardiff	6.12.1951	
Philip David North *1985–*	Newport	16. 5.1965	
Colonel Arthur O'Bree *1920–1923*	Poona, India	31. 5.1886	27.12.1943
Guy Nolan O'Daly *1938*	Bramley, Hants	4. 9.1908	
Rodney Craig Ontong *1975–* (Border, Transvaal, N. Transvaal)	Johannesburg	9. 9.1955	
Arthur James Osborne *1901–1906*	unknown	unknown	unknown
Richard John Parkhouse *1939*	Clydach	1910	
William Gilbert Anthony Parkhouse *1948–1964* (England)	Swansea	12.10.1925	
Duncan Brian Pauline *1986* (Surrey, Scotland)	Aberdeen	15.12.1960	
Dr Cecil Joseph Herbert Pearson *1922* (Devon)	Poplar, London	22. 1.1888	14. 9.1971
Albert Edward Peatfield *1903* (England XI)	Retford	1874	12.12.1953
W. Penfold *1908*	unknown	unknown	unknown
Arthur Lionel Bertie Perkins *1925–1933*	Swansea	19.10.1905	
Neil James Perry *1979–1981*	Sutton, Surrey	27. 5.1958	
Martin Phillips *1897*	unknown	unknown	unknown
Francis Brewster Pinch *1920–1926* (Wales)	Bodmin	24. 2.1891	8.10.1961
Leonard Pitchford *1935* (Monmouthshire)	Wing, Bucks	4.12.1900	
James Edward Pleass *1947–1956*	Cardiff	21. 5.1923	
W. Poole *1903*	unknown	unknown	unknown
Arthur Porter *1936–1949*	Clayton-le-Moor, Lancs	25. 3.1914	
Tyrone Lyndon Powell *1976* (Norfolk, New Zealand U-23 XI)	Bargoed	17. 6.1953	
Trevor Preece *1902–1923*	Bridgend	1882	21. 9.1965
Preedy *1907–1909* (Devon)	unknown	unknown	unknown
James Stuart Pressdee *1949–1965* (N.E. Transvaal)	Mumbles	19. 6.1933	
Mark Richard Price *1984–1985*	Liverpool	20. 4.1960	
Capt. Hubert Cecil Collins Prichard *1899* (Gloucestershire)	Clifton, Bristol	6. 2.1865	12.11.1942
A. J. Pritchard *1920*	unknown	unknown	unknown
F. H. Pruen *1897*	unknown	unknown	unknown
William Wade Fitzherbert Pullen *1895* (Gloucestershire, Somerset)	Itchington, Glos.	24. 6.1866	9. 8.1937
Gilbert Leach Rattenbury *1905–1912* (Gloucestershire)	Cardiff	28. 2.1878	14. 8.1958
David Jordan Reason *1920–1922*	Neath	1897	17. 2.1955
Dr Thomas Francis Reason *1914–1923*	Neath	1890	15. 2.1935
George H. Reed *1934–1938*	unknown	1901	unknown
Alan Rees *1955–1968*	Port Talbot	17. 2.1938	

Edward Lennox Rees *1893–1896*	Southampton	1868	13.10.1911
Rev Richard Morgan Rees *1896–1904*	Pontypridd	22. 4.1875	1932
Stanley H. Rees *1901–1914*	unknown	unknown	unknown
Dr Edgar W. Reid *1890–1894*	Swansea	26. 6.1865	19. 9.1924
Graham Edward Arthur Reynolds *1970–1971*	Newport	23. 9.1937	
Hubert Ralph John Rhys *1929–1930* (Wales)	Aberdare	31. 8.1897	18. 3.1970
Gwyn Richards *1971–1979*	Maesteg	29.11.1951	
J. Richards *1920*	unknown	unknown	unknown
John Dansy Hurry Riches *1947*	Cardiff	30.12.1920	
Norman Vaughan Hurry Riches *1901–1934* (Wales)	Cardiff	9. 6.1883	6.11.1975
Thomas John Rippon *1947–1948*	Swansea	6. 7.1918	
George Lionel Robathan *1911* (Gloucestershire, Monmouthshire)	Brighton	1878	3. 8.1951
John Frederick Roberts *1934–1936*	Pontardawe	24. 2.1913	
Martin Leonard Roberts *1985–* (Cornwall)	Mullion, Cornwall	12. 4.1966	
Maurice Robinson *1946–1950* (Warwickshire)	Lisburn, Co. Antrim	16. 7.1921	
Theodore Robinson *1889–1891* (Somerset)	Beaminster, Dorset	16. 2.1866	4.10.1959
Paul Gerrard Peter Roebuck *1988–* (Cambridge University, Gloucestershire)	Bath	13.10.1963	
Basil Leonard Rogers *1923* (Bedfordshire, Oxfordshire)	Bedford	20. 6.1896	1975
E. J. Rooney *1890*	unknown	unknown	unknown
R. Rooney *1899–1901*	unknown	unknown	unknown
Samuel Rooney *1893–1894*	unknown	unknown	unknown
Charles James Castell *1982–1984* (Kent)	Hong Kong	27.11.1951	
Corporal R. E. Rowntree *1899*	unknown	unknown	unknown
William Russell *1897–1906*	Norfolk	1867	8. 3.1908
Francis Peter Ryan *1922–1931* (Hampshire, Wales)	New Jersey	14.11.1888	5. 1.1954
Astley William Samuel *1889–1896*	Llandeilo	1860	unknown
Glyndwr Ninian Thomas Watkin Samuel *1936*	Swansea	26.10.1917	4.1985
Stuart A. Sant *1893*	unknown	unknown	unknown
Major Edmunds Saulez *1893*	unknown	1865	
Thomas D. Schofield *1893–1896*	Bridgend	1865	2. 1.1928
Scott *1895*	unknown	unknown	unknown
Michael Walter William Selvey *1983–1984* (Surrey, Cambridge University, Middlesex, Orange Free State, England)	Chiswick	25. 4.1948	
Hon. R. G. Seymour *1905*	unknown	unknown	unknown
J. E. Sharples *1922*	unknown	unknown	unknown
Ravishankar Jayadritha Shastri *1987–* (India)	Bombay	27. 5.1962	
George Bernard Shaw *1951–1955*	Treharris	24.10.1931	8.1984
Alfred James Shea *1928*	Briton Ferry	7.11.1898	5.1969
William Dennis Shea *1947–1948*	Briton Ferry	7. 2.1924	22. 9.1982
Donald John Shepherd *1950–1972*	Port Eynon	12. 8.1927	

E. Shepherd *1890*	unknown	unknown	unknown
Lord Samuel Charles Silkin *1938*	Neath	6. 3.1918	17. 8.1988
(Cambridge University)			
Arthur John Silverlock *1900*	South Hackney	12.1867	19. 3.1904
(South Wales, Monmouthshire)			
William Douglas Slade *1961–1967*	Briton Ferry	27. 9.1941	
Cyril Cecil Smart *1927–1946*	Lacock, Wilts	23. 7.1898	21. 5.1975
(Warwickshire)			
Christopher Lyall Smith *1979*	Durban,	15.10.1958	
(Hampshire, England)	S. Africa		
Douglas James Smith *1905–1907*	Batley	29. 5.1873	16. 8.1949
(Somerset, Worcestershire)			
Ian Smith *1985–*	Chopwell	11. 3.1967	
A. S. Snell *1920*	unknown	unknown	unknown
John William Solanky *1972–1976*	Dar-es-Salaam,	30. 6.1942	
(East Africa, Devon)	Tanzania		
H. G. Soloman *1901*	unknown	unknown	unknown
Charles Richard Spencer *1925*	Llandough	21. 6.1903	29. 9.1941
(Oxford University)			
Helm Spencer *1923–1925*	Padiman, Lancs	31.12.1891	1974
(Lancashire, Wales)			
Cecil Willmington Spiller *1922*	Cardiff	19. 8.1900	1974
William Spiller *1921–1923*	St Fagans	8. 7.1866	9. 6.1970
Stapleton *1909*	unknown	unknown	unknown
John Frederick Steele *1984–1986*	Broom Edge	23. 7.1946	
(Staffordshire, Leicestershire, Natal)			
Theophile Lecompte Stewart *1923*	Brisbane	9. 5.1891	14.12.1952
James Stone *1922–1923*	Southampton	29.11.1876	15.11.1942
George Storer *1891*	unknown	unknown	unknown
J. H. Storrie *1920*	unknown	unknown	unknown
Dennis Sullivan *1922–1928*	Mitcham	28. 1.1883	28.12.1968
(Surrey, Wales)			
George W. Swain *1893–1894*	unknown	unknown	unknown
Peter Douglas Swart *1978–1979*	Bulawayo,	27. 4.1946	
(Rhodesia, W. Province, Boland)	Rhodesia		
Edward Rhys Sweet-Escott *1904–1921*	Brompton	27. 7.1879	1. 7.1956
	Ralph,		
	Somerset		
Henry Herbert Sweet-Escott *1909*	Bridgwater	13.10.1885	27.12.1954
Ralph Bond Sweet-Escott *1891–1902*	Penkridge	11. 1.1869	10.11.1907
William Sidney Rice Sweet-Escott *1891–1899*	Bedford	10.10.1867	29.10.1926
Henry George Symonds *1908–1925*	Cardiff	24. 6.1889	1. 1.1945
(South Wales, Wales)			
John Robert Tait *1913–1926*	Scotland	20.11.1886	13. 4.1945
(Wales)			
Cyril Tamplin *1947*	Cardiff	27. 5.1921	
Herbert William Tayler *1920–1927*	Aldsworth,	6.12.1887	17. 4.1984
(Gloucestershire)	Glos.		
Henry Thomas Taylor *1932–1934*	Cardiff	7. 7.1911	20. 7.1970
Alec Guy Thackeray *1901–1906*	Cardiff	1882	26. 7.1909
Daniel Richard Thissen *1889–1900*	Swansea	1857	12.11.1928
Albert Edward Thomas *1913*	Ruthin	7. 6.1893	21. 3.1965
(Northamptonshire, South Wales)			

Arthur Emlyn Thomas *1925*	Briton Ferry	7. 5.1895	11. 2.1953
Dillwyn Thomas *1939*	Neath	13. 2.1905	
David John Thomas *1932*	Swansea	25.11.1911	
Gwyn Thomas *1922*	Pontardawe	1892	10. 1.1984
Harold T. Thomas *1894–1908*	unknown	unknown	unknown
John Gregory Thomas *1979–*	Trebanos	12. 8.1960	
(Border, E. Province, England, MCC)			
Dr L. Gwyn Thomas *1910–1920*	unknown	unknown	unknown
N. D. Thomas *1920*	unknown	unknown	unknown
Richard James Thomas *1974*	Griffithstown	18. 6.1944	
Sergeant Thomas *1908*	unknown	unknown	unknown
W. M. Thomas *1890*	unknown	unknown	unknown
Paul Adrian Todd *1987–*	Morton, Notts	12. 3.1953	
(Nottinghamshire, Lincolnshire, Minor Counties)			
Harry Tomlinson *1920–1923*	Barwell, Leics	1886	29.11.1944
William Mervyn Stanley Trick *1946–1950*	Briton Ferry	31.10.1916	
Bertrand Turnbull *1911–1914*	Cardiff	1887	17.11.1943
(Gloucestershire)			
Maurice Joseph Lawson Turnbull *1924–1939*	Cardiff	16. 3.1906	5. 8.1944
(Cambridge University and England)			
Cecil Thomas Tyson *1926*	Brompton, Yorks	24. 1.1889	3. 4.1940
(Yorkshire)			
Cornelius Johannes Petrus Gerhardus Van Zyl *1987–1988*	Bloemfontein	1.10.1961	
(Orange Free State)			
Hugh Wyndham Vaughan-Thomas *1933*	Swansea	13. 5.1910	20.10.1986
Capt Charles Lewis Veal *1910*	Bridgend	29. 8.1876	1. 6.1929
(MCC)			
Arthur Waite *1904*	unknown	unknown	unknown
Peter Michael Walker *1956–1972*	Clifton, Bristol	17. 2.1936	
(Transvaal, W. Province, England)			
Cyril Frederick Walters *1923–1928*	Bedlinog	28. 8.1905	
(Worcestershire, England)			
Donald J. Ward *1954–1962*	Trealaw	30. 8.1934	
Claude Charles Warner *1923*	Cardiff	31. 3.1882	29.12.1965
Steven Llewellyn Watkin *1986–*	Maesteg	15. 9.1964	
Albert John ('Allan') Watkins *1939–1962*	Usk	21. 4.1922	
(England)			
William Martin Watkins *1950*	Swansea	18. 1.1923	
W. Hastings Watson *1889–1893*	unknown	unknown	unknown
Gwilym John Hubert Went *1934*	Barry	25. 3.1914	
Oswald Stephen ('Ossie') Wheatley *1961–1970*	Low Fell, Gateshead	28. 5.1935	
(Cambridge University, Warwickshire)			
David William ('Butch') White *1972*	Sutton Coldfield	14.12.1935	
(Hampshire, England)			
M. E. White *1909*	unknown	unknown	unknown
William Kenneth Whitehill *1960*	Newport	13. 6.1934	
Eric Ioan Emlyn Whitman *1923*	Barry	31. 7.1909	
(Cambridgeshire)			
Thomas Aubrey Leyshon Whittington *1901–1923*	Neath	29. 7.1881	19. 7.1944
(MCC, West of England)			

Alan Haydn Wilkins *1976–1983* (Gloucestershire, Transvaal)	Cardiff	22. 8.1953	
William Wilkinson *1889* (Nottinghamshire)	Kimberley, Notts	5. 7.1859	6.10.1940
Dyson Bransby Williams *1901–1921* (changed name to Dyson Brock)	Killay	1877	18. 4.1922
David Lawrence Williams *1969–1976*	Tonna	20.11.1946	
F. I. Williams *1920*	unknown	unknown	unknown
Iestyn Williams *1890–1893*	unknown	1865	16. 6.1922
Ieuan Williams *1931*	Brynamman	17. 3.1909	3. 3.1964
Lewis Erskine Wyndham Williams *1928–1930*	Bonvilstan	28.11.1900	24. 4.1974
William Henry Williams *1889–1893*	Pontlottyn	1873	9. 1.1936
Hon Archer Windsor-Clive *1908–1909* (Cambridge University)	Reddich	6.11.1890	25. 8.1914
Arthur Wolfe *1895*	unknown	unknown	unknown
Wilfred Wooller *1938–1962* (Cambridge University, Denbighshire)	Rhos-on-Sea	20.11.1912	
Francis Frederick Worsley *1922–1923*	Kensington	2. 6.1902	15. 9.1949
Thomas Hywel Bruce Yorath *1891–1893*	Cardiff	9. 9.1868	unknown
William L. Yorath *1889–1890*	unknown	unknown	unknown
George Avery Young *1892–1893*	Cardiff	1863	23. 1.1900
Younis Ahmed *1984–1986* (Surrey, Pakistan, South Australia, Worcestershire)	Jullunder, India	20.10.1947	

BROTHERS

The following brothers have played for Glamorgan

J. and W. J. Bancroft
J. H. and W. H. Brain
J. H. P. and M. B. Brain
D. E. and G. Davies
D. R. and H. G. Davies
F. J. and R. C. Davis
P. M. T. and V. T. Hill
T. S. and J. Johns

D. E. and F. N. Jones
A. and E. W. Jones
R. and S. Lowe
H. G. and J. G. Moore-Gwyn
A. N. and J. T. Morgan
E. N. and W. G. Morgan
H. H., R. B. and W. S. R. Sweet-Escott

FATHERS AND SONS

The following fathers and sons have played for Glamorgan

W. Bancroft (junior) and W. J. Bancroft (in the match v Colts XXJ at Swansea, 1892)
W. H. and J. H. P. Brain
W. H. and M. B. Brain
H. and A. B. Creber
E. U. and A. C. R. David

V. T. and M. L. Hill
H. H. and K. S. Jarrett
N. V. H. and J. D. H. Riches
A. J. and W. D. Shea

OTHER PLAYERS

The following also played in friendlies and trial games during the 1890s and 1900s

NAME AND EXTENT OF CAREER (Other counties and clubs in brackets)	BIRTHPLACE	DATE OF BIRTH	DATE OF DEATH
J. G. Ardaseer *1907*	unknown	unknown	unknown
William Bancroft (junior) *1892*	unknown	unknown	unknown
Norman Witchell Biggs *1893*	Cardiff	3.11.1870	27. 2.1908
A. Bircham *1893*	unknown	unknown	unknown
F. Casbourne *1893*	unknown	unknown	unknown
William Cope *1893* (later Lord Cope of St Mellons)	Roath	18. 8.1870	15. 7.1946
Sir John Wesley Courtis *1893*	Williamstown, Australia	19. 2.1859	19.12.1939
Rhys Thomas Gabe *1907*	Llangennech	22. 6.1880	15. 9.1967
H. Lewin *1893*	unknown	unknown	unknown
Samuel Moss *1892* (Staffordshire)	unknown	1867	7. 8.1923
Sir George Walter Roffey *1893*	Brentford	21. 5.1870	13. 3.1940
Arthur Waldron *1891*	unknown	unknown	unknown
Rev Arthur Hawtrey Watson *1891* (Lincolnshire, Suffolk)	Derbyshire	18. 6.1865	7. 9.1952
Llewellyn J. Williams *1893*	unknown	unknown	unknown

LIMITED-OVER PLAYERS

The following have played for Glamorgan only in limited-overs games and have not appeared in first-class cricket.

NAME AND EXTENT OF CAREER	BIRTHPLACE	DATE OF BIRTH	DATE OF DEATH
Kenneth McKoy Valentine Francis *1973*	St Kitts, West Indies	14. 3.1950	
Kim Thomas Norkett *1974*	Malta	24.12.1955	

CAPPED PLAYERS AND CLUB COLOURS

The definition of a capped player in the pre first-class era is somewhat ambiguous. Rule 1 of the old Club rules states that 'any member of the club after playing in four county matches in one season shall be entitled to wear the county cap and blazer'. Therefore there is an important difference with the modern practice of awarding a cap for consistent, or outstanding, performances. Consequently, most of the regular players were deemed as 'capped' and wore the club cap, which in those days was green, with a red dragon motif. Several changes occurred in the 1930s following Turnbull and Clay becoming the Club's leading administrators. The colours were changed to blue and gold, and the daffodil emblem was adopted (it had been introduced as the Welsh national emblem by David Lloyd George during the First World War). In 1934 the Club rules on capped players were changed to 'only those members and players awarded them by the selection committee shall be entitled to wear the County cap and blazer'. Even so, the awarding of a cap was not recorded in the minutes or record books until after the Second World War.

1946	W. E. Jones, A. Porter, M. Robinson
1947	B. L. Muncer, A. J. Watkins, P. B. Clift
1948	J. Eaglestone, N. G. Hever, W. G. A. Parkhouse
1951	J. E. McConnon
1952	J. E. Pleass, D. J. Shepherd
1954	B. Hedges
1955	J. S. Pressdee
1956	L. N. Devereux
1958	P. M. Walker
1959	D. G. L. Evans
1960	J. B. Evans, A. R. Lewis
1961	D. Ward, O. S. Wheatley
1962	A. Jones
1963	A. Rees
1965	I. J. Jones, E. Lewis
1967	A. E. Cordle, E. W. Jones
1968	M. J. Khan
1969	B. A. Davis, R. C. Davis, M. A. Nash
1971	R. C. Fredericks, D. L. Williams
1973	J. W. Solanky
1974	L. W. Hill
1976	G. Richards
1977	J. A. Hopkins, M. J. Llewellyn
1979	R. C. Ontong, P. D. Swart, R. N. S. Hobbs
1980	Javed Miandad, N. G. Featherstone
1981	E. A. Moseley
1982	B. J. Lloyd, D. A. Francis
1983	M. W. W. Selvey, C. J. C. Rowe, A. L. Jones
1984	J. F. Steele
1985	Younis Ahmed, T. Davies, G. C. Holmes
1986	H. Morris, J. G. Thomas
1987	S. R. Barwick, A. R. Butcher, M. P. Maynard, C. P. Metson
1988	R. J. Shastri, J. Derrick

BENEFITS AND TESTIMONIALS

The following players have been awarded benefits and/or testimonials.

		£			£
1930	W. E. Bates	602	1961	J. E. McConnon	
1935	D. Davies	659	1963	B. Hedges	4,402
1936	J. Mercer	729	1964	J. S. Pressdee	
1938	E. Davies	689	1966	P. M. Walker	4,500
1939	A. H. Dyson	529	1968	D. J. Shepherd	5,000
1946	C. Smart	556	1969	D. G. L. Evans	3,500
1947	D. E. Davies	1,800	1972	A. Jones	10,000
1948	A. H. Dyson	1,600	1973	A. R. Lewis	
1950	G. Lavis	2,248	1975	E. W. Jones	17,000
1952	H. G. Davies	4,500	1977	A. E. Cordle	8,000
1953	W. E. Jones	4,460	1978	M. A. Nash	18,000

		£			£
1954	B. L. Muncer	3,556	1980	A. Jones	35,000
1955	A. J. Watkins	4,750	1982	P. B. Clift	
1957	W. G. A. Parkhouse	3,750	1984	E. W. Jones	
1959	P. B. Clift	3,000	1986	J. A. Hopkins	35,230
1960	D. J. Shepherd	3,200	1989	R. C. Ontong	

CAPTAINS OF GLAMORGAN

1889	E. U. David, W. H. Gwynn, W. Morgan
1890	W. H. Williams, W. H. Gwynn, A. W. Morris, W. D. Llewelyn
1891	J. H. Brain, W. D. Llewelyn
1892–1907	J. H. Brain
1908	J. H. Brain, T. A. L. Whittington, A. Gibson
1909–1912	T. A. L. Whittington
1913–1914	N. V. H. Riches
1919–1920	T. A. L. Whittington
1921	N. V. H. Riches
1922–1923	T. A. L. Whittington
1924–1927	J. C. Clay
1928	T. Arnott
1929	N. V. H. Riches, J. C. Clay
1930–1939	M. J. L. Turnbull
1946	J. C. Clay
1947–1960	W. Wooller
1961–1966	O. S. Wheatley
1967–1972	A. R. Lewis
1973	Majid Khan
1974	Majid Khan, A. Jones
1975	Majid Khan
1976	Majid Khan, A. Jones
1977–1978	A. Jones
1979	R. N. S. Hobbs
1980–1981	M. A. Nash
1982	Javed Miandad, B. J. Lloyd
1983	M. W. W. Selvey
1984	M. W. W. Selvey, R. C. Ontong
1985	R. C. Ontong
1986	R. C. Ontong, H. Morris
1987	H. Morris

TEST PLAYERS

The following Glamorgan cricketers have played in Test cricket whilst with the Club.

J. C. Clay	England (1935, 1 cap)
W. W. Davis	W. Indies (1982/3–)
R. C. Fredericks	W. Indies (1968/9–1976/7, 59 caps)
Javed Miandad	Pakistan (1976/7–)
I. J. Jones	England (1963/4–1967/8, 15 caps)
C. L. King	W. Indies (1976–1980/1, 9 caps)
A. R. Lewis	England (1972/3–1973, 9 caps)
M. P. Maynard	England (1988–)

J. E. McConnon	England (1954, 2 caps)
Majid Khan	Pakistan (1964/5–1982/3, 63 caps)
A. D. G. Matthews	England (1937, 1 cap)
W. G. A. Parkhouse	England (1950–1959, 7 caps)
R. J. Shastri	India (1980/1–)
J. G. Thomas	England (1986–)
M. J. L. Turnbull	England (1929/30–1936, 9 caps)
P. M. Walker	England (1960, 3 caps)
A. J. Watkins	England (1948–1952, 15 caps)

Alan Jones also played for England against The Rest of the World in 1970 in a match not now recognised as a Test match, whilst Ezra Moseley and Corrie Van Zyl have played in unofficial Tests in South Africa (South Africa *v.* West Indies).

The following Glamorgan cricketers played in Tests before joining, or after leaving the Club.

A. R. Butcher	England (1979, 1 cap)
T. W. Cartwright	England (1964/5, 5 caps)
B. A. Davis	W. Indies (1964/5, 4 caps)
R. N. S. Hobbs	England (1967–1971, 7 caps)
M. W. W. Selvey	England (1976–1976/7, 3 caps)
C. L. Smith	England (1983–)
C. F. Walters	England (1933–1934, 11 caps)
D. W. White	England (1961/2, 2 caps)
Younis Ahmed	Pakistan (1969/70–)

RUGBY PLAYERS

The following Glamorgan cricketers have also played rugby for Wales.

J. Bancroft	Wales 1908–1913 (18 caps), Swansea
W. J. Bancroft	Wales 1889–1900 (33 caps), Swansea
T. M. Barlow	Wales 1884 (1 cap), Cardiff
N. W. Biggs	Wales 1888–1894 (8 caps), Cardiff, Bath, Richmond, Barbarians
S. H. Biggs	Wales 1895–1900 (9 caps), Cardiff
R. W. Boon	Wales 1929–1932 (12 caps), Cardiff, London Welsh, Dunfermline, Barbarians
P. F. Bush	Wales 1905–1910 (8 caps), Cardiff, Penygraig, British Lions
W. Cope	Wales 1896 (1 cap), Cardiff, Cambridge University, Blackheath, Barbarians
D. W. Evans	Wales 1889–1891 (5 caps), Cardiff, Oxford University, British Lions, Barbarians
R. T. Gabe	Wales 1901–1908 (24 caps), Llanelli, Llangennech, Cardiff, British Lions
R. A. Gibbs	Wales 1906–1911 (16 caps), Cardiff, Penarth, Barbarians
W. H. Gwynn	Wales 1884–1885 (5 caps), Swansea (Secretary of WRU 1892–1896)
H. M. Ingledew	Wales 1890–1891 (3 caps), Cardiff, Barbarians
K. S. Jarrett	Wales 1967–1969 (10 caps), Abertillery, Newport and British Lions (to South Africa, 1968)
V. G. J. Jenkins	Wales 1932–1938 (14 caps), Oxford University, London Welsh, Bridgend, Kent, Cardiff, Barbarians and British Lions (to South Africa, 1938)
W. E. Jones	Wales (wartime international), Penarth, Gloucester, Neath

Dr E. Morgan	Wales 1902–1908 (16 caps), Cardiff, London Welsh, Newport, Guy's Hospital, British Lions
W. G. Morgan	Wales 1926–1929 (8 caps), Swansea, Cambridge University, Cardiff, Guy's Hospital and Barbarians
A. Rees	Wales 1962 (3 caps), Maesteg, Llanelli (rugby league for Leeds)
W. Spiller	Wales 1910–1913 (10 caps), Cardiff
R. B. Sweet-Escott	Wales 1891–1895 (3 caps), Cardiff, Blackheath, Penarth, Barbarians
M. J. L. Turnbull	Wales 1932 (2 caps), Cardiff, Cambridge University
W. H. Williams	Wales 1900–1901 (4 caps), Newport, London Welsh
W. Wooller	Wales 1932–1938 (18 caps), Cambridge University, Sale, Cardiff, Barbarians
G. A. Young	Wales 1886 (2 caps), Cardiff

The following Glamorgan cricketers have also played club rugby.

T. Arnott	Cardiff
M. K. Davies	Aberavon
R. G. Duckfield	Maesteg
R. D. L. Dudley-Jones	Cardiff
A. R. Gabe-Jones	Cardiff
P. W. Gatehouse	Caerphilly
E. R. K. Glover	Glamorgan Wanderers
W. E. Harris	Swansea Police Union
B. Hedges	Pontypridd and Swansea
G. Hughes	Cambridge University
S. P. James	Lydney
A. R. Lewis	Neath, Gloucester and Cambridge University
A. D. G. Matthews	Northampton, Penarth and East Midlands (Final Welsh Trial 1928)
E. N. Morgan	Cardiff
H. E. Morgan	Penarth
W. P. Morgan	Neath
H. Morris	Aberavon and Newport
K. T. Norkett	Newport and Ebbw Vale
W. G. A. Parkhouse	Swansea
E. W. Reid	Swansea and Guys Hospital
C. F. Walters	Swansea
A. H. Wilkins	Cardiff and Glamorgan Wanderers
W. L. Yorath	Cardiff

ASSOCIATION FOOTBALLERS

The following Glamorgan cricketers have also played League football.

W. E. Bates	Leeds United and Bolton Wanderers
E. F. Carless	Cardiff City and Plymouth Argyle
P. A. Cottey	Swansea City and Merthyr Town
G. J. Harris	Mansfield Town and Swansea Town
L. W. Hill	Newport County and Swansea Town
J. J. Hills	Cardiff City, Swansea Town and Fulham
J. E. McConnon	Aston Villa and Lovells Athletic
S. W. Montgomery	Cardiff City, Southend, Newport County and Hull City
J. S. Pressdee	Swansea Town (schoolboy international for Wales)
A. J. Watkins	Plymouth Argyle

STATISTICAL SECTION

UMPIRES

The following Glamorgan cricketers have become first-class umpires.

J. T. Bell	D. E. Davies (also Tests)	A. A. Jones
W. Bestwick	D. G. L. Evans (also Tests)	K. J. Lyons
D. Davies (also Tests)	J. J. Hills	J. Stone

BLUES

The following Glamorgan cricketers have gained cricket blues.

Oxford		Cambridge	
J. H. Brain	1884–1887	A. C. Burnett	1949
W. H. Brain	1891–1893	W. H. Griffiths	1946–1948
	(also a soccer blue)	R. J. Hadley	1971–1973
F. J. Davis	1963	S. P. Henderson	1982–1983
G. Evans	1939	G. Hughes	1965
L. D. Hildyard	1884–1886	A. R. Lewis	1960–1962
V. T. Hill	1892		(also a rugby blue)
V. G. J. Jenkins	1933	M. J. Khan	1970–1972
	(also a rugby blue)	J. T. Morgan	1928–1930
W. D. Llewelyn	1890–1891	M. W. W. Selvey	1971
		M. J. L. Turnbull	1926–1929
			(also a rugby blue)
		O. S. Wheatley	1957–1958
		Hon. A. Windsor-Clive	1910–1912
		W. Wooller	1935–1936
			(also a rugby blue)

TEST SELECTORS

The following Glamorgan players have acted as Test selectors for England.

M. J. L. Turnbull	1938–1939	W. Wooller	1955–1961
J. C. Clay	1947–1948	O. S. Wheatley	1973–1974

MISCELLANEOUS

T. L. Brierley	emigrated to Canada at the end of the 1948 season, and later toured England with the Canadian team in 1954
P. F. Bush	emigrated to France and acted as the French Consul in Nantes
H. L. Carr	became a leading journalist with *The News of the World*, and was a good golfer and billiards player
J. W. Courtis	was Lord Mayor of Cardiff in 1911
D. W. Evans	acted as legal adviser to King Edward VII and was knighted in 1925
R. C. Fredericks	is now a Minister of Sport in the Guyanan government
A. E. Freethy and T. D. Schofield	were well known rugby referees and officials of the WRU

L. J. Harris	founded the Primary Club and acted as its secretary for many years
V. T. Hill	was the President of Somerset CCC in 1930
H. M. Ingledew	was a founding member of the Barbarians RFC and played a leading role in the acquisition of the Arms Park from the Bute Estate during the 1920s
A. D. G. Matthews	represented Wales at table tennis and coached cricket at Cambridge University between 1934 and 1950
Serg. Thomas	was a policeman based in Neath, and was a leading member of the town's cricket club
L. E. W. ('Tip') Williams	was the founder of the South Wales Hunts CC
F. F. Worsley	worked for the BBC after his retirement and produced the ITMA programme ('It's That Man Again')
J. C. Clay	was a director of Chepstow Racecourse and has a steeplechase named after him which is run every year at the Gwent course
D. W. Hughes	was headmaster of Rydal School, Gwynedd, for many years after the Second World War

CAREER RECORDS OF GLAMORGAN
PLAYERS 1889–1988

Name	Inns	NO	Runs	HS	Avge	100s	O	M	Runs	Wkts	Avge	5wI	Best
Abel T. E.	55	1	821	107	15.20	1	76.5	14	258	8	32.25	—	3/42
Alexander H. G.	7	2	42	14	8.40	—							
Allin A. W.	16	8	108	32	13.50	—	333.3	96	1011	44	22.97	4	8/63
Anderson R. M. B.	1	0	0	0	—	—	18.0	4	60	0	—	—	—
Arkell T. M.	2	0	15	8	7.50	—							
Armstrong G. D.	42	11	426	64	13.74	—	655.3	122	2423	72	33.65	2	6/91
Arnott T.	321	25	4726	153	15.96	3	3697.3	642	11435	361	31.68	10	7/40
Arundale H.	4	0	25	9	6.25	—	—	—	—	0+1	—	—	1+
Bainton H.	2	1	89	72★	44.50	—	2.0	0	22	0	—	—	—
Bancroft J.	32	7	199	40	7.96	—							
Bancroft W. J.	358	20	8353	157	24.71	7	44.1	12	153	9+1	17.00	—	3/30
Barlow T. M.	18	0	233	75	12.94	—							
Barry I.	1	1	24	24★	—	—							
Barwick S. R.	107	42	562	30	8.65	—	2776.5	649	8146	241	33.80	8	8/42
Base S. J.	25	8	180	38	10.59	—	426.0	77	1434	49	29.26	2	5/67
Bastien, S.	6	2	57	36★	14.25	—	119.1	35	289	8	36.13	1	5/90
Bates W. E.	510	15	12802	200★	25.86	10	2217.4	213	8707	239	36.43	4	8/93
Batty A. M.	2	1	9	9★	—	—							
Baxter H. W.	4	1	72	56★	24.00	—							
Beasley H. O. C.	6	1	26	10	5.20	—							
Bell J. T.	281	18	7324	225	27.84	10	43.2	3	205	2	102.50	—	1/2
Bennett F.	3	1	21	14★	10.50	—							
Bestwick W.	5	3	6	3★	3.00	—	142.1	37	233	21	11.10	1	5/34
Bevan J. M.	1	0	3	3	3.00	—							
Biggs C. F.	2	0	14	9	7.00	—	7.0	3	14	0	—	—	—
Biggs S. H.	48	12	487	82	13.53	—	761.2	179	2026	116	17.47	7	8/48
Billings E. A.	21	2	269	62	14.16	—							
Binch F.	1	0	16	16	16.00	—	15.0	1	68	1	68.00	—	1/15
Blackmore D.	1	0	34	34	34.00	—							
Boon R. W.	19	2	229	33	13.47	—	10.0	0	40	0	—	—	—
Bowen E.	5	1	40	22	10.00	—	5.0	2	14	0	—	—	—
Bowen G. E.	4	0	41	17	10.25	—	8.0	0	17	0	—	—	—
Brain J. H.	223	18	5283	144	25.77	4	88.4	14	275	19+1	14.47	3	6/60
Brain J. H. P.	16	2	152	42	10.86	—							
Brain M. B.	2	0	9	9	4.50	—							
Brain W. H.	158	16	2263	113	15.94	2							
Brierley T. L.	292	25	4760	116★	17.82	3	5.0	0	33	0	—	—	—
Burnett A. C.	11	0	71	17	6.45	—							
Burton	6	2	17	13	4.25	—	62.0	15	131	8+1	16.38	2	5/63
Bush P. F.	5	0	7	5	1.40	—	3.0	0	16	1	16.00	—	1/16
Butcher A. R.	67	4	2291	166	36.37	4	75.0	11	250	8	31.25	—	3/35
Cadogan J. P.	4	1	108	46	36.00	—							
Cameron A. W.	25	3	288	39	13.09	—	117.2	7	429	21	20.43	1	6/35
Cann M. J.	10	3	118	28	16.86	—	38.5	6	173	5	34.60	—	2/20
Carless E. F.	3	—	35	25	11.66	—							
Carr H. L.	1	0	6	6	6.00	—							
Carrington	1	0	10	10	10.00	—							
Cartwright T. W.	11	2	76	22★	8.44	—	131.2	52	258	10	25.80	—	4/46

Chandless, J.	7	0	70	20	10.00	—	129.0	32	283	10	28.30	—	3/13
Clarke F.	41	15	98	31	3.76	—	648.0	143	1868	50	37.36	1	5/66
Clarke J. G.	58	6	785	95	15.10	—	55.3	8	197	12	16.41	1	5/11
Clay J. C.	536	88	6868	115★	15.33	2	9911.1	2326	25181	1292	19.49	105	9/54
Clift P. B.	306	21	6055	125★	21.24	7	216.2	38	675	11	61.36	—	3/6
Clough H.	1	0	15	15	15.00	—	30.0	8	22	1	22.00	—	1/22
Colley R. H.	1	0	0	0	—	—	16.0	9	30	0	—	—	—
Cooper E.	12	1	63	14	5.73	—	174.0	33	522	17	30.71	—	5/45
Cope J. J.	5	1	27	14★	6.75	—							
Cording G. E.	61	5	813	101	14.52	1							
Cordle A. E.	433	76	5239	81	14.67	—	7013.5	1615	19281	701	27.50	19	9/49
Cottey P. A.	38	5	788	92	23.88	—							
Creber A. B.	2	0	7	4	3.50	—							
Creber H.	300	108	1779	52	9.27	—	7245.0	1776	19570	1225+56	15.98	66	9/91
Crowther P. G.	14	0	185	99	13.21	—	7.0	1	22	1	22.00	—	1/22
Cullen J. S.	2	0	21	14	10.50	—							
Daniels S. A. B.	23	10	227	72	17.46	—	312.2	55	1162	28	41.50	—	3/33
Dauncey J. G.	4	0	54	34	13.50	—							
David A. C. R.	4	0	22	11	5.50	—	4.0	0	30	1	30.00	—	1/30
David E. U.	50	3	531	48	11.30	—	77.0	17	226	10	22.60	—	4/48
David R. F. A.	5	0	20	17	4.00	—							
Davies C. B.	1	0	1	1	1.000	—							
Davies D.	681	61	15008	216	24.20	16	3661.4	774	9404	271	34.70	4	6/50
Davies D. A.	64	16	600	55	12.50	—	185.5	15	760	14	54.28	—	3/63
Davies D. E. (1892)	1	0	6	6	6.00	—							
Davies D. E. (1924–)	1016	79	26102	287★	27.85	31	10263.4	2359	26030	885	29.41	32	6/24
Davies D. R.	1	0	7	7	7.00	—							
Davies G. (1932)	9	1	77	44	9.62	—	52.0	15	134	3	44.66	—	2/18
Davies G. (1947)	2	0	9	7	5.50	—							
Davies H. D.	70	26	247	28	5.61	—	1103.1	214	3659	115	31.81	4	6/85
Davies H. G.	596	95	6515	80	13.00	—	3.0	0	20	1	20.00	—	1/20
Davies J. A.	2	0	11	11	5.50	—							
Davies M. K.	2	1	14	12	14.00	—							
Davies M. N.	1	0	0	0	—	—							
Davies T.	121	36	1775	75	20.88	—							
Davies T. C.	6	4	9	5	4.50	—	211.1	41	625	18	34.72	—	3/22
Davies W. A.	3	0	0	0	—	—	11	6	19	1+6	19.00	—	3†
Davies W. D. E.	12	1	122	32	11.09	—	13.0	1	60	0	—	—	—
Davies W. G.	58	0	674	64	11.62	—	143.4	50	646	16	40.37	—	2/23
Davies W. H.	10	2	33	8★	4.12	—	58.3	16	130	3	43.33	—	2/35
Davis B. A.	103	8	2848	103	29.87	1	74.0	17	229	4	57.25	—	1/2
Davis F. J.	24	7	189	28★	11.11	—	233.3	82	674	18	37.44	1	5/72
Davis J. D. D.	1	0	27	27	27.00	—							
Davis R. C.	369	30	7363	134	21.71	5	2868.0	700	7793	241	32.33	6	6/62
Davis W. W.	51	21	471	50	15.70	—	1315.2	285	4211	142	29.65	6	7/70
Derrick J.	114	33	1759	78★	21.72	—	1495.0	326	4650	125	37.20	2	6/54
Devereux L. N.	187	25	3292	108★	20.32	1	725.4	224	1768	72	24.55	2	6/29
Dickinson H. J.	13	6	37	14★	5.28	—	102.0	16	335	6	55.83	—	3/91
Donelly C. W.	2	0	0	0	—	—	4.0	1	13	1	13.00	—	1/13
Donovan J.	21	3	235	98★	13.05	—	3.0	0	17	0	—	—	—
Donovan M.					did not bat or bowl in one game								
Downey J.					did not bat or bowl in one game								

301

Duckfield R. G.	301	39	6894	280*	26.31	9	53.0	1	255	0	—	—	—
Dudley-Jones R. D. L.	7	2	15	5	3.00	—	88.5	9	351	13	27.00	—	4/31
Duncan A. A.	3	1	16	15	8.00	—							
Dunford, W. B.	1	1	0	0*	—	—							
Dunn F. W.	2	0	1	1	0.50	—							
Dyson A. H.	696	37	17920	208	27.19	24	34.0	2	160	1	160.00	—	1/9
Eaglestone J. T.	80	7	1092	72	14.95	—							
Edrich B. R.	80	8	1246	74	17.30	—	8.0	3	12	0	—	—	—
Edwards A. M. E.	1	0	0	0	—	—	21.0	4	74	3	23.66	—	2/34
Edwards J. P.	2	0	5	4	2.50	—	50.0	11	142	5	28.40	—	2.35
Edwards W. A.	3	0	38	37	12.66	—							
Eldridge A. G.	32	8	190	32	7.91	—	558.4	192	1309	102+11	12.83	12	8/43
Elers, C. G. C.	11	4	259	151	37.00	1							
Ellis G. P.	139	10	2673	116	20.72	1	470.4	107	1418	24	59.08	—	2/20
Ellis H. A.	6	1	112	41	22.40	—							
Emery W.	4	0	5	5	1.25	—	34.0	6	111	2	55.50	—	1/41
Evans D. G. L.	364	91	2875	46*	10.53	—	4.0	0	12	0	—	—	—
Evans D. W.	1	0	2	2	2.00	—							
Evans G.	14	1	164	36	12.61	—	74.0	3	331	5	66.20	—	1/27
Evans H. P.	8	1	85	49	12.14	—							
Evans J. B.	129	19	1515	62*	13.77	—	2332.0	505	6670	246	27.11	10	8/42
Evans T.	2	1	0	0*	—	—	5.2	0	25	0	—	—	—
Evans W. H.	2	0	2	2	1.00	—							
Every T.	198	44	2518	116	18.35	1	8.0	0	49	0	—	—	—
Farr C.	1	0	2	2	2.00	—							
Featherstone N. G.	73	11	2120	113*	34.19	3	170	47	525	12	43.75	1	5/90
Fenwick L.	1	0	26	26	26.00	—	4.0	0	24	0	—	—	—
Fletcher E. V.	2	0	5	5	2.50	—							
Francis D. A.	237	36	4938	142*	24.57	3	5.0	0	31	0	—	—	—
Fredericks R. C.	80	8	2991	228*	41.54	7	207.1	45	667	20	33.35	—	3/37
Freethy A. E.	18	2	213	31	13.31	—	—						
Gabe-Jones A. R.	1	1	6	6*	—	—							
Gage H. F.	3	0	44	32	14.66	—	9.0	2	26	2	13.00	—	2/26
Gatehouse P. W.	23	8	85	20	5.66	—	475.4	84	1551	53	29.26	3	7/94
Geary F. W.	4	0	3	2	0.75	—	13.0	3	24	0	—	—	—
Gemmill W. N.	93	4	1208	77	13.57	—	25.0	4	104	0	—	—	—
Geoghegan J. P. A.	20	5	274	82	18.27	—	34.0	11	82	6	13.67	—	4.57
Gibbs R. A.	55	7	961	95	20.02	—							
Gibson A.	86	9	1158	66	15.04	—	6.0	0	31	0+2	—	—	2†
Gibson W. D.	1	1	7	7*	—	—							
Glover E. R. K.	73	23	406	62	8.12	—	1207.5	175	4284	118	36.30	3	5/79
Good D. C.	5	2	47	21	15.66	—	60.0	11	225	7	32.14	—	2/34
Green R. C.	1	1	3	3*	—	—	31.5	9	92	2	46.00	—	2/65
Griffiths W. H.	11	1	34	12	3.77	—	173.3	30	538	17	31.64	—	4/61
Gwynn D. G. P.	6	0	20	12	3.33	—							
Gwynn W. H.	4	0	72	27	18.00	—	22.4	6	61	3	20.33	—	2/15
Hacker W. S.	110	29	828	64	10.22	—	2694.0	461	5212	361+8	14.44	22	7/84
Hadley R. J.	3	2	4	4*	4.00	—	32.5	7	93	7	13.28	1	5/32
Haines C. V. G.	20	2	350	59	19.44	—	10.0	2	33	1	33.00	—	1/15
Hansford G.	3	0	24	12	8.00	—							
Harris A.	91	3	1698	110	19.29	2	1.0	1	0	0	—	—	—

Harris G. J.	1	0	0	0	—	—							
Harris K. H.	3	0	77	36	25.67	—	2.0	0	24	0	—	—	—
Harris L. J.	4	2	7	5	3.50	—	51.0	7	183	5	36.60	—	3/39
Harris W. E.	8	0	59	25	7.37	—	8.0	1	43	0	—	—	—
Harrison G. B.	17	0	109	34	6.41	—	2.3	0	10	0	—	—	—
Harrison S. C.	6	0	32	15	5.33	—	93.0	15	314	7	44.85	—	3/35
Hedges B.	744	41	17733	182	25.22	21	94.0	24	260	3	86.66	—	1-16
Henderson S. P.	45	7	1204	135*	31.68	3	16.0	2	96	2	48.00	—	2/48
Hever N. G.	166	74	869	40	9.45	—	3138.0	629	7400	318	23.27	11	7/55
Hickey D. J.	9	5	19	9*	4.75	—	281.5	39	1102	24	45.91	1	5/57
Hickley V. A.	15	1	256	65	18.29	—							
Hildyard L. D.	2	0	5	5	2.50	—							
Hill E. E.	1	1	18	18*	—	—							
Hill L. W.	130	20	2690	96*	24.45	—	8.4	1	44	0	—	—	—
Hill M. L.	6	1	110	35	22.00	—							
Hill P. M. T.	2	0	14	13	7.00	—	1.0	0	8	0	—	—	—
Hill R. K.	1	0	0	0	—	—	29.0	8	58	1	58.00	—	1/34
Hill V. T.	10	0	46	17	4.60	—							
Hills J. J.	165	7	3252	166	20.58	6							
Hinwood J. W. J.	5	0	18	10	3.60	—	69.0	12	280	6	46.67	—	3/99
Hirst J. O.	9	0	85	43	9.44	—							
Hoare W. R.	2	0	14	14	7.00	—							
Hobbs R. N. S.	44	19	246	49*	9.84	—	773.3	204	2370	65	36.46	2	5/67
Hodges A. E.	2	0	3	3	1.50	—							
Holmes G. C.	281	42	6591	117	27.58	8	1049.4	203	3636	80	45.45	2	5/30
Holmes T.	2	0	0	0	—	—							
Hopkins J. A.	524	32	13610	230	27.66	18	26.0	3	148	0	—	—	—
Hordley T. J.	10	4	31	9	5.16	—	171.0	50	397	26	15.27	—	4/19
Horsfall R.	9	0	76	21	8.44	—							
Horspool J. J.	7	2	45	11	9.00	—							
Howard A. R.	97	2	1153	63	12.13	—	18.0	2	70	0	—	—	—
Howells P.	2	0	6	6	3.00	—							
Hughes D. W.	25	6	216	70*	11.37	—	352.5	46	1255	38	33.03	2	5/70
Hughes G.	22	4	228	92	12.66	—	218.0	75	560	12	46.66	—	3/20
Hughes T. E.	1	0	0	0	—	—							
Hughes W. D.	8	2	58	28*	9.67	—	126	21	437	14	31.21	—	4/56
Ingledew H. M.	7	0	114	20	16.28	—	21.0	2	73	2	36.50	—	2/37
Jacob N. E.	15	0	87	19	5.80	—	7.0	0	42	0+4	—	—	4†
James D. H.	1	0	17	17	17.00	—	24.0	4	59	1	59.00	—	1/59
James E. H.	11	0	87	41	7.91	—	141.1	17	419	31	13.52	1	5/24
James E. L.	12	4	232	62*	29.00	—	14.0	1	45	1	45.00	—	1/8
James S. P.	13	1	246	106	20.50	1							
Jarrett H. H.	1	0	0	0	—	—	9	1	45	4	11.25	—	3/18
Jarrett K. S.	3	1	27	18*	13.50	—	12.0	2	76	0	—	—	—
Javed Miandad	135	22	6531	212*	57.80	17	254.3	57	851	21	40.52	—	3.52
Jenkins H.	2	1	81	65	81.00	—							
Jenkins L.	2	0	7	7	3.50	—							
Jenkins V. G. J.	69	9	1072	65	17.87	—	10.1	0	54	2	27.00	—	1/13
Jenkins W. L. T.	20	1	155	39	8.15	—							
Johns J.	5	1	4	3	0.80	—	46.0	6	164	13	12.62	2	6/44
Johns T. S.	2	2	14	8*	—	—	—	—	—	0+9	—	—	6†
Johnson C. R. H.	17	3	170	31	12.14	—	37.0	8	141	2	70.50	—	1/43

Jones A.	1102	71	34056	204★	33.03	52	58.5	15	249	1	249.00	—	1/41
Jones A. A.	17	5	64	12	5.33	—	514.0	90	1841	49	37.57	—	5/51
Jones A. L.	278	24	6548	132	25.78	5	15.5	0	152	1	152.00	—	1/60
Jones D. A.	1	0	6	6	6.00	—	14.0	3	43	2	21.50	—	2/22
Jones D. E.	9	0	78	25	8.67	—	6.0	0	21	0	—	—	—
Jones E. C. (1934–)	142	30	2016	132	18.00	2	1036.1	165	3299	102	32.14	6	7/79
Jones E. C. (1926)	1	0	0	0	—								
Jones E. W. (1961–)	591	119	8341	146★	17.67	3	0.3	0	5	0	—	—	—
Jones E. W. (1890–)	108	6	2433	152	23.85	1	15.0	5	53	0+2	—	—	2†
Jones F. N.	11	2	69	28	7.67	—							
Jones H.	2	0	3	2	1.50	—							
Jones H. O.	3	3	10	7	—		10.0	0	53	0	—	—	—
Jones I. J.	180	69	395	20	3.55	—	3904.4	979	9583	408	23.48	16	8/11
Jones J. M.	13	1	326	75	27.16	—							
Jones J. W.	21	6	310	108★	20.67	1	43.3	3	169	7+1	24.14	—	3/40
Jones O.	28	1	412	79	15.26	—	214.2	46	588	28+3	21.00	—	4/9
Jones R. G.	5	2	29	17★	9.66	—	70.5	29	132	18	7.33	—	5/42
Jones T. C.	6	0	36	21	6.00	—							
Jones W. E. (1946–)	1	0	0	0	—		94.0	9	342	13	26.30	1	7/92
Jones W. E. (1929–)	73	30	300	27	6.97	—	1020.2	202	2754	77	35.76	3	6.93
Jones W. E. (1937–)	555	63	13270	212★	27.00	11	1926.2	438	5620	189	29.73	3	5/50
Jones W. M.	15	3	116	51★	9.66	—	58.5	9	214	6	35.66	—	3/11
Joseph A. F.	2	0	8	8	4.00	—							
Judge P. F.	67	24	332	40	7.12	—	1175.3	221	3475	138	25.18	3	8/75
Kindersley C. E.	2	0	0	0	—								
King C. L.	27	1	811	78	31.19	—	259.1	58	730	20	36.50	—	4/31
Kingston G. C.	15	2	161	26	12.38	—	60.0	12	210	4	52.20	—	2/18
Lambert W.	19	8	38	7	3.45	—	314.3	62	842	59	14.27	2	5/16
Landers E.	2	0	7	7	3.50	—							
Lavis G.	312	43	4957	154	18.42	3	2741	515	7768	156	49.79	—	4/55
Lawlor P. J.	2	0	8	8	4.00	—	13.0	2	50	1	50.00	—	1/36
Letcher H. B.	158	16	2287	156	16.11	1	783.4	201	2209	105	21.04	3	7/66
Lewis A. R.	546	52	15003	223	30.37	21	55.1	3	306	4	76.50	—	3/18
Lewis B.	45	5	333	38	8.32	—	670.1	160	2001	82	24.40	6	7/28
Lewis D. W.	17	6	107	29★	9.72	—	286.0	58	901	21	42.90	—	4/42
Lewis E. J.	150	10	2169	80	15.49	—	1297.3	363	3821	151	25.30	7	8/89
Lewis H. T.	2	0	20	12	10.00	—							
Lewis K. H.	48	14	312	34	9.17	—	695.0	126	2044	55	37.16	—	4/25
Lewis R. A.	15	2	172	52	13.23	—	42.0	15	104	3+3	34.67	—	1/17
Lewis S. A.	1	0	4	4	4.00	—							
Lewis W. E.	5	1	24	10	6.00	—							
Lindley J.	8	1	57	30★	8.14	—	128.4	47	237	19+7	12.47	2	5/54
Ling A. J. P.	13	3	192	41★	19.20	—	2.0	0	12	0	—	—	—
Linton J. E. F.	4	0	3	2	0.75	—	25.0	4	82	1	82.00	—	1/34
Llewellyn M. J.	215	30	4288	129★	23.17	3	227.1	62	615	23	26.73	—	4/35
Llewelyn J. T. D.	2	1	5	3★	5.00	—							
Llewelyn W. D.	23	0	418	99	18.17	—	54.2	11	156	6+5	26.00	—	3/30
Lloyd B. J.	184	47	1631	48	11.90	—	3418.3	779	10133	247	41.02	3	8/70
Long J. P.	8	0	57	20	7.12	—	4.0	0	17	0	—	—	—
Lowe R.	85	7	1580	87	20.26	—	301.1	72	795	65+1	12.23	2	6/37
Lowe S.	101	33	672	36★	9.88	—	2093.4	760	5429	342+3	15.87	21	8/96
Lyons K. J.	99	14	1673	92	19.68	—	81.1	13	252	2	126.00	—	1/36

McConnon J. E.	350	38	4514	95	1470	—	5913.2	1593	15656	799	19.59	49	8/36
McFarlane L. L.	6	2	12	8	3.00	—	259.0	42	1008	16	63.00	—	4/100
Mack A. J.	23	10	60	18	4.61	—	352.0	70	1129	37	30.51	—	4/28
Mackay J. F.	1	0	2	2	2.00	—	10.0	3	16	1	16.00	—	1/8
Madden-Gaskell J. C. P.	2	0	39	22	19.50	—							
Majid Khan	270	17	9610	204	37.98	21	723.3	216	1674	51	32.82	—	4/48
Malone S. J.	6	1	4	2	0.80	—	174.1	23	654	13	50.31	1	5/38
Mann A. H.	7	0	120	58	17.14	—							
Marley K. R.	2	0	82	49	41.00	—							
Marsh W. E.	6	1	39	13	7.80	—	64.1	6	290	8	36.25	—	3/70
Martin E. G.	4	0	11	8	2.75	—	22.0	4	77	1+4	77.00	—	4†
Martyn O. B.	2	0	15	12	7.50	—							
Mathias F. W.	46	5	457	58	11.14	—	16.0	0	84	1	84.00	—	1/28
Matthews A. D. G.	71	24	691	37	14.70	—	1473.1	352	3607	227	15.88	16	7/57
Maxwell J.	79	12	1666	113*	24.87	3	774.4	148	2430	179	13.58	9	6/26
Maynard M. P.	82	9	2826	160	38.71	5	31.1	4	106	4	26.50	—	3/21
Meggitt F. C.	2	0	4	4	2.00	—							
Mendelson W.	4	0	33	19	8.25	—							
Mercer J.	578	100	5730	72	11.98	—	13813.5	3242	34058	1460	23.32	98	10/51
Metson C. P.	67	15	844	81	16.23	—							
Miller H. D. S.	40	3	433	81	11.70	—	514.2	126	1350	48	28.12	1	7/48
Mizen C. A.	4	1	33	12	11.00	—	5.0	1	15	0	—	—	—
Monkhouse S.	9	4	23	15	4.60	—	149.0	24	481	16	30.06	—	3/37
Montgomery S. W.	43	2	763	117	18.60	1	37.0	10	99	6	16.50	—	3/29
Moore-Gwyn H. G.	16	1	229	63	15.26	—							
Moore-Gwyn J. G.	2	0	4	4	2.00	—							
Morgan A. N.	9	0	83	35	9.22	—	64.0	8	263	3	87.66	—	2.93
Morgan E.	6	1	10	5	2.00	—							
Morgan E. N.	1	0	1	1	1.00	—							
Morgan F. W.	1	0	3	3	3.00	—	12.0	2	33	1	33.00	—	1/33
Morgan H. E.	148	5	2859	254	19.99	4	31.0	7	90	6+9	15.00	—	3/50
Morgan H. W.	3	1	11	5	5.50	—	22.0	4	58	2	29.00	—	1/27
Morgan J. T.	52	3	792	103*	16.16	1	168.5	32	535	11	48.63	—	3/16
Morgan T. R.	96	10	1343	87*	15.62	—	5.5	0	27	0	—	—	—
Morgan W.	32	1	547	91	17.65	—	471.4	106	1115	70+9	15.93	5	7/79
Morgan W. G.	66	11	976	91*	17.75	—	59.3	4	257	3	85.66	—	1/15
Morgan W. P.	2	0	4	4	2.00	—	1.0	1	0	0	—	—	—
Morris A. W.	21	1	332	51	16.60	—	3.0	0	14	2	7.00	—	2/14
Morris F. H.	6	1	53	15*	10.60	—							
Morris H.	185	21	5037	143	30.71	6	38.2	6	228	2	114.00	—	1/6
Morris I.	25	2	253	38	11.00	—	28.0	4	141	4	35.25	—	2/30
Morris V. L.	34	1	417	42	12.64	—							
Morris W. P.	88	7	1288	85	15.90	—	126.2	27	388	25+12	15.52	1	9/28
Moseley E. A.	43	10	655	70*	19.85	—	910.0	195	2729	114	23.94	5	6/23
Moss E.	2	0	15	10	7.50	—	25.0	4	70	2	35.00	—	2/70
Moynihan W. A.	1	0	4	4	4.00	—							
Mullens D.	2	1	4	4*	4.00	—	15	1	55	2	27.50	—	2/55
Mullins A.	2	0	9	6	4.50	—	34.0	2	57	2	28.50	—	2/44
Muncer B. L.	333	46	6460	135	22.50	4	6642.2	1807	14462	708	20.42	42	9/62
Murray J. F.	2	1	101	78*	50.50	—							
Nash A.	225	45	1302	44	7.23	—	4969.3	1567	11872	763+22	15.56	72	9/33

305

Nash M. A.	467	67	7120	130	17.81	2	9193.3	2426	25601	991	25.83	45	9/56
Nicholl L. D.	8	0	206	91	25.75	—	1.0	0	6	1	6.00	—	1/6
Needham P. J. E.	1	0	4	4	4.00	—	41.5	11	105	2	52.50	—	1/49
North P. D.	20	7	168	41*	12.92	—	304.0	79	780	19	41.05	—	4/43
O'Bree A.	46	2	770	116	17.50	1						—	—
O'Daly G. N.	1	0	9	9	9.00	—	7.0	1	17	0	—	—	—
Ontong R. C.	408	65	10771	204*	31.40	18	5575.0	1255	16918	525	32.22	20	8/67
Osborne A. J.	68	6	987	110	15.92	1	324.1	82	1006	62+2	16.23	2	6/40
Parkhouse R. J.	1	0	0	0	—	—						—	—
Parkhouse W. G. A.	759	48	22619	201	31.81	32	37.1	8	125	2	62.50	—	1/4
Parvez Mir	2	0	16	10	8.00	—	4.0	0	21	0	—	—	—
Pauline D. B.	20	0	455	97	22.75	—	14.0	0	67	2	33.50	—	2/48
Pearson C. J. H.	2	0	9	9	4.50	—	4.0	0	12	0	—	—	—
Peatfield A. E.	9	0	120	44	13.33	—							
Penfold W.	2	1	10	9*	5.00	—							
Perkins A. L. B.	10	3	102	26*	14.57	—							
Perry N. J.	12	4	19	6	2.37	—	282.3	73	920	21	43.80	—	3/51
Phillips M.	4	1	5	3	1.66	—	17.0	2	39	2	19.50	—	—
Pinch F. B.	78	5	1223	138*	16.75	2	500.0	108	1503	51+1	29.47	—	4/48
Pitchford L.	3	1	24	14*	12.00	—	3.0	1	4	0	—	—	—
Pleass J. E.	253	31	4293	102*	19.30	1	4.0	0	15	0	—	—	—
Poole W.	2	1	2	2*	1.00	—	44.0	6	136	10	13.60	—	—
Porter A.	64	7	1292	105	22.66	2	161.0	24	480	16	30.00	—	4/25
Powell T. L.	2	0	0	0	—	—							
Preece T.	27	3	359	73	14.96	—							
Preedy	32	7	344	42*	13.77	—	305.3	56	766	52	14.73	3	6/50
Pressdee	543	83	13411	150*	29.16	12	3666.2	1095	8988	405	22.18	19	9/43
Price M. R.	13	4	144	36	16.00	—	289.4	66	806	19	42.42	—	4/60
Prichard H. C. C.	7	1	106	50	17.67	—							
Pritchard A. J.	1	0	2	2	2.00	—	—	—	—	0+2	—	—	2†
Pruen F. H.	1	0	21	21	21.00	—							
Pullen W. W. F.	7	0	190	77	27.14	—							
Rattenbury G. L.	35	6	412	55	14.21	—	385.0	81	1085	50	21.70	1	5/50
Reason D. J.	15	3	122	32*	10.17	—	10.0	0	30	1+1	30.00	—	1†
Reason T. F.	14	2	220	90*	18.33	—	7.0	1	34	0	—	—	—
Reed G. H.	25	12	65	11	5.00	—	704.4	133	1941	62	31.30	1	5/30
Rees A.	372	53	7681	111*	24.07	2	94.3	11	398	6	66.33	—	3/68
Rees E. L.	15	5	44	17	4.40	—	158.4	50	347	21+4	16.52	1	6/42
Rees R. M.	9	0	75	25	8.33	—							
Rees S. H.	59	1	747	82	12.88	—	3.0	0	24	0	—	—	—
Reid E. W.	7	0	64	14	9.14	—	43.0	11	95	7	13.57	1	5/39
Reynolds G. E. A.	3	2	37	23*	37.00	—	32.0	14	75	2	37.50	—	2/24
Rhys H. R. J.	13	1	147	35	12.25	—							
Richards G.	174	26	3370	102*	22.77	1	691.3	135	2257	48	47.02	1	5/55
Richards J.	2	0	22	19	11.00	—							
Riches J. D. H.	2	0	5	4	2.50	—							
Riches N. V. H.	362	38	11722	217*	36.18	20	27.3	1	101	1+1	101.00	—	1†
Rippon T. J.	4	2	45	30	22.50	—							
Robathan G. L.	12	0	95	30	7.92								
Roberts J. F.	6	1	86	47*	17.20	—							
Roberts M. L.	3	0	14	8	4.67	—							
Robinson M.	106	7	2139	190	21.60	2	128.0	18	432	13	33.23	—	3/17
Robinson T.	24	1	411	70	17.86	—	345.5	92	693	51	13.59	5	6/26

Name	Inns	NO	Runs	HS	Avge	100	Overs	Mdns	Runs	Wkts	Avge	5wi	BB
Roebuck P. G. P.	4	0	60	46	15.00	—							
Rogers B. L.	4	1	46	16*	15.33	—	10.0	0	33	1	33.00	—	1/22
Rooney E. J.	4	0	19	11	4.75	—	19.0	3	53	3	17.67	—	2/23
Rooney R.	14	3	237	54*	21.54	—	2.0	0	4	0	—	—	—
Rooney S.	7	0	64	34	9.11	—	25.4	3	73	2	36.50	—	2/73
Rowe C. J. C.	83	10	1947	105	26.67	1	874.0	189	2826	69	40.95	—	4/29
Rowntree R. E.	3	0	8	7	2.66	—	40.0	3	128	4	32.00	—	2/28
Russell W.	154	12	2673	143	18.82	1	1934.2	768	3848	265+7	14.52	3	6/36
Ryan F. P.	312	100	1699	46	8.01	—	6589.2	1317	19053	913	20.86	79	8/41
Samuel A. W.	24	8	201	46*	12.56	—	404.2	95	870	48	18.13	1	5/62
Samuel G. N. T. W.	4	0	41	22	10.25	—							
Sant S. A.	2	0	21	21	10.50	—							
Saulez E.	11	0	257	80	23.36	—							
Schofield T. D.	5	1	3	2	0.75	—							
Scott	2	0	20	12	10.00	—							
Selvey M. W. W.	42	11	361	63	11.65	—	941.1	207	3000	87	34.48	4	6/31
Seymour R. G.	4	0	14	8	3.50	—							
Sharples J. E.	1	0	0	0	—	—	1.0	0	1	0	—	—	—
Shastri R. J.	40	4	1330	157	36.94	2	723.3	187	1760	54	32.59	2	7/49
Shaw G. B.	20	13	30	11	4.28	—	229.2	36	706	26	27.15	2	5/38
Shea A. J.	3	0	22	10	7.33	—	41.0	7	171	1	171.00	—	1/130
Shea W. D.	3	1	27	18*	13.50	—	51.0	5	180	5	36.00	—	4/68
Shepherd D. J.	816	241	5610	73	9.75	—	21514.2	7334	45571	2174	20.95	122	9/47
Shepherd E.	2	0	10	8	5.00	—							
Silkin S. C.	2	0	2	2	1.00	—	9.0	0	60	1	60.00	—	1/27
Silverlock A. J.	1	0	0	0	—	—	9.0	0	42	0	—	—	—
Slade W. D.	116	11	1482	73*	14.11	—	504.3	146	1493	32	46.65	—	4/144
Smart C. C.	301	35	8069	151*	30.34	9	2097.4	302	6943	169	41.08	1	5/39
Smith C. L.	2	1	81	67	81.00	—							
Smith D. J.	25	1	365	69	15.21	—	31.0	10	91	4	22.75	—	4/78
Smith I.	30	5	315	45	12.60	—	280.1	54	1022	21	48.67	—	3/65
Snell A. S.	2	0	1	1	0.50	—							
Solanky J. W.	134	22	2263	73	20.20	—	1617.5	397	4514	176	25.64	8	6/63
Soloman H. G.	1	0	38	38	38.00	—							
Spencer C. R.	1	0	0	0	—	—							
Spencer H.	68	2	743	56	11.25	—	844.5	170	2270	101	22.47	4	7/33
Spiller C. W.	4	0	20	14	5.00	—	43.0	8	144	4	36.00	—	3/50
Spiller W.	29	1	458	104	16.36	1	4.0	0	31	0	—	—	—
Stapleton	3	0	11	6	3.67	—							
Steele J. F.	70	20	1385	100*	27.70	1	1044.1	262	3031	88	34.44	4	5/42
Stewart T. L.	2	0	4	4	2.00	—							
Stone J.	48	2	1047	108	22.76	1							
Stone J. H.	1	0	0	0	—	—	13.3	1	65	4	16.25	—	3/27
Storer G.	1	0	0	0	—	—	26.0	11	41	1	41.00	—	1/41
Sullivan D.	166	55	811	47*	7.30	—							
Swain G. W.	1	0	12	12	12.00	—							
Swart P. D.	73	8	1996	122	30.70	4	512.3	123	1785	64	27.89	—	4/24
Sweet-Escott E. R.	106	12	2025	129	21.54	2	27.0	3	91	5	18.20	—	4/67
Sweet-Escott H. H.	3	0	10	7	3.33	—							
Sweet-Escott R. B.	40	4	565	75	15.69	—	17.0	3	47	1	47.00	—	1/12
Sweet-Escott W. S. R.	58	12	636	82	13.83	—	535.4	136	1466	70+4	20.94	4	7/41
Symonds H. G.	95	8	1392	76	16.00	—	53.0	0	231	5	46.20	—	2/41

Name	Inns	NO	Runs	HS	Avge	100	Overs	Mdns	Runs	Wkts	Avge	5wi	Best
Tait J. R.	130	4	2630	96	20.87	—	45.0	8	207	4	51.75	—	1/5
Tamplin C.	4	2	56	40*	28.00	—							
Tayler H. W.	21	3	279	44	15.50	—							
Taylor H. T.	4	1	17	16*	5.66	—	2.0	0	11	0	—	—	—
Thackeray A. G.	15	1	327	78	23.35	—	—	—	—	0+1	—	—	1†
Thissen D. R.	28	3	304	44*	12.16	—							
Thomas A. E. (1913)	2	0	27	26	13.00	—							
Thomas A. E. (1925)	2	0	15	11	7.50	—							
Thomas D.	2	1	14	14*	14.00	—	27.0	4	99	5	19.80	1	5/64
Thomas D. J.	1	1	10	10*	—	—	17.0	1	63	0	—	—	—
Thomas G.	2	0	27	21	13.50	—							
Thomas H. T.	15	0	104	25	6.93	—							
Thomas J. G.	139	24	2137	110	18.58	2	2244.5	386	8230	256	32.15	9	6/68
Thomas L. G.	29	1	348	44	12.43	—							
Thomas N. D.	2	0	15	15	7.50	—							
Thomas R. J.	1	1	8	8*	—	—	10.2	2	40	1	40.00	—	1/40
Thomas, Serg.	3	0	24	18	8.00	—							
Thomas, W. M.	2	0	13	9	6.50	—	4.0	0	18	0	—	—	—
Todd P. A.	24	0	470	135	19.58	1							
Tomlinson H.	19	0	387	73	20.37	—	48.0	10	163	1	163.00	—	1/30
Trick W. M. S.	22	11	52	15	4.72	—	515.3	196	1087	56	19.41	4	6/29
Turnbull B.	3	0	13	12	4.33	—							
Turnbull M. J. L.	504	25	14431	233	30.12	22	46.4	2	266	2	133.00	—	1/4
Tyson C. J.	4	0	88	79	22.00	—	15.0	1	32	0	—	—	—
Van Zyl C. J. P. G.	10	1	115	35	12.78	—	286.1	67	850	17	50.00	—	3/35
Vaughan-Thomas H. W.	1	0	3	3	3.00	—							
Veal C. L.	3	0	32	21	10.66	—							
Waite A.	2	1	34	30*	34.00	—							
Walker P. M.	738	106	16510	152*	26.12	12	8879.0	2749	21652	771	28.08	22	7/58
Walters C. F.	133	9	2146	116	17.31	2	5.2	0	37	0	—	—	—
Ward D. J.	206	33	2496	86	14.42	—	1796.2	448	4987	187	26.66	5	7/60
Warner C. C.	2	1	14	7*	14.00	—	15	2	47	0	—	—	—
Watkin S. L.	19	7	115	23	9.58	—	543.3	128	1505	48	31.35	2	8/59
Watkins A. J.	649	76	17419	170*	30.39	29	7397.5	2027	17683	774	22.84	24	7/28
Watkins W. M.	1	0	3	3	3.00	—							
Watson W. H.	12	1	199	58	18.09	—							
Went G. J. H.	2	1	14	14*	14.00	—	5.0	1	14	0	—	—	
Wheatley O. S.	227	87	799	30	5.70	—	6262.2	1988	13356	715	18.67	37	9/60
White D. W.	1	0	8	8	8.00	—	17.4	2	32	1	32.00	—	1/32
White M. E.	1	0	17	17	17.00	—							
Whitehill W. K.	11	3	60	16	7.50	—							
Whiteman E. I. E.	3	0	27	16	9.00	—	53.0	8	172	3	57.33	—	2/113
Whittington T. A. L.	218	11	4563	188	22.04	4	7.5	1	53	3	17.67	—	3/26
Wilkins A. H.	73	22	502	70	9.84	—	1252.2	234	4204	135	31.14	6	6/74
Wilkinson W.	3	0	29	19	9.66	—	104.5	355	149	12	12.42	—	4/10
Williams D. B.	27	2	360	43	14.40	—							
Williams, D. L.	144	72	399	37*	5.54	—	3535.4	816	9839	363	27.10	13	7/60
Williams F. I.	2	0	24	24	12.00	—							
Williams I. (1890–)	6	0	24	16	4.00	—	3.0	0	11	0	—	—	—
Williams I. (1931)	4	0	10	7	2.50	—							
Williams L. E. W.	8	2	145	53*	24.16	—	7.0	1	42	0	—	—	—

Williams W. H.	11	3	108	37	13.50	—	19.0	4	47	1	47.00	—	1/16
Windsor-Clive A.	8	0	31	15	3.88	—							
Wolfe A.	1	0	9	9	9.00	—							
Wooller W.	630	72	12692	128	22.75	5	9118.5	2332	23513	887	26.50	40	8/45
Worsley F. F.	3	0	34	21	11.33	—							
Yorath T. H. B.	11	3	115	29	14.38	—	4.0	0	21	0	—	—	—
Yorath W. L.	6	0	45	21	7.50	—							
Young G. A.	5	1	105	61	26.25	—							
Younis Ahmed	88	14	3635	177	49.12	8	106.4	29	294	2	147.00	—	1/38

NOTES:

1. The career figures are for all the first-class games played by Glamorgan since 1921, plus the inter-county and major representative matches between 1889 and 1920 (see following section).

2. Unfortunately, a complete series of scorebooks has not survived for the period since 1889 and for a few seasons around the turn of the century, the individual figures were obtained from the *Western Mail* and the *South Wales Daily News* (*Wisden* only gives seasonal averages for the pre-1921 period). Unfortunately some bowling figures have been omitted from several newspaper reports, or there are discrepancies between these newspaper sources. Consequently, for a few players it has been impossible to obtain complete bowling figures, in terms of overs, maiden and runs conceded. The wickets taken in these games can be gained from the scorecards and are denoted above by a + sign. In addition, there is doubt in a few cases when the best bowling performance occurred, because the number of wickets taken in these matches where runs conceded are missing, equals those taken in games where full figures are available. These are denoted by a † sign after the number of wickets.

SUMMARY OF ALL INTER-COUNTY AND MAJOR REPRESENTATIVE GAMES, 1889–1920

(home games first in each column)

	89	90	91	92	93	94	95	96	97	98	99	00	01	02	03	04	05	06	07	08	09	10	11	12	13	14	20
Warwickshire	L–	D–																									W–
MCC & Ground		LL	LW	WW	LL	LL	D–	WL	L–	W–	W–	D–	A–	–D		D–	W–	LL		W–			–L	DL	WL	WL	WW
Surrey Club & Ground	–W	–L	WW	WW	WL	DD	DW	WD	DD	LW	WW	WW	WW	WW	WD	WW	DD	LL	WW	LW	WL	WW	WW	WW	WL	LD	WD
Monmouthshire		WL	WW	WW	WW	WL		WD	WD	LW	WW	WW	WW	WW	WW	WW	WL	DD	WW	WW	WW	L–	DD	LL			
Somerset		LL																									
Gloucestershire			DL																								
Devon			DD	DL	WL			WD	WL		WW	WW	WW														
Wiltshire				DW	WD	LW	WL	WD	WL	WW	WW	WL	LW	WW	WW	WW	WL	WL	WL	WW	WW	LW	WW	WW	WW	WA†	WW
Herefordshire					DW	L–		WW					L–											WL			
South Africa																											
South Wales CC							W–					D–															
V. T. Hills XI							D–					DD															
Worcestershire									L–	LD	DL	L–															
Cornwall										WW	WW	WW							WW	WW	WW	L–					
Berkshire										WD	WL		WW	WL	WW	WL	WW										–D
W. M. Brownlee's XI												D–		W–													
Northamptonshire												DD		LD*													
Public School Nondescripts														LD*		W–											
Philadelphians																	DW	WW									
Northumberland																	WL	WW	–W								
Durham																		–W	W–	WW	WW	WW	WW	WL			
Carmarthenshire																			L–								
Dorset																				–L	W–	W–	–L				
Lancashire II																							DD	LL			
Staffordshire																						WW	W–				
Oxford Harlequins																						–L					
Notts II																						WW	WW				
Hertfordshire																							WW				
Sussex II																						–L					
Buckinghamshire																								D–	WW		
H. Webb's XII																									–L		
Kent II																										WA†	
Norfolk																										WL	WL
Essex II																											W–
Cheshire																											
J. H. P. Brains XI																											
W	1	3	3	5	4	2	1	4	4	4	9	6	7	5	7	7	7	7	9	9	8	9	8	4	6	4	9
L	2	1	2	1	1	5	3	2	2	2	1	1	2	3	7	3	3	4	1	3	2	4	2	1	3	3	2
D	1	6	3	4	1	–	–	6	5	–	–	5	3	6	2	1	2	1	1	1	1	1	2	4	1	2	2
A	–	1	1	–	–	–	–	–	–	–	–	–	1	–	–	–	–	–	–	–	–	–	–	–	–	1	–
Position in Minor County Championship								2nd	2nd	4th	3rd	1st	5th	4th	4th	3rd	8th	8th	2nd	2nd	2nd	3rd	5th	10th	2nd	6th	6th

*Both games played at Cardiff Arms Park   †Abandoned owing to the declaration of war

The following matches in the 1889–1920 period have *not* been included in the table above, or in the records section:

18, 19 May 1891 Glamorgan *v* Glamorgan Colts XXII at Cardiff (Drawn)

13, 14 May 1892 Glamorgan *v* Glamorgan Colts XXI at Swansea (Glamorgan won by 2 wkts)

22, 23 May 1893 Glamorgan *v* Glamorgan Colts XXII at Cardiff (Glamorgan won by 8 wkts)

23, 24 August 1893 Glamorgan *v* A Cardiff and District XI at Cardiff (Cardiff won by 107 runs)

16, 17 July 1894 South Wales *v* E. M. Grace's Gloucestershire XI at Cardiff (South Wales won by 55 runs)

4, 5 August 1902 Glamorgan/Wiltshire XI *v* Australians at Cardiff (Australia won by 6 wkts)

3, 4 August 1904 Gentlemen of Glamorgan *v* Players of Glamorgan at Cardiff (Drawn)

2, 3 May 1905 South Wales *v* Yorkshire at Cardiff (Yorkshire won by 70 runs)

5, 6 July 1905 Gentlemen of Glamorgan *v* Gentlemen of Essex at Neath (Drawn)

7, 8 August 1905 South Wales *v* Australians at Cardiff (Drawn)

4 September 1905 Glamorgan *v* Llanelli CC at Llanelli (Llanelli won by 17 runs)

3, 4 May 1906 South Wales *v* Yorkshire at Cardiff (Drawn)

5, 6 July 1906 Gentlemen of Glamorgan *v* Gentlemen of Essex at Neath (Essex won by 10 wkts)

9, 10 July 1906 South Wales *v* West Indians at Cardiff (West Indians won by 278 runs)

1, 2 August 1906 Glamorgan *v* Glamorgan Colts XVIII at Cardiff (Drawn)

12, 13 June 1907 Gentlemen of Glamorgan *v* Players of Glamorgan at Cardiff (Players won by 51 runs)

4, 5 July 1907 Gentlemen of Glamorgan *v* Gentlemen of Essex at Neath (Drawn)

14, 15 August 1907 South Wales *v* Lancashire Nomads at Cardiff (Drawn)

26, 27 August 1907 South Wales *v* South Africans at Cardiff (South Africans won by an innings and 66 runs)

7, 8 July 1908 South Wales *v* Philadelphians at Cardiff (Philadelphians won by 38 runs)

2, 3, 4 August 1909 South Wales *v* Australians at Cardiff (Australia won by 8 wkts)

5, 6 June 1911 South Wales *v* All-India at Cardiff (South Wales won by 7 wkts)

20, 21, 22 June 1912 South Wales *v* South Africans at Swansea (South Africans won by 230 runs)

24, 25, 26 August 1912 South Wales *v* Australians at Cardiff (Abandoned – rain)

6, 7 September 1912 Gentlemen of Glamorgan *v* Players of Glamorgan at Neath (Drawn)

12, 13 June 1913 Gentlemen of Glamorgan *v* Players of Glamorgan at Neath (Players won by 40 runs)

15, 16 July 1913 Gentlemen of Glamorgan *v* Gentlemen of Carmarthenshire at Llanelli (Drawn)

23 July 1913 Glamorgan *v* Maesteg CC at Maesteg (Glamorgan won by 288 runs)

14, 15 August 1913 Gentlemen of Glamorgan *v* Gentlemen of Carmarthenshire at Swansea (Glamorgan won by 137 runs)

21, 22 July 1914 Gentlemen of Glamorgan *v* Gentlemen of Carmarthenshire at Swansea (Drawn)

27, 28 July 1914 Gentlemen of Glamorgan *v* Gentlemen of Carmarthenshire at Llanelli (Carmarthenshire won by 8 wkts)

30, 31 July 1914 Glamorgan *v* Combined Briton Ferry Town and Steelworks XI at Neath (Glamorgan won by 49 runs)

21, 22 August 1914 Gentlemen of Glamorgan *v* Weston and District XI at Weston (Glamorgan by an innings and 64 runs)

3 June 1920 Glamorgan *v* Cardiff High School Old Boys at Cardiff (Glamorgan won by 18 runs)

17, 18 June 1920 Gentlemen of Glamorgan *v* Players of Glamorgan at Neath (Players won on 1st innings)

RESULTS OF COUNTY CHAMPIONSHIP MATCHES 1921–1988

(Home matches first in each column)

Year	D	E	GL	HA	K	LA	LE	MX	NH	NT	SM	SY	SX	WA	WO	YO	P	W	L	D	A	Pos
1921	LL		LL	LL		LD	LL			LL		LD		WL		WL	18	2	14	2	—	17th
1922	LL		DL	LL		LL	DL		LL	LL	LW		LL		LD	LL	22	1	18	3	—	16th
1923	DL		WL	DL		LL	DL		WL	LL	DL	LL	LL		DL	LL	24	2	17	5	—	16th
1924	WW		DL			WL	WD		DL	DL	AW	LL		LL	LDL	−L	22	5	11	5	1	13th
1925	WL	LD	LL			LL	LL		LL	LL	LD	DL	LL	DL	LL	DL	26	1	20	5	—	17th
1926	DW	LL	LW			DL	LD		LW	WL	WD	WD		WW	DW	LL	24	9	9	6	—	8th
1927	LD	DD	DD			LA	LD		AL	WL	DD	DL	DD	DL	DD	LD	26	1	8	15	2	15th
1928	LD	DD	LD			DD	DD		LD	LL	WD	DD	LD	DL	WD	LD	26	2	9	15	—	15th
1929	DD	DL	LL	LL		LL	LL		DL	LL	WW	LL	LW	LL	DL	DL	28	3	19	6	—	17th
1930	WW	DL	LL	DL		LD	DD		WD	LL	DL	DD	DL	WD	WD	DD	28	5	9	14	—	11th
1931	DL	DL	DD	DL		LD	DD	DL	WL		DD	WL	LD	LW	WD	LL	28	4	11	13	—	15th
1932		LD	WD	DL	LL	DD	WL	LL		DL	DL	WL	DD	LL	DD	DD	28	3	12	13	—	15th
1933		LL	LD			DD	DL	DD	DL	DD	DD		DL	DD	WL	LL	24	1	9	14	—	16th
1934		DL	LD		LL	DL	DL	DL	WD		WD	DW		DL	DD	DD	24	3	8	13	—	13th
1935		LD	LL	WD	LL	LD	WW		WD	DL	LD		WW	LL	DD	DL	26	6	11	9	—	13th
1936		DL	LL	LL	LD	DL	WD		DD	DD	DL	LD	DL		LD	LD	26	1	12	13	—	16th
1937		WW	LD	WW	WD	DD	WW		WW	DD	LD	DL	LW	DL	WL	DL	28	11	7	10	—	7th
1938		DL	DL	WW	WL	DL	DD		DW		WD		LD	LD	LD	LL	24	5	9	10	—	16th
1939		DW	DW	DD	LD	DL	DD		DW	WD	DW	LD	DL	WL	DL	LL	28	6	8	14	—	13th
1946	WL	DL	WL	W−	−D	DW	−W	L−	DL	D−	WD	WD	DW	−W	LW	LL	26	10	8	8	—	6th
1947	DL	WD	DL	−W	W−	DD	D−	−L	WD	−D	WW	WL	WL	D−	DL	LL	26	8	8	10	—	9th
1948	−L	WW	D−	WWWW	DD	LL	LD	DD	WD	WW	W−	W−	WL	−W	−D		26	13	5	8	—	1st
1949	W−	WD	−D	DD	WL	DD	DD	DD	WL	DD	WL	−D	−L	DW	W−	L−	26	7	6	13	—	8th
1950	WD	WL	DW	DD	−W	LL	LW	WD	DD	D−	DD	DD	DD		−D	D−	28	6	4	18	—	11th
1951	WW	LD	DD	DD	D−	DW	DW	DD	WD	−D	DD	LW	DW	DL	W−	−L	28	8	4	16	—	5th
1952	DW	DL	LL	LD	WD	LD	W−	−W	WD	WD	D−	LW	−D	LD	DD		28	8	7	13	—	7th
1953	WD	WD	DD	LD	WD	DL	−D	D−	DL	DW	WD	−L	DD	W−	WD	WD	28	8	4	16	—	10th
1954	LW	DD	DW	DD	D−	LL	WD	DW	WW	−W	WW	DW	DL	WL	−D	D−	28	11	5	12	—	4th
1955	LD	LD	DL	LL	−L	DD	LL	LL	LD	D−	WW	LL	DD	WL	W−	−W	28	5	14	9	—	16th
1956	LA	WD	LL	WW	WL	DL	W−	−L	DW	LD	DD	L−	DD	−D	DL	DD	28	6	9	12	1	13th
1957	DD	DD	LL	AD	WW	LW	−W	L−	LW	WW	WL	−L	DD	L−	WD	LW	28	10	8	9	1	9th
1958	LD	DL	WW	LL	W−	DD	LL	DL	LW	−W	LD	DL	DD	−D	D−		28	5	11	12	—	15th
1959	WD	DL	WW	DL	−L	WD	WL	WD	WL	D−	WW	LD	WL	WD	W−	−L	28	12	8	8	—	6th
1960	WD	LL	DL	LD	DD	DW	WW	LL	WL	LD	WL	SX	WL	WL	WL	WL	32	9	14	9	—	11th
1961	DW	DD	LL	LW	LD	DD	WL	DL	LW	WW	WD	WW	LL	LD	LL	LD	32	9	12	11	—	14th
1962	LL	WD	LW	DL	DL	WW	DW	DD	DL	LD	LL	DL	DD	DL	LD	WL	32	6	13	13	—	14th
1963	DW	DW	WL	DW	DL	WL	W−	−D	DW	WD	LD	W−	DL	−L	WW	LL	28	11	8	9	—	2nd
1964	DD	DD	WD	DD	WD	DD	−L	D−	WD	DW	DW	−L	DW	D−	LL	LL	28	7	7	14	—	11th
1965	LL	LD	WD	DD	W−	WWWW	LD	LD	−W	DW	WD	WD	WW	DD	−L	W−	28	12	6	10	—	3rd
1966	WW	DD	DL	WD	−D	WD	DL	DD	WD	D−	LL	LD	DW	DL	L−	−L	28	6	8	14	—	14th
1967	LD	DD	DD	DD	WL	DL	D−	LD	WD	WD	−W	DL	L−	DD	LD	DD	28	4	7	17	—	14th
1968	LD	AL	DD	WW	LL	WW	D−	−D	DW	LA	WW	W−	WD	−W	DD	LW	28	11	6	9	2	3rd
1969	DW	WD	WW	DD	−D	DD	D−	W−	−W	−D	WD	−D	WW	D−	WW	D−	24	11	—	13	—	1st
1970	WL	DW	WW	DD	W−	DD	−L	−D	D−	L−	WW	D−	WL	−L	LD	−W	24	9	6	9	—	2nd
1971	−D	LL	DA	DD	−W	L−	LL	DD	WD	DD	DD	−D	D−	L−	WD	W−	24	3	5	15	1	15th
1972	−D	L−	DD	DW	−L	−D	D−	L−	D−	LD	D−	DD	L−	DL	−L		20	1	7	12	—	13th
1973	L−	−D	DL	LD	W−	L−	W−	−D	−L	W−	LL	D−	−L	D−	DD	W−	20	4	8	8	—	11th
1974	−D	D−	LA	WD	−L	−D	W−	L−	D−	D−	LL	−D	D−	−D	LL	−D	20	2	7	10	1	16th
1975	L−	−L	WD	LW	W−	−L	−L	−L	−D	DL	L−	−W	W−	DW	D−		20	7	8	5	—	9th
1976	−W	D−	DL	−L	−D	D−	L−	L−	L−	−D	W−	WD	LD	−L			20	3	10	7	—	17th
1977	D−	−L	LW	DW	L−	D−	LD	−L	−A	−D	DD	−L	−D	DD	DW	L−	22	3	7	11	1	14th
1978	−L	D−	DL	DL	−L	−D	DD	−L	W−	D−	L−	−D	DD	DW	−L		22	3	8	11	—	13th
1979	D−	−L	DD	DL	L−	D−	−L	−A	LD	−L	−D	LD	DL	D−			22	—	10	11	1	17th
1980	−D	D−	WW	−D	DW	−D	DD	L−	−D	−D	DD	L−	WD	AD	−D		22	4	4	13	1	12th
1981	L−	−L	AD	DL	D−	L−	DD	−L	−L	−L	DD	L−	−L	WW	LD	W−	22	3	10	8	1	14th
1982	−D	L−	DW	LL	−D	−L	LL	L−	D−	DD	−L	D−	DD	DD	−D		22	1	8	13	—	16th
1983	L−	DL	LL	−D	LD	DD	−L	DD	D−	W−	−L	LL	DW	−D			24	2	10	12	—	15th
1984	DD	−D	DD	D−	−D	D−	D−	DL	W−	−L	WD	DD	−D	DW	DW	DD	24	4	2	18	—	13th
1985	−L	D−	DD	WL	D−	−D	DD	D−	−D	DW	DW	−W	DL	DD	DD	L−	24	4	4	16	—	12th
1986	L−	LW	LD	−D	DD	DD	−W	−D	DD	L−	DD	D−	−L	LD	LL	−D	24	2	7	15	—	17th
1987	LD	−D	LL	D−	−L	W−	D−	DD	L−	−L	DL	LL	−D	DD	WD	WD	24	3	9	12	—	13th
1988	D−	−D	AL	LD	L−	L−	DD	−D	−L	−L	DD	D−	−D	DW	LL	D−	22	1	8	12	1	17th

PLAYING RECORD AGAINST EACH COUNTY IN THE CHAMPIONSHIP, 1921–1988

	Total		Home				Away			
	P	W	D	L	A	W	D	L	A
Derbyshire	89	12	15	18		11	20	13	1
Essex	99	10	26	12	1	6	23	22	
Gloucestershire	119	11	27	21	2	12	20	26	2
Hampshire	102	10	26	14	1	11	23	18	
Kent	72	16	8	11		5	16	16	
Lancashire	107	9	29	17		7	27	18	
Leicestershire	103	14	25	13		11	18	22	
Middlesex	67	3	18	12		2	17	15	
Northants	104	18	21	14	1	12	19	20	2
Notts	87	9	21	14		9	18	16	
Somerset	123	21	25	15	1	15	32	15	
Surrey	86	11	16	16		6	19	18	
Sussex	99	11	27	12		11	17	21	
Warwickshire	99	13	25	12		8	21	20	
Worcestershire	113	17	22	17	1	10	29	18	
Yorkshire	92	7	17	22		4	18	24	

RESULTS OF OTHER FIRST-CLASS MATCHES 1921–1988
(Year of game in brackets)

Australia: W2 (64, 68); L3 (26, 56, 75); D13 (21, 30, 34, 38, 48, 53, 61, 61, 64, 72, 77, 81, 85)

West Indies: W2 (23, 39); L9 (33, 39, 50, 57, 57, 63, 73, 76, 84); D8 (28, 33, 50, 63, 66, 69, 80)

South Africa: W1 (51); L8 (29, 35, 47, 47, 51, 55, 60, 60); D5 (24, 29, 35, 55, 65)

New Zealand: W2 (37, 37); L4 (27, 31, 58, 73); D8 (31, 49, 49, 58, 65, 69, 78, 86)

India: W2 (36, 59); L5 (32, 46, 59, 71, 79); D5 (32, 46, 52, 52, 65)

Pakistan: W2 (62, 71); L2 (74, 82); D5 (54, 54, 62, 67, 87)

Sri Lanka: D2 (79, 81)

Zimbabwe: D1 (85)

Oxford University: W11 (61, 67, 69, 70, 71, 76, 77, 78, 79, 84, 86); L2 (28, 30); D7 (38, 68, 81, 82, 83, 85, 87)

Cambridge University: W5 (65, 68, 71, 72, 84); L2 (34, 70); D15 (29, 34, 38, 62, 63, 64, 66, 69, 72, 73, 75, 77, 82, 83, 88)

Nottinghamshire (non-championship friendlies): L1 (31); D1 (31)

Somerset (non-championship friendlies): W1 (48); D2 (49, 50)

Combined Universities: W1 (22)

Leveson-Gowers XI: D3 (24, 25, 26)

Sir J. Cahn's XI: W1 (38); D (36)

Combined Services: W3 (50, 51, 56); L (48, 52)

All-England XI: D1 (48)

South of England XI: W1 (48)

Gentlemen of Ireland: D1 (53)

Windward Islands: D1 (70)

Trinidad: L1 (70)

Jamaica: D1 (70)

MCC: L1 (70)

RESULTS OF THE WARTIME FRIENDLIES ARRANGED BY THE GLAMORGAN COMMITTEE (1942–1945)

22 August 1942 at Arms Park: Western Command (158) tied with Southern Command (158)

12 June 1943 at Barry: Glamorgan (109) beat an Anti-Aircraft XI (87) by 22 runs

2 August 1943 at Arms Park: Glamorgan (267) beat an Army XI (138) by 129 runs

3 August 1943 at Arms Park: 'Glamorgan Past' (215) beat 'Glamorgan Future' (159) by 56 runs

14 August 1943 at Barry: Glamorgan (101) beat an RAF XI (75) by 26 runs

29 May 1944 at Arms Park: A British Empire XI (152-9) beat Glamorgan (109) by 43 runs

10 June 1944 at Bristol: Glamorgan (193-6) drew with the West of England (135-8)

24 June 1944 at Pontypridd: Western Command (188) beat Glamorgan (117) by 71 runs

8 July 1944 at Barry: Glamorgan (151-5) beat Learie Constantine's West Indies XI (147) by 5 wkts

15 July 1944 at Arms Park: The RAF (243-3) beat Glamorgan (152) by 91 runs

5 August 1944 at Barry: Glamorgan (248-6) beat West of England (193) by 55 runs

7 August 1944 at Newport: Glamorgan (210) beat the Army (175) by 35 runs

12 August 1944 at Arms Park: Glamorgan (136) beat the National Fire Service (99) by 37 runs

19 August 1944 at Swansea: Glamorgan (203-7) drew with The National Fire Service (130-6)

26 August 1944 at Newport: Glamorgan (248-9) beat an Anti-Aircraft XI (118) by 130 runs

16 September 1944 at Briton Ferry: Glamorgan (172-6) beat West of England (138) by 34 runs

21, 22 May 1945 at Arms Park: The RAAF (128 and 89) beat Glamorgan (112 and 49) by 56 runs
9 June 1945 at Newport: A London Counties XI (150-8) beat Glamorgan (72) by 78 runs
16 June 1945 at Briton Ferry: Glamorgan (271) beat Western Command (68) by 203 runs
30 June 1945 at Arms Park: The RAF (200) drew with Glamorgan (183-8)
14 July 1945 at Barry: Glamorgan (127) beat Learie Constantine's West Indies XI (110) by 17 runs
21 July 1945 at Swansea: Glamorgan (133-4) drew with the New Zealand Services (rain)
28 July 1945 at Pontypridd: Glamorgan (213-9) beat the National Fire Service (32) by 181 runs
6, 7 August 1945 at Swansea: Glamorgan (283 and 163-6) drew with the Army (196)
18 August 1945 at Arms Park: West of England (219-8) beat Glamorgan (126) by 93 runs

(None of the above are classified as first-class matches)

RESULTS OF ALL SUNDAY LEAGUE MATCHES 1969–1988

	DE	ES	GS	HA	KE	LA	LE	MX	NH	NT	SM	SY	SX	WA	WO	YO	W	L	A	T	Pos
1969	W	L	L	W	L	L	W	L	W	W	W	L	L	W	L	L	7	9	–	–	10th
1970	L	L	L	L	W	L	L	A	W	W	W	L	A	L	L	W	5	9	2	–	14th
1971	A	L	L	W	W	W	L	W	A	L	L	W	W	W	L	L	7	7	2	–	10th
1972	L	L	W	A	L	L	L	L	L	L	L	A	W	L	L	L	2	12	2	–	17th
1973	L	W	W	A	L	L	L	W	W	L	L	L	W	A	L	L	5	9	2	–	13th
1974	L	W	L	L	L	L	L	L	W	W	L	L	A	L	W	W	5	10	1	–	14th
1975	L	L	W	L	L	L	W	L	W	L	T	W	L	L	L	L	4	11	–	1	17th
1976	L	L	W	W	L	L	W	L	W	L	W	L	L	L	L	L	5	11	–	–	16th
1977	L	L	W	L	A	W	L	W	W	W	L	L	A	W	L	W	7	7	2	–	8th
1978	L	A	W	L	W	L	L	W	L	L	L	L	W	W	A	W	6	8	2	–	10th
1979	L	W	L	L	L	W	L	L	W	L	W	L	W	W	L	L	6	10	–	–	12th
1980	L	W	L	A	L	W	L	L	L	W	L	A	L	L	L	W	4	10	2	–	17th
1981	L	L	W	L	A	L	W	W	W	L	L	A	L	W	L	W	6	8	2	–	10th
1982	W	L	A	L	L	L	A	W	W	L	L	W	L	W	W	A	6	7	3	–	10th
1983	W	L	L	L	L	W	L	A	L	W	L	W	L	A	W	W	6	8	2	–	10th
1984	W	L	W	L	W	L	L	A	W	W	L	L	L	L	A	W	6	8	2	–	9th
1985	A	L	L	A	L	T	L	W	A	L	W	L	L	A	W	W	4	7	4	1	14th
1986	W	L	W	L	L	W	W	L	W	A	L	L	L	W	L	L	6	9	1	–	12th
1987	L	L	L	W	L	W	A	L	W	L	W	A	L	L	L	W	5	9	2	–	14th
1988	W	W	L	L	L	A	L	A	W	W	W	W	T	W	L	W	8	5	2	1	6th

RESULTS IN THE BENSON AND HEDGES CUP 1972–1988

1972 Beat MC (South), SM, HA, lost to GS; *Quarter-Final*: lost to WA by 5 wkts

1973 Beat HA, MC (South), GS, lost to SM; *Quarter-Final*: lost to LA by 159 runs

1974 Beat MC (South), lost to GS, SM, HA

1975 Beat GS, lost to SM, HA, SY

1976 Beat HA, LA, lost to WA, DE

1977 Beat WA, MC (West), WO, lost to DE; *Quarter-Final*: lost to HA by 6 wkts

1978 Beat WO, CU, HA, lost to SM; *Quarter-Final*: lost to WA by 46 runs

1979 Beat GL, WD, lost to DE, game *v* MC (South), abandoned; *Quarter-Final*: lost to DE by 6 wkts

1980 Beat GL, MC, lost to ES, SX

1981 Beat ES, lost to SM, KE, game *v* CU abandoned

1982 Beat CU, lost to GS, SM, MX

1983 Beat CU, lost to KE, games *v* SY and MX abandoned

1984 Beat MX, lost to SM, SX, KE

1985 Beat MC, SM, lost to HA, KE

1986 Lost to GS, SM, ES, SX

1987 Beat SX, lost to SY, MC, KE

1988 Beat SM, CS, GS, lost to HA; *Quarter-Final*: beat NT by 6 wkts; *Semi-Final*: lost to DE by 14 runs

RESULTS OF GILLETTE CUP/
NATWEST TROPHY MATCHES,
1963–1988

1963 Beat Somerset, lost to Worcestershire
1964 Beat Worcestershire and Essex, lost to Lancashire in the Quarter-Final
1965 Lost to Surrey
1966 Beat Northamptonshire, lost to Warwickshire
1967 Lost to Hampshire
1968 Lost to Northamptonshire
1969 Beat Northamptonshire and Hertfordshire, lost to Derbyshire in the Quarter-Final
1970 Beat Cornwall, lost to Surrey
1971 Beat Staffordshire, lost to Essex
1972 Beat Northamptonshire and Buckinghamshire, lost to Warwickshire in the Quarter-Final
1973 Lost to Gloucestershire
1974 Lost to Lincolnshire
1975 Lost to Hampshire
1976 Lost to Warwickshire
1977 Beat Worcestershire, Surrey and Leicestershire, lost to Middlesex in the Final
1978 Lost to Somerset
1979 Lost to Kent
1980 Lost to Sussex
1981 Beat Oxfordshire, lost to Hampshire
1982 Lost to Warwickshire
1983 Beat Norfolk, lost to Hampshire
1984 Lost to Nottinghamshire
1985 Beat Scotland and Sussex, lost to Worcestershire in the Quarter-Final
1986 Beat Staffordshire, lost to Sussex
1987 Beat Cheshire, lost to Yorkshire
1988 Beat Scotland and Lancashire, lost to Surrey in the Quarter-Final

GROUNDS AND GROUND RECORDS

Glamorgan have staged first-class and minor county matches at the following 13 venues:

1. The Welsh county played at the *Arms Park, Cardiff* from 1889 until 1966, when the ground was redeveloped as the Welsh National Rugby Stadium. The ground is situated in the centre of the city on the east bank of the River Taff, and takes its name from a former coaching inn called the Cardiff Arms Hotel—the 'park' being the land behind the hotel. The area was owned by the Marquess of Bute, who allowed people to use the Park for recreational pursuits. The first record of cricket being played there dates back to August 1848, and the ground was also used by Llewelyn's Glamorganshire XI and the SWCC in the years before the formation of the County Club.

2. The *St Helen's* ground in Swansea lies a mile and a half to the west of the city centre, on the foreshore of Swansea Bay. Its name is derived from a convent belonging to an order of Augustinian Nuns which stood there in the medieval period. The whole area was purchased by Swansea Cricket and Football Club in 1873, and turned into a sports ground. Glamorgan first played at St Helen's against the MCC in 1890, though there are records of cricket being played in Swansea dating back to 1780. The ground was purchased by Swansea City Corporation in 1939, who lease it to Glamorgan for their West area fixtures.

3. Glamorgan first played at *The Gnoll*, Neath, in 1908 against Carmarthenshire. The ground lies half a mile to the north of the town, in an area which formerly was part of the grounds of Gnoll House, the home of a wealthy family of industrialists, who turned it into a sporting complex in the 1870s. The initial first-class game at The Gnoll was the match with Essex in 1934.

4. *Ynysangharad Park, Pontypridd* entered the first-class calendar in 1926. It forms part of a parkland area to the east of the town which was laid out in 1923 as a memorial to the area's servicemen who were killed in the First World War. The last first-class game staged at Pontypridd was in 1972, though a Sunday League fixture took place there in Centenary Year.

5. *Cowbridge* is a small market town and dormitory suburb some 12 miles to the west of Cardiff, and its cricket ground staged four games between 1931 and 1932 as the County sought new areas of support.

6. *Stradey Park* is situated about a mile to the west of the centre of Llanelli, where a cricket club has been in existence since 1837. The Park formed part of the grounds of Stradey Castle, the home of the Mansel Lewis family, and has been used by Llanelli CC on a regular basis since 1874. Glamorgan played County Championship matches at the ground between 1933 and 1965, though one-day matches have been staged there in 1987 and 1988.

7. Glamorgan first played at *Rodney Parade, Newport* in 1935 after the Club's affiliation with Monmouthshire. The ground belongs to Newport Athletic Club and lies in the centre of the town, on the east bank of the River Usk. The final first-class game at Newport was against Warwickshire in 1965, though the County revisited the ground in Centenary Year for a Sunday League game.

8. The *Eugene Cross Park* ground in Ebbw Vale staged many of Monmouthshire's games in the Minor County Championship in the 1920s and 1930s, as well as Glamorgan's second eleven matches in the same competition before the Second World War. The ground is owned by the town's Welfare Association and named after Sir Eugene Cross, its former Chairman. It staged County Championship fixtures between 1946 and 1968, and apart from 1983, has been used for an annual Sunday League game. The ground lies three-quarters of a mile from the town centre, and with an altitude of 878 feet, is amongst the highest county ground in the country.

9. The Steel Company of Wales ground at *Margam* lies adjacent to their steelworks at Port

Talbot, close to junction 38 of the M4. A cricket club was formed by the steel company in the 1920s, and has used the Margam ground since 1947. It was allocated the friendly with the Gentlemen of Ireland in 1953, and staged a number of fixtures between 1961 and 1963.

10. *Colwyn Bay* CC have used the ground, near the seafront at Rhos-on-Sea, since its formation in 1924. It was also used by Wales and Denbighshire for matches in the 1920s and 1930s, and staged Glamorgan fixtures between 1966 and 1974. It was also allocated the West Indian tourists fixture in 1984 with the League Cricket Conference.

11. *Sophia Gardens, Cardiff* became Glamorgan's new home in the capital in 1967 following the move from the Arms Park. It lies in another area of parkland, under a mile from the city centre, on the west bank of the Taff. The area was formerly owned by the Bute Estate, and takes is name from the second Marquess's wife, Sophia who laid out the gardens in the 1850s for the inhabitants of Cardiff. The Bute Estate gave all of their land in the city to Cardiff Corporation in 1947, and since 1964 the sports ground has been leased by Cardiff Athletic Club.

12. Glamorgan played one game in 1971 at the *Llandarcy* ground owned by the BP Oil Refinery Ltd, some two miles to the south-west of Neath. It has staged second team fixtures since 1965, and is the home ground of Glamorgan Colts, who play in the SWCA.

13. The most recent addition to Glamorgan's list of first-class venues is *Abergavenny*. The Pen-y-Pound ground lies to the north of the delightful market town, and has staged cricket since 1896, having been formerly owned by the Marquess of Abergavenney, who was the President of Kent CCC in 1878. Glamorgan first visited the ground for a Sunday League game in 1981, and since 1983 it has staged an annual three-day game.

Glamorgan have also used six other venues for non first-class and one-day matches:

(a) Barry Athletic Club's ground for wartime fixtures between 1943 and 1945, plus the two-day game in 1950 with the RAF.
(b) Briton Ferry Town CC's ground for two wartime friendlies in 1944 and 1945, and the Monmouthshire game in 1920.
(c) The Maindy Barracks ground in Cardiff for the friendly with the RAF in 1949.
(d) Llandudno CC's ground for a Sunday League match with Leicestershire in 1969.
(e) The University College of Wales' Vicarage Field ground in Aberystwyth for the Sunday League fixture against Essex in 1977.
(f) The Hoover Sports ground at Merthyr Tydfil for the Sunday League game against Kent in 1988.

PLAYING RECORD AT EACH GROUND

[CC = County Championship matches; F = Other First-Class Friendlies; MC = Minor County games (1889–1920); LO = Limited-Overs fixtures (JPL/RAL/B & H/GC/NWT)].

Ground		P	W	L	D	Aban
Arms Park, Cardiff	CC	208	52	68	87	1
	F	36	8	9	19	—
	MC	103	55	25	21	2
	LO	1	1	—	—	—
St Helen's, Swansea	CC	296	68	99	127	2
	F	64	8	20	35	—
	MC	42	30	7	5	—
	LO	87	41	43	—	3

Ground	Type					
The Gnoll, Neath	CC	37	12	10	15	—
	F	1	—	—	1	—
	MC	5	5	—	—	—
	LO	6	2	4	—	—
Ynysangharad Park, Pontypridd	CC	34	8	9	16	1
	F	5	3	2	8	
	LO	3	1	1	—	1
Cowbridge	CC	4	3	—	1	—
Stradey Park, Llanelli	CC	23	10	3	10	—
	LO	1				
Newport	CC	25	7	9	9	—
	F	2	2	—	—	—
	LO	2	2	—	—	—
Ebbw Vale	CC	24	9	3	12	—
	LO	19	9	9	—	1
Margam	CC	3	1	1	1	—
	F	2	—	—	2	—
Colwyn Bay	CC	5	1	—	4	—
	F	2	1	—	1	—
	LO	2	—	2	—	—
Sophia Gardens, Cardiff	CC	121	21	36	63	1
	F	6	—	2	4	—
	LO	87	27	49	—	11
Llandudno	LO	1	1	—	—	—
BP Llandarcy	F	1	1	—	—	—
Aberystwyth	LO	1	—	1	—	—
Abergavenny	CC	4	—	2	2	—
	LO	2	1	1	—	—
Merthyr Tydfil	LO	1				

FIRST-CLASS RECORDS AT EACH GROUND

Highest and Lowest Totals – For and Against

Ground						
Arms Park, Cardiff	587-8d	v Derbyshire	1951	541	by Gloucestershire	1931
	26	v Lancashire	1958	40	by Derbyshire	1946
St Helen's, Swansea	547-6d	v Northamptonshire	1933	544-4d	by West Indies	1976
	36	v Hampshire	1922	40	by Somerset	1968
Newport	577-4	v Gloucestershire	1939	505-5d	by Gloucestershire	1939
	69	v Yorkshire	1949	69	by Sir J. Cahn's XI	1938
Pontypridd	421	v Warwickshire	1937	398	by Nottinghamshire	1929
	68	v Leicestershire	1929	53	by Somerset	1946
Neath	409-3d	v Australians	1985	347-4d	by Warwickshire	1959
	43	v Essex	1935	57	by Surrey	1937
Llanelli	434-6d	v Worcestershire	1933	298	by Sussex	1951
	96	v Lancashire	1949	71	by Worcestershire	1938
Cowbridge	338	v Leicestershire	1932	173-5d	by Essex	1931
	89	v Essex	1931	40	by Somerset	1932
Ebbw Vale	322	v Essex	1949	354-9d	by Essex	1954
	64	v Essex	1962	33	by Leicestershire	1965
Margam	298	v Camb University	1963	161	by Sussex	1960
	49	v Gloucestershire	1962	67	by Gents of Ireland	1953

Sophia Gardens, Cardiff	543-8d	v Somerset	1988	529-8d	by Northampton-shire	1983
	43	v Leicestershire	1971	52	by Hampshire	1968
Colwyn Bay	326-6d	v Sussex	1974	315-6	by Sussex	1974
	183	v Derbyshire	1966	118	by Derbyshire	1966
Llandarcy	299	v Oxford University	1971	204	by Oxford University	1971
	133	v Oxford University	1971	182	by Oxford University	1971
Abergavenny	386	v Leicestershire	1987	394-6d	by Worcestershire	1983
	168	v Derbyshire	1986	143-7d	by Derbyshire	1986

Highest Individual Innings — For and Against

Arms Park, Cardiff	205	M. J. L. Turnbull v Nottinghamshire	1932
	248*	A. Sandham for Surrey	1928
St Helen's, Swansea	233	M. J. L. Turnbull v Worcestershire	1937
	257	A. H. Bakewell for Northamptonshire	1923
Newport	287*	D. E. Davies v Gloucestershire	1939
	302	W. R. Hammond for Gloucestershire	1939
Pontypridd	150*	J. S. Pressdee v Cambridge University	1965
	154	C. J. Barnett for Gloucestershire	1933
Neath	200*	Javed Miandad v Australians	1985
	219*	G. A. Hick for Worcestershire	1986
Llanelli	161	W. G. A. Parkhouse v Gloucestershire	1950
	118	P. H. Parfitt for Middlesex	1961
Cowbridge	103	D. E. Davies v Leicestershire	1932
	52	L. C. Eastman for Essex	1931
Ebbw Vale	118*	J. S. Pressdee v Essex	1949
	132	H. Horton for Hampshire	1959
Margam	90	B. Hedges v Cambridge University	1963
	54	E. J. Craig for Cambridge University	1963
Sophia Gardens, Cardiff	177	Younis Ahmed v Middlesex	1985
	252	W. Larkins for Northamptonshire	1983
Colwyn Bay	112	A. R. Lewis v Cambridge University	1968
	121*	M. G. Griffith for Sussex	1974
Llandarcy	94	R. C. Fredericks v Oxford University	1971
	62	G. Robinson for Oxford University	1971
Abergavenny	135	A. R. Butcher v Leicestershire	1987
	159	G. A. Hick for Worcestershire	1988

Best Bowling in an Innings — For and Against

Arms Park, Cardiff	9-47	D. J. Shepherd v Northamptonshire	1954
	10-40	W. Bestwick for Derbyshire	1921
St Helen's, Swansea	9-43	J. S. Pressdee v Yorkshire	1965
	9-60	H. Verity for Yorkshire	1930
Newport	7-74	J. E. McConnon v Essex	1960
	9-77	D. Shackleton for Hampshire	1953
Pontypridd	8-60	J. Mercer v South Africa	1929
	10-18	G. Geary for Leicestershire	1929
Neath	8-42	B. L. Muncer v Somerset	1949
	9-39	D. J. Halfyard for Kent	1957

Llanelli	9-54	J. C. Clay v Northamptonshire	1935
	8-43	V. E. Jackson for Leicestershire	1956
Cowbridge	5-22	J. C. Clay v Northamptonshire	1931
	7-100	G. Geary for Leicestershire	1932
Ebbw Vale	9-60	O. S. Wheatley v Sussex	1968
	6-29	K. Preston for Essex	1962
Margam	7-32	J. B. Evans v Leicestershire	1961
	5-10	J. B. Mortimore for Gloucestershire	1962
Sophia Gardens, Cardiff	8-63	A. W. Allin v Sussex	1976
	9-57	P. I. Pocock for Surrey	1979
Colwyn Bay	9-49	A. E. Cordle v Leicestershire	1969
	7-47	D. C. Morgan for Derbyshire	1966
Llandarcy	4-43	D. L. Williams v Oxford University	1971
	4-45	M. S. J. Burton for Oxford University	1971
Abergavenny	3-36	G. C. Holmes v Worcestershire	1985
	3-31	D. E. Malcolm for Derbyshire	1986

Best Bowling in a Match – For and Against

Arms Park, Cardiff	14-153	J. E. McConnon v Derbyshire	1951
	14-69	A. V. Bedser for Surrey	1956
St Helen's, Swansea	17-212	J. C. Clay v Worcestershire	1937
	15-52	V. W. C. Jupp for Northamptonshire	1925
Newport	12-180	J. C. Clay v Somerset	1937
	13-99	T. W. Goddard for Gloucestershire	1937
Pontypridd	14-119	J. Mercer v South Africa	1929
	16-96	G. Geary for Leicestershire	1929
Neath	12-94	B. L. Muncer v Somerset	1949
	13-51	A. E. Moss for Middlesex	1960
Llanelli	15-86	J. C. Clay v Northamptonshire	1935
	12-94	R. N. S. Hobbs for Essex	1965
Cowbridge	9-47	J. C. Clay v Somerset	1932
	7-100	G. Geary for Leicestershire	1932
Ebbw Vale	11-115	O. S. Wheatley v Sussex	1968
	10-97	K. Preston for Essex	1962
Margam	11-51	D. J. Shepherd v Gloucestershire	1962
	7-33	C. Cook for Gloucestershire	1962
Sophia Gardens, Cardiff	13-127	R. C. Ontong v Nottinghamshire	1986
	13-102	D. L. Underwood for Kent	1979
Colwyn Bay	13-110	A. E. Cordle v Leicestershire	1969
	9-82	D. C. Morgan for Derbyshire	1966
Llandarcy	4-40	M. J. Llewellyn v Oxford University	1971
	7-99	M. S. J. Burton for Oxford University	1971
Abergavenny	5-152	R. J. Shastri v Leicestershire	1987
	3-31	D. E. Malcolm for Derbyshire	1986

RECORD ATTENDANCE AT THE MAJOR GROUNDS (ONE DAY'S PLAY)

Arms Park: 15,000 v Middlesex, 1948
St Helen's: 50,000 v Australia, 1948
Sophia Gardens: 11,500 v Somerset (JPSL), 1976

TEAM RECORDS

HIGHEST AND LOWEST TOTALS BY GLAMORGAN AGAINST ALL FIRST-CLASS COUNTIES AND MAJOR TOURING TEAMS

Opponents	Highest	Year	Lowest	Year
Derbyshire	587-8 dec *at* Arms Park	1951	49 *at* Sophia Gardens	1967
Essex	586-5 dec *at* Brentwood	1948	43 *at* Neath	1935
Gloucestershire	577-4 *at* Newport	1939	49 *at* Margam	1962
Hampshire	488-8 dec *at* Arms Park	1938	36 *at* Swansea	1922
Kent	492 *at* Tonbridge	1939	46 *at* Sophia Gardens	1979
Lancashire	425 *at* Old Trafford	1938	22 *at* Liverpool	1924
Leicestershire	469-7 dec *at* Leicester	1937	24 *at* Leicester	1971
Middlesex	475-5 dec *at* Sophia Gardens	1985	83 *at* Swansea	1965
Northants	547-6 dec *at* Swansea	1933	54 *at* Arms Park	1921
Nottinghamshire	502 *at* Arms Park	1932	47 *at* Arms Park	1922
Somerset	574-7 *at* Newport	1939	52 *at* Neath	1963
Surrey	550-6 dec *at* The Oval	1936	31 *at* The Oval	1957
Sussex	447 *at* Hove	1985	41 *at* Hove	1925
Warwickshire	524-9 dec *at* Edgbaston	1980	40 *at* Arms Park	1929
Worcestershire	506-8 dec *at* Swansea	1929	61 *at* Neath	1936
Yorkshire	349-7 *at* Middlesbrough	1976	48 *at* Arms Park	1924
Oxford Univ.	456 *at* Oxford	1985	128 *at* Oxford	1930
Cambridge Univ.	416-8 dec *at* Swansea	1975	141 *at* Cambridge	1964
Australia	409-3 dec *at* Neath	1985	99 *at* Swansea	1930
New Zealand	340 *at* Swansea	1937	69 *at* Arms Park	1958
India	317 *at* Swansea	1979	81 *at* Arms Park	1932
South Africa	301 *at* Swansea	1965	64 *at* Swansea	1955
West Indies	493 *at* Arms Park	1933	77 *at* Arms Park	1957
Pakistan	363-6 dec *at* Swansea	1962	107 *at* Swansea	1974
Sri Lanka	272 *at* Swansea	1979	168 *at* Sophia Gardens	1981

THE FOLLOWING LARGE AND LOW TOTALS WERE ALSO RECORDED BY GLAMORGAN BETWEEN 1889 AND 1920

540 *v* Devon at Exeter, 1907
538 *v* Monmouthshire at Arms Park, 1901
531-9 dec *v* Carmarthenshire at Swansea, 1910
500 *v* Carmarthenshire at Swansea, 1911
489 *v* Berkshire at Swansea, 1903
460-4 dec *v* Dorset at Blandford, 1907
452 *v* Buckinghamshire at Neath, 1911

20 *v* Wiltshire at Chippenham, 1905
27 *v* Somerset at Bath, 1890
36 *v* Worcestershire at Arms Park, 1910
42 *v* Somerset at Arms Park, 1910
44 *v* Wiltshire at Chippenham, 1903
45 *v* Surrey II at The Oval, 1902
49 *v* Monmouthshire at Arms Park, 1914

HIGHEST AND LOWEST TOTALS AGAINST GLAMORGAN BY ALL FIRST-CLASS COUNTIES AND MAJOR TOURING TEAMS

Opponents	Highest	Venue and Year	Lowest	Venue and Year
Derbyshire	439	Chesterfield, 1927	40	Arms Park, 1946
Essex	499-8 dec	Swansea, 1928	74	Leyton, 1966
Gloucestershire	653-6 dec	Bristol, 1928	55	Cheltenham, 1964
Hampshire	495	Bournemouth, 1976	52	Sophia Gardens, 1968
Kent	490	Gravesend, 1934	49	Swansea, 1949
Lancashire	564-9 dec	Old Trafford, 1938	49	Liverpool, 1924
Leicestershire	456-4	Leicester, 1975	33	Ebbw Vale, 1965
Middlesex	484	Lords, 1932	99	Swansea, 1959
Northants	529-8 dec	Sophia Gardens, 1983	59	Cowbridge, 1931
Nottinghamshire	564-6 dec	Trent Bridge, 1926	44	Ebbw Vale, 1963
Somerset	463	Taunton, 1982	40	Cowbridge 1932/Swansea 1968
Surrey	560-8 dec	The Oval, 1947	59	Arms Park, 1948
Sussex	540-6 dec	Eastbourne, 1938	35	Horsham, 1946
Warwickshire	543-8 dec	Edgbaston, 1927	61	Neath, 1959
Worcestershire	506-5 dec	Worcester, 1934	63	Swansea, 1921
Yorkshire	579-6 dec	Huddersfield, 1925	83	Sheffield, 1946
Oxford Univ.	494	Oxford, 1928	65	Oxford, 1977
Cambridge Univ.	513-5 dec	Cowbridge, 1934	104	Margam, 1963
Australia	461-8	Swansea, 1921	101	Swansea, 1964
New Zealand	378-5 dec	Swansea, 1986	110	Swansea, 1937
India	376-6 dec	Arms Park, 1946	87	Swansea, 1932
South Africa	479-8 dec	Arms Park, 1947	83	Swansea, 1951
West Indies	544-4 dec	Swansea, 1976	96	Swansea, 1939
Pakistan	359-8 dec	Swansea, 1974	158	Arms Park, 1962/Swansea 1971
Sri Lanka	309-9 dec	Swansea, 1979	185-7	Sophia Gardens, 1981

THE FOLLOWING LARGE AND LOW TOTALS WERE ALSO RECORDED AGAINST GLAMORGAN BETWEEN 1889 AND 1920

Highest

446-5 dec *by* MCC and Ground at Lord's, 1896
435 *by* Monmouthshire at Arms Park, 1908
417-8 dec *by* Durham at Sunderland, 1914
380-7 dec *by* Cheshire at Aigburgh, 1920
363 *by* Staffordshire at Stoke, 1911
355 *by* Devon at Exeter, 1892
352-9 dec *by* Berkshire at Reading, 1905
351-9 dec *by* Surrey II at The Oval, 1920
351 *by* Gloucestershire at Bristol, 1891

Lowest

32 *by* Carmarthenshire at Llanelli, 1910
38 *by* Monmouthshire at Newport, 1901
41 *by* Wiltshire at Chippenham, 1908
45 *by* Surrey II at Arms Park, 1920
48 *by* Monmouthshire at Newport, 1901
48 *by* Wiltshire at Chippenhan, 1904
53 *by* Monmouthshire at Arms Park, 1899
54 *by* Wiltshire at Arms Park, 1911

INDIVIDUAL RECORDS

HIGHEST SCORE AND BEST BOWLING IN AN INNINGS FOR GLAMORGAN AGAINST ALL FIRST-CLASS COUNTIES AND MAJOR TOURING TEAMS

Opponents	Highest score		Best bowling	
Derbyshire	170	N. V. H. Riches at Swansea, 1924	8-41	F. P. Ryan at Arms Park, 1925
Essex	215	D. E. Davies at Brentwood, 1948	9-59	J. C. Clay at Westcliff, 1937
Gloucestershire	287*	D. E. Davies at Newport, 1939	8-36	B. L. Muncer at Cheltenham, 1947
Hampshire	204*	A. Jones at Basingstoke, 1980	9-56	M. A. Nash at Basingstoke, 1975
Kent	223	A. R. Lewis at Gravesend, 1966	8-61	J. S. Pressdee at Dover, 1963
Lancashire	191*	A. H. Dyson at Arms Park, 1934	8-49	B. L. Muncer at Llanelli, 1949
Leicestershire	212*	Javed Miandad at Swansea, 1984	9-49	A. E. Cordle at Colwyn Bay, 1969
Middlesex	204*	R. C. Ontong at Swansea, 1984	8-84	D. J. Shepherd at Swansea, 1957
Northamptonshire	228*	R. C. Fredericks at Swansea, 1972	9-47	D. J. Shepherd at Arms Park, 1954
Nottinghamshire	205	M. J. L. Turnbull at Arms Park, 1932	8-36	J. E. McConnon at Trent Bridge, 1953
Somerset	216*	D. Davies at Newport, 1939	8-42	J. B. Evans at Arms Park, 1961
Surrey	280*	R. J. Duckfield at The Oval, 1936	9-97	B. L. Muncer at Arms Park, 1947
Sussex	170*	A. H. Dyson at Eastbourne, 1938	9-60	O. S. Wheatley at Ebbw Vale, 1968
Warwickshire	181	Javed Miandad at Edgbaston, 1980	8-40	D. J. Shepherd at Swansea, 1960
Worcestershire	233	M. J. L. Turnbull at Swansea, 1937	9-66	J. C. Clay at Swansea, 1937
Yorkshire	156*	A. Jones at Middlesbrough, 1976	9-43	J. S. Pressdee at Swansea, 1965
Oxford Univ.	182	B. Hedges at Oxford, 1967	7-38	S. R. Barwick at Oxford, 1984
Cambridge Univ.	150*	J. S. Pressdee at Pontypridd, 1965	7-72	J. Mercer at Cambridge, 1929
Australia	200*	Javed Miandad at Neath, 1985	7-165	J. E. McConnon at Swansea, 1953
New Zealand	169	A. R. Lewis at Arms Park, 1965	6-41	E. C. Jones at Arms Park, 1937
India	113	J. S. Pressdee at Arms Park, 1959	8-43	J. C. Clay at Swansea, 1936
South Africa	146*	A. R. Lewis at Swansea, 1965	8-45	D. J. Shepherd at Swansea, 1960

325

STATISTICAL SECTION

West Indies	161*	A. Jones at Swansea, 1966	7-21 A. D. G. Matthews at Swansea, 1939
Pakistan	144	B. Hedges at Swansea, 1962	5-29 A. E. Cordle at Swansea, 1967
Sri Lanka	83	N. G. Featherstone at Sophia Gardens, 1981	6-62 R. C. Ontong at Sophia Gardens, 1981

HIGHEST SCORE AND BEST BOWLING IN AN INNINGS AGAINST GLAMORGAN FOR ALL FIRST-CLASS COUNTIES AND MAJOR TOURING TEAMS

Opponents	Highest score		Best bowling
Derbyshire	213*	P. N. Kirsten at Derby, 1980	10-40 W. Bestwick at Arms Park, 1921
Essex	222	L. G. Crawley at Swansea, 1928	8-38 K. Farnes at Clacton, 1938
Gloucestershire	302*	W. R. Hammond at Bristol, 1934	8-25 W. R. Hammond at Clifton, 1930
Hampshire	227	J. Arnold at Arms Park, 1932	9-77 D. Shackleton at Newport, 1953
Kent	187	W. H. Ashdown at Arms Park, 1936	9-39 D. J. Halfyard at Neath, 1957
Lancashire	239	G. E. Tyldesley at Arms Park, 1934	8-41 C. Parkin at Blackpool, 1923
Leicestershire	210*	M. R. Hallam at Leicester, 1959	10-18 G. Geary at Pontypridd, 1929
Middlesex	200	R. A. Gale at Newport, 1962	9-61 W. W. Daniel at Swansea, 1982
Northamptonshire	257	A. H. Bakewell at Swansea, 1933	8-18 V. W. C. Jupp at Swansea, 1925
Nottingham	242	W. W. Keeton at Trent Bridge, 1932	8-26 F. Barratt at Arms Park, 1922
Somerset	190	G. Atkinson at Bath, 1960	9-51 J. C. White at Bath, 1932
Surrey	248*	A. Sandham at Arms Park, 1928	9-57 P. I. Pocock at Sophia Gardens, 1974
Sussex	250*	J. Langridge at Hove, 1933	8-30 M. W. Tate at Horsham, 1923
Warwickshire	243*	A. I. Kallicharran at Edgbaston, 1983	9-93 W. E. Hollies at Edgbaston, 1939
Worcestershire	219*	G. A. Hick at Neath, 1986	9-40 R. T. D. Perks at Stourbridge, 1939
Yorkshire	197	L. Hutton at Swansea, 1947	9-50 H. Verity at Swansea, 1930
Oxford Univ.	133	D. B. Pithey at Oxford, 1961	6-42 C. K. Hill-Wood at Oxford, 1930
Cambridge Univ.	200*	E. T. Killick at Cambridge, 1929	8-68 K. I. Hodgson at Cambridge, 1982
Australia	228*	W. Woodfull at Swansea, 1934	7-37 W. J. O'Reilly at Swansea, 1934
New Zealand	169*	W. M. Wallace at Swansea, 1949	6-21 G. F. Cresswell at Swansea, 1949
India	112	G. R. Viswanath at Swansea, 1979	8-33 G. S. Ramchand at Arms Park, 1952

326

South Africa	153	E. A. B. Rowan at Arms Park, 1935	7–36	C. L. Vincent at Pontypridd, 1929
West Indies	201★	C. H. Lloyd at Swansea, 1969/1976	8–73	E. T. Willett at Swansea, 1973
Pakistan	163★	Mudassar Nazar at Swansea, 1982	7–37	Intikhab Alam at Swansea, 1971
Sri Lanka	76★	D. S. de Silva at Swansea, 1979	5–34	L. W. Kaluperuma at Sophia Gardens, 1981

HIGHEST AND LOWEST TOTALS BY GLAMORGAN IN LIMITED-OVERS CRICKET

40-overs competition	277-6	*v* Derbyshire at Ebbw Vale, 1984
	42	*v* Derbyshire at Swansea, 1979
55-overs competition	245-7	*v* Hampshire at Swansea, 1976
	68	*v* Lancashire at Old Trafford, 1973
60-overs competition	283-3	*v* Warwickshire at Edgbaston, 1976
	76	*v* Northamptonshire at Northampton, 1968

HIGHEST AND LOWEST TOTALS AGAINST GLAMORGAN IN LIMITED-OVERS CRICKET

40-overs competition	310-5	*by* Essex at Southend, 1983
	85	*by* Warwickshire at Swansea, 1972
55-overs competition	294-9	*by* Hampshire at Southampton, 1985
	59	*by* Combined Universities at Cambridge, 1983
60-overs competition	371-4	*by* Hampshire at Southampton, 1975
	67	*by* Northamptonshire at Northampton, 1966

HUNDREDS FOR GLAMORGAN IN LIMITED-OVERS CRICKET

40-overs competition:	110	*by* A. Jones *v* Gloucestershire at Sophia Gardens, 1978
	101★	*by* D. A. Francis *v* Warwickshire at Edgbaston, 1980
	107	*by* Javed Miandad *v* Leicestershire at Leicester, 1981
	100	*by* R. C. Ontong *v* Northamptonshire at Abergavenny, 1982
	130★	*by* J. A. Hopkins *v* Somerset at Bath, 1983
	103★	*by* Younis Ahmed *v* Derbyshire at Ebbw Vale, 1984
	100	*by* H. Morris *v* Derbyshire at Ebbw Vale, 1986
55-overs competition:	103★	*by* M. A. Nash *v* Hampshire at Swansea, 1976
	103★	*by* J. A. Hopkins *v* Minor Counties at Swansea, 1980
	115	*by* H. Morris *v* Kent at Sophia Gardens, 1987
	115	*by* M. P. Maynard *v* Combined Universities at Sophia Gardens, 1988
	108	*by* M. P. Maynard *v* Nottinghamshire at Sophia Gardens, 1988
60-overs competition:	103★	*by* B. Hedges *v* Somerset at Arms Park, 1963
	124★	*by* A. Jones *v* Warwickshire at Edgbaston, 1976

327

CARRYING BAT THROUGHOUT A COMPLETED INNINGS IN FIRST-CLASS MATCHES

Score	Innings total	Batsman	Opponents and venue	Year
177*	347	N. V. H. Riches	Leicestershire at Leicester	1921
85*	161	N. V. H. Riches	Yorkshire at Leeds	1922
22*	68	T. R. Morgan	Yorkshire at Arms Park	1922
14*	47	T. R. Morgan	Nottinghamshire at Arms Park	1922
13*	42	T. R. Morgan	Lancashire at Swansea	1922
87*	188	T. R. Morgan	Leicestershire at Leicester	1923
100*	161	D. Davies	Worcestershire at Worcester	1923
72*	164	J. T. Bell	Essex at Arms Park	1926
200*	390	W. E. Bates	Worcestershire at Kidderminster	1927
73*	160	W. E. Bates	Northamptonshire at Swansea	1928
775*	156	A. H. Dyson	Northamptonshire at Kettering	1931
109*	204	A. H. Dyson	Middlesex at Arms Park	1932
191*	352	A. H. Dyson	Lancashire at Arms Park	1934
75*	142	D. E. Davies	South Africa at Arms Park	1935
155*	340	D. E. Davies	Somerset at Weston-super-Mare	1935
110*	210	A. H. Dyson	Sir J. Cahn's XI at Newport	1938
99*	196	A. H. Dyson	Gloucestershire at Newport	1939
60*	152	W. G. A. Parkhouse	Lancashire at Swansea	1954
166*	364	A. Jones	Nottinghamshire at Trent Bridge	1967
109*	240	J. A. Hopkins	Derbyshire at Swansea	1983
113*	262	A. R. Butcher	Derbyshire at Sophia Gardens	1987

A HUNDRED IN EACH INNINGS IN FIRST-CLASS MATCHES

Scores	Batsman	Opponents	Year
105 and 111	W. E. Bates	Essex at Leyton	1927
121 and 148	W. G. A. Parkhouse	Somerset at Arms Park	1950
187* and 105*	A. Jones	Somerset at Glastonbury	1963
132 and 156*	A. Jones	Yorkshire at Middlesbrough	1976
147 and 100	A. Jones	Hampshire at Swansea	1978
137* and 106	Javed Miandad	Somerset at Swansea	1981
115 and 105	H. Morris	Warwickshire at Edgbaston	1987
100* and 107	G. C. Holmes	Somerset at Taunton	1988

A HUNDRED IN FIRST INNINGS FOR GLAMORGAN IN FIRST-CLASS MATCHES

138* F. B. Pinch v Worcestershire at Swansea, 1921 (on first-class debut)

145* R. C. Fredericks v Nottinghamshire at Trent Bridge, 1971

140* Javed Miandad v Essex at Swansea, 1980

158* Younis Ahmed v Oxford University at The Parks, 1984

102 M. P. Maynard v Yorkshire at Swansea, 1985 (on first-class debut)

328

HIGHEST AGGREGATE OF RUNS FOR GLAMORGAN IN A SEASON IN FIRST-CLASS MATCHES

Aggregate	Average	Batsman	Year
2083	69.43	Javed Miandad	1981
2071	49.31	W. G. A. Parkhouse	1959
2052	41.87	A. R. Lewis	1966
2026	32.15	B. Hedges	1961
1954	39.87	D. E. Davies	1937
1911	34.74	J. S. Pressdee	1962
1898	35.14	J. S. Pressdee	1961
1885	40.97	A. H. Dyson	1938
1865	34.53	A. Jones	1966
1857	34.38	A. Jones	1963
1851	35.59	B. Hedges	1962
1814	37.02	A. Jones	1967
1811	36.95	A. L. Jones	1984
1805	38.40	A. Jones	1965

HIGHEST BATTING AVERAGE IN A SEASON IN FIRST-CLASS MATCHES

Average	Batsman and aggregate	Year
69.43	Javed Miandad (2,083 runs)	1981
66.60	Majid Khan (1,332 runs)	1972
64.00	Javed Miandad (832 runs)	1984
59.77	N. V. H. Riches (538 runs)	1928
54.07	Javed Miandad (1,460 runs)	1980

MOST HUNDREDS IN A SEASON IN FIRST-CLASS MATCHES

Hundreds	Batsman	Year
8	Javed Miandad	1981
7	W. G. A. Parkhouse	1950
6	W. G. A. Parkhouse	1959
6	Majid Khan	1972

THREE CENTURIES IN SUCCESSIVE INNINGS IN FIRST-CLASS MATCHES

Batsman	Year	Scores and opponents
D. Davies	1928	126* v Sussex at Swansea; 103 v Northamptonshire at Northampton; 165* v Sussex at Eastbourne
W. G. A. Parkhouse	1950	121 and 148 v Somerset at Arms Park; 127 v Combined Services at Arms Park
Javed Miandad	1981	105 v Warwickshire at Sophia Gardens; 137* and 106 v Somerset at Swansea

1,000 FIRST-CLASS RUNS FOR GLAMORGAN IN A SEASON

Batsman	No of times	Years
W. E. Bates	(7)	1923, 1926, 1927, 1928, 1929, 1930, 1931
J. T. Bell	(3)	1926, 1928, 1929
T. L. Brierley	(1)	1938
A. R. Butcher	(2)	1987, 1988
P. B. Clift	(3)	1949, 1951, 1952
D. Davies	(7)	1928, 1930, 1931, 1932, 1933, 1936, 1938
D. E. Davies	(16)	1932, 1933, 1934, 1935, 1936, 1937, 1938, 1939, 1946, 1947, 1948, 1949, 1950, 1951, 1952, 1953
B. A. Davis	(2)	1969, 1970
R. C. Davis	(1)	1975
L. N. Devereux	(1)	1957
R. J. Duckfield	(3)	1933, 1934, 1937
A. H. Dyson	(10)	1931, 1932, 1933, 1934, 1935, 1937, 1938, 1939, 1946, 1947
N. G. Featherstone	(2)	1980, 1981
R. C. Fredericks	(2)	1971, 1972
D. A. Francis	(1)	1982
A. Harris	(1)	1962
G. C. Holmes	(3)	1984, 1985, 1986
B. Hedges	(9)	1954, 1956, 1957, 1958, 1959, 1960, 1961, 1962, 1963
J. A. Hopkins	(7)	1977, 1978, 1979, 1980, 1981, 1983, 1984
A. Jones	(23)	1961, 1962, 1963, 1964, 1965, 1966, 1967, 1968, 1969, 1970, 1971, 1972, 1973, 1974, 1975, 1976, 1977, 1978, 1979, 1980, 1981, 1982, 1983
A. L. Jones	(2)	1983, 1984
W. E. Jones	(7)	1946, 1948, 1950, 1951, 1953, 1954, 1955
Majid Khan	(5)	1968, 1969, 1972, 1973, 1975
A. R. Lewis	(9)	1963, 1964, 1965, 1966, 1967, 1968, 1969, 1970, 1971
M. P. Maynard	(3)	1986, 1987, 1988
H. Morris	(2)	1986, 1987
Javed Miandad	(3)	1980, 1981, 1985
B. L. Muncer	(1)	1952
R. C. Ontong	(5)	1979, 1982, 1983, 1984, 1985
W. G. A. Parkhouse	(15)	1948, 1949, 1950, 1951, 1952, 1953, 1954, 1955, 1956, 1957, 1958, 1959, 1960, 1961, 1962
J. S. Pressdee	(6)	1959, 1961, 1962, 1963, 1964, 1965
A. Rees	(4)	1962, 1963, 1964, 1967
N. V. H. Riches	(1)	1921
C. J. C. Rowe	(1)	1982
C. C. Smart	(5)	1934, 1935, 1936, 1937, 1939
P. D. Swart	(1)	1978
M. J. Turnbull	(8)	1930, 1931, 1932, 1933, 1934, 1935, 1937, 1939
P. M. Walker	(11)	1958, 1959, 1961, 1962, 1964, 1965, 1966, 1967, 1968, 1970, 1971
A. J. Watkins	(13)	1947, 1948, 1949, 1950, 1951, 1952, 1953, 1954, 1955, 1957, 1958, 1959, 1960
W. Wooller	(4)	1947, 1951, 1953, 1954
Younis Ahmed	(2)	1984, 1985

EARLIEST DATES FOR REACHING A 1,000 RUNS IN A SEASON

17 June	W. G. A. Parkhouse	1950 and 1959
23 June	W. E. Jones	1948

EARLIEST DATE FOR REACHING 2,000 RUNS IN A SEASON

Date	Batsman	Year
25 August	A. R. Lewis	1966

INDIVIDUAL BATTING RECORDS

SCORES OF OVER 200 FOR GLAMORGAN IN FIRST-CLASS CRICKET

Score	Player	Opponents and venue	Year
287★	D. E. Davies	Gloucestershire at Newport	1939
280★	R. J. Duckfield	Surrey at The Oval	1936
233	M. J. L. Turnbull	Worcestershire at Swansea	1937
230	J. A. Hopkins	Worcestershire at Worcester	1977
228★	R. C. Fredericks	Northamptonshire at Swansea	1972
225	J. T. Bell	Worcestershire at Dudley	1926
223	A. R. Lewis	Kent at Gravesend	1966
216	D. Davies	Somerset at Newport	1939
215	D. E. Davies	Essex at Brentwood	1948
212★	Javed Miandad	Leicestershire at Swansea	1984
212★	W. E. Jones	Essex at Brentwood	1948
208	A. H. Dyson	Surrey at The Oval	1932
207	W. E. Jones	Kent at Gravesend	1948
205	M. J. L. Turnbull	Nottinghamshire at Arms Park	1932
204★	R. C. Ontong	Middlesex at Swansea	1984
204	Majid Khan	Surrey at The Oval	1972
204★	A. Jones	Hampshire at Basingstoke	1980
201	W. G. A. Parkhouse	Kent at Swansea	1956
200★	W. E. Bates	Worcestershire at Kidderminster	1927
200★	M. J. L. Turnbull	Northamptonshire at Swansea	1933
200★	Javed Miandad	Somerset at Taunton	1981
200★	Javed Miandad	Essex at Colchester (Castle Park)	1981
200★	Javed Miandad	Australia at Neath	1985

Three double centuries were scored in the period 1889–1920:

254	H. E. Morgan	Monmouthshire at Arms Park	1901
217★	N. V. H Riches	Dorset at Blandford	1907
207	W. J. Bancroft	Berkshire at Swansea	1903

A HUNDRED BEFORE LUNCH IN FIRST-CLASS MATCHES

Batsman	Pre-lunch	Final score	Opponents and venue	Year
A. H. Dyson	104	104	Kent at Swansea	1937
J. S. Pressdee	107★	107★	Kent at Dartford .	1959
J. S. Pressdee	102★	115	Sussex at Arms Park	1961
Majid Khan	147	147	West Indies at Swansea	1969
Majid Khan	114★	156	Worcestershire at Sophia Gardens	1969
Majid Khan	113	113	Warwickshire at Edgbaston	1972
M. A. Nash	115★	130	Surrey at The Oval	1976
Javed Miandad	131★	181	Warwickshire at Edgbaston	1980
M. P. Maynard	106★	160	Somerset at Weston-super-Mare	1987
M. P. Maynard	108★	108★	Worcestershire at Abergavenny	1988

FAST SCORING IN FIRST-CLASS MATCHES

Fastest Fifty:	M. P. Maynard, 50 in 14 mins *v* Yorkshire at Sophia Gardens, 1987
Fastest Hundred:	W. G. A. Parkhouse, 100★ in 70 mins *v* Northamptonshire at Northampton, 1961
	Majid Khan, 100★ in 70 mins *v* Warwickshire at Edgbaston, 1972
Fastest Double Hundred:	M. J. L. Turnbull, 200★ in 188 mins *v* Worcestershire at Swansea, 1937

MOST RUNS OFF ONE OVER

Runs (over)	Batsman and bowler	Opponents and venue	Year
32 (664664)	C. C. Smart off G. Hill	Hampshire at Arms Park	1935
31 (62460661)	J. Mercer off R. Howorth	Worcestershire at Arms Park	1939
30 (464466)	M. P. Maynard off K. Sharp	Yorkshire at Sophia Gardens	1987
28 (644446)	J. E. McConnon off N. Thomson	Sussex at Arms Park	1955
28 (066466)	Javed Miandad off Asif Din	Warwickshire at Sophia Gardens	1981
26 (04604660)	D. E. Davies off G. V. Gunn	Nottinghamshire at Swansea	1939
26 (666242)	D. J. Shepherd off E. Smith	Derbyshire at Arms Park	1961

INDIVIDUAL BOWLING RECORDS

HAT-TRICKS FOR GLAMORGAN IN FIRST-CLASS MATCHES

Bowler	Opponents and venue	Year
T. Arnott	Somerset at Arms Park	1926
J. Mercer	Surrey at The Oval	1932
D. E. Davies	Leicestershire at Leicester	1937
J. E. McConnon	South Africa at Swansea	1951
I. J. Jones	Yorkshire at Harrogate	1962
D. J. Shepherd	Northamptonshire at Swansea	1964
O. S. Wheatley	Somerset at Taunton	1968
Majid Khan	Oxford University at Oxford	1969

A. J. Watkins took four wickets with five successive balls against Derbyshire at Chesterfield, 1954.

HAT-TRICKS FOR GLAMORGAN IN LIMITED-OVERS GAMES

Bowler	Opponents and venue	Year (Competition)
M. A. Nash	Worcestershire at Worcester	1975 (JPL)
A. E. Cordle	Hampshire at Portsmouth	1979 (JPL)
E. A. Moseley	Kent at Sophia Gardens	1981 (BRH)
G. C. Holmes	Nottinghamshire at Ebbw Vale	1987 (RAL)

BEST BOWLING FIGURES IN FIRST-CLASS CRICKET FOR GLAMORGAN

In an innings:

Analysis	Bowler	Opponents and venue	Year
10-51	J. Mercer	Worcestershire at Worcester	1936
9-43	J. S. Pressdee	Yorkshire at Swansea	1965
9-47	D. J. Shepherd	Northamptonshire at Arms Park	1954
9-48	D. J. Shepherd	Yorkshire at Swansea	1965
9-49	A. E. Cordle	Leicestershire at Colwyn Bay	1969
9-54	J. C. Clay	Northamptonshire at Llanelli	1935
9-56	M. A. Nash	Hampshire at Basingstoke	1975
9-59	J. C. Clay	Essex at Westcliff	1937
9-60	O. S. Wheatley	Sussex at Ebbw Vale	1968
9-62	B. L. Muncer	Essex at Brentwood	1948
9-66	J. C. Clay	Worcestershire at Swansea	1937
9-93	A. Nash	Sussex at Swansea	1922
9-97	B. L. Muncer	Surrey at Arms Park	1947

In a match:

Analysis	Bowler	Opponents and venue	Year
17-212	J. C. Clay	Worcestershire at Swansea	1937
15-86	J. C. Clay	Northamptonshire at Llanelli	1935
15-116	A. Nash	Worcestershire at Swansea	1921
15-161	B. L. Muncer	Essex at Brentwood	1948
15-201	B. L. Muncer	Sussex at Swansea	1948

BEST BOWLING FIGURES IN LIMITED-OVERS CRICKET FOR GLAMORGAN

In 40-over games:

Analysis	Bowler	Opponents and venue	Year
6-36	G. C. Kingston	Derbyshire at Ebbw Vale	1969
6-29	M. A. Nash	Worcestershire at Worcester	1975

In 55-over games:

Analysis	Bowler	Opponents and venue	Year
5-30	D. L. Williams	Hampshire at Bournemouth	1972
5-17	A. H. Wilkins	Worcestershire at Worcester	1978
5-29	W. W. Davis	Middlesex at Sophia Gardens	1984
5-30	R. C. Ontong	Somerset at Taunton	1985

In 60-over games:

5-24	Majid Khan	Northamptonshire at Northampton	1969
5-21	P. M. Walker	Cornwall at Truro	1970
5-31	M. A. Nash	Oxfordshire at Oxford	1981
5-24	G. C. Holmes	Scotland at Edinburgh	1985
5-17	J. G. Thomas	Sussex at Sophia Gardens	1985
5-32	S. Monkhouse	Cheshire at Sophia Gardens	1987
5-13	R. J. Shastri	Scotland at Edinburgh	1988

HIGHEST NUMBER OF FIRST-CLASS WICKETS IN A SEASON FOR GLAMORGAN

Total (average)	Bowler	Year
176 (17.34)	J. C. Clay	1937
168 (14.03)	D. J. Shepherd	1956
156 (17.12)	B. L. Muncer	1948
142 (17.52)	D. J. Shepherd	1960
137 (20.35)	J. Mercer	1929
136 (16.07)	J. E. McConnon	1951
133 (17.46)	F. P. Ryan	1925
133 (21.79)	D. J. Shepherd	1961
133 (18.57)	O. S. Wheatley	1962
130 (12.40)	J. C. Clay	1946
129 (16.15)	J. Mercer	1926
127 (21.11)	F. P. Ryan	1930
127 (19.37)	J. Mercer	1936
126 (18.83)	D. J. Shepherd	1963

BEST FIRST-CLASS BOWLING AVERAGES IN A SEASON FOR GLAMORGAN

Average	Bowler and No of wickets	Year
12.95	O. S. Wheatley (82 wkts)	1968
13.16	A. D. G. Matthews (30 wkts)	1938
13.30	J. C. Clay (65 wkts)	1935
13.40	J. C. Clay (130 wkts)	1946
13.66	A. D. G. Matthews (45 wkts)	1937

BOWLERS TO HAVE TAKEN OVER 100 FIRST-CLASS WICKETS IN A SEASON FOR GLAMORGAN

Bowler	No of times	Years
J. C. Clay	(3)	1934, 1937, 1946
D. E. Davies	(2)	1935, 1937
J. Mercer	(6)	1926, 1929, 1930, 1932, 1935, 1936
B. L. Muncer	(4)	1947, 1948, 1949, 1952
J. E. McConnon	(3)	1951, 1954, 1959
J. S. Pressdee	(1)	1963
F. P. Ryan	(5)	1923, 1924, 1925, 1926, 1930
D. J. Shepherd	(12)	1952, 1956, 1957, 1959, 1960, 1961, 1962, 1963, 1965, 1966, 1967, 1970.

A. J. Watkins	(1)	1955
O. S. Wheatley	(3)	1961, 1962, 1966
W. Wooller	(2)	1949, 1954

EARLIEST DATE FOR TAKING 100 WICKETS IN A SEASON

Date	Bowler	Year
2 July	D. J. Shepherd	1956
9 July	B. L. Muncer	1948

MOST BALLS BOWLED IN AN INNINGS IN FIRST-CLASS GAMES FOR GLAMORGAN

	Analysis						
Balls	O	M	R	W	Bowler	Opponents and venue	Years
346	57.4	26	106	6	D. J. Shepherd	Derbyshire at Swansea	1970
337	56.1	26	76	4	J. E. McConnon	Northamptonshire at Northampton	1958
331	55.1	20	87	6	D. J. Shepherd	Hampshire at Bournemouth	1963
330	55.0	21	105	3	D. E. Davies	Middlesex at Arms Park	1932
330	55.0	20	84	3	J. S. Pressdee	Northamptonshire at Northampton	1965
320	40.0	9	132	6	D. E. Davies	Warwickshire at Edgbaston	1939

MOST BALLS BOWLED IN A FIRST-CLASS MATCH FOR GLAMORGAN

	Analysis						
Balls	O	M	R	W	Bowler	Opponents and venue	Year
545	90.5	28	201	15	B. L. Muncer	Sussex at Swansea	1948
516	86.0	17	229	5	B. J. Lloyd	Cambridge University at Swansea	1975
508	84.4	34	155	10	J. E. McConnon	Northamptonshire at Northampton	1958
504	84.0	31	175	7	J. C. Clay	Nottinghamshire at Swansea	1933
487	81.4	26	154	10	D. J. Shepherd	Hampshire at Bournemouth	1963
486	81.0	32	216	10	M. A. Nash	Warwickshire at Edgbaston	1980

WICKET WITH FIRST BALL IN FIRST-CLASS CRICKET FOR GLAMORGAN

Bowler	Opponents and venue	Year
J. Johns	Somerset at Arms Park	1922
W. G. Davies	Surrey at The Oval	1958

MOST MAIDEN OVERS IN SUCCESSION IN FIRST-CLASS GAMES FOR GLAMORGAN

Overs	Bowler	Opponents and venue (No of balls)	Year
14	P. M. Walker	Somerset at Glastonbury (84 balls)	1969
12	J. E. McConnon	Derbyshire at Arms Park (78 balls)	1958
12	D. J. Shepherd	Hampshire at Southampton (76 balls)	1968

RECORD PARTNERSHIPS

RECORD PARTNERSHIPS IN FIRST-CLASS MATCHES

For Glamorgan:

Wicket	Partnership	Batsmen	Opponents and venue	Year
1st	330	R. C. Fredericks *and* A. Jones	Northamptonshire at Swansea	1972
2nd	249	S. P. James *and* H. Morris	Oxford University at the Parks	1987
3rd	313	D. E. Davies *and* W. E. Jones	Essex at Brentwood	1948
4th	306★	Javed Miandad *and* Younis Ahmed	Australians at Neath	1985
5th	264	M. Robinson *and* S. W. Montgomery	Hampshire at Bournemouth	1949
6th	230	W. E. Jones *and* B. L. Muncer	Worcestershire at Worcester	1953
7th	195★	W. Wooller *and* W. E. Jones	Lancashire at Liverpool	1947
8th	202	D. Davies *and* J. J. Hills	Sussex at Eastbourne	1928
9th	203★	J. J. Hills *and* J. C. Clay	Worcestershire at Swansea	1929
10th	143	T. Davies *and* S. A. B. Daniels	Gloucestershire at Swansea	1982

Against Glamorgan:

1st	335	B. Dudleston *and* J. F. Steele *for* Leicestershire (Leicester)		1975
2nd	344	A. Sandham *and* R. J. Gregory *for* Surrey (The Oval)		1937
3rd	323★	H. Sutcliffe *and* M. Leyland *for* Yorkshire (Huddersfield)		1928
4th	315	W. G. Quaife *and* J. H. Parsons *for* Warwickshire (Edgbaston)		1927
5th	335	B. F. Butcher *and* C. H. Lloyd *for* West Indians (Swansea)		1969
6th	276	M. Leyland *and* E. Robinson *for* Yorkshire (Swansea)		1926
7th	182	D. Bennett *and* J. T. Murray *for* Middlesex (Lord's)		1961
8th	192	S. Turner *and* R. N. S. Hobbs *for* Essex (Ilford)		1968
9th	161	G. J. Whittaker *and* W. S. Surridge *for* Surrey (The Oval)		1951
10th	148	B. Bellamy *and* V. Murdin *for* Northamptonshire (Northampton)		1925

RECORD PARTNERSHIP IN 40-OVER GAMES

For Glamorgan:

Wicket	Partnership	Batsmen	Opponents and venue	Year
1st	138	A. Jones *and* J. A. Hopkins	Essex at Swansea	1980
2nd	123	J. A. Hopkins *and* G. C. Holmes	Gloucestershire at Sophia Gardens	1986
3rd	154	R. C. Ontong *and* Javed Miandad	Kent at Canterbury	1982
4th	137★	A. Jones *and* P. D. Swart	Surrey at The Oval	1978
5th	134	A. Jones *and* G. Richards	Gloucestershire at Sophia Gardens	1978
6th	83	Javed Miandad *and* J. G. Thomas	Nottinghamshire at Trent Bridge	1983
7th	76	A. E. Cordle *and* J. W. Solanky	Leicestershire at Sophia Gardens	1974
8th	88	B. A. Davis *and* M. A. Nash	Kent at Swansea	1970
9th	62★	J. F. Steele *and* S. R. Barwick	Worcestershire at Worcester	1986
10th	41	J. W. Solanky *and* D. L. Williams	Kent at Swansea	1973

Against Glamorgan:

1st	177	G. M. Turner *and* J. M. Parker *for* Worcestershire at Worcester	1973
2nd	116★	P. J. Graves *and* Javed Miandad *for* Sussex at Swansea	1979
3rd	162	M. J. Harris *and* B. Hassan *for* Nottinghamshire at Trent Bridge	1972
4th	178	J. J. Whitaker *and* P. Willey *for* Leicestershire at Swansea	1984
5th	107	J. Sullivan *and* A. Kennedy *for* Lancashire at Old Trafford	1974
6th	88	B. W. Reidy *and* G. Fowler *for* Lancashire at Old Trafford	1980
7th	97★	G. Cook *and* G. Sharp *for* Northamptonshire at Northampton	1983
8th	47★	M. S. Turner *and* C. H. Dredge *for* Somerset at Sophia Gardens	1986
9th	65	C. W. J. Athey *and* S. Oldham *for* Yorkshire at Sophia Gardens	1977
10th	38	R. G. Williams *and* J. C. J. Dye *for* Northamptonshire at Sophia Gardens	1976

RECORD PARTNERSHIP IN 55-OVER GAMES

For Glamorgan:

Wicket	Partnership	Batsmen	Opponents and venue	Year
1st	176★	A. Jones *and* J. A. Hopkins	Minor Counties at Swansea	1980
2nd	109	A. Jones *and* D. A. Francis	Warwickshire at Edgbaston	1977
3rd	187	J. A. Hopkins *and* M. P. Maynard	Nottinghamshire at Sophia Gardens	1988
4th	121	A. R. Lewis *and* M. J. Llewellyn	Hampshire at Swansea	1973
5th	81	R. C. Ontong *and* J. F. Steele	Somerset at Swansea	1984
6th	114	M. J. Khan *and* G. P. Ellis	Gloucestershire at Bristol	1975
7th	117	Javed Miandad *and* E. W. Jones	Combined Univs. at Cambridge	1983
8th	102	R. C. Ontong *and* J. Derrick	Kent at Sophia Gardens	1985
9th	44	E. W. Jones *and* A. E. Cordle	Warwickshire at Edgbaston	1978
10th	18	A. J. Mack *and* A. A. Jones	Essex at Chelmsford	1980

Against Glamorgan:

1st	158	V. P. Terry *and* C. L. Smith *for* Hampshire at Southampton	1988
2nd	148	C. G. Greenidge *and* M. C. J. Nicholas *for* Hampshire at Southampton	1985
3rd	157	D. R. Turner *and* T. E. Jesty *for* Hampshire at Swansea	1977
4th	100	J. M. Parks *and* B. C. Rose *for* Somerset at Yeovil	1973
5th	108	K. W. R. Fletcher *and* D. R. Pringle *for* Essex at Chelmsford	1986
6th	65★	V. J. Marks *and* D. I. Breakwell *for* Somerset at Taunton	1979
7th	95	I. T. Botham *and* T. Gard *for* Somerset at Taunton	1986
8th	44	P. Sainsbury *and* G. R. Stephenson *for* Hampshire at Swansea	1976
9th	28	S. J. G. Doggart *and* M. Cullinan *for* Combined Univs. at Cambridge	1983
10th	24	N. Phillip *and* J. K. Lever *for* Essex at Swansea	1981

RECORD PARTNERSHIP IN 60-OVER GAMES

For Glamorgan:

Wicket	Partnership	Batsmen	Opponents and venue	Year
1st	144	A. Jones *and* R. C. Fredericks	Northamptonshire at Northampton	1972
2nd	108	A. R. Jones *and* H. Morris	Lancashire at Sophia Gardens	1988
3rd	132	A. Jones *and* P. M. Walker	Staffordshire at Stoke	1971

337

4th	107	J. S. Pressdee *and* A. Rees	Essex at Neath	1964
5th	129	A. R. Lewis *and* E. W. Jones	Hertfordshire at Swansea	1969
6th	102	H. Morris *and* R. C. Ontong	Worcestershire at Swansea	1985
7th	58	P. M. Walker *and* E. W. Jones	Warwickshire at Edgbaston	1972
8th	71	R. C. Ontong *and* T. Davies	Staffordshire at Stone	1986
9th	87	M. A. Nash *and* A. E. Cordle	Lincolnshire at Swansea	1974
10th	44	J. W. Solanky *and* G. D. Armstrong	Hampshire at Southampton	1975

Against Glamorgan:

1st	210	B. A. Richards *and* C. G. Greenidge *for* Hampshire at Southampton	1975
2nd	135	G. D. Mendis *and* P. W. G. Parker *for* Sussex at Hove	1980
3rd	135	A. M. Green *and* Imran Khan *for* Sussex at Hove	1986
4th	82	G. W. Johnson *and* A. G. E. Ealham *for* Kent at Swansea	1979
5th	116	T. W. Graveney *and* R. G. Broadbent *for* Worcestershire at Neath	1963
6th	94	A. I. Kallicharran *and* N. M. McVicker *for* Warwickshire at Edgbaston	1972
7th	49	C. M. Wells *and* I. J. Gould *for* Sussex at Sophia Gardens	1985
8th	64★	R. Illingworth *and* P. Booth *for* Leicestershire at Swansea	1977
9th	75	B. A. Langford *and* D. G. Doughty *for* Somerset at Cardiff Arms Park	1963
10th	28★	J. D. Appleyard *and* B. G. Collins *for* Hertfordshire at Swansea	1969

LEADING RUNSCORERS AND WICKET-TAKERS FOR GLAMORGAN IN LIMITED-OVERS CRICKET

40-overs competition:

Batsman	Runs	Bowler	Wickets
A. Jones	4,702	M. A. Nash	215
J. A. Hopkins	3,980	A. E. Cordle	164
R. C. Ontong	2,771	D. L. Williams	142
Javed Miandad	2,238	R. C. Ontong	130
Majid Khan	1,958	G. C. Holmes	92
G. C. Holmes	1,835	J. G. Thomas	87
A. L. Jones	1,642	J. W. Solanky	73

55-overs competition:

A. Jones	1,282	M. A. Nash	64
J. A. Hopkins	1,251	R. C. Ontong	48
R. C. Ontong	898	A. C. Cordle	34
Javed Miandad	629	D. L. Williams	30
M. J. Llewellyn	590	S. R. Barwick	29

60-overs competition:

A. Jones	1,077	M. A. Nash	41
R. C. Ontong	480	D. J. Shepherd	23
A. R. Lewis	442	I. J. Jones	22
P. M. Walker	426	A. E. Cordle	19
J. A. Hopkins	394	D. L. Williams	18
E. W. Jones	358	P. M. Walker	16

WICKET-KEEPING RECORDS

MOST DIMISSALS IN AN INNINGS OF A FIRST-CLASS MATCH FOR GLAMORGAN

Dismissals	(ct-st)	Wicket-keeper	Opponents and Venue	Year
7	(6-1)	E. W. Jones	Cambridge University at Cambridge	1970
6	(5-1)	H. G. Davies	Leicestershire at Leicester	1939
6	(6-0)	D. G. L. Evans	Yorkshire at Swansea	1967
6	(6-0)	E. W. Jones	Essex at Sophia Gardens	1982
6	(6-0)	C. P. Metson	Leicestershire at Neath	1988

MOST DISMISSALS IN A FIRST-CLASS MATCH FOR GLAMORGAN

Wickets	(ct-st)	Wicket-keeper	Opponents and venue	Year
8	(6-2)	H. G. Davies	South Africa at Swansea	1955
8	(8-0)	E. W. Jones	Warwicks at Edgbaston	1970
8	(8-0)	E. W. Jones	Essex at Sophia Gardens	1982

MOST DISMISSALS IN FIRST-CLASS GAMES IN A SEASON FOR GLAMORGAN

Wickets	(ct-st)	Wicket-keeper	Year
94	(85-9)	E. W. Jones	1970
89	(78-11)	D. G. L. Evans	1963
82	(59-23)	H. G. Davies	1955
82	(78-4)	D. G. L. Evans	1962
79	(74-5)	D. G. L. Evans	1961
75	(62-13)	D. G. L. Evans	1965
75	(69-6)	E. W. Jones	1968

Most catches in a season: E. W. Jones 85 in 1970
Most stumpings in a season: T. L. Brierley 24 in 1937

MOST DISMISSALS IN A CAREER IN FIRST-CLASS GAMES FOR GLAMORGAN

Total	Caught	Stumped	Wicket-keeper
933	840	93	E. W. Jones
782	580	202	H. G. Davies
558	503	55	D. G. L. Evans
225	153	72	T. L. Brierley
212	128	84	D. Sullivan
192	165	27	T. Davies
178	108	70	T. Every
113	99	14	C. P. Metson
95	92	3	J. J. Hills
45	39	6	N. V. H. Riches
38	26	12	J. Stone

20	12	8	J. M. Jones
18	16	2	G. E. Cording
17	10	7	V. G. J. Jenkins
11	9	2	J. T. Morgan
10	8	2	W. L. T. Jenkins

HIGHEST FIRST-CLASS TOTAL WITHOUT CONCEDING A BYE

Total	Wicket-keeper	Opponents and Venue	Year
422-8 dec	H. G. Davies	Gloucestershire at Swansea	1957
415-8 dec	E. W. Jones	Gloucestershire at Swansea	1974
412-8 dec	E. W. Jones	Hampshire at Portsmouth	1970
406-3 dec	H. G. Davies	Essex at Westcliff	1953

FIELDING RECORDS

MOST CATCHES BY A FIELDER IN AN INNINGS OF A FIRST-CLASS MATCH

Catches	Fielder	Opponents and venue	Year
5	W. E. Bates	Warwickshire at Edgbaston	1928
5	R. C. Davis	Northamptonshire at Sophia Gardens	1970
5	J. A. Hopkins	Worcestershire at Sophia Gardens	1976
5	G. Hughes	Essex at Swansea	1964
5	P. M. Walker	Leicestershire at Swansea	1960
5	P. M. Walker	Derbyshire at Chesterfield	1961
5	P. M. Walker	Nottinghamshire at Newport	1961
5	P. M. Walker	Derbyshire at Swansea	1970

MOST CATCHES BY A FIELDER IN A FIRST-CLASS MATCH

Catches	Fielder	Opponents and venue	Year
8	P. M. Walker	Derbyshire at Swansea	1970
7	G. Hughes	Essex at Swansea	1964
7	P. M. Walker	Northamptonshire at Northampton	1960
7	P. M. Walker	Nottinghamshire at Newport	1961

MOST CATCHES IN FIRST-CLASS GAMES DURING A SEASON

Catches	Fielder	Year
67	P. M. Walker	1961
64	P. M. Walker	1959
62	P. M. Walker	1960
54	P. M. Walker	1965

OVER 100 CATCHES IN FIRST-CLASS GAMES DURING A CAREER

Catches	Fielder
656	P. M. Walker
392	W. Wooller
390	A. J. Watkins
344	J. S. Pressdee
312	W. G. A. Parkhouse
276	A. Jones
253	M. J. L. Turnbull
241	D. J. Shepherd
211	D. E. Davies
210	J. A. Hopkins
208	R. C. Davis
193	D. Davies
182	W. E. Bates
171	J. C. Clay
169	P. B. Clift
155	A. R. Lewis
	Majid Khan
148	M. A. Nash
143	J. E. McConnon
141	A. E. Cordle
124	J. Mercer
123	C. C. Smart
117	W. E. Jones
114	R. C. Ontong
113	A. Rees
111	B. L. Muncer
104	A. L. Jones
100	W. D. Slade

ALL-ROUND RECORDS

A CENTURY AND OVER 10 WICKETS IN A FIRST-CLASS MATCH

Player	Score	Analyses	Opponents and venue	Year
R. C. Ontong	130	5-39 and 8-67	Nottinghamshire at Trent Bridge	1985
B. L. Muncer	107*	5-34 and 5-23	Derbyshire at Chesterfield	1951

1000 RUNS AND 100 WICKETS IN FIRST-CLASS GAMES DURING A SEASON

Player	Runs (average)	Wickets (average)	Year
D. E. Davies	1,326 (28.21)	100 (21.07)	1935
D. E. Davies	1,954 (39.87)	101 (22.41)	1937

B. L. Muncer	1,076 (24.45)	100 (17.53)	1952
J. S. Pressdee	1,435 (34.17)	104 (21.04)	1963
A. J. Watkins	1,114 (24.22)	113 (20.09)	1955
W. Wooller	1,059 (24.06)	107 (18.42)	1954

LARGEST MARGINS OF VICTORY IN FIRST-CLASS GAMES

Margin	Opponents and venue	Year
Innings and 190 runs	Essex at Brentwood	1948
Innings and 186 runs	Leicestershire at Cowbridge	1932
Innings and 174 runs	Somerset at Swansea	1953
Innings and 157 runs	Kent at Sophia Gardens	1967
Innings and 153 runs	Somerset at Cowbridge	1932
Innings and 152 runs	Kent at Swansea	1937
332 runs	New Zealand at Swansea	1937
278 runs	Kent at Swansea	1948
262 runs	Northamptonshire at Arms Park	1954
238 runs	Oxford University at Oxford	1978
232 runs	Gloucestershire at Swansea	1923

LARGEST MARGINS OF DEFEAT IN FIRST-CLASS GAMES

Margins	Opponents and venue	Year
Innings and 331 runs	by Surrey at Arms Park	1936
Innings and 327 runs	by Nottinghamshire at Trent Bridge	1929
Innings and 270 runs	by Sussex at Horsham	1923
Innings and 258 runs	by Yorkshire at Arms Park	1922
Innings and 226 runs	by West Indies at Swansea	1984
326 runs	by Sussex at Hove	1925
317 runs	by Nottinghamshire at Trent Bridge	1925
301 runs	by Nottinghamshire at Trent Bridge	1931
298 runs	by Surrey at Swansea	1924
297 runs	by Northamptonshire at Northampton	1925
296 runs	by Gloucestershire at Bristol	1925

LARGEST MARGINS OF VICTORY IN GAMES BETWEEN 1889 AND 1920

Margin	Opponents and venue	Year
Innings and 327 runs	Berkshire at Swansea	1903
Innings and 327 runs	Carmarthenshire at Swansea	1910
Innings and 259 runs	Carmarthenshire at Llanelli	1908
Innings and 254 runs	Monmouthshire at Swansea	1904
Innings and 233 runs	Dorset at Blandford	1907
Innings and 227 runs	Public School Nondescripts at Swansea	1901
Innings and 226 runs	Carmarthenshire at Swansea	1911
Innings and 223 runs	Devon at Exeter	1907
Innings and 215 runs	Monmouthshire at Cardiff Arms Park	1901
272 runs	Carmarthenshire at Llanelli	1910
233 runs	Cornwall at Swansea	1897

LARGEST MARGINS OF DEFEAT IN GAMES BETWEEN 1889 AND 1920

Margin	Opponents and venue	Year
Innings and 233 runs	Surrey II at The Oval	1906
Innings and 217 runs	Gloucestershire Club and Ground at Bristol	1891
295 runs	Durham at West Hartlepool	1905

LARGEST MARGINS OF VICTORY IN LIMITED-OVERS CRICKET

40-overs games:	148 runs	*v* Northamptonshire at Wellingborough, 1975
	10 wkts	*v* Warwickshire at Edgbaston, 1988
55-overs games:	166 runs	*v* Combined Universities at Cambridge, 1983
	10 wkts	*v* Minor Counties at Swansea, 1980
60-overs games:	85 runs	*v* Hertfordshire at Swansea, 1969
	9 wkts	*v* Northamptonshire at Northampton, 1966

LARGEST MARGINS OF DEFEAT IN LIMITED-OVERS CRICKET

40-overs games:	160 runs	*v* Derbyshire at Swansea, 1979
	10 wkts	*v* Leicestershire at Leicester, 1972
	10 wkts	*v* Middlesex at Lords, 1976
55-overs games:	159 runs	*v* Lancashire at Old Trafford, 1973
	10 wkts	*v* Hampshire at Southampton, 1988
60-overs games:	164 runs	*v* Hampshire at Southampton, 1975
	9 wkts	*v* Derbyshire at Sophia Gardens, 1969
	9 wkts	*v* Yorkshire at Headingley, 1987

NARROWEST MARGIN OF VICTORY IN FIRST-CLASS GAMES

Margin	Opponents and venue	Year
1 wkt	Essex at Arms Park	1956
1 run	Worcestershire at Swansea	1953
1 run	Essex at Swansea	1969
2 runs	Middlesex at Swansea	1959
9 runs	Oxford University at Oxford	1967

NARROWEST MARGIN OF DEFEAT IN FIRST-CLASS GAMES

Margin	Opponents and venue	Year
1 wkt	*by* Gloucestershire at Bristol	1936
1 wkt	*by* Worcestershire at Stourbridge	1939
1 wkt	*by* Essex at Westcliff	1952
1 wkt	*by* Middlesex at Arms Park	1955

1 wkt	*by* Kent at Dartford	1959
1 wkt	*by* Yorkshire at Bradford	1960
1 wkt	*by* Leicestershire at Leicester	1961
1 wkt	*by* Gloucestershire at Bristol	1973
3 runs	*by* Worcestershire at Llanelli	1938
4 runs	*by* Yorkshire at Arms Park	1957
5 runs	*by* Derbyshire at Arms Park	1954
8 runs	*by* Gloucestershire at Swansea	1926
8 runs	*by* Worcestershire at Neath	1936

NARROWEST MARGIN OF VICTORY IN GAMES BETWEEN 1889 AND 1920

Margin	*Opponents and venue*	*Year*
1 wkt	Monmouthshire at Swansea	1902
1 wkt	Berkshire at Reading	1903

NARROWEST MARGIN OF DEFEAT IN GAMES BETWEEN 1889 AND 1920

| 1 wkt | *by* Devon at Arms Park | 1905 |

NARROWEST MARGIN OF VICTORY IN LIMITED-OVER CRICKET

40-over games:	1 run	*v* Yorkshire at Bradford, 1970
		v Somerset at Sophia Gardens, 1976
		v Warwickshire at Swansea, 1977
		v Surrey at Ebbw Vale, 1979
		v Worcestershire at Worcester, 1982
55-over games:	1 run	*v* Combined Universities at Oxford, 1978
		v Gloucestershire at Bristol, 1980
60-over games:	1 wkt	*v* Worcestershire at Newport, 1964

NARROWEST MARGIN OF DEFEAT IN LIMITED-OVERS CRICKET

40-over games:	1 run	*by* Essex at Swansea, 1969
		by Surrey at Byfleet, 1971
		by Derbyshire at Buxton, 1973
		by Hampshire at Sophia Gardens, 1984
		by Derbyshire at Cheadle, 1987
	1 wkt	*by* Somerset at Taunton, 1973
		by Hampshire at Bournemouth, 1983

55-over games: Scores level and losing more wickets, *by* Somerset at Cardiff, 1978

344

UNUSUAL DISMISSALS

Handled Ball: A. Rees, *v* Middlesex at Lords, 1965
Run out by the bowler: G. Barker, by W. Wooller *v* Essex at Arms Park, 1958
Stumped by a substitute: P. M. Walker, by L. A. Johnson (for K. V. Andrew), *v* Northamptonshire at Northampton, 1959
Stumped by a substitute: A. L. Jones, by G. Sharp (for G. Cook), *v* Northamptonshire at Northampton, 1983
Stumped off a wide: R. C. Ontong, by R. J. Parks off T. M. Tremlett in the Sunday League match *v* Hampshire at Cardiff, 1986

OVER 200 FIRST-CLASS APPEARANCES FOR GLAMORGAN

Appearances	Player
647	D. J. Shepherd
612	D. E. Davies
610	A. Jones
437	P. M. Walker
435	W. G. A. Parkhouse
423	H. G. Davies
422	B. Hedges
412	A. H. Dyson
412	J. Mercer
411	D. Davies
407	A. J. Watkins
405	E. W. Jones
400	W. Wooller
358	J. C. Clay
340	W. E. Jones
335	M. A. Nash
322	J. S. Pressdee
315	A. R. Lewis
314	M. J. L. Turnbull
312	A. E. Cordle
299	J. A. Hopkins
283	W. E. Bates
270	D. G. L. Evans
252	R. C. Ontong
243	J. E. McConnon
224	B. L. Muncer
216	A. Rees
215	F. P. Ryan
213	R. C. Davis
206	G. Lavis
206	O. S. Wheatley

OFFICERS OF THE CLUB 1888–1988

President:

1888–1900	The Marquess of Bute
1901–1905	Lord Windsor
1906–1922	The Earl of Plymouth
1923–1924	Sir Harry Webb
1925–1933	Daniel Radcliffe
1934–1939	The Earl of Plymouth
	(post not filled 1940–1946)
1947–1959	H. H. Merrett
1960–1973	J. C. Clay
1974–1978	Lord Brecon
1979–	Judge Rowe Harding

Patron:

1923–1929	The Earl of Plymouth
1930–1933	The Earl of Plymouth and A. M. Talbot-Fletcher
1934–1939	A. M. Talbot-Fletcher and the Earl of Dumfries
	(post not filled 1940–1946)
1947–1950	Sir W. Reardon-Smith and D. M. Evans-Bevan
1951–1965	D. M. Evans-Bevan
1966–1973	D. M. Evans-Bevan and Lord Brecon
1974–1980	Sir Edward Lewis
	(post not filled 1981–1985)
1986–	HRH The Prince of Wales

Chairman:

1921	T. D. Schofield
1922–1927	Sir S. H. Byass
1928–1939	Bertrand Turnbull
1940–1958	Col J. M. Bevan
1959–1976	Judge Rowe Harding
1977–1983	O. S. Wheatley
1984–1987	G. Craven
1988–	A. R. Lewis

Secretary (Honorary Post 1888–1920):

1888–1892	W. L. Yorath
1893	M. S. Foulger and J. H. Brain
1894–1903	J. H. Brain
1904–1908	J. H. Brain and H. B. Letcher
1909–1922	T. A. L. Whittington
1923–1932	A. Gibson
1933–1939	M. J. L. Turnbull
1940–1945	A. E. Brown
1946	J. C. Clay
1947–1977	W. Wooller
1978–1982	P. B. Clift
1983–	P. G. Carling

Treasurer:

1888–1892	J. T. D. Llewelyn
1893	W. D. Llewelyn and T. M. Barlow
1894–1903	T. M. Barlow
1904–1912	H. M. Ingledew
1913–1921	D. B. Williams
1922–1924	W. L. Renwick
1925–1932	E. A. Tyler
1933–1938	J. C. Clay and R. E. Arnott
1939–1946	A. E. Brown
1946–1948	G. V. Wynne-Jones
1949–1983	R. R. Davies
1984–1986	W. R. Matthews
1987–	W. H. Cawdron

Trustees:

1953–1970	Col J. M. Bevan, N. V. H. Riches, J. C. Clay
1971–1973	T. E. Billing, N. V. H. Riches, J. C. Clay
1974–1975	T. E. Billing, N. V. H. Riches, J. H. Bowen
1976–1978	T. E. Billing, J. R. Mullens, J. H. Bowen
1979–1982	T. E. Billing, W. R. Matthews, J. H. Bowen
1983	T. E. Billing, W. R. Matthews
1984–1986	G. Craven, W. R. Matthews, R. R. Davies
1987	G. Craven, O. S. Wheatley, R. R. Davies
1988–	G. Craven, O. S. Wheatley, W. Wooller

BIBLIOGRAPHY

David Rayvern Allen (ed.): *Arlott: his writings on the game* (Willow Books, 1984)

John Arlott: *Cricket Journal No. 3 – Cricket on Trial* (Heinemann, 1960)

John Arlott: *Cricket: The Great Captains* (Pelham, 1971)

John Arlott: *Indian Summer* (Longman, 1947)

John Arlott: *Vintage Summer – 1947* (Eyre and Spottiswood, 1967)

Bailey, Thorn and Wynne-Thomas: *The Who's Who of Cricketers* (Newnes Books, 1984)

Trevor Bailey: *Championship Cricket* (Longman, 1961)

Robert Brooke: *Who's Who of English first-class cricketers 1945–1984* (Collins Willow, 1985)

Lionel Brown: *Victor Trumper and the 1902 Australians* (Secker and Warburg, 1981)

Cardiff CC 1867–1967

John Edwards: *Dai Davies – Not Out 78* (Dyfed Publishers, 1975)

David Foot: *Sunshine, Sixes and Cider* (David and Charles, 1986)

Glamorgan CCC Yearbooks 1933–1988

Benny Green (ed.): *The Wisden Book of Obituaries* (MacDonald Queene Anne, 1986)

Arthur Haygarth: *Cricket Scores and Biographies*

Alan Jones: *Hooked On Opening* (Gomer Press (Llandysul), 1984)

Frank Lee: *Cricket, Lovely Cricket* (Stanley Paul, 1960)

David Lemmon (ed.): *Pelham Cricket Year* (Pelham Books, 1979)

Tony Lewis: *Playing Days* (Stanley Paul, 1985)

Llanelli CC: *100 Years of Cricket at Stradey Park* (Llanelli CC, 1974)

Christopher Martin-Jenkins: *The Complete Who's Who of Test Cricketers* (Orbis, 1980)

Brinley Matthews: *The Swansea Story* (Swansea Cricket and Football Club, 1968)

Allan Meredith: *A Hard Slog – The History of the South Wales Cricket Association, 1926–1986* (Towy Press (Llandeilo), 1987)

J. H. Morgan: *Glamorgan* (Convoy Press, 1953)

Playfair Cricket Annual 1951–1988

D. T. and J. B. Smith: *South Wales Cricket Club, 1859–1886*

South Wales Cricketers Magazine 1948–1953

E. W. Swanton: *Barclays World of Cricket* (Collins, 1980)

Wayne Thomas: *Glamorgan C.C.C. – The Book of Records, 1921–1976* (Davies and Sons (Woking), 1977)

Peter Walker: *Cricket Conversations* (Pelham Books, 1978)

Roy Webber: *Who's Who in World Cricket* (Hodder and Stoughton, 1952)

Roy Webber: *County Cricket Championship – a History of the Competition since 1873* (Phoenix Sports Books, 1957)

Webber and Arnott: *Glamorgan C.C.C., 1921–1947* (The Cricket Book Society, 1948)

Wisden Cricketers' Almanack 1898–1988

Wilf Wooller: *A History of County Cricket – Glamorgan* (Arthur Barker, 1971)

ACKNOWLEDGEMENTS

The compilation and writing of this book would not have been possible, or so enjoyable, had it not been for the support and co-operation of a number of people, starting with Richard Wigmore of Christopher Helm Ltd, who initially invited me to undertake the project and has given me constant guidance throughout. Gerard Elias, the Hon Appeals Director of the Club's centenary committee, kindly gave his blessing that this would be the official centenary history of Glamorgan, and I am most grateful to the club for their assistance, in particular to Secretary Phil Carling, and Mike Fatkin, a member of the administrative staff, for providing unrestricted access to the Club's records. My sincere thanks also to Tony Lewis, the Chairman of the Club in centenary year, for writing the introduction and giving a personal view of what it means to play for the Welsh county.

Several individuals have generously given their time to help solve my many queries, especially on the events of the last century, and the statistical section of the book would be less comprehensive if I had not been fortunate enough to have their help, in particular David Smith, whose library and knowledge of early Welsh cricketers and the South Wales Cricket Club is second to none. I fully appreciate his many hours of checking biographical details and dates of games, and for reading the final manuscript. Brian Lile also greatly assisted in the compilation of the pre-1921 records and averages, and willingly searched the seemingly unending records housed at the National Library of Wales at Aberystwyth. I am most grateful for his efforts, and his knack of tracking down needles in very large haystacks, and coming up with the answers when I doubted very much if they could be found!

A number of members of the Association of Cricket Statisticians and leading researchers have also given me considerable support. My thanks to Peter Wynne-Thomas for his wise guidance on a variety of matters, to Philip Bailey, Philip Thorn, Robert Brooke, Vic Isaacs and Les Hatton for assistance with the post-1921 biographical details and statistics, and to Jack Burrell, especially for details on the somewhat obscure professionals around the turn of the century. Hugh Morgan and Bob Harragan kindly helped in tracking down some of the personalities and events before 1888, whilst Wayne Thomas and Byron Denning, the current Glamorgan scorer, assisted with the first-class records and statistics. In addition, Duncan Pierce kindly supplied details on the various Glamorgan cricketers who have played other sports, in particular rugby and football, and assisted with the search for birth and death records at St Catherine's House.

I am grateful to Lawrence Hourahane, the former Assistant Secretary of the Club, for reading the early manuscripts and offering constructive advice, based on his wide knowledge of the Club's affairs. Allan Devonald of Peter Llewellyn (Photocopying) Ltd kindly provided a word processor and I am most appreciative of the sterling efforts of the office staff at Sophia Gardens in running off the processor discs on their printers.

My thanks to Chris Brain for allowing me to delve through the trunks of documents in his family's possession which contain the many letters J. H. Brain wrote and received whilst acting as the Club's captain and secretary. Similarly, John Riches gave me a host of interesting anecdotes and insights into his father's career with Glamorgan, whilst Tony Lewis, Ossie Wheatley, Don Shepherd, Ernie Harris, Kevin Lyons, Phil Clift, Jim Pleass, Wilf Wooller, Roger Davis, Alan Jones and Peter Walker all helped with information on other incidents in the Club's history.

I am extremely grateful for the help I received from several people in obtaining photographs, especially John Billot of the *Western Mail* for giving access to the newspaper's archives and his own cigarette card collection, and to Ron Harries for loaning me several of his own items of Glamorgan memorabilia, in particular on Maurice Turnbull. My thanks also to Bill Meale, the historian of Penarth RFC for the photographs of Herbie Morgan, to Onllwyn Brace and Maggie Titterton of the Sports Department of the BBC in Cardiff for access to film and photographic archives at Broadcasting House, Llandaff, and to David Hill for the early photograph of the Swansea ground. Mike Poloway and Steve Goodwin generously assisted with the photography, and I am very grateful for the help of Morton Davies, in particular with the superb colour shot of St. Helen's, Swansea, on the jacket.

Others who I would like to thank include Edward Bevan, David Foot, Michael Hill, Ron Jones, Alan Meredith (SWCA), Ches Evans (Welsh Cricket Association), Philip DeFriez, and members of my family for their kind help with the proofs. Ted Crowe and Jonathan Morgan, two of my colleagues at Blundell's, both gave valuable information on a number of players and suggested contacts, whilst I am grateful that Jeremy Salter, my head of department, and headmaster John Rees understand my 'obsession' with Glamorgan cricket!

My thanks to the archivists at the Glamorgan Record Office, Dyfed Record Office, the Welsh Folk Museum and Church House; to the librarians in the Reference Department of Cardiff Central Library, J. Vivian Hughes, the Local Studies Librarian at Swansea Library and Dr John Alban, the Swansea City Archivist; and to all the registrars and officials of a number of schools and colleges for information on their pupils who have appeared for the county.

The following club officials also kindly answered my queries: Colin Adams and Jeffrey Bird (Cowbridge), Chris Despres (St Fagan's), Dai Samuel and Gwyn Grattan (Neath), John Warner (Chepstow), Dr R. B. Kemp (Aberystwyth), B. H. Hurst (Colwyn Bay), Peter Reynolds (Margam), Arthur Porter (Newport), and the late Llewellyn Williams (Swansea). Lastly, but by no means least, my sincere thanks to my wife Debra for her support and encouragement throughout the writing of this book.

Photographs not acknowledged in the text are reproduced by kind permission of Glamorgan County Cricket Club and of the following sources:
Cardiff Central Library (pages 47, 144)
John Riches (page 58)
John Billot (page 65)
Blundell's School (page 75)
Central Photos Ltd (page 115)
Ron Harries (page 121)

Andrew Hignell
Tiverton, Devon
September 1988

INDEX